CONSTITUTIONALLY CONFORMING INTERPRETATION – COMPARATIVE PERSPECTIVES
VOLUME 2: CONNECTIONS AND ANALYSIS

This is the second part of a two-volume set, which presents an in-depth investigation into the canon of constitutionally conforming interpretation.

This second volume builds upon the insights of the first volume, which includes national reports on the use of constitutional interpretation. In Volume 2, the analysis is extended beyond the national context, discussing its application in the supranational and international contexts, including in EU law and the domestic use of international law. It presents several critical perspectives, challenging the legitimacy of constitutionally conforming interpretation, and looks at the invisible constitution, constitutional amendments, and the impact of legalism. The volume is rounded off by three comparative analyses, which formulate universally applicable insights.

Together with Volume 1, this book fills an important gap in legal scholarship and sets the stage for cross-national discourse on this critical legal method.

Hart Studies in Constitutional Theory: Volume 10

Hart Studies in Constitutional Theory

Series Editors

Authors writing for this series cover a wide range of perspectives, methods, and regions, to enhance our understanding of constitutions as central institutions of modern public life. Taken together, the books in this series aim to challenge established wisdom and advance original ideas.

This series is a natural home for books interrogating the concepts and structures of constitutions on the national, the supranational and the international level. Its guiding philosophy is that the task of constitutional theory is not only to delineate the basic structures of government and to protect human rights, but also more broadly to offer methods for grappling with the social, political, and economic problems societies face today.

The series is open to theoretical, normative, analytical, empirical and comparative approaches, stemming from legal studies as well as from political philosophy and political science. In its ambition to become a global forum for debate about constitutional theory, the series editors welcome submissions for monographs as well as edited volumes from all parts of the world.

Recent titles in this series:

Proportionality and Facts in Constitutional Adjudication
Anne Carter

The Methodology of Constitutional Theory
Edited by Dimitrios Kyritsis and Stuart Lakin

A Constitutionalist Approach to the European Convention on Human Rights: The Legitimacy of Evolutive and Static Interpretation
Lisa Sonnleitner

Judicial Avoidance: Balancing Competences in Constitutional Adjudication
Carolina Alves das Chagas

Constitutionally Conforming Interpretation – Comparative Perspectives: Volume 1: National Reports
Edited by Matthias Klatt

Equality Before the Law: Equal Dignity, Wrongful Discrimination, and the Rule of Law
Michael P Foran

Constitutional Courts and Judicial Review: Between Law and Politics
Dieter Grimm

Essays on Freedom and Proportionality
Edited by Dimitrios Kyritsis

The Distorting Lens of Convergent Constitutional Theory
Peter Cane

Constitutionally Conforming Interpretation – Comparative Perspectives

Volume 2: Connections and Analysis

Edited by
Matthias Klatt

• HART •
OXFORD • LONDON • NEW YORK • NEW DELHI • SYDNEY

HART PUBLISHING

Bloomsbury Publishing Plc

Kemp House, Chawley Park, Cumnor Hill, Oxford, OX2 9PH, UK

1385 Broadway, New York, NY 10018, USA

Bloomsbury Publishing Ireland Limited, 29 Earlsfort Terrace, Dublin 2, D02 AY28, Ireland

HART PUBLISHING, the Hart/Stag logo, BLOOMSBURY and the Diana logo are trademarks of Bloomsbury Publishing Plc

First published in Great Britain 2025

A catalogue record for this book is available from the British Library.

A catalogue record for this book is available from the Library of Congress.

Library of Congress Control Number: 2023941386

ISBN: HB: 978-1-50995-380-6
ePDF: 978-1-50995-382-0
ePub: 978-1-50995-381-3

Typeset by Compuscript Ltd, Shannon

For product safety related questions contact productsafety@bloomsbury.com

To find out more about our authors and books visit www.hartpublishing.co.uk. Here you will find extracts, author information, details of forthcoming events and the option to sign up for our newsletters.

SERIES EDITORS' FOREWORD

Interpreters of the law seek to align the meaning of statutes as much as possible with the constitution, thereby ensuring that everyday legal practice conforms with constitutional supremacy. This is the companion to an earlier volume that examined the application of the method of constitution-conforming interpretation in a variety of national legal systems from around the world. The present collection widens the focus in a twofold manner. It broadens the spatial perspective beyond the boundaries of the nation-state to encompass the international context, while it also presents critical perspectives that address the disadvantages of constitution-conforming interpretation. Such a comparative analysis enriches and expands upon existing scholarship.

The two volumes complement each other and are worth reading together. The contributors to the second volume engage with the contributions in the first volume, meticulously examining the findings set out therein and finding connections with their own scholarly projects. The result is that the question of constitution-conforming interpretation is surveyed and analysed from a variety of viewpoints, improving our understanding of this technique as a whole.

Comparative constitutional law turns into constitutional theory when analysing the similarities and differences between constitutional systems – including their historical and cultural contexts – leads to deeper, more fundamental questions that are universal and enduring. Readers are encouraged to approach the chapters in this volume as efforts to do just that.

Maartje De Visser
Charles Barzun
Matthias Klatt
Singapore/Charlottesville/Graz, March 2025

PREFACE

This volume concludes the research project that began with a first volume: Matthias Klatt (ed), *Constitutionally Conforming Interpretation – Comparative Perspectives. Volume 1: National Reports* (Oxford, Hart Publishing, 2023), Hart Studies in Constitutional Theory, Vol 5.

While the first volume consisted of a total of 19 country reports, we now present connections and analyses. These new contributions build on the country reports and in many cases refer to them. In this way, we have created a dense, far-reaching and integrated overview of the main lines of discussion.

The chapters in Part I are devoted to the use of CCI in an international context, both in European Union law and in international law. It is regrettable that two chapters, which would have been of significant value, were omitted from this volume. These were the chapters on the convention-conforming interpretation in the systems of the European Convention on Human Rights and of the Inter-American Human Rights System.

Part II presents critical perspectives that examine the fundamental principles of CCI from a variety of viewpoints or focus on specific CCI application scenarios. Additionally, the chapter by Sommer and Roznai can be regarded as a country report on Israel, bringing the total number of countries analysed in this study to 20.

Part III presents comparative analyses. The authors synthesise the findings of both volumes from an overarching perspective, thereby formulating a comprehensive summary of the entire research project.

I am indebted to the entire team at the Graz Jurisprudence Research Centre for their invaluable support. I would be remiss if I did not extend my gratitude to Ms Marlene Anzenberger, who edited this volume with great care and perseverance. I would also like to express my gratitude to the speakers and discussants who participated in a special workshop at the annual conference of the International Society of Public Law ICon-S in Madrid during the summer of 2023.

I dedicate this volume to the memory of Fred Schauer, a brilliant scholar whose contribution to our inaugural volume was exemplary, and whose insights on constitutional avoidance were an important source of inspiration for me when I first conceived of this project.

Matthias Klatt
Graz, December 2024

CONTENTS

PART III
COMPARISON AND ANALYSIS

EDITOR AND AUTHOR BIOGRAPHIES – VOL 2

Virgílio Afonso da Silva is Professor of Law and director of the research cluster 'Constitution, Politics & Institutions' at the University of São Paulo. He is the recipient of a scholarship for distinguished researchers from the Brazilian Research Council. His articles and book chapters on balancing and proportionality, judicial review, human rights and socio-economic rights have been published in Brazil and in leading international journals. He is the author of *The Constitution of Brazil: a contextual analysis* (Hart Publishing, 2019).

Antonia Baraggia is Assistant Professor of Comparative Law at the Department of National and Supranational Public Law at the University of Milan, Italy. She is Principal Investigator of the project CONFEDERAL on fiscal federalism and social rights. She authored three books and several publications in Italian and English, eg on the effects of the financial crisis on national constitutional systems and on the European Union, on fundamental rights protection in comparative perspective and on the dialogue among Courts.

Stéphane Beaulac is Professor of International Law and of Constitutional Law at the University of Montreal, Canada. He holds a Ph.D. in International Law from the University of Cambridge, where he also earned an LL.M. (first class honour) in Comparative Constitutional Law. Beaulac has clerked at the Supreme Court of Canada and is the author of numerous law books and over 100 papers, published, among others, by OUP, CUP, Routledge, Springer and Hart.

Eion Carolan is a Full Professor at University College Dublin, Ireland, where he is Director of the UCD Centre for Constitutional Studies. He is currently leading 'The Foundations Project' (www.foundations.ac), an ERC-funded research programme examining the foundations of constitutional resilience and the rule of law across Europe and Latin America.

Oran Doyle is a Research Professor at the Institutum Iurisprudentiae of the Academia Sinica, Taiwan, and a Professor in law at Trinity College Dublin, Ireland. He works in the field of comparative constitutional law and theory, with a particular focus on constitutional amendment. He is the author of *The Constitution of Ireland: A Contextual Analysis* (Hart Publishing, 2018).

Alfonso García Figueroa is a Spanish Professor of Legal Philosophy at the Faculty of Law in Toledo (UCLM, Spain). His research interests span legal theory, legal argumentation, philosophy of religion, philosophy of sport and political philosophy. He is author of many books, among them *Principios y positivismo jurídico* (1997), *Criaturas de la moralidad* (2009), *Pleitos divinos* (2014) and *Moral de victoria* (2021). He has worked as an ethics expert for the Research Executive Agency of the European Commission.

Matthias Klatt serves as the Director of Graz Jurisprudence, which is the Research Centre for Legal Philosophy and Global Constitutionalism at the University of Graz in Austria. In addition to this role, he holds the esteemed Chair of Jurisprudence. Prior to his current appointment, Professor Klatt held an Assistant Professorship in Public Law, European Law, International Law, and Legal Philosophy at the University of Hamburg. He also served as the Juliana Cuyler Matthews Junior Research Fellow at New College, Oxford. His research has been disseminated in six different languages.

Cormac Mac Amhlaigh is Professor of Public Law at Edinburgh University in Scotland. He writes generally on issues of constitutional theory and has recently published a book advancing a novel pluralist constitutional theory.

Michel Rosenfeld is the University Professor of Law and Comparative Democracy, and the Justice Sydney L. Robins Professor of Human Rights at the Cardozo School of Law in New York City. He was the founding editor-in-chief of the *International Journal of Constitutional Law* (ICON) from 2001 to 2014, and president of the International Association of Constitutional Law (1999–2004). His most recent book is *A Pluralist Theory of Constitutional Justice: Assessing Liberal Democracy in Times of Rising Populism and Illiberalism.*

Yaniv Roznai is Associate Professor at the Harry Radzyner Law School, Interdisciplinary Center (IDC) Herzliya, Israel. He holds an LL.B. from IDC and LL.M. and Ph.D. degrees from the LSE. Roznai was a post-doctoral fellow at NYU and at the University of Haifa. He is the Co-Founding Chair of the Israeli Association of Legislation and an elected member of the Council of ICON-S. His scholarship focuses on comparative constitutional law, constitutional theory, legisprudence, and public international law.

Hillel Sommer is Senior Lecturer at the Radzyner School Law School, Israel. He researches and teaches Constitutional Law and Marketing and Advertising Law. At IDC, Sommer served as first Dean of Student Affairs and as Vice Dean of the Law School. Further, Sommer advised the Knesset's Constitution, Law and Justice Commission in its most recent attempt to draft a Constitution for the State of Israel. Sommer is the recipient of a Fulbright Fellowship for his studies at Yale.

Silvia Suteu is Associate Professor at the Faculty of Laws, University College London (UCL). She specialises in comparative constitutional law and constitutional theory, with a focus on comparative constitutional change, gender equality, and participatory constitutionalism, on which she has published widely. Her monograph, *Eternity Clauses in Democratic Constitutionalism*, was published by Oxford University Press in 2021 and won the 2023 ICON-S Book Prize.

Jure Vidmar holds the Chair of Public International Law at Maastricht University. He is also a Member of the Permanent Court of Arbitration in The Hague, Member of the OSCE Court of Conciliation and Arbitration in Geneva, and is appointed to the Pool of Arbitrators and Trade and Sustainable Development Experts under the EU's Trade Agreements with Third Countries. He has also served as Judge ad hoc of the European Court of Human Rights.

PART I

CCI in the International Context

1

Conforming Interpretation in the EU Through the Lens of the CJEU's Case Law

ANTONIA BARAGGIA

I. Introduction

Conforming interpretation is an increasingly common interpretive canon in contexts that see the interaction of different legal systems no longer organised on the classic hierarchical criterion.

It is an interpretive technique that has a regulative function in the relations between different and competing legalities, necessary for the resilience of multi-level systems and corresponding to the new 'post-national constellation'[1] defined by the intersection of national law, EU law and international law. It is a particularly effective tool for ensuring consistency between different norms within the same system or for managing conflicts that inevitably arise where two or more legal systems intersect.

In Union law, particularly considering the case law of the Court of Justice, we find both types of applications.[2]

The first, which we can call *internal* conforming interpretation, requires that the judges interpret the EU law in light of the provision of the Treaties and of the EU Charter of Fundamental Rights (CFR), as in the case *ZZ v Secretary of State for the Home Department*, where the CJEU argued that 'it must be determined whether and to what extent Articles 30(2) and 31 of Directive 2004/38, the provisions of which must be interpreted in a manner which complies with the requirements flowing from Article 47 of the Charter, permit the grounds of a decision taken under Article 27 of the directive not to be disclosed precisely and in full [...] The interpretation of Articles 30(2) and 31 of Directive 2004/38, read in

[1] Jürgen Habermas, *La costellazione postnazionale: mercato globale, nazioni e democrazia* (Milano, Feltrinelli, 1999).

[2] Matthias Klatt, 'The Legitimacy of Constitutionally Conforming Interpretation' in Matthias Klatt (ed), *Constitutional Conforming Interpretation – Comparative Perspectives Volume 1: National Reports* (Oxford, Hart Publishing, 2023) s I.

the light of Article 47 of the Charter, cannot have the effect of failing to meet the level of protection that is guaranteed.'[3]

In this case, it is a conforming interpretation within the European legal system, analogous to the constitutional conforming interpretation found in many national systems, aimed at ensuring compliance of subordinate norms with the higher-ranking source.

It is a different case with the second *genus* of conforming interpretation, which does not operate within a hierarchically ordered system of sources but in a context of plurality of legal systems, without a hierarchical ordering criterion. Both the conforming interpretation of national law to EU law and the conforming interpretation of EU law to international law belong to this genus. In both cases, these are situations characterised by a kind of inter-legality, in the light of which conforming interpretation is not so much functional to respect the hierarchy of sources as to settle, as far as possible, antinomies and contrasts by way of interpretation, even where there is no clear hierarchical ordering.

The CJEU's jurisprudence on conforming interpretation should be read considering this systemic function. It is a jurisprudence that recognises in the hands of national authorities (judges first and foremost, but also executives and legislators) a real duty to interpret national legislation in accordance with EU law, when it is possible. Only if any possibility of conforming interpretation is precluded, national authorities should disapply – as an extrema ratio – national law incompatible with the EU law.[4] Indeed, in cases where such an interpretation proves impracticable, the domestic court will have to, as appropriate, disapply the national rule irretrievably conflicting with EU law,[5] and/or trigger the judgment of constitutional legitimacy of said norm for a conflict with the interposed parameter of constitutional rank.

However, a principle that seems to introduce an ordering and pacifying criterion for tensions can itself become a source of 'disorder' and conflict.

Consider, for example, the case where the conforming interpretation of a national norm leads the latter to be in conflict with the national Constitution.

In this case, how to resolve such a conflict? By virtue of the primacy of EU law, could one accept a violation of the constitution by the norm in question, when it is well understood that it does not concern the fundamental non-derogable national constitutional principles, the so-called counter-limits? The counter-limits doctrine, as is known, was elaborated by the Italian Constitutional Court to stress how 'the fundamental principles of the constitutional order and

[3] Case C-300/11 *ZZ v Secretary of State for the Home Department* ECLI:EU:C:2013:363, [2013] QB 1136, paras 50, 52.

[4] Case C-282/10 *Dominguez* ECLI:EU:C:2012:33, [2012] 2 CMLR 14, para 23: '[T]he question whether a national provision must be disapplied in as much as it conflicts with European Union law arises only if no compatible interpretation of that provision proves possible.'

[5] Cases C-106/77 *Amministrazione delle finanze dello Stato v S.p.A. Simmenthal* ECLI:EU:C:1978:49, [1978] ECR 629; *Dominguez* (n 4); C-176/12 *Association de médiation sociale* ECLI:EU:C:2014:2, [2014] 2 CMLR 41; C-573/17 *Popławski* ECLI:EU:C:2019:530.

inalienable human rights constitute a "limit to the introduction (…) of generally recognised norms of international law, to which the Italian legal order conforms under Article 10, para. 1 of the Constitution" (Judgment No. 48/1979 and No. 73/2011) and serve as "counter-limits" to the entry of European Union law […] In other words, they stand for the qualifying fundamental elements of the constitutional order. As such, they fall outside the scope of constitutional review'.[6] Or, on the contrary, weakening the primacy of EU law, should one opt for a declaration that the rule is unconstitutional as interpreted in light of the conforming interpretation? As we can see, the terrain of conforming interpretation is far from free of pitfalls. Indeed, as stated by the literature, 'despite the success of this instrument, it still remains mysterious in its foundation, content, scope, and legal nature.'[7]

All these elements may change in light of the specific perspective of the actor invoking and applying conforming interpretation: for the CJEU, for example, the foundation of conforming interpretation may be found in the principle of sincere cooperation and in the primacy of EU law; for national courts, especially apex court, it may be found in the constitutional provision that recognised EU law as a source of law ordinary legislation must comply with. Even if you look at the scope, while for the EU consistent interpretation aims at affirming the primacy of EU law and to achieve a kind of harmonisation of the different legislations, for national courts it is one of the different tools to avoid a conflict between domestic and EU law.[8]

As Advocate General Tizzano argued, 'the duty of consistent interpretation is one of the "structural" effects of [European] law which, together with the more "invasive" device of direct effect, enables national law to be brought into line with the substance and aims of [European] law. Because it is structural in nature, the duty applies with respect to all sources of [European] law, whether constituted by primary or secondary legislation, and whether embodied in acts whose legal effects are binding or not.'[9]

The purpose of this chapter is to trace the emergence of the principle of conforming interpretation in the EU, taking the perspective of the Court of Justice: it will highlight the developments of this instrument from its origins (and its narrow application to the EU directives) to its most recent uses (with regard in particular to the issue of the EU fundamental values and European identity).

[6] It. Const. Court, judgment no. 238/2014, Conclusions in Point of Law, para 3.2.

[7] Enzo Cannizzaro, 'Interpretazione conforme fra tecniche ermeneutiche ed effetti normativi' in Alessandro Bernardi (ed), *L'interpretazione conforme al diritto dell'Unione europea profili e limiti di un vincolo problematico* (Napoli, Jovene, 2015) 3.

[8] Elisabetta Lamarque, 'L'interpretazione conforme al diritto dell'Unione europea secondo la Corte costituzionale italiana' in Bernardi (ibid) 91; Elisabetta Lamarque, 'The Italian Courts and Interpretation in Conformity With the Constitution, EU Law and the ECHR' (2012) 4 *Rivista AIC* 1.

[9] Case C-144/04 *Mangold* ECLI:EU:C:2005:420, [2005] ECR I-9981, para 117.

II. Conforming Interpretation to EU Directives

As has often been the case with other relevant concepts in the evolution of European Union law, when we speak of conforming interpretation, we are dealing with a concept first introduced and developed in jurisprudence by the Court of Justice (CJEU) in order to reconcile the tensions inherent in a composite system. Consistent interpretation can be considered one of the different 'judiciary-based principles governing the interplay between EU law and domestic legal orders: effectiveness, primacy, effective judicial protection, direct effect.'[10]

In particular, the very first application of consistent interpretation in the EU dealt with the duty that national courts have, as part of the Member State responsible for the fulfilment of EU obligations, to interpret national law in light of EU law, namely directives.[11] The use of consistent interpretation achieves indirectly, via judicial interpretation of national law, the result obtainable through direct effect of directives where that principle cannot be applied. This is the reason why the use of conforming interpretation vis à vis EU directives has also been defined as 'indirect effect'.

The principle was developed by the Court of Justice case law in *Von Colson*[12] and its scope was widened in *Marleasing*[13] and further detailed in copious case law, which has rooted the duty of consistent interpretation in the very nature of the EU.

Let's proceed in order recalling the main steps of the CJEU case law crafting the duty of consistent interpretation.

The case of *Von Colson and Kamann v Land Nordrhein-Westfalen* (C-14/83) is widely recognised as the leading case for the development of the principle of conforming interpretation in the EU. The case helped establish how national courts should apply EU law, even when national laws are not explicitly aligned with EU directives. As it is well-known, the case involved two female social workers, Renate Von Colson and Sabine Kamann, who applied for a position at a men's prison in Germany, managed by Land Nordrhein-Westfalen. Despite being qualified, they were not considered for the position due to their gender. They argued that this was contrary to the Council Directive 76/207/EEC on the implementation of the principle of equal treatment for men and women as regards access to employment, vocational training, and promotion, and working conditions.

The key legal question was whether the German government had failed to properly implement the EU directive on equal treatment, which required Member States to abolish all forms of gender discrimination in employment. The CJEU,

[10] Daniele Gallo, 'Rethinking Direct Effect and Its Evolution: A Proposal' (2022) 1 *European Law Open* 576, 577.

[11] Gerrit Betlem, 'The Doctrine of Consistent Interpretation: Managing Legal Uncertainty' (2022) 22(3) *Oxford Journal of Legal Studies* 397.

[12] Case C-14/83 *Sabine von Colson and Elisabeth Kamann v Land Nordrhein-Westfalen* ECLI:EU:C:1984:153, [1984] ECR 1891.

[13] Case C-106/89 *Marleasing SA v La Comercial Internacional de Alimentación SA* ECLI:EU:C:1990:395, [1990] ECR I-4135.

for the first time, explicitly introduced the principle of consistent interpretation, instructing national courts to interpret and apply their national law in light of the text and purpose of the directive. The Court stated that it was the obligation of the national court to interpret its national law in light of the wording and the purpose of the directive to achieve the result sought by the directive.

The principle was further developed in the *Marleasing* decision, which had wide-reaching implications for the application of EU law within Member States, extending the principle of conforming interpretation even in the case that national laws were adopted before the EU directive: 'in applying national law, whether the prevision in question were adopted before or after the directive, the national court called upon to interpret it is required to do so, as far as possible, in the light of the wording and purpose of the directive.'[14]

The principle of conforming interpretation even seems to override the duty to disapply national law that is incompatible with EU law:[15] as the Court has stated in Case C-282/10 *Dominguez*, paragraph 23: 'the question whether a national provision must be disapplied in as much as it conflicts with European Union law arises only if no compatible interpretation of that provision proves possible.'

The duty of consistent interpretation, therefore, is an extraordinary tool to affirm the primacy of EU, and it is inherently linked to the very nature of the EU system, since it 'enables the national courts to ensure, in the context of their jurisdiction, the full effectiveness of European Union law when deciding the disputes before them.'[16] Primacy, nonetheless, does not portray a hierarchical structure as in national orders, where the subordinate norm is invalid, but rather conveys a preference, or prevalence, among an inter-legality of sources.

While the duty of conforming interpretation develops, initially, regarding directives, progressively the Court of Justice has extended this duty to all Union laws, whether they are binding or not: the duty also applies in relation to the EU Treaties, general principles of EU law, regulations and even recommendations.[17]

In *Van Munster*, for example the Court affirmed that all binding norms of EU law are to be subject to the practice of consistent interpretation: 'when, for the purpose of applying a provision of domestic law, a national court has to characterise a social security benefit awarded under the statutory scheme of another Member State, it should interpret its own legislation in the light of the aims of Articles 48 to 51 of the Treaty and, as far as is at all possible, prevent its interpretation from being such as to discourage a migrant worker from actually exercising his right to freedom of movement.'

[14] ibid.

[15] Bruno de Witte, 'Direct Effect, Primacy, and the Nature of the Legal Order' in Paul Craig and Gráinne de Búrca (eds), *The Evolution of EU Law* (Oxford, Oxford University Press, 2021) 207.

[16] See Joined Cases C-397/01 to C-403/01 *Pfeiffer and Others* ECLI:EU:C:2004:584, [2004] ECR I-8835, para 114; *Dominguez* (n 4) para 24; Case C-306/12 *Spedition Welter GmbH v Avanssur SA* ECLI:EU:C:2013:650, [2014] RTR 5.

[17] Paul Craig and Gráinne de Búrca (eds), *EU Law. Text, cases, and materials* (Oxford, Oxford University Press, 2011) 200–11.

In the *Pupino* case[18] the Court has applied the duty of conforming interpretation to the framework decisions enacted under the Third Pillar, even though they lacked direct effect. Moreover, in *Pupino* the Court explicitly recognised the normative basis for conforming interpretation in the principle of loyal cooperation: 'It would be difficult for the Union to carry out its task effectively if the principle of loyal cooperation, requiring in particular that Member States take all appropriate measures, whether general or particular, to ensure fulfilment of their obligations under European Union law, were not also binding in the area of police and judicial cooperation in criminal matters, which is moreover entirely based on cooperation between the Member States and the institutions.'[19]

Indeed, the foundation of the duty of consistent interpretation is commonly found in Article 4(3) of the Treaty on European Union (TEU): 'Pursuant to the principle of sincere cooperation, the Union and the Member States shall, in full mutual respect, assist each other in carrying out tasks which flow from the Treaties. The Member States shall take any appropriate measure, general or particular, to ensure fulfilment of the obligations arising out of the Treaties or resulting from the acts of the institutions of the Union. The Member States shall facilitate the achievement of the Union's tasks and refrain from any measure which could jeopardise the attainment of the Union's objectives.'

Conforming interpretation is therefore a cooperative instrument, that aims to solve conflicts of law before resorting to the most severe action of disapplication of national law or even the declaration of unconstitutionality of the national law on the basis of the interposed parameter of EU law.

A paramount question, in this regard, is whether such duty of consistent interpretation merely falls upon national judges or upon the General Court (GC), too, when interpreting national law, as first stated in *Corneli*.[20] An extension of the duty to the GC raises several doubts, *in primis* the impossibility of it to refer for a preliminary ruling *ex* Article 267 TFEU to the CJEU, but also the potential scenario of the GC ruling against national consolidated jurisprudence based on non-consistent interpretation – a task, the latter, which, as already clarified by the CJEU, should not pertain to EU judges.[21]

Of course, there are some limits imposed on the use of conforming interpretation in light of the fragile equilibrium on which the relations between the EU and the Member States are built.[22] A consistent interpretation of national law is subject to the general principles of EU law.[23] These limits have been recognised by the CJEU itself, for example in the already mentioned *Pupino* case. Here the Court argued

[18] Stefan Lorenzmeier, 'The Legal Effect of Framework Decisions – A Case-Note on the Pupino Decision of the European Court of Justice' (2006) 12 *Zeitschrift für Internationale Strafrechtsdogmatik* 583.

[19] Case C-105/03 *Pupino* ECLI:EU:C:2005:386, [2005] 3 WLR 1102, para 45.

[20] Case T-502/19 *Corneli* ECLI:EU:T:2022:402, [2023] 2 CMLR 19.

[21] See Ilaria Anrò, 'Il diritto nazionale al vaglio della CGUE nell'ambito del Meccanismo di Vigilanza Unico, tra primato e nuovi modelli di integrazione' (2024) 1 *Quaderni AISDUE* 19.

[22] Sacha Prechal, *Directives in EC Law* (Oxford, Oxford European Union Law Library, 2005) 194.

[23] Case C-80/86 *Kolpinghuis Nijmegen* ECLI:EU:C:1987:431, [1987] ECR 3969, para 13.

that the obligation of conforming interpretation on the national court is limited by general principles of law, particularly those of legal certainty and non-retroactivity.

Moreover, conforming interpretation is limited also with regard to the national law: as Shutze argues, 'national courts are (…) not required to stretch the medium of national law beyond breaking point.'

In other words, the principle of conforming interpretation cannot serve as the basis for an interpretation of national law *contra legem*.

This principle requires that the national court does 'whatever lies within its jurisdiction, having regard to the whole body of rules of national law.'[24]

This latter statement by the court discloses some possible critical aspects of conforming interpretation. In particular, it seems difficult, if the national court is asked to consider the 'whole of national law', to distinguish conforming interpretation from systematic interpretation.

Whereas conforming interpretation, properly understood, requires the adoption of an interpretation in accordance with a particular provision of law, systematic interpretation requires conformity in relation to an entire normative system. In other words, prima facie, conforming interpretation would be a systematic technique, taking a particular norm as a parameter and isolating it from its context.[25]

However, the distinction between conforming interpretation and systematic interpretation is not always so clear, especially when we look at conforming interpretation to the EU Charter of Fundamental Rights or to the EU values of Article 2, the latter being one of the most innovative and fascinating developments in the relationship between the EU and its Member States.

Indeed, through the ever-expanding use of conforming interpretation even in the realm of EU values, the EU is capable of extending its own legal influence even in purely internal matters. Considering this, conforming interpretation can be considered a powerful federalising tool deployed by the EU.

If this is certainly the case, the tool of conforming interpretation is a kind of two-faced Janus: we should not underestimate that at the end of the day, the national courts are tasked to decide whether they can interpret the domestic law in conformity with the EU law, according to their specific interpretative techniques.[26] This feature brings national courts to the forefront of the evolution of the EU as a plural constitutional system, which develops thanks to the constant interactions between different and autonomous legal systems. As AG Maduro argued, conforming interpretation seems to require national courts to 'reconcile the irreconcilable: how to protect the Constitution within the domestic legal order without breaching the primordial requirement of the primacy of Community law?'.

[24] Joined Cases C-387/01 to C-403/01 *Pfeiffer* (n 16), para 118; see also *Pupino* (n 19).

[25] Cannizzaro (n 7).

[26] As Prechal (n 22) 194 argued, '[w]hen searching for an answer to the question whether consistent interpretation is possible or not, and thus when addressing the issue of the discretion of the national courts under national law, the crucial factor is the approach, or methods or rules of interpretation or construction prevailing within the Member State concerned.'

In reality this is the very essence of the EU as a community of law, as AG Maduro, once again, maintains: 'what the Conseil d'État is asking the Court to do is not to verify the conformity of a Community act with certain national constitutional values – which it could not do anyway – but to review its lawfulness in the light of analogous European constitutional values. It is through this process that what at first sight appeared to be irreconcilable has in fact been reconciled. The European Union and the national legal orders are founded on the same fundamental legal values. While it is the duty of the national courts to guarantee the observance of those values within the scope of their constitutions, it is the responsibility of the Court to do likewise within the Community legal order.'[27]

III. Conforming Interpretation to the Charter of Fundamental Rights

The entry into force of the Charter of Nice has introduced a new binding source of rights that poses new challenges for consistent interpretation. The Charter has set up a basis for a new phase for the CJEU, focused on the protection of fundamental rights in a complex area of intersection between EU law and national constitutional provisions.[28]

Even before the entry into force of a binding Charter, the jurisdiction of the ECJ over fundamental rights issues has developed through unwritten general principles and, primarily, from the impulses of the Member States. We can recall that the original motivation for the protection of fundamental rights in the EU was the German courts' insistence that EU law respects fundamental rights, and this was reflected in the ECJ's early jurisprudence in *Stauder* and *Internationale Handelsgesellschaft*. Nevertheless, the advent of the Charter has opened a new path in the relationship between the ECJ and national constitutional courts.

The evolution of the EU as a community of rights and not only of the market has challenged the traditional monopoly of the constitutional courts in protecting human rights in the domestic domain. As Sarmiento pointed out, 'the role of the Charter as a paramount reference of EU law grants new interpretive powers to the Court of Justice, but it does so in an area much cherished by national constitutional courts.'[29]

What is the role of consistent interpretation by national courts in the realm of the application of the Charter of Fundamental Rights?

[27] Case C-127/07 *Société Arcelor Atlantique et Lorraine and Others v Premier Ministre and Others* ECLI:EU:C:2008:728, [2008] ECR I-9895, Opinion of AG Poiares Maduro, para 15.

[28] See Aida Torres Pérez, 'The Challenges for Constitutional Courts as Guardians of Fundamental Rights in the European Union' in Patricia Popelier, Armen Mazmanyan and Werner Vandenbruwaene (eds), *The Role of Constitutional Courts in Multilevel Governance* (Cambridge, Intersentia, 2013) 49.

[29] Daniel Sarmiento, 'Who is afraid of the Charter?' (2013) 50(5) *Common Market Law Review* 1267, 1268.

The Charter has been recognised as having binding force as the EU Treaty, so national authorities have the same duty of conforming interpretation as regarding any other source of law of the EU.

Moreover, the Court has recognised that 'in accordance with a general principle of interpretation, an EU measure must be interpreted, as far as possible, in such a way as not to affect its validity and in conformity with primary law as a whole and, in particular, with the provisions of the Charter.'[30]

However, the field of fundamental rights is quite sensitive, because it is traditionally a matter of constitutional law at national level; consequently, the duty of consistent interpretation, applied to the realm of fundamental rights, may trigger some antinomic reaction, especially when the EU and national standards differ.

To properly assess the extent of the duty of consistent interpretation vis à vis the EU catalogue of fundamental rights, it is notable to stress that the Charter has a limited scope of application: as is well-known, Article 51 CFR states that 'the provisions of this Charter are addressed to the Member States only when they are implementing Union law.'

So, the duty of conforming interpretation can be applied to national courts only within the scope of application of Article 51 CFR.[31]

However, such a formula does not help in unravelling the knot, since its interpretation is highly controversial.[32]

Before dealing with the textual interpretation of this formula, it would be useful to highlight the main aspects of well-known ECJ doctrine on the scope of the application of fundamental rights (and specifically of the general principle of EU law), developed before the adoption of the Charter of Nice. Two paradigms were affirmed by the ECJ: the Member States are bound to respect EU fundamental rights only when they implement EU law (*Wachauf*)[33] or when they derogate from EU law (ERT).[34]

Nevertheless, the true meaning of this formula is debated in scholarship and even the ECJ's jurisprudence has not been unambiguous. First of all, the explanations of the Charter[35] seem to lead to a broader interpretation, stating that the

[30] Case C-358/17 *UBS Europe SE and Alain Hondequin and Others v DV and Others* ECLI:EU:C:2018:715, [2019] Bus LR 61, para 51.

[31] Koen Lenaerts and José Antonio Gutiérrez-Fons, 'The Place of the Charter in the EU Constitutional Edifice' in Steve Peers et al (eds), *The EU Charter of Fundamental Rights. A Commentary* (Oxford, Hart Publishing, 2013).

[32] See Filippo Fontanelli, 'The Implementation of European Union Law by Member States Under Article 51(1) of the Charter of Fundamental Rights' (2014) 20(2) *Columbia Journal of European Law* 194.

[33] Case C-5/88 *Hubert Wachauf v Bundesamt für Ernährung und Forstwirtschaft* ECLI:EU:C:1989:321, [1989] ECR 2609.

[34] Case C-260/89 *Elliniki Radiophonia Tiléorassi AE and Panellinia Omospondia Syllogon Prossopikou v Dimotiki Etairia Pliroforissis and Sotirios Kouvelas and Nicolaos Avdellas and others* ECLI:EU:C:1991:254, [1991] ECR I-2925.

[35] Explanations Relating to the Charter of Fundamental Rights, art 51(2) 2007 OJ (C 303 02).

Charter is binding on Member States acting 'within the scope of Union law',[36] codifying in such a way previous ECJ case law on the binding nature of the general principle of EU law for Member States.

Second, ECJ case law has varied. In the *Iida*[37] case, for example, the Court seemed to confirm a stricter interpretation of Article 51, applying it only when a Member State is implementing Union law. Also in the *Ymeraga*[38] case, the Court affirmed that the refusal by a national authority to grant a right of residence as a family member of a Union citizen is not 'a situation involving the implementation of European Union law within the meaning of Article 51 of the Charter.'

In contrast, in the leading case on the issue, the *Åkerberg Fransson*[39] case, the ECJ stated that, whenever Member States act 'within the scope of EU law', they are bound to respect the fundamental rights framed in the EU Charter and that the ECJ represents the last interpretive authority. A stricter interpretation was then advanced in the *Siragusa*[40] case: here the ECJ affirmed that the concept of implementing EU law demands a 'certain degree of connection between national legislation and EU law itself.' As it has been noted, looking at the result of the *Siragusa* case, 'the Court declared it had no jurisdiction – the Court also seems to be willing to let fundamental rights cases be decided at the national level, when there is no convincing connection to EU law which would establish its own jurisdiction.'[41]

As we can see, the space given to the interpretation of the scope of Article 51 is quite wide,[42] and the concept of 'implementing EU law' remains indeterminate and vague, subject to the fluctuations of the Court. However, the scope of application of the Charter introduces a substantive limitation to the duty of consistent interpretation vis à vis the Charter's provisions by national courts.

A second interesting aspect of the use of conforming interpretation deals with the issues of the horizontal effect of the Charter's provisions[43] and in particular with the possibility to invoke the Charter's rights in disputes among private parties.

[36] ibid: 'It follows unambiguously from the case law of the Court of Justice that the requirement to respect fundamental rights defined in the context of the Union is only binding on the Member States when they act in the scope of Union law' (judgment of 13 July 1989, Case 5/88 *Wachauf* (ibid); judgment of 18 June 1991, Case C-260/89 *ERT* ECLI:EU:C:1991:254, [1991] ECR I-2925; judgment of 18 December 1997, Case C-309/96 *Annibaldi* ECLI:EU:C:1997:631, [1997] ECR I-7493).

[37] Case C-40/11 *Yoshikazu Iida v Stadt Ulm* ECLI:EU:C:2012:691, [2013] 2 WLR 788.

[38] Case C-87/12 *Kreshnik Ymeraga v Ministre du Travail* ECLI:EU:C:2013:291, [2013] 3 CMLR 33.

[39] Case C-617/10 *Åklagaren v Hans Åkerberg Fransson* ECLI:EU:C:2013:105, [2013] 2 CMLR 46.

[40] Case C-206/13 *Cruciano Siragusa v Regione Sicilia* ECLI:EU:C:2014:126, [2014] 3 CMLR 13.

[41] Benedikt Pirker, 'Case C-206/13 Siragusa: A further piece for the Åkerberg Fransson jigsaw puzzle' (*European Law Blog*, 12 March 2014), available at www.europeanlawblog.eu/pub/case-c-20613-siragusa-a-further-piece-for-the-akerberg-fransson-jigsaw-puzzle/release/1.

[42] See eg Jan Komarek, 'National Constitutional Courts in the European Constitutional Democracy' (2014) 12(3) *International Journal of Constitutional Law* 525.

[43] Sacha Prechal, 'Horizontal direct effect of the Charter of Fundamental Rights of the EU' (2020) 66 *Revista de Derecho Comunitario Europeo* 407.

In *Egenberger*[44] the Court was called into question to assess whether the national legislation was compatible with Directive 2000/78, establishing a general framework for equal treatment in employment and occupation, with regard to discrimination on grounds of religious beliefs.

The Court argued that despite the fact that Directive 2000/78 had no horizontal effect and that it was not certain whether consistent interpretation of national law was possible, the prohibition of any discrimination on grounds of religion or belief is mandatory as a general principle of EU law, laid down in Article 21(1) of the Charter, and it is sufficient in itself to confer on individuals a right which they may rely on as such in disputes between them in a field covered by EU law.

Moreover, the Court recognises that, like Article 21 of the Charter, Article 47 of the Charter on the right to effective judicial protection is sufficient in itself and does not need to be made more specific by provisions of EU or national law to confer on individuals a right which they may rely on as such.

For these reasons, if consistent interpretation of national law is not possible, the referring court must ensure judicial protection of the right conferred by Articles 21 and 47 CFR and guarantee the full effectiveness of the Articles even in disputes between individuals, by disapplying, if need be, any contrary provision of national law.

IV. Conforming Interpretation and EU Values: Toward a 'Value Conforming Interpretation'?

One of the most pressing challenges of conforming interpretation is dealing with the new course inaugurated by the CJEU on the normative nature of EU fundamental values, namely with the cases of the *Portuguese judges*,[45] *Repubblika*,[46] *LM*[47] and C-156/21 and C-157/21.

With the Portuguese Judges case, the court turned an 'austerity measures case into a rule of law' case,[48] operationalising the principle of judicial independence through Article 19 TEU.

The Court reasoning starts with a quite innovative interpretation of the scope of application of Article 19 TEU, when it affirms that 'that provision relates to "the fields covered by Union law", irrespective of whether the Member States are implementing Union law, within the meaning of Article 51(1) of the Charter.'

[44] Case C-414/16 *Vera Egenberger v Evangelisches Werk für Diakonie und Entwicklung e.V.* ECLI:EU:C:2018:257, [2019] 1 CMLR 9.

[45] Case C-64/16 *Associação Sindical Dos Juízes Portoghesi* ECLI:EU:C:2018:117, [2018] 3 CMLR 16.

[46] Case C-896/19 *Czech Republic* ECLI:EU:C:2021:311, [2021] 3 CMLR 18.

[47] Case C-216/18 *PPU LM* ECLI:EU:C:2018:586, [2019] 1 WLR 1004.

[48] Matteo Bonelli and Monica Claes, 'Judicial Serendipity: How Portuguese Judges Came to the Rescue of the Polish Judiciary' (2018) 14(3) *European Constitutional Law Review* 622–643.

So, the scope of application of Article 19 TEU is broader than the substantive scope of application of the Charter: as it has been noted, under this interpretation, 'the mere fact of being a court or tribunal with the competence to potentially decide on the interpretation or application of Union law is sufficient to come within the material scope of Article 19 TEU.'[49]

The latter, according to the CJEU, gives 'concrete expression' to the value of the rule of law stated in Article 2 TEU and it entrusts the responsibility for ensuring judicial review in the EU legal order not only to the Court of Justice but also to national courts and tribunals.

Under this narrative, national courts are part of the EU judiciary, and they fulfil the duty of ensuring that in the interpretation and application of the Treaties the law is observed and, in light of this, Article 19 TEU includes the obligation to uphold judicial independence at national level.

The operationalisation of Article 19 was just the first step of what we can define as an example of transformative case law of the CJEU, which was further realised in the twin decisions dealing with the legality of Regulation 2020/2092 on the so called 'rule of law conditionality mechanism'.

In upholding the validity of the Regulation 2020/2092, the CJEU outlined the contours within which relations between the EU and its Member States are developed, marked by respect for the fundamental values of the Union that were accepted and shared by the states at the time of their voluntary accession to the European project. In continuity with previous jurisprudence aimed at giving substance to the EU values, one of the most important consequences of the judgments is the elaboration of the normative nature of the values of the rule of law, which can be operationalised in principles and rules set out by Regulation 2020/2092.

This has been a slow progression that has led to the sanctioning of the normative and not just merely value-political nature of the Union's values under Article 2 TEU: these values, intrinsically connected to each other, become, in fact, the vector of binding forecasts for states, failure to comply with which can be sanctioned at the jurisdictional level.

The Court of Justice thus inaugurated, after an incremental process,[50] a new constitutional phase in the relations between the Union and the Member States, on the one hand through reference to the identity of the European Union as a common legal order, and, on the other hand, through recognition of the normative nature of the values of Article 2 TEU, which 'are embodied in principles that entail legally binding obligations on member states.'[51]

[49] ibid.

[50] Armin von Bogdandy et al, 'A Constitutional Moment for the European Rule of Law: The Importance of Red Lines' in Armin von Bogdandy et al (eds), *Defending Checks and Balances in EU Member States* (Berlin, Springer, 2021) 385ff.

[51] Case C-156/21 *Hungary v Parliament and Council* ECLI:EU:C:2021:974, [2023] 4 WLR 32, para 232.

In particular, the Court states, respect for the principles of the rule of law 'constitutes an obligation as to the result to be achieved' by the Member States, 'which (…) flows directly from the commitments undertaken by the Member States vis-à-vis each other and with regard to the European Union.'[52]

Speaking of the obligation of result, the Court seems to apply the language of directives to the rule of law: this is a deliberate choice[53] that the Court has already made, but only with reference to Article 19 TEU in some cases concerning respect for the rule of law.[54]

Never had it gone so far as to use such terminology in reference to Article 2 TEU. This stark configuration of the normative value of Article 2 TEU, moreover, has broad implications beyond the rule of law. It could also relate to principles outside the values of Article 2 TEU, such as non-discrimination and the principle of equality. The Luxembourg courts are clear on this point: 'although Article 2 TEU refers separately to the rule of law as a value common to the member states and to the principle of non-discrimination, it is clear that a member state whose society is characterised by discrimination cannot be regarded as guaranteeing respect for the rule of law within the meaning of that common value.'[55]

Recognition of the applicability of the values of Article 2 TEU thus leads the Court to define the nature, structural features and ultimate reason why the Union stands, particularly by playing on the delicate strings of the concept of identity.

According to the Court, the values enshrined in Article 2 TEU are 'an integral part of the very identity of the European Union as a common legal order. Therefore, the European Union must be able to defend those values, within the limits of its powers under the Treaties.'[56]

The conceptualisation of European identity is placed in tension with national identities so that, in case of conflict, European identity cannot be contradicted or denied by national identities: as has been argued, in light of this case law, there is no room for unconstitutional identities in the EU.[57]

This new course of the CJEU opens a new path for the role of conforming interpretation in the EU. According to this new turn of the CJEU case law, it is

[52] Case C-157/21 *Poland v Parliament and Council* ECLI:EU:C:2021:975, para 169, [2022] 4 WLR 105; Case C-156/21 *Hungary v Parliament and Council* ECLI:EU:C:2021:974, [2023] 4 WLR 32, para 231.

[53] See Jakopo Alberti, 'Adelante, presto, con Juicio. First Considerations on the Court of Justice Rulings Establishing the Legitimacy of the "Conditionality Regulation"' (2022) 2 *Eurojus* 25.

[54] See Cases C-83/19, C-127/19, C-195/19, C-291/19, C-355/19 and C-397/19 ECLI:EU:C:2021:393, [2021] 3 CMLR 27 concerning Romania and Case C-487/19 ECLI:EU:C:2021:798, [2022] 2 CMLR 9 concerning Poland.

[55] *Hungary v Parliament and Council* (n 51), para 229.

[56] *Hungary v Parliament and Council* (n 51), para 127; Case C-157/21 *Poland v Parliament and Council* ECLI:EU:C:2021:975, [2022] 4 WLR 105, para 145.

[57] Pietro Faraguna and Tímena Drinóczi, *Constitutional Identity in and on EU Terms* (Verfassungsblog, 21 February 2022), available at verfassungsblog.de/constitutional-identity-in-and-on-eu-terms; Pietro Faraguna, 'Constitutional Identity and General International Law' in Giuseppe Puma (ed), *Diritto internazionale e sistema delle fonti Tra modello centrrato e modello diffuso del controllo di costituzionalità* (Bari, Cacucci, 2020) 39ff.

even more true that 'Article 2 TEU entails a duty of value-conform interpretation of national law resting on national judges. As such, national judges and individuals can rely on Article 2 TEU to counter illiberal developments and attacks on the Union's common values in their Member States.'[58]

As von Bogdandy argues, '[t]he activation of Article 2 TEU has far-reaching effects. Its application could bring about a massive power shift to the detriment of the Member States' autonomy, identity, and diversity.'[59]

The turn toward a value conforming *interpretation* may open a new path for the future use of this interpretative tool within the relation between the EU and the Member State, substantially expanding the scope of EU law.

V. The Future of Conforming Interpretation in the EU Legal Sphere

What role does the canon of conforming interpretation play today in the EU legal order?

Whereas in domestic law it responds to the need to ensure the primacy of the Constitution, which is hierarchically superior to ordinary laws, in the case of EU law it becomes a fundamental instrument of inter-legal linkage, capable on the one hand of ensuring the primacy and effectiveness of EU law, and on the other of conferring on national judges a great deal of interpretive power. It is thus a key instrument given the pluralist and non-hierarchical nature of the EU system.

On the other hand, like all instruments that aim at recomposing normative tensions, it runs the risk, in its concrete application, of influencing the dynamics of relations between the different levels involved.

If the original call for conforming interpretation with reference to secondary law could certainly serve the objective of ensuring the primacy and effectiveness of EU law at the national level, the more recent development towards an obligation to interpret in conformity with fundamental values and rights raises some questions, especially if it is read, as this chapter has attempted to do, in the light of the affirmation of 'transformative' ECJ jurisprudence.

Indeed, the use of conforming interpretation, as it has been observed, 'involves a shift of power within national judicial systems. It strengthens the power of the Court of Justice, which could uniformly impose its version of fundamental rights and the principles of separation of powers on national ordinary courts. By interpreting European rules against the background of their national implementation,

[58] Michal Bobek and Jeremias Adams-Prassl, *The EU Charter of Fundamental Rights in the Member States* (Oxford, Hart Publishing, 2022) 64.

[59] Armin von Bogdandy and Luke Dimitrios Spieker, 'EU Values as Constraints and Facilitators in Democratic Transitions' in Michal Bobek et al (eds), *Transition 2.0. Re-establishing Constitutional Democracy in EU Member States* (Baden-Baden, Nomos, 2023).

the Court of Justice considerably extends the impact of its case law throughout the national legal systems.'[60]

This is even more true with regard to the recent developments that have brought the EU values of Article 2 TEU into sharper focus.

In the light of this possible consequence of the extension of the application of the principle of conforming interpretation, it is worth discussing a proposal put forward by a group of prominent scholars aimed at recognising the fundamental role of the national court in the construction of the EU legal order.

They proposed a 'reverse' preliminary ruling procedure: 'Whenever an encroachment on the national identity of a Member State is at stake, the Court must not ignore it (…). The ECJ is hardly in a position to fulfil this task without an input from national constitutional courts on the interpretation of national constitutional values, which are part of the values enshrined in Article 2 TEU. In order to complete this circle, a genuine dialogue, which is not a one-way street but a two-way street, is needed. Ideally, such a dialogue would take the form of a reference from the ECJ to the national court which is competent to give a binding decision on the interpretation of the national constitution.'[61]

This proposal for a reverse preliminary ruling procedure could represent an application of the principle of mutual cooperation and open up a new application of the duty of conforming interpretation with regard to the ECJ vis-à-vis the Member States.

It is not only this direction of cooperation that corresponds to the nature of the EU as a plural legal space. In addition, as has been noted, 'if the ECJ were to develop solutions jointly with the constitutional courts, it would very likely contribute to a higher level of acceptance and confidence in the European structures and institutions, deprive the opponents of European integration of an important argument, and integration as such would gain momentum.'[62]

The realisation of a community of values is a joint effort that must involve both the transformative role of the ECJ and the role of national courts, which act to bring the specificity of national identities into the EU discourse. The tool of conforming interpretation may prove to be a fundamental instrument, as in the domestic contexts, to foster this mutual interaction and to foster the EU evolution as a proper constitutional legal framework.

[60] Zdeněk Kühn, 'Centralized Judicial Review and the Problem of its "Over Centralization"' in Bobek et al (ibid) 292.

[61] Christoph Grabenwarter et al, 'The Role of the Constitutional Courts in the European Judicial Network' (2021) 27(1) *European Public Law* 43–62.

[62] ibid.

2

EU Constitutional Conflicts and Constitutionally Conforming Interpretation

CORMAC MAC AMHLAIGH

I. Introduction

Intersystemic interactions between EU law and national constitutional law – popularly framed in terms of 'constitutional pluralism' – have become a mainstay of contemporary constitutional practice in the EU. Originating in early judgments of the German Federal Constitutional Court (GFCC) concerned with the potential for EU law to violate fundamental rights protected by the German constitution,[1] it has exploded into a well-developed form of constitutional adjudication accompanied by a vast literature.[2] As befitting of a juridical phenomenon which has been developing for 50 years, the interactions between EU law and national constitutional law have changed and evolved over time. In the current iteration of intersystemic interactions, the GFCC has continued to be a protagonist with some particularly aggressive recent judgments which seem to represent a hardening rather than a softening of the more ecumenical approach it had taken in previous years.[3] The German approach has been replicated continent-wide by 'copy-cat' judgments from apex courts of other EU Member States which have adopted very similar arguments to resolve questions surrounding the possibility of EU law violating core constitutional provisions.[4] Perhaps most ominously, the growth and popularity of an interactive approach to the relationship between EU law and national constitutional law has been exploited by political movements in

[1] Solange I, BVerfGE 37, 291, 29 May 1974; Solange II, BVerfGE 73, 339, 22 October 1986. See also Neil MacCormick, 'The Maastricht-Urteil: Sovereignty Now' (1995) 1 *European Law Journal* 259.

[2] For an overview of the field, see Gareth Davies and Matej Avbelj (eds), *Research Handbook on Legal Pluralism and EU Law* (Cheltenham, Edward Elgar, 2018).

[3] Peter Hilpold, 'So Long Solange? The PSPP Judgment of the German Constitutional Court and the Conflict between the German and the European "Popular Spirit"' (2021) 23 *Cambridge Yearbook of European Legal Studies* 159.

[4] Cormac Mac Amhlaigh, 'Pluralising Constitutional Pluralism' in Andrew Halpin and Nicole Roughan (eds), *In Pursuit of Pluralist Jurisprudence* (Cambridge, Cambridge University Press, 2017).

certain EU Member States intent on regressing from what are understood to be the common constitutional values of the EU.[5] With regard to the latter development, intersystemic interactions between EU law and national constitutional law characterised in terms of two legal systems arranged heterarchically without the presumptive authority of one over the other,[6] has encouraged values-regressive political actors to defy attempts by the EU institutions to stem or even reverse their regressive constitutional reforms.[7] More generally, what this iteration reveals is that after 50 years, the interactive model of the relationship between EU law and domestic constitutional law remains in a state of flux and irresolution – no side has definitively settled the question of how interactions should be managed nor potential conflicts avoided in every case.

There is much that can be said about these developments, but I will not contribute to the vast literature on the topic in general terms. Rather, for current purposes, this chapter will examine the relevance of the preoccupations of the current volume, constitutionally conforming interpretation (CCI), to the question of the interactive model of intersystemic relations in the EU context. The chapter argues that there are two ways of thinking about the relevance of CCI to intersystemic relations between EU law and national law which track the major fault-line in constitutional pluralist literature. On the one hand we have *regulated* cases of intersystemic interaction, whereby potential conflicts can be resolved according to legal norms.[8] On the other hand we have *unregulated* cases of intersystemic interaction whereby potential conflicts are resolved according to politics.[9] Prima facie it seems that CCI is of potential relevance to the former – where there is still a 'constitution' *to conform to* – rather than the latter where there are no standards which can act as the 'constitution' for the purposes of conforming interpretations.[10] However, I will argue

[5] Roger D Kelemen and Laurent Pech, 'The Uses and Abuses of Constitutional Pluralism: Undermining the Rule of Law in the Name of Constitutional Identity in Hungary and Poland' (2019) 21 *Cambridge Yearbook of European Legal Studies* 59.

[6] Cormac Mac Amhlaigh, 'The Anatomy of Constitutional Pluralism in the European Union' in Davies and Avbelj (n 2) 62.

[7] So much so, that one of the Polish Government's White Papers on the reform of the judiciary directly referenced the progenitor of constitutional pluralism, Neil MacCormick, as part of the inspiration for its approach: 'This special character of the European legal system – comprised of national systems AND *acquis Communautaire* was best described by a Scottish law philosopher, Neil MacCormick. In his commentary to the German Federal Constitutional Tribunal in its ruling over the Treaty of Maastricht (case Brunner) where one can find roots for the nowadays ample and developed theory of constitutional pluralism.' The Chancellery of the Prime Minister, White Paper on the Reform of the Polish Judiciary (Warsaw, 7 March 2018), available at www.premier.gov.pl/en/news/news/the-government-presents-a-white-paperon-the-reforms-of-the-polish-justice-system.html, para 173. See Kelemen and Pech (n 5) 71.

[8] Such as MacCormick's 'pluralism under international law' whereby interactions were to be resolved according to the prescriptions of general international law. Neil MacCormick, *Questioning Sovereignty: Law, State and Nation in the European Commonwealth* (Oxford, Oxford University Press, 1999) 117.

[9] Again, MacCormick's early characterisation of 'radical pluralism' is an exemplar of this. MacCormick (n 8) 118. See also Nico Krisch, 'Who Is Afraid of Radical Pluralism? Legal Order and Political Stability in the Postnational Space' (2011) 24 *Ratio Juris* 386.

[10] See Matthias Klatt, 'The Legitimacy of Constitutionally Conforming Interpretation' in Matthias Klatt (ed), *Constitutionally Conforming Interpretation – Comparative Perspectives Volume 1: National Reports* (Oxford, Hart Publishing, 2023).

that CCI is also relevant to putatively unregulated cases of intersystemic interactions. In the latter case, drawing on Dworkin's interpretive approach to theoretical disagreements, CCI is recast in terms of an interpretive approach to intersystemic interactions. This denotes a shift from interactions based on what it identifies as criterial concepts to an approach based on interpretive concepts whereby the political value at stake in intersystemic interactions is emphasised and disagreements about the resolution of potential conflicts recast as rival best interpretations of that value. This has the result of emphasising the normativity of intersystemic interactions in the EU context even in putatively unregulated cases, as well as helping us understand pathological approaches to intersystemic interactions which fundamentally fail to recognise the political value governing such interactions.[11]

II. Regulated Cases: Inter-systemic Interaction and Conforming Constitutional Interpretation

The relevance of CCI to *regulated* cases of intersystemic interaction is generally uncontroversial and has been practised and theorised in many different contexts, particularly in the relationship between domestic law and general international law. Generally speaking, the focus and relevant 'constitution' here is considered to be the international legal system and domestic legal norms are to be interpreted in a way which conforms with the requirements of international law.[12] However, CCI can occur in the other direction too, where the relevant 'constitution' involves the domestic law of states. For example, supranational and international courts themselves can frequently deploy a form of CCI with respect to international legal norms to manage interactions between legal systems for the same purposes as domestic courts. An example of this tendency would be aspects of the ways in which the European Court of Human Rights deploys its margin of appreciation doctrine to respect national constitutional and policy preferences.[13]

Following Klatt's formulation of the orthodox account of CCI in terms of its four conditions – ambiguity, minimal divergent interpretation, minimal conforming interpretation and fidelity to the norm being interpreted – and taking the classic case of a domestic court considering the interpretation of a norm of the domestic constitutional order which has the capacity to conflict with a binding norm of international law, the relevance of CCI to regulated cases of intersystemic interactions would go something like this: where a norm of national law which potentially conflicts with a norm of international law is ambiguous, where one interpretation

[11] See s V.

[12] See eg Nick Friedman, 'United Kingdom. In the Shadow of Parliamentary Sovereignty: The Human Rights Act and the Principle of Legality' in Klatt (n 10).

[13] See generally Janneke Gerards, 'Pluralism, Deference and the Margin of Appreciation Doctrine' (2011) 17 *European Law Journal* 80.

potentially conflicts with the international norm, another interpretation conforms with the international norm, and none of the candidate interpretations (particularly the conforming interpretation) does violence to the normative content of the norm being interpreted,[14] CCI encourages the court to opt for the interpretation which conforms with the international legal norm as the most legitimate method of deciding intersystemic interactions. Here the legitimacy of CCI lies in the fact that it preserves the role of the courts under the separation of powers through its reliance on a rigorous legal method to resolve intersystemic interactions, respects the integrity of both legal orders, pays due deference to democratic considerations where the norm in question is the product of a democratically representative legislature, and, perhaps most importantly, avoids conflicts between the norms of distinct systems and therefore preserves rule of law-related values.[15]

In this regard, intersystemic interactions such as those between EU and national constitutional law are compatible with the standard legal-theoretical assumptions of CCI including the presumption of constitutionality, the unity of the legal system and particularly *favor legis*.[16] However, the one distinction between the role of CCI in *intersystemic* interactions, when compared with *infrasystemic* interactions between, say, a lower level statute and a higher level constitutional provision of the same legal system,[17] is that in the former case, the result of an inability to resolve any potential conflicts by adopting CCI[18] is the *disapplication* rather than the *voiding* of the conflicting norm where that norm is not a norm of the system. This has to do with the fact that few, if any, legal systems claim the jurisdictional power to void the norm of another legal system, particularly the international legal system.[19] Rather, the limits of the ability of courts to resolve potential conflicts where CCI is impossible is to *disapply* or otherwise nullify the *effect* of the conflicting norm within the relevant jurisdiction without any attempt to invalidate the norm in question.[20]

In intersystemic interactions, then, CCI can provide a useful tool to bolster the legitimacy of judicial decision-making by promoting values associated with the

[14] What this actually means in practice is ambiguous. Klatt argues that an interpretation 'must not wholly rewrite the normative content of the interpreted norm' and must not effectively usurp the legislative power. Klatt (n 10) s II(A). There are further details to be sketched in here but this broad idea of fidelity to the content of the norm will suffice for current purposes.

[15] Something which has been of concern to sceptics of constitutional pluralism. See eg Julio Baquero-Cruz, 'The Legacy of the Maastricht-Urteil and the Pluralist Movement' (2008) 14 *European Law Journal* 389.

[16] Klatt (n 10) s III. It is also the settled doctrine of the CJEU that 'national law must be interpreted in conformity with EU law.' See Joined Cases C-83/19, C-127/19, C-195/19, C-291/19, C-355/19 and C397/19 *Asociaţia 'Forumul Judecătorilor din România'* ECLI:EU:C:2021:393, [2021] 3 CMLR 27, para 246.

[17] Klatt (n 10).

[18] Due to the lack of ambiguity, no conforming interpretation which is not faithful to the normative content of the norm in question is possible.

[19] This jurisdictional self-limitation is an expression of dualist approaches to international law which are almost universal among states. For discussion of its theoretical implications for international law see Cormac Mac Amhlaigh, *New Constitutional Horizons: Towards a Pluralist Constitutional Theory* (Oxford, Oxford University Press, 2022) ch 3.

[20] Which is precisely what the GFCC threated in the PSPP case. See Hilpold (n 3) 179.

rule of law and ensuring that any conflicts between legal systems – again, paradigmatically between state law and international law – are resolved by recourse to legal norms and legal adjudication rather than politics. This is particularly relevant to the international arena where the legitimacy of international courts tends to be more heavily contested than state courts.[21] Even if conflict remains unavoidable due to the absence of the conditions necessary to permit a CCI, CCI ensures that all attempts were made to resolve conflicts according to the law, before brute politics is used to resolve the dispute.

III. Unregulated Cases

Under what we can call the 'circumstances of constitutional pluralism'[22] the possibility of norm conflicts in intersystemic interactions are becoming increasingly likely and recent examples from EU law show how a direct, and in a number of cases deliberate and provocative confrontational judicial politics can emerge where there seems to be little in the way of legal norms and methods which could manage the relationship between the interacting systems.[23] From the earliest iterations of constitutional pluralism, it was acknowledged that it may not always be possible to resolve potential conflicts according to legal standards and legal methods. As noted above, the idea of unregulated intersystemic interactions was first identified by Neil MacCormick (the progenitor of constitutional pluralism as a theory of intersystemic interactions in the EU) in a scenario which he identified as 'radical pluralism'.[24] Radical pluralism posits intersystemic interactions in terms of *heterarchically* arranged legal systems without the presumptive authority of one over the other.[25] In the absence of a *hierarchy* of systems which might furnish a clear conflicts norm such as *lex superiori derogat legi inferiori* to resolve potential conflicts, there is no clear norm-based path out of direct conflict between their norms. As such, the position of interacting heterarchical systems is 'all there is to be said as a matter of *law*'.[26] The radical pluralist position acknowledges that 'not every legal problem can be solved legally'.[27] Any resolution of direct conflict, whereby the normative position of an individual is such that they are both, say, prohibited

[21] Andreas Follesdal, 'Survey Article: The Legitimacy of International Courts' (2020) 28 *Journal of Political Philosophy* 476.

[22] See Mac Amhlaigh, *New Constitutional Horizons: Towards a Pluralist Constitutional Theory* (n 19) ch 1.

[23] See Hilpold (n 3). Specifically on the Polish Courts' judgments challenging EU law, see Mikolaj Barczentewicz and Marcin Matczak, 'Poland. Constitutionally Conforming Interpretation in Times of Constitutional Crisis' in Klatt (n 10) and Aleksandra Gliszczyńska-Grabias and Wojciech Sadurski, 'Is It Polexit Yet? Comment on Case K 3/21 of 7 October 2021 by the Constitutional Tribunal of Poland' (2023) 19 *European Constitutional Law Review* 163.

[24] MacCormick (n 8) 117.

[25] Mac Amhlaigh, 'The Anatomy of Constitutional Pluralism in the European Union' (n 6).

[26] MacCormick (n 8) 119.

[27] ibid.

and permitted from undertaking an action, is avoided, in the main, by judicial circumspection and *political* as much as legal judgment.[28] Radical pluralism sees unregulated cases of intersystemic interactions as coming down, ultimately, to 'political action'[29] including political action by courts. There is only so much that CCI can do, it seems, to manage unregulated interactions in a norm-based way.

For some, the lack of regulation of intersystemic interactions are a cause for celebration. Krisch, for example, has argued that the type of interactions emerging from unregulated cases is a positive development allowing for more pluralism and diversity in supranational law.[30] Unregulated pluralism, Krisch argues, leaves a space for adaption, contestation and mutual checks and balances.[31] Unregulated cases of interaction do, however, come with risks. First, there is an obvious risk to the standard legitimacy associated with judicial decision making (which is exploited by CCI as outlined above). Judicial decision-making is strongly supported by the values of the rule of law which includes the idea that, where normative positions are changed due to a judicial decision, they are changed according to the law – that is based on an interpretation of extant legal norms – rather than purely political action by courts. Where judicial decisions are made in the absence of clear normative guidance – such as in unregulated cases of interaction – much of the legitimacy of judicial decision-making falls away which can put the very legitimacy of individual courts in question.[32] Second, an unregulated *politics* of conflicts-resolution in the absence of specific normative guidance runs the risk of descending into mere power or unjustified coercion which violates key constitutional values and undermines the very point of *constitutional* governance.[33] Where intersystemic interactions are unregulated, it leaves scope for powerful political actors – including powerful courts such as the GFCC – to unjustifiably coerce less powerful actors which can have all sorts of normative and political implications including for the democracy of Member States, state sovereignty and the liberty and equality of citizens. This is particularly relevant to the EU context where a significant part of the success of the integration project has involved a clear rejection of pure inter-state balance of power politics where more powerful states subdue weaker states and supranational organisations or vice versa.[34] The formal equality of Member States alongside the central role of law in managing interstate relations remains a significant pillar of the EU's legitimacy.

[28] ibid.

[29] ibid.

[30] Nico Krisch, *Beyond Constitutionalism: The Pluralist Structure of Postnational Law* (Oxford, Oxford University Press, 2010); Krisch (n 9).

[31] Krisch (n 9) ch 3.

[32] See Baquero-Cruz (n 15). Similar concerns inform the idea of 'judicial activism' in domestic constitutional systems. Keenan D Kmiec, 'The Origin and Current Meanings of "Judicial Activism"' (2004) 92 *California Law Review* 1441.

[33] Cormac Mac Amhlaigh, 'Harmonising Global Constitutionalism' (2016) 5 *Global Constitutionalism* 173.

[34] Loïc Azoulai, '"Integration through Law" and Us' (2016) 14 *International Journal of Constitutional Law* 449.

Resolving unregulated intersystemic interactions by political means – even, and perhaps particularly, where these political means are adopted by judicial actors – can pull at these threads of legitimacy potentially resulting in the unravelling of the legitimacy of the integration project.[35] Finally, and relatedly, in developments that may not have been foreseen when MacCormick and particularly Krisch were celebrating the promises of radical pluralism, unregulated cases run a real risk of violating the common constitutional values of the EU and its Member States.[36] If law and constitutional values have a 'civilising effect' on interstate relations in the EU constitutional sphere, then their absence in unregulated intersystemic interactions can make the introduction of uncivilising elements such as the violation of core common constitutional values more likely just as we have seen with regard to the Polish government's celebration of unregulated conflicts to support its resistance to attempts by the EU courts to stem its violation of common constitutional values.[37] Many proposals have therefore been advanced to 're-regulate' unregulated intersystemic interactions which may see a role for CCI in the management of even unregulated interactions.[38] However, such solutions have failed to take the disagreement around solutions seriously and fail to identify the key terms of trade between the interacting legal systems in question.[39] In the ensuing section it will be argued that we can envisage a role of CCI in the management of unregulated interactions which takes the disagreement around such interactions seriously if we take an interpretive approach to the political value of EU law in intersystemic interactions in the EU context.[40]

IV. Constitutionally Conforming Interpretation and Unregulated Cases: An Interpretive Approach

The characterisation of unregulated intersystemic interactions is frequently presented in terms of a disagreement about the appropriate nature and locus of authority and in particular which level of governance, or perhaps more accurately which court, *should* have the final say on the norms applicable in the conglomerate

[35] Cormac Mac Amhlaigh, 'Eppur Esiste!: Legitimacy and Longevity in the EU's Long Decade of Crisis' in Matej Avbelj (ed), *The Future of EU Constitutionalism* (Oxford, Hart Publishing, 2023); Federico Fabbrini, 'After the OMT Case: The Supremacy of EU Law as the Guarantee of the Equality of the Member States' (2015) 16 *German Law Journal* 1003.

[36] Mac Amhlaigh, 'Eppur Esiste!: Legitimacy and Longevity in the EU's Long Decade of Crisis' (n 35); see also Kim Lane Scheppele, Dimitry Vladimirovich Kochenov and Barbara Grabowska-Moroz, 'EU Values Are Law, after All: Enforcing EU Values through Systemic Infringement Actions by the European Commission and the Member States of the European Union' (2020) 39 *Yearbook of European Law* 3.

[37] See above (n 7).

[38] See s IV.

[39] See Mac Amhlaigh, 'Pluralising Constitutional Pluralism' (n 4).

[40] For a full exposition of this approach to intersystemic interactions, see Mac Amhlaigh, *New Constitutional Horizons: Towards a Pluralist Constitutional Theory* (n 19) ch 8.

system that is the EU's legal order.[41] A variety of solutions have been advanced which attempt to provide an answer to this question. Alongside the more radical pluralist 'prescriptions' of MacCormick or Krisch outlined above where resolutions should occur on an ad hoc and mutually accommodative basis, implying that normative theory has a limited, or no, role,[42] others have, in a CCI vein, argued for a strict supremacy of EU law,[43] where EU law should provide something like second order content-independent reasons for resolving the conflict in favour of EU law each time;[44] or advanced solutions based on a supremacy of international law or based on an overlapping consensus and deliberative solutions.[45] However, each of these types of solutions present their own problems. The risks associated with radical pluralism have already been outlined above. With respect to the other, more normative (and CCI friendly) solutions, however, the problem lies in their failure to take the realities of these interactions seriously. These interactions are characterised by disagreement, including disagreement about which norms should apply to the interaction in order to resolve a potential conflict. As such, these putative solutions to resolve such conflicts merely replicate the disagreement about the resolution of such interactions rather resolving them in a normative way as the subject of the disagreement cannot operate to resolve the disagreement about that very subject.

Therefore, in thinking about the management of unregulated cases, we must both take the realities of disagreement and absence of a shared set of specific conflicts norms seriously, while at the same time trying to identify standards of management which allow us to distinguish between more legitimate – involving relevant normative considerations – and illegitimate – purely political and therefore potentially coercive – forms of management of conflicts in such interactions. This standard, then, can provide an outline of an incipient or intimated normative standard – a 'constitution' to allow for some form of CCI – for the management of conflicts in unregulated intersystemic interactions. Here I argue that Dworkin's interpretive approach to law provides a particularly useful methodology to achieve these aims.

Dworkin famously attacked legal positivist accounts of the concept of law as 'semantic theories of law' by arguing that they failed to capture the types of disagreements which actually emerge in legal practice, particularly among the judiciary.[46] Given the fact that positivists (at least in the Hartian vein) insist on

[41] See eg Gunnar Beck, 'The Lisbon Judgment of the German Constitutional Court, the Primacy of EU Law and the Problem of Kompetenz-Kompetenz: A Conflict between Right and Right in Which There Is No Praetor' (2011) 17 *European Law Journal* 470.

[42] MacCormick (n 8) 119.

[43] Roger D Kelemen, 'On the Unsustainability of Constitutional Pluralism: European Supremacy and the Survival of the Eurozone' (2016) 23 *Maastricht Journal of European and Comparative Law* 136.

[44] Cormac Mac Amhlaigh, 'Concepts of Law in Integration Through Law' in Daniel Augenstein (ed), *'Integration through Law' Revisited: The Making of the European Polity* (London, Routledge, 2012).

[45] MacCormick (n 8); Charles F Sabel and Oliver H Gerstenberg, 'Constitutionalising an Overlapping Consensus: The ECJ and the Emergence of a Coordinate Constitutional Order' (2010) 16 *European Law Review* 511.

[46] Ronald Dworkin, *Law's Empire* (Cambridge, Belknap Press, 1986) ch 1.

consensus among officials around what counts as law for the concept of law,[47] for Dworkin, positivists must understand the actual disagreements judges have in an unattractive way: they are disagreeing about the meaning of the word 'law'.[48] However, as they are using different necessary and sufficient conditions to argue for a particular meaning of the word 'law', they are not actually disagreeing at all, they are talking past each other.[49] It was based on this unsatisfactory state of theoretical disagreements about law that Dworkin went on to develop his well-known, valued-based conception of law in terms of 'law as integrity'.[50]

Much of the disagreement around the resolution of unregulated cases of inter-systemic interactions can be understood, it is argued, according to this characterisation of disagreement. We could understand interactions in unregulated cases as rival claims as to what the term 'law' or many of the common words used in such disagreements – such as 'demos', 'sovereignty', 'masters of the treaties', 'primacy', 'supremacy' or 'constitutional identity'[51] – *really* means. However, given that those involved are using different criteria as to what those words mean, there is no substantive disagreement at all; the interlocutors – mainly, but not exclusively, courts – are simply talking past each other. This type of pseudo disagreement in EU inter-systemic interactions has been aptly captured by Culver and Giudice in the following terms:

> [I]f the highest decision-making authorities are each claiming supremacy to interpret the relation between Member State law and EU law, what [are claimed to be] interacting systems look more like *two hierarchical systems talking past each other.* (Emphasis Added) Both systems include both the norms of Member States and the EU, but they differ in their view of which norms are supreme and who has supreme authority to interpret the norms. *So where is the interaction*?[52]

Characterising the arguments advanced in the context of unregulated intersystemic interaction involving EU law and national law in this way makes them, in Dworkin's words, 'pointless in the most trivial and irritating way'.[53] As Dworkin emphasises, law, and the role of courts in interpreting and applying it, 'is not a grotesque joke';[54] it matters that we understand what the law requires and what courts say in interpreting it given that, ultimately, coercion trails on the coat-tails

[47] Particularly around the 'rule of recognition' which specifies 'some feature or features possession of which by a suggested rule is taken as conclusive affirmative indication that it is a rule of the group to be supported by the social pressure it exerts'. HLA Hart, *The Concept of Law*, 2nd edn (Oxford, Clarendon Press, 1994) 97. See Dworkin (n 46) 34.

[48] Dworkin, *Law's Empire* (n 46) 31–33.

[49] ibid 43–44.

[50] ibid ch 7.

[51] For a study of the use and abuse of constitutional identity in the EU context, See Julian Scholtes, *The Abuse of Constitutional Identity in the European Union* (Oxford, Oxford University Press, 2023).

[52] Keith Culver and Michael Giudice, 'Not a System but an Order: An Inter-Institutional View of European Union Law' in Julie Dickson and Pavlos Eleftheriadis (eds), *Philosophical Foundations of European Union Law* (Oxford, Oxford University Press, 2012) 66.

[53] Dworkin, *Law's Empire* (n 46) 44.

[54] ibid.

of a judicial decision.[55] If we take seriously, as Dworkin does, the idea that law's function is to legitimate coercion, it is necessary, therefore, to understand the disagreements emerging from what we have been calling unregulated intersystemic interactions as a form of *substantive* disagreement with a view to approximating some sort of normative resolution of such interactions which can serve to justify, in part, the potential coercion which follows the judgment.[56] We therefore need to understand these disagreements as good faith *substantive* disagreements about some sort of criteria shared between the interlocutors which allows substantive disagreement to get off the ground. As Dworkin advises, the way to do this is to think of the concepts deployed in support of one or other side of the disagreement, such as in disagreements surrounding the concept of law, as *interpretive* rather than *criterial* concepts. Criterial concepts generally yield precise criteria, such as the criteria of an equilateral triangle involving a figure with three equal sides. However, interpretive concepts are concepts which we use, share, debate and disagree about *despite the fact that we do not have precise agreement about what their criteria are.*[57] Interpretive concepts presuppose an interpretive attitude which recognises that a particular object or practice such as law has some point; that it 'serves some interest or purpose or enforces some principle' in short, that it 'has value'.[58] Disagreement surrounding interpretive concepts, then, can be understood as rival representations about what presents that point or value 'in its best light',[59] thereby avoiding a descent into pseudo disagreement borne of a purely semantic approach.

This attitude imbues the object of our inquiry with a sense of meaning beyond the mere enumeration of its core features and, crucially, provides a basis of *agreement* – that a concept has an identifiable political value – about which substantive disagreement can then get off the ground in the form of rival best interpretations of that value. Thus, in order to view unregulated intersystemic interactions in terms of substantive, rather than semantic or pseudo, disagreement, we need to adopt an interpretive approach to such interactions and the concepts deployed therein. Disagreement about the characterisation and management of unregulated intersystemic interactions should be considered, both by theorists as well as participants in the practice, as engagement around a common question of value in order for them to be understood to be *interacting* and allow substantive disagreement to emerge which is then explained by differences in how to show that value in its best light.

Our gambit here is to suggest that the best way to make sense of unregulated intersystemic interactions between EU law and national constitutional law as a form of substantive rather than semantic or pseudo disagreement – and therefore

[55] Or, in the alternative, it matters that we understand what the law requires because of its central role in guiding action which may or may not relate to values such as human dignity. Contrast Joseph Raz, 'The Rule of Law and Its Virtue' in Joseph Raz, *The Authority of Law* (Oxford, Oxford University Press, 2009) with Jeremy Waldron, 'The Concept and the Rule of Law' (2008) 43(1) *Georgia Law Review* 1.

[56] Dworkin, *Law's Empire* (n 46) ch 2.

[57] Ronald Dworkin, *Justice for Hedgehogs* (London, Belknap Press, 2011) 160.

[58] Dworkin, *Law's Empire* (n 46) 47.

[59] Ronald Dworkin, *Justice in Robes* (London, Belknap Press, 2006) 155.

make them more amenable to CCI – is to understand the disagreement as rival best interpretations of the value of EU law.[60] In the context of the contemporary EU, the political value of EU law can be understood in terms of the ability of particular transcontinental institutions to respond to the challenges raised by contemporary globalisation and in particular the scale and capacity problems associated with unilateral state action conditioned by the requirements of legality.[61] These include a variety of governance questions whether relating to trade, environmental protection, climate change, tax evasion, security or more generally, in Dworkin's words, the prevention of 'economic, commercial, medical or environmental disaster.'[62] The disagreements involved in intersystemic interactions in EU law, then, can be understood as best interpretations of the presentation of that capacious value. For some, especially the EU Courts and their supporters, it is the political autonomy of the EU institutions and its legal system, the interpretive autonomy of the EU courts as well as the primacy of its legal system which ensures equality and the values of the rule of law in the integration process, which presents the political value of EU law in its best light. For others, it is state consent, state-based democracy, the presentation of EU Member States as 'Masters of the Treaties' and the values associated with transnational legality – and in particular, the requirement that EU institutions exercise their powers within the confines of the legal restrictions put in place by the EU's Member States as understood by their apex courts[63] – which provides the best interpretation of the political value of EU law. Crucially, the deployment of these concepts constitutes best interpretations of what the value of EU law requires rather than the assertion of stipulative conditions which result in semantic or pseudo disagreement and therefore unjustified coercion.

Taking our general interpretive approach to putatively unregulated intersystemic interactions, then, encourages us to recast these putative 'interactions' not as 'laundry lists'[64] of stipulative criteria of legitimate authority resulting in the pseudo- or semantic disagreement outlined above, but as an *interpretive disagreement about what presents the political value of EU law in its best light*. Summarising the interpretive account of unregulated intersystemic interactions, then, we can view intersystemic interactions between EU law and state law as based on an *agreement* of the political value of EU law and its broad aims of legally-regulated continental 'peace and prosperity'[65] which are then presented as rival conceptions of what

[60] Mac Amhlaigh, *New Constitutional Horizons* (n 19) 219–23.

[61] Another way to motivate this thought is to see EU institutions as providing a satisfactory answer to what Bernard Williams called the 'first political question' in an acceptable way, where the 'first political question' here refers to *supranational* rather than *national* politics. For discussion, see Mac Amhlaigh, 'Eppur Esiste!: Legitimacy and Longevity in the EU's Long Decade of Crisis' (n 35).

[62] Ronald Dworkin, 'A New Philosophy for International Law' (2013) 41 *Philosophy and Public Affairs* 2, 17–18.

[63] Hilpold (n 3).

[64] Mattias Kumm, 'The Jurisprudence of Constitutional Conflict: Constitutional Supremacy in Europe before and after the Constitutional Treaty' (2005) 11 *European Law Journal* 262, 276.

[65] Joseph Weiler, *The Constitution of Europe: 'Do the New Clothes Have an Emperor?' And Other Essays on European Integration* (Cambridge, Cambridge University Press, 1999) 246.

participants in the disagreement believe to be their most appealing formulation. This allows us to understand disagreements involving unregulated intersystemic interactions in terms of substantive rather than pseudo disagreements where a shared agreement of the value of such interactions precedes the disagreement making such disagreement substantive and meaningful.

Approaching unregulated intersystemic interactions in an interpretive way not only allows us to make sense of such interactions as a form of substantive disagreement, it also helps us to understand how different values and best interpretations thereof relate to each other. Once we start down the path of taking an interpretive approach to concepts of political value, there is an inexorability about thinking of value in holistic terms. As Dworkin notes, the interpretive enterprise 'weaves together hosts of values and assumptions of very different kinds' which are 'drawn from very different kinds of judgment or experience'.[66] It is therefore 'pervasively holistic'.[67] Engaging in an inquiry into political value, then, involves finding the 'place of each value in a larger and mutually supporting web … that displays supporting connections among moral and political values generally and then places these in the still larger context of ethics'.[68]

For current purposes, the interpretive approach, and its associated holistic emphasis, demands that the various 'best interpretations' of EU law, whether in terms of the autonomy or supremacy of the EU legal system, Member State consent or transnational legality, attempt to integrate their best interpretations with the other interpretations at stake. Thinking of unregulated intersystemic interactions in this interpretive way highlights the fact that disagreement in the circumstances which give rise to EU constitutional conflicts are substantive disagreements, and not pseudo- disagreements. Perhaps more importantly, it exposes and emphasises the 'normative core'[69] of unregulated intersystemic interactions, understood as *agreement* as to the political value of EU law in the context of disagreement of its 'best interpretation' as well as a shared commitment to the political value of EU law.

V. Interpretive Intersystemic Interactions as Constitutionally Conforming Interpretation

Once viewed in this way, unregulated intersystemic interactions appear increasingly, if somewhat loosely, regulated in a way which can leave room for a CCI

[66] Dworkin, *Justice for Hedgehogs* (n 57) 154.

[67] Dworkin, *Justice for Hedgehogs* (n 57) 154.

[68] Dworkin, *Justice in Robes* (n 59) 168. See also Luke MacInnis, 'Dworkin's Unity of Value: An Interpretation and Defense' (2020) 26 *Res Publica* 403. For a development of the implications of this holism for the concept of transnational constitutionalism, see Mac Amhlaigh, *New Constitutional Horizons* (n 19) ch 8.

[69] Jessica C Lawrence, 'Constitutional Pluralism's Unspoken Normative Core' (2019) 21 *Cambridge Yearbook of European Legal Studies* 24.

approach to these types of interactions. In taking an interpretive approach to unregulated intersystemic interactions in the manner suggested here, we not only make sense of the types of disagreements which emerge in this context as substantive disagreements, but we also have a normative basis for a CCI which can be applied to such conflicts and resolve them in a principled way, rather than engaging in pseudo or semantic disagreement with its attendant risk of potentially coercive interaction. Here our CCI involves understanding the political value of EU law as the basis for regulating such interactions, disagreements about their resolution and avoidance of conflict as being based on rival 'best interpretations' of that value, as well as a tendency towards coherence and holism. As a form of CCI it provides a trans- constitutional framework of value which can furnish the relevant 'constitution' to allow a CCI to get off the ground in these types of cases.

Furthermore, and being attentive to the particular concerns of the current volume, the interpretive approach to putatively unregulated intersystemic interactions defended here can be understood to be based on the same legal theoretical foundations as other forms of CCI.[70] First of all, and perhaps most obviously, it is based on a sense of the unity of the law, even if reasonably loosely, which 'guides all interpretations'[71] and provides the necessary 'consistency and coherence'[72] by avoiding unregulated norm conflicts. However, the unity here is not of the formal variety such as the hierarchy of norms of the Vienna school, but relates, rather, to a coherence of value such as that identified by Klatt.[73] Second, this approach, relying as it does on best interpretations of value, encourages a 'presumption of constitutionality' on all sides of the disagreement in the sense that the different 'best interpretations' of the value of EU constitutional authority are prima facie valid interpretations. As the interlocutors are engaged in providing rival interpretations of the presentation of a *common constitutional value* in its best light, which ultimately tends towards a unity of value, there is a necessary presumption of 'constitutionality' of each rival interpretation. Finally, the interpretive approach to intersystemic interactions outlined here shares the rule of law-based justification of the *favor legis* principle. As the 'direction of thought' in this general approach tends towards 'unity, not fragmentation',[74] and entails an obligation to integrate rival best conceptions of the value of EU constitutional authority, the participants in the interpretive exercise should understand themselves to be interpreting a common value even where they diverge, as well as strive to integrate divergent interpretations as far as possible.

Framing disagreement about EU intersystemic interactions in these terms is, itself, interpretive: it attempts to provide a 'best interpretation' of disagreements

[70] Klatt (n 10) s III(A).

[71] ibid s III(B).

[72] ibid.

[73] ibid. The idea that the holistic interpretive approach advanced here can be understood as supported by the unity of law-based justification of CCI gains support from Klatt's elaboration of the unity of the legal system in terms of Dworkinian integrity.

[74] Dworkin, *Justice for Hedgehogs* (n 57) 119.

emerging from unregulated intersystemic interactions. The account defended here therefore excludes disagreements which do not share an agreed paradigm informing understandings of intersystemic interactions between EU law and national law of the value of EU law about which disagreement about 'best interpretations' can emerge. The attempts by value-regressive political movements in certain EU Member States in recent times provide us with good examples of approaches to intersystemic interactions which seem to reject this paradigm, such as the provocative decision of the captured[75] Polish Constitutional Tribunal of 7 October 2021.[76] This notorious decision found that aspects of the EU treaties violated the Polish constitution,[77] including some of the fundamental features of the EU's legal system such as the very foundation and purpose of the EU,[78] the principle of sincere co-operation and mutual respect in the carrying out of Treaty obligations,[79] the establishment and jurisdiction of the EU Courts to ensure that legal obligations are complied with,[80] as well as the fundamental values of the EU including human dignity, freedom, democracy, equality, the rule of law and respect for human and minority rights.[81] It has been described by eminent commentators in the following terms:

> It is difficult to find any similar negation of the rule of law, of the principle of sincere cooperation among the member states and of the principle of effective judicial protection established by the European Court of Justice, uttered by a constitutional court of any other member state of the EU.[82]

Taking an interpretive approach to this putative intersystemic interaction, yields two plausible interpretations. One does not show such decisions as forms of substantive disagreement in their best light at all. On this interpretation there is no attempt to engage in good faith substantive disagreement on the part of the Polish Constitutional Tribunal. The Court here cares little about justifying the coercion which follows from judicial decisions such that the Court is comfortable with the law being a 'grotesque joke' in Dworkin's terms. An alternative interpretation could try to view this decision in its best light as an attempt at good faith substantive disagreement, but one which is particularly wrong-headed. On this, more charitable, interpretation of the arguments of the Polish Court, we could allow for the good faith of the Court in its engagement but decide that its interpretation of the value at stake is grossly mistaken. Dworkin paints of picture of what a good faith, but

[75] I use the term here to signify a lack of independence from political branches of government, and in particular the executive, such that it cannot be considered an 'independent and impartial tribunal' in the meaning of art 6 of the European Convention of Human Rights. The European Court of Human Rights agrees; see No. 4907/2018, Xero Flor w Polsce sp. z o.o. v Poland, Judgment of 7 May 2021.

[76] Gliszczyńska-Grabias and Sadurski (n 23).

[77] ibid 165–66.

[78] art 1 TEU.

[79] art 4(3) TEU.

[80] art 19 TEU.

[81] art 2 TEU.

[82] Gliszczyńska-Grabias and Sadurski (n 23) 164.

fundamentally mistaken, interpretation of a shared value might look like. Where we assume that an interlocutor advances an interpretation of our practices in good faith and as a form of substantive disagreement, but which seems like a radical departure from its agreed understanding, Dworkin argues that they may not be contradicting themselves nor speak thoughts 'no one can understand'.[83] We may understand them 'only too well' he argues and 'it is not inconceivable (though it is unlikely)' that they will be able to defend their views through a radical interpretation of a practice 'that is otherwise so appealing that it persuades us to abandon what was formally a cardinal paradigm'.[84] However, on further interrogation of their interpretation, Dworkin argues that 'if we remain convinced that his views are not only wrong but fundamentally wrong' such that 'his radical interpretation has missed some main point any successful interpretation must recognize' we should dismiss their views as 'absurd'.[85] In such cases we have reasons to believe that such an argument or interpretation is 'deeply suspect'[86] and fails to capture the core value at stake in the practice.

An interpretation of the political value of EU law in intersystemic interactions which includes an attack on its authority as well as its foundational values could fit either of these interpretations. Even taking the more charitable interpretation, we can, I think, fairly easily 'remain convinced' that the captured Polish Constitutional Tribunal's interpretive offering of the paradigm of the value of EU law in this decision is 'not only wrong but fundamentally wrong'[87] and that in managing unregulated intersystemic interactions in the way that it has, the Court has 'missed some main point any successful interpretation'[88] of the value of EU law must recognise. As such, the decision can be understood at best, as fundamentally misguided, at worst as travesty of the ideals of law and a blithe disregard for justifying and legitimating coercion. Given the broader political context of Poland's 'constitutional breakdown'[89] within which the decision emerged, we may have good reasons to adopt the less charitable interpretation. Either way, the decision should be viewed as exceptional, failing to qualify as a form of genuine substantive disagreement which should be taken seriously in normative terms.

VI. Conclusion

CCI provides a useful tool to manage judicial discretion in interpreting and applying the law to ensure respect for certain core values such as the rule of law and the

[83] Dworkin, *Law's Empire* (n 46) 92.
[84] ibid.
[85] ibid.
[86] ibid 91.
[87] ibid 92.
[88] ibid.
[89] Wojciech Sadurski, *Poland's Constitutional Breakdown* (Oxford, Oxford University Press, 2019).

separation of powers. As much is clear from its deployment in domestic constitutional systems.[90] However, in an increasingly legally pluralist world, CCI can also serve to manage *intersystemic* interactions which have, arguably, left open a broader space for judicial discretion and the insertion of politics than is the case with the interpretation of norms which are exclusively internal to a legal system. As we have seen from recent judicial decisions involving interactions between EU law and national law, there is a serious risk that this space can be exploited to avoid respect for core values and advance particularly regressive political projects resulting in unjustified coercion. An interpretive approach to intersystemic interactions as a form of CCI such as that outlined here serves to reduce the space for regressive judicial politics by providing a bench-mark against which to examine putatively unregulated intersystemic interactions with a view to differentiating between legitimate and illegitimate interactions. This benchmark takes the form of the value of EU law about which all disagreements must plausibly relate. Interactions which have no plausible connection to the value of EU law can, then, be dismissed as recklessly coercive or, on a more charitable interpretation, as a good faith, but fundamentally wrong-headed, interpretation of the paradigm of the value of EU law. Taking an interpretive approach to intersystemic interactions as forms of constitutionally conforming interactions will not necessarily force bad-faith actors to engage in good faith with intersystemic interactions, nor may it even help improve wrong-headed good faith interpretations of the core substantive value of EU law. However, it does, at least, provide us with a tool to help us determine and understand what it means to act in bad faith and question the legitimacy of such interaction which is the first step in a long – potentially very long – journey to remedying the exploitation of unregulated intersystemic interactions for regressive and ultimately coercive purposes.

[90] See generally, Klatt (n 10).

3

Constitutionally Conforming Interpretation and the Constitutionalisation of International Law: Certain Public Law Elements Short of Constitutionalism

JURE VIDMAR

I. Introduction

Discussing the legitimacy of constitutionally conforming interpretation (CCI) in constitutionalised systems, Matthias Klatt argues that:

> All legal norms of a legal order form a unified entity controlled by the constitution, which is the highest law. This unity guides all interpretations … The unity of the legal system builds upon two elements: consistency and coherence. A legal system is consistent if its elements are not in logical contradiction with each other. Any conflict of norms compromises the consistency of a legal system, and it endangers the rule of law and its clarity, foreseeability, and guiding function.[1]

In his seminal work *The Concept of Law*, HLA Hart argued that international law was a simple set of primary rules without any systemic coherence significant for municipal legal orders.[2] The Report of the Study Group of the United Nations (UN) International Law Commission (ILC) on Fragmentation of International Law came to a similar conclusion: 'The international legal system has never enjoyed the kind of coherence that may have characterised the legal orders of States.'[3]

[1] Matthias Klatt, 'The Legitimacy of Constitutionally Conforming Interpretation' in Matthias Klatt, *Constitutionally Conforming Interpretation – Comparative Perspectives Volume 1: National Reports* (Oxford, Hart Publishing, 2023) s III(B).

[2] HLA Hart, *The Concept of Law*, 3rd edn (Oxford, Oxford University Press, 2012) ch 10.

[3] See Fragmentation of International Law: Difficulties Arising from the Diversification and Expansion of International Law, Report of the Study Group of the International Law Commission,

The lack of systemic coherence can lead to problems in the practical application of the rules of international law. As the Study Group of the ILC further observed:

> [T]he emergence of conflicting rules and overlapping legal regimes will undoubtedly create problems of coordination at the international level. But … no homogenous, hierarchical meta-system is realistically available to do away with such problems. International law will need to operate within an area where the demands of coherence and reasonable pluralism will point in different directions.[4]

International legal scholarship has tried to overcome the lack of systemic coherence by introducing certain concepts and principles from municipal legal systems. The project on international constitutionalism has been particularly prominent in this regard. Its proponents have indeed tried to conceptualise international law as a constitutionalised 'homogenous, hierarchical meta-system.'[5] But some critical voices have pointed out that any instances of a hierarchy of norms in international law are merely perceived, while the practical application of legal norms remains non-hierarchical in nature.[6]

The non-hierarchical understanding of international law in principle originates in the Hartian description of international law as a *non*-system, and then seeks to achieve at least some systemic coherence and unity through the development of the so-called conflict rules.[7] These are the rules that resolve conflicts between different norms and sub-regimes of the international legal order. Some well-known examples are the principles of *lex posterior derogat legi priori*,[8] *lex specialis derogat legi generali*,[9] and the more specific primacy rule contained in Article 103 of the Charter of the United Nations (UN Charter).[10] The constitutionalist understanding of international law is more ambitious, however, and looks beyond the merely technical effects of the conflict rules. It builds on the notion of there being a core international value system, which is also reflected in a constitutional hierarchy between the norms of international law.[11]

finalised by Mr Martti Koskenniemi, UN Doc A/CN.4/L.682 (13 April 2006) [The Fragmentation Report], para 493.

[4] ibid.

[5] ibid; cf Erika de Wet, 'The International Constitutional Order' (2006) 55 *International and Comparative Law Quarterly* 51; Jan Klabbers, Anne Peters and Geir Ulfstein, *The Constitutionalization of International Law* (Oxford, Oxford University Press, 2009).

[6] See Erika de Wet, 'Paradigmen in der internationalen Praxis: Normenhierarchie versus systemische Integration' in Bardo Fassbender, *Paradigmen im internationalen Recht: Implikationen der Weltfinanzkrise für das internationale Recht: mit Diskussion* (Heidelberg, CF Müller, 2012) 81; Nico Krisch, *Beyond Constitutionalism: The Pluralist Structure of Postnational Law* (Oxford, Oxford University Press, 2010).

[7] See the Fragmentation Report (n 3) 249–56.

[8] Erika de Wet, 'Paradigmen in der internationalen Praxis: Normenhierarchie versus systemische Integration' in Bardo Fassbender et al *Berichte DGVR Bd 45* (Heidelberg, CF Müller, 2012) 2, available at dgfir.de/workspace/media/documents/berdgvr-2010-de-wet-thesen.pdf.

[9] ibid.

[10] UN Charter (1945) art 103.

[11] de Wet (n 5).

The idea of a constitutional hierarchy is primarily not based in the type of a source of international law as reflected in Article 38(1) of the Statute of the International Court of Justice (ICJ) (eg treaty law v customary international law), but in the standing of the norm itself. In this vein, it is often argued that the UN Charter is a constitutional instrument of the international community,[12] while other constitutional values and norms may be primarily derived from international human rights law, in particular those of *jus cogens* and *erga omnes* character.[13]

Focusing on interpretation and judicial practice, this chapter argues that the constitutional understanding of international law remains merely theoretical and is probably too ambitious for the current state of international law. This is not to say that international law completely lacks an overarching systemic framework or unity. Rather, the systemic framework of international law is not hierarchical or constitutional in nature. The rules of international law are interpreted in conformity with certain rudimentary systemic public law elements. There is a very minimalistic understanding of an 'international community as a whole' which makes international law more than a mere nexus of bilateral private-law type of obligations.[14]

As noted by James Crawford, 'at least some obligations are universal in scope, and cannot be reduced to bundles of bilateral interstate relations.'[15] Sarah Thin further explains:

> Despite Hart's rather infamous comments to the effect that international law is better described as a 'mere set' of rules rather than a system, there is increasing acceptance of the systemic nature of international law. The comparative lack of institutional development and coherence is no longer as great a barrier, and the essential 'rules of the game' … are increasingly accepted as equivalent to the source of essential authority found in domestic systems.[16]

It is argued in this chapter that general principles of law, obligations *erga omnes* and *jus cogens* norms provide for a rudimentary public law framework, which enables an application and systematisation of treaty and customary law. Such an application and systematisation takes place through the process of interpretation, and particularly through the method known as systemic integration.[17] But there is no pre-existing constitutional hierarchy in international law and the label constitutionalism remains devoid of any practical meaning in the interpretation and application of international law.

[12] Ronald St J Macdonald, 'The Charter of the United Nations as a World Constitution' (2000) 75 *International Law Studies* 263.

[13] de Wet (n 5) 54–59.

[14] Sarah Thin, *Beyond Bilateralism: A Theory of State Responsibility for Breaches of Non-Bilateral Obligations* (Cheltenham, Edward Elgar, 2024) 211–12.

[15] James Crawford, 'Responsibility to the International Community as a Whole' (2001) 8 *Indiana Journal of Global Legal Studies* 307.

[16] Thin (n 14) 215.

[17] Campbell McLachlan, 'The Principle of Systemic Integration and Article 31(3)(c) of the Vienna Convention' (2005) 54 *International and Comparative Law Quarterly* 279.

This chapter now continues with developing the idea that international law remains a state-centric legal system, which operates in the private law paradigm. In its essence, international law works as a system of private law obligations between states. Subsequently, the chapter turns to certain public law elements, which enable international law to function as a system. In the end, the chapter argues against a constitutional understanding of the international legal system.

II. State Centrism and the Private Law Paradigm

International law is a legal system derived from states. This is not to say that actors other than states do not exist in this system.[18] But states are those actors which have full international legal capacity. This also follows from the formal sources of law: It is states which conclude international treaties in the sense of the Vienna Convention on the Law of Treaties (VCLT);[19] and it is state practice, combined with *opinio juris* (again derived from states) which form customary international law.[20]

International treaties can be of various kinds. They can be bilateral, multilateral or indeed so multilateral that they are virtually universal. They can regulate something quite technical and specific, such as construction of a system of locks on a river in the border area between two states,[21] or establish something as complex as the United Nations (UN),[22] or the European Union (EU).[23] Treaties between states can thus create international organisations and other legal creatures with their own organs which can also make autonomous decisions,[24] at least to some extent, and some more than others – depending on what states have agreed to in the underlying treaty. Exercising their treaty powers, states may sometimes even create a Frankenstein over whom they lose control.[25]

When the UN Security Council adopts a legally-binding resolution, its binding nature is anchored in Chapter VII of the UN Charter which is an international

[18] ibid.

[19] The Vienna Convention on the Law of Treaties (VCLT (1969) art 1.

[20] *Case Concerning Military and Paramilitary Activities in and Against Nicaragua* (Judgment) General List No 70 [1986] ICJ, (The *Nicaragua* case), para 184.

[21] *Case Concerning the Gabčíkovo-Nagymaros Project (Hungary v Slovakia)* (Judgment) General List No 92 [1997] ICJ, (The *Gabčíkovo-Nagymaros* case), para 15.

[22] UN Charter.

[23] Consolidated Version of the Treaty on European Union (TEU) (2007).

[24] UN Charter arts 39–42; TEU arts 13–22.

[25] Andrew Guzman, 'International Organizations and the Frankenstein Problem' (2013) 24 *European Journal of International Law* 999, 1025, arguing that 'States sometimes create their own form of artificial life, the international organisation (IO). Dr Frankenstein created his monster in an attempt to improve on a world populated only by humans. States create IOs with the hope of enhancing international cooperation beyond what can be achieved by states alone. Like Frankenstein's monster, IOs created by states may behave differently from the way they are expected to. There is always a risk that an IO will impact the system in ways that harm, rather than help, the interests of states. An IO can become a monster.'

treaty. Hence, even the law-making powers of the UN can be traced back to states, or more specifically, to the very specific treaty which has been ratified by nearly all states in the world.[26] At the same time, it is a selection of states who vote in the Security Council; this is not an autonomous organ devoid of state influence.[27] The General Assembly resolutions are not legally binding, but they may be relevant for the identification of customary international law.[28] And it is again states who vote in the General Assembly. This body may be, inter alia, seen as a provider of secretarial services for the identification of international custom. It is always difficult to identify what states believe for the purposes of *opinio juris*, but the General Assembly is probably the most prominent place where states go on the record, and do so in a collective setting.

In terms of legal capacity, international law-*making* appears to be a prerogative of states, although sometimes this happens indirectly and through international organisations.[29] How about law-*breaking*? Is this also only a prerogative of states? Here, we come to the question of capacity to commit an internationally wrongful act. It appears that in most circumstances only an act of state is capable of being an internationally wrongful act.

In the *Reparations Advisory Opinion*, the International Court of Justice (ICJ) acknowledged that rights and duties under international law were not only inherent in states but also in international organisations.[30] The Court importantly added that this does not mean that the level of these rights and duties is the same as that of states, but that even international organisations have international legal capacity for the purposes of their functioning. The ICJ reasoned: 'The subjects of law in any legal system are not necessarily identical in their nature or in the extent of their rights, and their nature depends upon the needs of the community.'[31] After establishing that the UN had international personality, the Court continued:

> That is not the same thing as saying that it is a State, which it certainly is not, or that its legal personality and rights and duties are the same as those of a State. Still less is it the same thing as saying that it is 'a super-State,' whatever that expression may mean. It does not even imply that all its rights and duties must be upon the international plane, any more than all the rights and duties of a State must be upon that plane. What it does mean is that it is a subject of international law and capable of possessing international rights and duties, and that it has capacity to maintain its rights by bringing international claims.[32]

[26] UN Members, available at www.un.org/en/member-states.

[27] UN Charter arts 23–32.

[28] The *Nicaragua* case (n 20), para 188.

[29] ibid.

[30] *Reparation for Injuries Suffered in the Service of the United Nations* (Advisory Opinion) General List No 4 [1949] ICJ (The *Reparations* Advisory Opinion) 174.

[31] ibid 8.

[32] ibid 9.

The rise of international human rights law also gives international legal subjectivity to individuals,[33] as does international refugee law,[34] while international criminal law sanctions individuals as perpetrators of war crimes and crimes against humanity.[35] But one should not forget that even in these instances treaties concluded by states still are in the background, as well as customary international law which is shaped and formed by states.[36] Moreover, actors such as international organisations in principle can enter into international treaties and thus create international legal obligations.[37] But their treaty-making capacity is limited by their functional purposes and international organisations are in practice not bound by very many international legal obligations.

International law is thus for the most part a system of legal obligations derived from contractual relations between states. While treaties are generally considered to be contracts between states, they are not the only source of international law that generates contractual relations. Customary international law creates a nexus of contractual-type of obligations that is conceptually similar to the nexus of inter-state obligations created by multilateral treaties.[38] Despite their multilateral nature, custom and multilateral treaties still govern the horizontal relations between states, albeit those of more than two states. Custom and (multilateral) treaties do not create a vertical public law type of a relationship between states and the over-arching public authority.

The structure of international legal obligations in international law thus follows the logic of private law. Moreover, in his work *Private Law Analogies in International Law*, Hersch Lauterpacht noted:

> It is not only the vast subject of treaties and the analogy to private law rules governing their formation, validity and termination … and not only the theories of acquisition of territory (the Roman law rules of possession and occupation). There are few branches of the international law of peace which are not affected by this problem. The international law of tort and the theory of state responsibility; the measure of damages, the question of interest moratory and compensatory; the theory of succession; the doctrine of prescription;

[33] Robert McCorquodale, 'An Inclusive International Legal System' (2004) 17 *Leiden Journal of International Law* 477–504.

[34] Convention Relation to the Status of Refugees (1951) art 1.

[35] *Trial of the Major War Criminals before the International Military Tribunal Volume 1* (Nurnberg 1947), para 223, recognising that '[c]rimes against international law are committed by men, not by abstract entities, and only by punishing individuals who commit such crimes can the provision of international law be enforced.'

[36] Rome Statute of the International Criminal Court (1998). This treaty has been ratified by 123 *states.* Art 5 of this international *treaty* defines war crimes, crimes against humanity and genocide as crimes for which the Court can – subject to some other conditions – exercise its jurisdiction over individuals.

[37] Jose Alvarez, *International Organizations as Law-Makers* (Oxford, Oxford University Press, 2006); Olivier Corten and Pierre Klein, 'Are Agreements between States and Non-State Entities Rooted in the International Legal Order?' in Enzo Cannizzaro (ed), *The Law of Treaties Beyond the Vienna Convention* (Oxford, Oxford University Press, 2011) 3–24.

[38] The Vienna Convention on the Law of Treaties between States and International Organizations or between International Organizations (1986).

> quasi contracts; international servitudes; leases; international mandates ... the private law rules of arbitration., procedure and evidence, especially those of estoppel, of res iudicata and of the burden of proof – they all come within the scope of the problem.[39]

Lauterpacht's observation is as accurate today as it was nearly 100 years ago. The law of state responsibility is indeed much more developed today than it was 100 years ago, and the ILC's work on the matter drew very heavily from the theories of torts and delicts.[40] It would be quite plausible to describe the law of state responsibility as a system of torts between states. International judicial bodies to a large extent still operate on the logic that falls closer to private law arbitrations than to public judiciary in domestic systems. Indeed, not only international arbitrations, also international courts, such as the International Court of Justice (ICJ), require party consent and contain a number of arbitral features. And the concept of territorialism in international law is heavily based in the rules governing possession in (Roman) private law.[41]

What is evidently absent in the nature and structure of international law is an overarching political community and a political theory that would govern the relationship between that community and the state. In domestic legal system, the horizontal private law type of relations are supplemented by the vertical public law relationship between the state and the individual. But in international law, there appears to be no obvious vertical relationship between the international community and states as its subjects, and no political theory that would govern this relationship. This is why international law does not provide for, for example, a fully-fledged judicial system. International adjudication is not based in a fully-fledged public law of the international community, but in 'contractual' consent expressed by states in international treaties. International adjudication is thus limited to the extent of such private law type of consent.

Nevertheless, in order for international law to function as a system, certain public law elements had to be imported and imagined. This chapter now turns to the idea of there being an international community as a whole. It will be considered what public legal dimensions such an idea has and how the idea influences the interpretation and application of international law.

III. The International Community as a Whole

The private law paradigm in principle makes international law a network of bilateral obligations between states. However, as James Crawford noted, 'at least some

[39] Hersch Lauterpacht, *The Function of Law in the International Community* (Oxford, Oxford University Press, 1933) 3–4.

[40] James Crawford, 'The ILC's Articles on Responsibility of States for Internationally Wrongful Acts: A Retrospect' (2002) 96 *American Journal of International Law* 874, 876–77.

[41] Cedric Ryngaert, and Duco W Hora Siccama, 'Ascertaining Customary International Law: An Inquiry into the Methods Used by Domestic Courts' (2018) 65 *Netherlands International Law Review* 1, 1–25.

obligations are universal in scope, and cannot be reduced to bundles of bilateral interstate relations.'[42] It is argued in this chapter that general principles of law, obligations *erga omnes* and *jus cogens* norms provide for at least a rudimentary public law framework, which enables an application and systematisation of treaty and customary law.

The use of phrases such as 'the international community as a whole' may be seen as a silent adoption of the idea of public law within the international legal order. Such phrasings introduce a sense of a community, but does this have any implications for how international law operates? The debate seems to be have been squeezed between two somewhat difficult concepts: obligations *erga omnes* and norms of *jus cogens*.[43] The norms most commonly associated with these two concepts are the prohibitions of torture, slavery, racial discrimination, aggression, genocide and the right of self-determination (or rather prohibition of colonialism).[44] Instead of looking for hierarchical – or even constitutional – superiority of these concepts,[45] international legal theory needs to identify their theoretical foundations and asks what these foundations tell us about the idea of public law which is lingering in the background.

In one explanation, all non-bilateral obligations have an *erga omnes* character.[46] This view is problematic as it ignores the ICJ's reference to the 'importance of the rights involved', contained in the *Barcelona Traction* dictum. The 'importance' is a substantive issue and can only be defined by the special character of the obligations at stake. Maurizio Ragazzi argues that the obligations of this character have two components: 'the moral content' and the 'required degree of support by the international community.'[47] The concept of obligations *erga omnes* thus reflects the notion of a value-loaded international community interest. However, when establishing importance for the international community as a whole, the ICJ has only given circular references and rather generally invoked norms and principles of international law. In *East Timor*, the Court accepted the *erga omnes* character of the right of self-determination by arguing that self-determination was 'one of the essential principles of contemporary international law'.[48] *East Timor* thus defines the 'importance' identified in *Barcelona Traction* as something which is 'essential'. Such circularities are of little help where one needs to explain which norms are the

[42] James Crawford, 'Responsibility to the International Community as a Whole' (2001) 8 *Indiana Journal of Global Legal Studies* 307.

[43] See Erika de Wet, '"Jus Cogens" and "Obligations Erga Omnes"' in Dinah Shelton (ed), *The Oxford Handbook of International Human Rights Law* (Oxford, Oxford University Press, 2013) 541.

[44] Articles on Responsibility of States for Internationally Wrongful Acts (ARSIWA), with commentaries, UN Doc A/56/10 (2001), Commentary to art 26.

[45] cf Erika de Wet and Jure Vidmar (eds), *Hierarchy in International Law: The Place of Human Rights* (Oxford, Oxford University Press, 2012).

[46] Claudia Annacker, 'The Legal Regime of Erga Omnes Obligations in International Law' (1993) 46 *Österreichische Zeitschrift für öffentliches Recht und Völkerrecht* 131, 136.

[47] Maurizio Ragazzi, *The Concept of International Obligations Erga Omnes* (Oxford, Clarendon Press, 1997) 163.

[48] *East Timor (Portugal v Australia)* [1995] ICJ Rep 90, para 29.

concern of the 'international community as a whole', why that is so, and how is that manifested in the international legal *system*.

The ICJ has also been unable to identify obligations *erga omnes*, their content and underpinnings, on the basis of the formal sources of law alone. As Maurizio Ragazzi has put it, obligations *erga omnes* reflect 'an exceptionless [sic] moral norm (or moral absolute) prohibiting an act which, in moral terms, is intrinsically evil (*malum in se*)'.[49] According to Ragazzi, obligations *erga omnes* are binding not only because states agree that they are, but even more importantly, 'because nobody can claim exceptions from moral absolutes'.[50] The second claim, that 'moral absolute' operates as a direct source of international law, remains debatable. It is nevertheless undisputed that the concept of obligations *erga omnes* has its underpinnings in strong moral values and it is these underpinnings that shape international law making.

Although the concept of obligations *erga omnes* is value-loaded, it is not seen as a hierarchically superior international law. The Report of the Study Group of the International Law Commission on Fragmentation of International Law defines the concept along the following lines:

> A norm which is creative of obligations *erga omnes* is owed to the 'international community as a whole' and all States – irrespective of their particular interest in the matter – are entitled to invoke State responsibility in case of breach. The *erga omnes* nature of an obligation, however, indicates no clear superiority of that obligation over other obligations. Although in practice norms recognized as having an *erga omnes* validity set up undoubtedly important obligations, this importance does not translate into a hierarchical superiority ...[51]

Obligations *erga omnes* may thus be seen as a legal manifestation of certain shared community values in the international community, or of an international public order. While the concept may encompass 'moral absolutes', it does not take any hierarchical precedence over other rules of international law. The legal effects of these obligations remain unclear. It thus also remains unclear how these shared community values (the international public order) are accommodated within the international legal system. It does appear that obligations *erga omnes* and their community interest are systemic in nature; they reflect a sense of a system and community values which stretch beyond the pure bilateral or contractual logic of international law.

There is a great deal of criticism that after the introduction obligations *erga omnes* in *Barcelona Traction*, the ICJ did not develop this concept further and its normative effects thus remain unclear.[52] With regard to constitionalised legal systems, Klatt

[49] Ragazzi (n 47) 183.
[50] ibid.
[51] Fragmentation Report (n 3), para 380.
[52] See Craig Eggett and Sarah Thin, 'Clarification and Conflation: Obligations Erga Omnes in the Chagos Opinion' (2019) *EJIL Talk*, available at www.ejiltalk.org/clarification-and-conflation-obligations-erga-omnes-in-the-chagos-opinion/.

argues, that '[c]oherence [of a legal system] relates to the internal relations among the fundamental values of a legal system. While consistency is concerned with logical and formal aspects of unity, coherence allows us to comprehend substantive ties between the elements of a system.'[53] In international law, the problem is that the fundamental values of this particular legal *system* may well be reflected in the concept of obligations *erga omnes*, but the concept remains devoid of any direct legal effects. To build on Klatt, the substantive ties between the value-loaded *erga omnes* obligations and other elements of the international legal system are missing.

Although no specific rule may follow from the concept of *erga omnes* obligations directly, the concept introduces a systemic way of thinking and creates a vertical relationship between the states and the community. This element of public law influences the interpretation of treaties and custom: The obligations they generate are not necessarily only bilateral in nature, and international law also imposes certain systemic, community-oriented, boundaries on the creation and interpretative scope of international legal obligations.

A strong sense of an international community is also inherent in the concept of *jus cogens*. For a long time, the ICJ had been reluctant to employ the term *jus cogens* and was referring to an *erga omnes* character as virtually a synonym for *jus cogens*.[54] It is now somewhat difficult to separate the two concepts. The ICJ has not explored the content of obligations *erga omnes* beyond the overlap with *jus cogens*, which is itself a somewhat mysterious concept and will be further explored below.[55]

It is in the nature of *jus cogens* norms that they have an *erga omnes* effect.[56] Indeed, we are talking about jus cogens *norms* and erga omnes *obligations*. Arguably, *jus cogens* violations trigger *erga omnes* obligations – for the international community as a whole. Yet not all obligations *erga omnes* are to be found on the flipside of *jus cogens*.[57] Which obligations have an *erga omnes* but not *jus cogens* character remains unclear. Christian Tams concludes that '*[e]rga omnes* outside *jus cogens* is likely to remain uncharted territory until States begin to invoke the concept more commonly in formalised proceedings.'[58] Obligations *erga omnes* may be seen as a legal manifestation of the international community interest. To the extent of their overlap with norms of *jus cogens*, they may also be seen

[53] Klatt (n 1) s III(B).

[54] For more on the relationship between *jus cogens* and obligations *erga omnes* see Christian Tams, *Enforcing Obligations Erga Omnes in International Law* (Cambridge, Cambridge University Press, 2005) 157; de Wet (n 43) 57; Stefan Kadelbach, 'Jus Cogens, Obligations *Erga Omnes* and other Rules – The Identification of Fundamental Norms' in Christian Tomuschat and Jean-Marc Thouvenin (eds), *The Fundamental Norms of the International Legal Order: Jus Cogens and Obligations Erga Omnes* (Leiden, Nijhoff, 2006) 21–26; Michael Byers, 'Conceptualising the Relationship Between Jus Cogens and Erga Omnes Rules' (1997) 66 *Nordic Journal of International Law* 211, 213–19.

[55] For a survey of obligations for which the ICJ has established that they are of *erga omnes* character see Christian Tams, *Enforcing Obligations Erga Omnes in International Law* (Cambridge, Cambridge University Press, 2005) 117–18.

[56] See de Wet (n 43) 61.

[57] ibid.

[58] Tams (n 55) 157.

as an enforcement mechanism of the latter. It is wrong, however, to see obligations *erga omnes* as hierarchically superior law. Indeed, *erga omnes* obligations are not norms, but *obligations* created by a breach of *jus cogens* norms. As such, they do not have any independent legal force, but are secondary in nature and contingent of a breach of a certain norm. In this sense, a perceived hierarchical superiority of *erga omnes* obligations could only be a consequence of hierarchical superiority of *jus cogens* – if there existed such superiority. What implications does this have for the idea of an international public order?

As explained by Sarah Thin:

> If one state commits aggression against another state, or commits genocide on the territory of another state, such a violation would indeed appear to generate an injured state and a bilateral relationship of responsibility between those two states. However, such an act would be a violation of a community interest obligation and as such, would imply consequences that could beyond the bilateral model. The legal effect of community interest obligations, discussed in more detail in the following chapter, includes the generation of rights to invoke responsibility that go far beyond the bilateral relationship between two states. The exclusivity of the bilateral relationship of responsibility leaves no room for the legal expression of the community interest. The structures that we have developed around community interest norms and obligations, from *erga omnes* to *jus cogens*, break apart the exclusivity of the bilateral model and generate an extra-state interest. Community interest obligations and their legal effects transcend the bilateral model.[59]

Erga omnes obligations and *jus cogens* norms thus reflect a shift of paradigm from a strictly bilateral private-law-like international law to a more systemic and community-oriented model which adds at least a very basic and theoretical vertical relationship between states and the international community.

IV. The Rudimentary Public Law Structure

In municipal settings, public law and political theorists have defined and investigated the relationships between: (i) institutions of the state; and (ii) the state and the individual. This is necessarily different in international law where the actors involved differ from those at domestic level. Arguably, the relationship between the institutions of the international community have been addressed by the studies on fragmentation of international law.[60] These studies have addressed the problem of the relationship between the different regimes of international law built around different institutions (eg WTO law, international criminal law, international human rights law, international investment law), and have proposed a robust system of conflict rules to regulate the relationship between these regimes.[61]

[59] Thin (n 14) 69.
[60] See Fragmentation Report (n 3), para 493.
[61] ibid, paras 116–37.

At the same time, the vertical relationship between the state and the individual has remained either understudied or overtly influenced by municipal theories that are not always readily transposable to the international level.

Inspired by the rise of international human rights law and international criminal law after World War II, some scholars have started to place the individual in the centre of the international legal system and have conceptualised a domestic-like vertical relationship between the individual and the international community.[62] But international human rights and international criminal law are still derived from the law-making powers of states. The scope of these legal regimes depends on whether or not a particular state is a party to a certain treaty, whether it has filed reservations to that treaty, and sometimes also on how states have voted in the UN Security Council. In other words, the position of the individual in international law is not regulated by a public law of the international community, but by a private law system of treaty-created obligations between states.

If a public law of the international community existed, the vertical relationship in this system would need to be one between the international community and the state. On the international plane, it is the state which takes the position of the individual in a municipal public order. International human rights and international criminal law may well play an important role in the theory governing the vertical relationship between the international community and the state, but this is because the values of protecting human rights and punishing international crimes belong to the fundamental values of the international community as a whole.

International human rights and international criminal law in this public law model do not operate from the level of an individual, but from the overarching level of the community vis-à-vis the state. It needs to be asked whether the notion of 'the international community as a whole' can be conceptualised as a legal fiction to represent an international sovereign authority and develops a political theory of international law which defines the vertical relationship between the fictitious international sovereign – the international community as a whole – and the state. This section now demonstrates that the idea of public law is present in the concept of *jus cogens* and may be imported to international law also through the general principles of law.

A. *Jus Cogens*

In the 1969 Vienna Convention on the Law of Treaties (VCLT), the concept of *jus cogens* was for the first time unequivocally mentioned in international treaty law.[63] However, even in this instance it was only given a rather narrow power to void treaties. The Convention also remained silent on the content of the concept. Article 53

[62] See McCorquodale (n 33) 486; see also Anne Peters, 'Humanity as the A and Ω of Sovereignty' (2009) 20 *European Journal of International Law* 513.

[63] VCLT art 53.

of the VCLT, inter alia, provides that 'a peremptory norm of general international law is a norm accepted and recognized by the international community of States as a whole'.[64] The concept of peremptory norms thus also rests on the presumption of the existence of an international community of states with a shared interest. It is notable, however, that the VCLT qualified the notion of the international community with states, while the ICJ a year later, with regard to obligations *erga omnes*, only referred to the international community. The Court known for its restrictive interpretations of international law certainly did not omit 'states' accidentally.

In the Article 53 definition, a peremptory norm is subject to acceptance – by the international community of states as a whole – of the normative content as well as its peremptory character. Does this mean that *jus cogens* is an inherently treaty law concept? The concept indeed predates the 1969 VCLT and was invoked by writers even in the pre-World War II era.[65] At the time, it was unclear whether or not it was a concept generally operating in international law. This has now been generally accepted.[66] Even the VCLT reference to 'general international law' suggests that *jus cogens* is a concept grounded outside of treaty law but is capable of having systemic effects on the conclusion and interpretation of treaties.

The ILC draft conclusions on identification and legal consequences of peremptory norms of general international law, inter alia, provide: 'Customary international law is the most common basis for peremptory norms of general international law (*jus cogens*).'[67] This clearly indicates that *jus cogens* is normatively grounded in customary international law and may be seen as double custom: State practice and *opinio juris* need to accept both the content of the norm and its peremptory status.

Any norm of customary international law requires its acceptance by states through state practice and *opinio juris*. However, the acceptance of the special peremptory character, not only normative content, by 'the international community of states as a whole' points to the strong ethical underpinning of these norms.[68] Sandesh Sivakumaran argues that *jus cogens* represents a minimum threshold of the international value system.[69] The strong community-oriented ethical underpinning of *jus cogens* norms has implications for the law-making. International

[64] ibid.

[65] For a detailed account on the early writings on *jus cogens* see Dinah Shelton, 'Normative Hierarchy in International Law' (2006) 100 *American Journal of International Law* 291, 297–99.

[66] There are currently 111 state parties to the VCLT. Many of its provisions are nevertheless binding on non-parties to the Convention via customary international law. Although some states have refrained from ratification precisely because of art 53, there is little doubt that the article has customary international law status. Indeed, the status of permanent objector to *jus cogens* has not been accepted by the international community of states.

[67] ILC Draft Conclusions on Identification and Legal Consequence of Peremptory Norms of General International Law (Jus Cogens) (2022), Conclusion 5(1) [ILC Draft Conclusions].

[68] de Wet (n 43) 57.

[69] Sandesh Sivakumaran, 'Impact on the Structure of International Obligations' in Martin Scheinin and Menno Kamminga (eds), *The Impact of Human Rights Law on General International Law* (Oxford, Oxford University Press, 2009) 146.

law is, in principle, a consensus-based legal system. States create treaty obligations for themselves and at their free will. It is *state* practice and *opinio juris* which leads to the emergence of customary norms of international law, from which states again have an escape route through the concept of a persistent objector. In principle, it is only new states which become automatically bound by pre-existing customary law and even automatically accede to certain treaties previously governing their territory (eg human rights treaties).[70] Yet the peremptory status of certain norms, encompassing the minimum threshold of the international value system, also overrides some fundamental tenets of a consensus-based international law making.

The ethical underpinning of the peremptory norms can compensate for deficiencies in universal acceptance of these norms. In this context three examples appear to be particularly instructive: (1) The right to the freedom from torture is supported by very strong *opinio juris*, yet state practice is rather weak. There is nevertheless little doubt that the freedom from torture has a *jus cogens* status.[71] (2) Apartheid South Africa claimed that it was a persistent objector to the prohibition of racial discrimination. This claim was universally rejected on the basis that unlike ordinary customary law, peremptory law does not allow for the persistent objector's status.[72] (3) France used to claim that it had never consented to the concept of *jus cogens* as such.[73] This argument was rejected and now even France has accepted the binding nature of these norms in terms of both content and character.[74]

These examples reveal that with regard to peremptory norms, international law-making may work differently. As Robert McCorquodale argues, 'some human rights create legal obligations on a state irrespective of whether it has ratified a particular treaty, either because the human right is part of customary international law and so binding on all states or by virtue of a rule of *jus cogens*, which no state can derogate from or evade by contrary practice'.[75] Moreover, in *Furundzija*, the International Criminal Tribunal for the former Yugoslavia (ICTY) reasoned: 'Because of the importance of the values [which the prohibition of torture] protects, this principle has evolved into a peremptory norm of *jus cogens*, that is a norm that enjoys a higher rank in the international hierarchy than treaty law and even "ordinary" customary rules'.[76] The ILC Report has also noted: 'Peremptory norms of general international law (jus cogens) reflect and protect fundamental

[70] See Akbar Rasulov, 'Revisiting State Succession to Humanitarian Treaties: Is There a Case for Automaticity?' (2003) 14 *European Journal of International Law* 141.

[71] See Richard Garnett, 'The Defence of State Immunity for Acts of Torture' (1997) 18 *Australian Yearbook of International Law* 97, making the following argument: 'It may be argued … that the absolute nature of the conventional prohibitions, when coupled with the near universal *opinion juris* amongst states as to the illegality of the practice, may be a sufficient basis for concluding that torture is prohibited as a peremptory norm.'

[72] Byers (n 54) 222.

[73] ibid 229.

[74] See Alain Pellet, 'Comments in Response to Christine Chinkin and in Defense of Jus Cogens as the Best Bastion against the Excesses of Fragmentation' (2006) 27 *Finnish Yearbook of International Law* 83, 85.

[75] McCorquodale (n 33) 486.

[76] *Prosecutor v Anto Furundžija* (Judgment) IT-95–17/1, T Ch II (10 December 1998) 260, para 153.

values of the international community. They are universally applicable and are hierarchically superior to other rules of international law.'[77]

Despite these pronouncements, a hierarchical superiority of *jus cogens* remains a contested issue. It is notable that in the *Germany v Italy* decision on jurisdictional immunities, the ICJ did not accept any hierarchical superiority of *jus cogens*.[78] Even the ILC Report appears to limit the putative hierarchical superiority on law-making and the questions of interpretation. Conclusion 10 in principle repeats Articles 53 and 64 VCLT, and Conclusion 11 provides for some additional clarification on certain practicalities of these provisions:

> 2. A treaty which is in conflict with a new peremptory norm of general international law (jus cogens) becomes void and terminates in whole, unless:
>
> (a) the provisions that are in conflict with a peremptory norm of general international law (jus cogens) are separable from the remainder of the treaty with regard to their application;
>
> (b) it appears from the treaty or is otherwise established that acceptance of the said provisions was not an essential basis of the consent of the parties to be bound by the treaty as a whole; and
>
> (c) continued performance of the remainder of the treaty would not be unjust.[79]

While the wording of Article 53 VCLT is rather categorical, Conclusion 11 of the ILC Report provides for some reasonable safety valves. For example, it has been debated in scholarship and practice what the effects would be of a UN Security Council's Chapter VII resolution creative of an obligation to violate a peremptory norm. The generally accepted response was that such a resolution would be void,[80] but this does not necessarily mean that the UN Charter as such would also be void. Such a situation would be an example of severability in the sense of Conclusion 11(2)(a) of the ILC Report.

Conclusion 14 of the ILC Report addresses the effect of *jus cogens* on customary international law:

> 1. A rule of customary international law does not come into existence if it would conflict with an existing peremptory norm of general international law (jus cogens). This is without prejudice to the possible modification of a peremptory

[77] ILC Draft Conclusions, Conclusion 2.

[78] *Jurisdictional Immunities of the State (Germany v Italy)* [2012] ICJ Rep 99 [*Jurisdictional Immunities* case]. Consider para 93, where the ICJ provided the following reasoning with regard to the question of whether *jus cogens* takes precedence over immunities because of its special character. The ICJ noted that '[t]his argument … depends upon the existence of a conflict between a rule, or rules, of jus cogens, and the rule of customary law which requires one State to accord immunity to another.' The ICJ found that 'no such conflict exists.' This is so because '[t]he two sets of rules address different matters. The rules of State immunity are procedural in character and are confined to determining whether or not the courts of one State may exercise jurisdiction in respect of another State. They do not bear upon the question whether or not the conduct in respect of which the proceedings are brought was lawful or unlawful.'

[79] ILC Draft Conclusions, Conclusion 11(2).

[80] Antonios Tzanakopoulos, 'Collective Security and Human Rights' in Erika de Wet and Jure Vidmar (eds), *Hierarchy in International Law: The Place of Human Rights* (Oxford, Oxford University Press, 2012) 42.

norm of general international law (jus cogens) by a subsequent norm of general international law having the same character.

2. A rule of customary international law not of a peremptory character ceases to exist if and to the extent that it conflicts with a new peremptory norm of general international law (jus cogens).
3. The persistent objector rule does not apply to peremptory norms of general international law (jus cogens).[81]

Following the ILC's conclusions, when *jus cogens* norms are breached, the concept does not create remedies that would trump other international legal obligations.[82] What *jus cogens* does is that it prevents a certain obligation to develop either by law-making or subsequent interpretation. For example, Article 53 VCLT would void a treaty by virtue of which two or more states would conclude a treaty that would create an obligation to torture eg a terrorism suspect. Moreover, *jus cogens* prevents, for example, that the positive obligations under the right to life could be interpreted as an obligation to torture in order to extract information in the so-called ticking bomb scenario.[83] Such an obligation would be prevented under both customary and treaty law. But this is not a matter of hierarchical superiority or even constitutionalism. The hierarchical relationship remains mainly theoretical at best, as *jus cogens* does not appear to have any effects beyond voiding treaties and preventing certain customary obligations to develop or persist.

As such, the concept of *jus cogens* performs a role in international law that is quite similar to the concept of public law limitations on the freedom of contract in domestic settings. While one is in principle free to enter into a contractual relationship, public law imposes certain limitations to this freedom and prevents certain contractual obligations from coming into existence.[84] *Jus cogens* also prevents certain international legal obligations from coming into existence either by virtue of treaty or customary international law. In that sense, the concept of *jus cogens* has not come any further from what Alfred Verdross called 'forbidden treaties'.[85] One may now only need to look beyond treaties nowadays. It appears that *jus cogens* today any international law-making or interpretation of an existing source of international law that offends against *jus cogens*. Nothing more and nothing less.

Jus cogens thus provides for a rudimentary public law umbrella which can have interpretative effects on the system of international law even in the absence of its hierarchical superiority. Notably, neither Article 38(1) of the ICJ Statute nor

[81] ILC Draft Conclusions, Conclusion 14.

[82] ibid.

[83] See Michelle Farrell, *The Prohibition of Torture in Exceptional Circumstances* (Cambridge, Cambridge University Press, 2013) 82.

[84] See eg Hector MacQueen and Alfred Cockrell, 'Illegal Contracts' in Reinhard Zimmermann, Daniel Visser and Kenneth Reid (eds), *Mixed Legal Systems in Comparative Perspective: Property and Obligations in Scotland and South Africa Mixed Legal Systems in Comparative Perspective: Property and Obligations in Scotland and South Africa* (Oxford, Oxford University Press, 2005) 143.

[85] Alfred von Verdross, 'Forbidden Treaties in International Law: Comments on Professor Garner's Report on "The Law of Treaties"' (1937) 31 *American Journal of International Law* 571.

Article 31 VCLT create a pre-determined hierarchy of sources and/or norms. The concept of *jus cogens* has its value as an interpretative systemic element which reflects community values, and overrides state centrism and certain classical tenets of international law-making. The concept changes the traditional paradigm of international law as voluntary law and introduces a set of norms which can be legally binding on states even in the absence of their consent. It thus manifests a strong sense of the international community interest which prevails over the will of individual states. However, the *jus cogens* norms have not been given any effects of hierarchical superiority in international practice. They are the legal manifestation of the fundamental values of the international community, and ensure that an obligation to act against such values does not develop. *Jus cogens* is thus more about deterrence than proper hierarchy.

International legal doctrine has thus introduced certain concepts that imply the presence of a 'hierarchical meta system',[86] but it appears that Dino Krtitsiotis is right when he concludes that international law does not know how to accommodate these concepts. He argues: 'Our "international community" is "deep" enough to have conceived of the idea of *jus cogens* but not deep enough to know what to do with it. It is caught in the perennial mire of something called *erga omnes* (or obligations owed to the "community" as a whole), and continues to inch toward so-called crimes and offences against the "international order".'[87] The problem is that all these concepts envisage a strong sense of community and its values. While such a community sense may well limit the treaty-making capacity of states and influence the interpretation of treaty and customary obligations, the rudimentary public law elements in international law remain rather limited to a systemic prevention of certain international legal obligations from coming into effect. This is not a matter of hierarchy or constitutionalism, but rather a limitation on the law-making process and a systemic check on the private law logic of public international law.

B. General Principles of Law

General principles of law are a formal source of international law under Article 38(1)(c) of the ICJ Statute.[88] Unlike obligations *erga omnes* and *jus cogens* norms, general principles thus have a clear textual basis for their legal authority as a formal source of international law. Their normative value nevertheless appears to be somewhat undefined. Writers have particularly questioned whether general principles directly generate any international legal rules and obligations.[89]

[86] cf Fragmentation Report (n 3), para 493.

[87] Dino Kritsiotis, 'Imagining the International Community' (2002) 13 *European Journal of International Law* 961, 990.

[88] Statute of the International Court of Justice (1945) art 38(1).

[89] Craig Eggett, 'The Role of Principles and General Principles in the "Constitutional Processes" of International Law' (2019) 66 *Netherlands International Law Review* 197.

International treaty and customary international law can create an obligation in the sense: State A shall not do X, and state B shall do Y. It would be difficult to derive such obligations from a general principle of law only and exclusively. As argued by Gleider Hernandez, 'general principles normally enter judicial reasoning without formal reference or label.'[90] In other words, general principles of international law are often in the background of reasoning when other sources of international law are interpreted, but do not generate direct legal obligations.

In that sense, Hersch Lauterpacht wrote that the concept of general principles of law is 'in essential harmony with the attitude [...] of every legal community.'[91] Notably, Lauterpacht thus saw general principles as an element that underpins the sense of a legal community in international law. The reference to a legal community is very similar to what we understand nowadays under the term systemic integration. International law lacks coherence and characteristics of a legal system if it does not adopt certain internal rules that ensure at least a minimum threshold of its coherence.[92]

Craig Eggett has noted in this regard:

> The mode of creation of general principles of law is one of the issues where the lack of clarity in comparison with treaties and customary rules becomes very clear. For treaties, the rules of the ... [VCLT] set out the formal procedures for signature and ratification, and provide for certain conditions of validity. For the ascertainment of customary rules, the ICJ has built a body of case law stating and clarifying the well-known elements of state practice and *opinio juris*. There is as yet no such guidance for the ascertainment of general principles of law. Seeking to establish the criteria for the ascertainment of general principles can contribute the establishment of constitutional features in at least two ways. First, there is scope to rely on the concept of the 'international community' as a basis for the recognition of general principles. Increased clarity as to international lawmaking processes enhances its systemic coherence. Second, greater reliance on this source could allow for the creation of rules that are not exclusively dependent on the consent of states, and so seek to serve the interests of the community as opposed to solely those of states.[93]

It has been argued in this chapter that obligations *erga omnes* and *jus cogens* norms provide for a very rudimentary systemic public law element in the private law structure of public international law. Both concepts are built on the understanding of there being an international community underpinned by a minimum threshold of public community values. The role of general principles of law is even more complex in this regard. They bring elements of both public and private law into the international legal *system*.

[90] Gleider Hernández, *International Law* (Oxford, Oxford University Press, 2019) 33.

[91] Hersch Lauterpacht, *The Function of Law in the International Community* (Oxford, Oxford University Press, 1933) 74–75.

[92] The Fragmentation Report (n 3), para 15.

[93] Eggett (n 89) 208.

International judicial bodies had to import to international law a great deal of procedural principles in order to be able to exercise their judicial function.[94] The underlying treaties that create such judicial bodies do not and cannot anticipate every possible procedural issue that may arise in the future, and reliance on the general principles of international procedural law is thus instrumental. International criminal tribunals need to resort to general principles of criminal law in their work.[95] With respect of international treaties, certain private law analogies (eg general principles of contract law) maybe used in the process of interpretation and application.[96]

Discussing the rule of law principle, Thin argues that systemic integration of this principle:

> [O]pens the door to a very different role for international courts and tribunals. The end point of this reasoning is to see international courts and tribunals, or at least some particular courts and tribunals, as organs of the international community. They perform a systemic role in the interest of the community in the rule of law rather than purely in furtherance of individual state interests. This way we see the court(s) as above and beyond the will of states; as a form of public authority. Suddenly, the purpose of the judicial body is not only the settlement of the dispute, but also to ensure and enforce compliance with the law more generally … Such an aim could underlie broader functions, such as the existence of a broader advisory capacity or even judicial law-making in a gap-filling capacity.[97]

In other words, the application of general principles of law enables international courts and tribunals to act as systemic judicial bodies of the international community rather than mere dispute settlement mechanisms akin to private law arbitration.[98]

Eggett argues that 'general principles of law play a central role in the operation of the international legal system, so much so that they constitute systemic elements of international law.'[99] Indeed, it is well-established in doctrine and practice that individual sources of law cannot be read in isolation and need to be interpreted in line with other applicable sources in a particular situation.[100] The general principles of law are instrumental in the process of fitting the puzzles together. It is sometimes difficult to distinguish the effects of the general principles of law in the sense of Article 38(1)(c) of the ICJ Statute from those

[94] Craig Eggett, *General Principles as Systemic Elements of International Law* (PhD thesis, University of Maastricht, 2021) 141–44.

[95] ibid; see also Paolo Palchetti, 'Making and Enforcing Procedural Law at the International Court of Justice' (2019) 61 *Questions of International Law* 5.

[96] Hersch Lauterpacht, *Private Law Sources and Analogies of International Law* (London, Longmans, Green and Co, 1927).

[97] Thin (n 14) 183–84.

[98] Eggett (n 94) 142.

[99] ibid 169.

[100] See eg *Oil Platforms (Islamic Republic of Iran v United States of America)*, Judgment, [2003] ICJ Rep 161, 41.

under treaty or even customary international law. This is because a number of general principles are in any case also elaborated in treaties or have also become customary (eg *pacta sunt servanda* and *lex specialis*) under the VCLT and customary law of treaties. But it is not uncommon in international law that a certain legal rule or doctrine may follow from more than one source of law. After all, it is quite common that multilateral treaties overlap with custom. Although Article 38(1)(c) of the ICJ Statute is not their only point of entry into the international legal system, the general principles of law have an important systemic function in the interpretation and application of the rules and obligations of international law.

V. From Constitutionalism to Systemic Integration

It has been argued thus far that international law does not operate on the basis of a pre-determined constitutional hierarchy. There exists a rudimentary public law umbrella that provides for some systemic coherence of the largely private law paradigm of public international law. While some commentators have defined obligations *erga omnes* and *jus cogens* norms as elements of hierarchy and given them a higher status in the perceived constitutional structure of international law,[101] this chapter has rather shown that their systemic effect is not hierarchical in nature. Instead, these norms and obligations play a role in the process of interpretation and application of international law. This section demonstrates that international law does not seek unity and coherence like domestic constitutional systems. Some basic coherence is achieved through the process of interpretation of international law, but systemic integration does not equal constitutionalism.

A. Systemic Elements Short of Constitutionalism

Klatt argues that:

> The unity of a legal system is not the precondition of … [CCI]; it is its *result*. The interpreter *makes* the law consistent and coherent by interpreting it in a constitutionally conforming manner. The argument based on the unity of the legal system is not based on a cognitivist or descriptive perspective but on a normative and constructivist perspective. The unity of the legal system is not given but assigned to us as the main task of our academic endeavours.[102]

[101] cf de Wet (n 11).
[102] Klatt (n 1) s III(B).

In international law, not even the result necessarily leads to unity. The cacophony of the different (judicial) interpreters have led to a cacophony of results. As the ILC aptly observed in the Fragmentation Report:

> [T]he emergence of new and special types of law, 'self-contained regimes' and geographically or functionally limited treaty systems creates problems of coherence in international law. New types of specialized law do not emerge accidentally but seek to respond to new technical and functional requirements. The emergence of 'environmental law' is a response to growing concern over the state of the international environment. 'Trade law' develops as an instrument to regulate international economic relations. 'Human rights law' aims to protect the interests of individuals and 'international criminal law' gives legal expression to the 'fight against impunity'. Each rule complex or 'regime' comes with its own principles, its own form of expertise and its own 'ethos', not necessarily identical to the ethos of neighbouring specializations. 'Trade law' and 'environmental law', for example, have highly specific objectives and rely on principles that may often point in different directions. In order for the new law to be efficient, it often includes new types of treaty clauses or practices that may not be compatible with old general law or the law of some other specialized branch. Very often new rules or regimes develop precisely in order to deviate from what was earlier provided by the general law. When such deviations become general and frequent, the unity of the law suffers.[103]

But there is only so much unity one can expect of international law. As the ILC further observed in the Fragmentation Report, [s]uch deviations should not be understood as 'mistakes' of legal technique. They reflect the differing pursuits and preferences that actors in a pluralistic (global) society have.[104] Indeed, the specialised sub-regimes and regional arrangements have developed precisely because the *lex generalis* rules were too thin and *lex specialis* was developed. In that sense, international law does not pursue a particular social ideal or operate on the basis of a certain international political theory. It is rather that certain treaty sub-regimes are purely functional and pragmatic in nature. This is another reason why the label constitutionalism is of little help and is probably misplaced. In reality, there only exist certain systemic elements that reconcile some conflicts, but unity of international law is nether achieved nor sought.

The interpreters are at least bound by some minimalistic public law structure and the concept of systemic integration. The effects of *jus cogens* are most visible through the lens of Article 53 VCLT,[105] which has already been discussed, and the concept of systemic integration, to which this contribution now turns.

[103] Fragmentation Report (n 3), para 15.

[104] ibid, para 16.

[105] VCLT art 53 reads: 'A treaty is void if, at the time of its conclusion, it conflicts with a peremptory norm of general international law. For the purposes of the present Convention, a peremptory norm of general international law is a norm accepted and recognized by the international community of States as a whole as a norm from which no derogation is permitted and which can be modified only by a subsequent norm of general international law having the same character.'

B. Systemic Integration

Article 31(3)(c) provides that when treaties are interpreted, '[t]here shall be taken into account, together with the context … any relevant rules of international law applicable in the relations between the parties.'[106] It would indeed be difficult to reconcile international legal obligations between states if each individual source of law were read in isolation. Importantly, Article 31(3)(c) VCLT does not limit systemic integration to treaty law. The formulation 'any relevant rules of international law applicable,'[107] clearly accommodates legal obligations stemming from other sources of international law. In his seminal work on the law of treaties, Arnold McNair argued that treaties need to be 'applied and interpreted against the background of the general principles of international law,'[108] and Campbell McLachlan has noted:

> A treaty will normally be capable of interpretation and application according to its own terms and context. But in hard cases, it may be necessary to invoke an express justification for looking outside the four corners of a particular treaty to its place in a broader framework of international law, applying general principles of international law.[109]

In the *Oil Platforms case*, the International Court of Justice (ICJ) reasoned:

> [U]nder the general rules of treaty interpretation, as reflected in the 1969 Vienna Convention on the Law of Treaties, interpretation must take into account 'any relevant rules of international law applicable in the relations between the parties' (Article 31, paragraph 3 (c)). The Court cannot accept that Article XX, paragraph 1 (d), of the 1955 Treaty [of Amity between the United States and Iran] was intended to operate wholly independently of the relevant rules of international law on the use of force, so as to be capable of being successfully invoked, even in the limited context of a claim for breach of the Treaty, in relation to an unlawful use of force. The application of the relevant rules of international law relating to this question thus forms an integral part of the task of interpretation entrusted to the Court.[110]

In *Oil Platforms*, the ICJ operationalised Article 31(3)(c) VCLT and the systemic nature of international law. The provisions of international treaties should not be read in a legal vacuum – they ought to be interpreted with other rules of international law in mind. In this sense, the ICJ had previously established in *Right of Passage* that treaties ought to be 'interpreted as producing and as intended to produce effects in accordance with existing law and not in violation of it,'[111] and

[106] VCLT art 31(1)(c).
[107] ibid.
[108] Arnold McNair, *The Law of Treaties* (Oxford, Oxford University Press, 1961) 466.
[109] McLachlan (n 17) 281.
[110] *Oil Platforms (Islamic Republic of Iran v United States of America)*, Judgment, [2003] ICJ Rep 161, 41.
[111] *Right of Passage over Indian Territory (Portugal v India)* (Preliminary Objections) [1957] ICJ Rep 125, 142.

in the *Namibia* Advisory Opinion that 'an international instrument has to be applied within the framework of the entire legal system prevailing at the time of the interpretation'.[112]

In the absence of a constitutional metasystem known in domestic settings, systemic integration allows for some basic coherence in the process of interpretation and application of international law. As noted by the ILC Study Group in the Fragmentation Report, there is a need to:

> [T]o carry out interpretation such that the rules are seen in the light of some comprehensible and coherent objective, so as to prioritize concerns that are more important at the cost of less important objectives. This is all that article 31, paragraph 3 (c), requires: the integration into the process of legal reasoning – including reasoning by courts and tribunals – of a sense of coherence and meaningfulness. Success or failure here is measured by how the legal world views the outcome.[113]

However, as Adamantia Rachovitsa cautions:

> [T]he principle of systemic integration – either allegedly derived from Article 31 (3)(c) VCLT or as a stand-alone principle – cannot remedy the international courts' fragmented lens. The purpose of interpretation is not to integrate treaties into a coherent whole, but to introduce into the process of interpreting a treaty any relevant rules and to offer interpretive guidance (Article 31(3)(c) VCLT being one tool for accomplishing this).[114]

Indeed, systemic integration is no panacea and no comprehensive metasystem. It is not a solution that would harmonise or even constitutionalise international law. Nevertheless, systemic integration can provide for certain conceptual solutions and rudimentary public law tools for the interpretation of private law type of legal obligations. While a number of doctrinal writings have assumed that a system can only function if it is constitutionalised or otherwise hierarchical in nature,[115] McLachlan explains that 'the importance of the rules of customary international law and general principles of law … [in the systemic integration process] is not in their overriding character'.[116] Indeed, systemic integration is not about hierarchy and overriding, it is about reconciling two or more obligations and shaping their scopes by reading one into another.

[112] *Legal Consequences for States of the Continued Presence of South Africa in Namibia (South-West Africa) notwithstanding Security Council resolution 276 (1970)* (Advisory Opinion) [1971] ICJ Rep 16, 53.

[113] See Fragmentation of International Law: Difficulties Arising from the Diversification and Expansion of International Law, Report of the Study Group of the International Law Commission, finalised by Mr. Martti Koskenniemi, UN Doc A/CN.4/L.682 (13 April 2006) [The Fragmentation Report], para 419.

[114] Adamantia Rachovitsa, 'The Principle of Systemic Integration in International Human Rights Law' 66 *International and Comparative Law Quarterly* (2017) 557, 560.

[115] For an overview see de Wet (n 5) and Shelton (n 65) 291.

[116] McLachlan (n 17) 313.

VI. Conclusion

Public international law operates in a private law paradigm. In its essence, this is a system of contract-like and tort-like relations between states. The word public in public international law is a misnomer. A comprehensive public law framework is absent in this system and it is well-known that Hart described international law as a non-system.[117] Klatt argues that 'the unity of the legal system demands striving for consistency in the legal system. We must also remember that rational discourse's general obligation is not to contradict oneself.'[118] While it may be too ambitious to speak of international law as a constitutionalised legal order, there exist at least some elements that provide for conflict rules and seek to interpret away the most obvious contradictions.

In order for the international legal system to function some rudimentary elements of public law have been introduced to help regulate the private law relations between states. The interpretation technique of systemic integration is a tool for building a rudimentary public law structure in the system of international law. The systemic public law concepts at work here are general principles of law, obligations *erga omnes* and *jus cogens* norms.

It remains debatable whether the general principles of law as a source of international law are able of generating any direct legal rules and obligations. Their function has been said to be primarily systemic in nature. They are often lurking in the background when other sources of international law are applied and interpreted. They also provide coherence to international law and mitigate against Hart's assertion of international law being a non-system. Reliance on general principles has been particularly important in those situations where treaty and customary law was rather thin (eg to prevent *non liquet* in international adjudication)[119] or two or more obligations stemming from either treaty or custom appear to be in conflict.[120]

The concept of *jus cogens* is probably nothing different than the international law analogy to public law limitations on the freedom of contract. They provide for a limitation on state consent and prevent that certain obligations could develop which would offend against the minimum threshold of an international public order. Obligations *erga omnes* presume the existence of an international community or international society and create a vertical (public law type) relationship between states and the community. This relationship is very rudimentary and not underpinned by a comprehensive political and constitutional theory, the way this is ordinarily the case in municipal constitutional orders.

The label constitutionalism is of little help in international law. Interpretation in international law neither achieves nor strives for a constitutional-like coherence

[117] cf (n 2).
[118] Klatt (n 1) s IV(A).
[119] Eggett (n 94) 79.
[120] ibid 149.

and unity. Certain specialised and geographical treaty regimes are functional and pragmatic in nature, and do not pursue unitary community values. But certain systemic elements and the concept of systemic integration provide at least for a very basic minimum threshold of the international community and basic systemic functioning of international law.

It would thus be too far-fetched to speak of CCI in international law. At least if the label constitutionalism ought to mean something similar to constitutionalism at domestic or supranational level, in particular in the EU. Rather than constitutionalism proper, the interpretation and application of international law needs to conform with some minimalistic public law framework. In practice, this means that no source of international law may be created or interpreted contrary to *jus cogens*, existing sources should not be interpreted in isolation but by taking into account other international legal obligations, and systemic gaps should be filled by general principles of law.

While such structure of international law still is too shallow to be constitutional in nature, it does contain systemic qualities. Contrary to Hart's assertion, international law is not a non-system. Interpretation of international law is therefore system-conforming, and certain rudimentary public law elements have been added to this systemic picture.

4

Conforming Legal Interpretation Based on International Law: The Use of Unwritten Principles, the Example of Equality of Arms

STÉPHANE BEAULAC*

I. Preliminary Matters

The initial challenge in addressing these issues, of course, concerns the terminology used, which would oppose *unwritten* principles (presumably vague and uncertain), on the one hand, to *written* rules (deemed clear and precise), on the other. Setting up the problem as such, resorting to a simple binary reasoning, if not a simplistic dichotomy (be it genuine, exaggerated or false) brings to mind the classic Wittgensteinian insight,[1] that the limits of one's language are, indeed, the limits of one's world.[2] Dwelling on the same theme in his book *Eunomia*, University of Cambridge Professor Philip Allott once wrote that, '[o]ur words make our worlds', and that in fact, '[t]o choose our words is to choose a world'.[3]

* This chapter was written at the kind invitation of Matthias Klatt, director of the Research Centre for Legal Philosophy and Global Constitutionalism at the University of Graz (Austria), where I spent part of my sabbatical leave during the winter term of 2023, as a Land Steiermark Senior Fellow. The financial support of Graz Jurisprudence is hereby acknowledged, with thanks and appreciation. An early version of the chapter was presented as part of a Global Constitutionalism Colloquium 2022–23, organised by Mattias Kumm at the WZB Social Science Centre, in Berlin (Germany).

[1] Naturally, writing this chapter in Austria, at the University of Graz, it was quite fitting to start with a reference to one of its most celebrated contemporary philosophers, also an alumni of the University of Cambridge, like me.

[2] The quote from the original book: 'Die Grenzen meiner Sprache bedeuten die Grenzen meiner Welt' – see Ludwig Wittgenstein, *Tractatus Logico-Philosophicus* [reprinted with a few corrections] (New York, Harcourt, 1933) s 5(6).

[3] Philip Allott, *Eunomia – New Order for a New World* (Oxford, Oxford University Press, 1990) 6.

Short of dispensing with them,[4] let me suggest at the outset that it might be appropriate, perhaps more useful to see principles, along with rules,[5] on a spectrum, that is to say on a sort of continuum.[6] Thus beyond the written-unwritten dichotomy, (i) these norms could be sometimes expressly and directly linked to the language of the normative instrument (such as a constitution or an international treaty); (ii) while in many other instances they would be connected more or less remotely to the letter of the law; and finally, (iii) on rare occasions, while they would be deemed fundamental in a material sense,[7] there could be no textual support at all for them in the constitution or in conventional law.

For our purposes, it is mainly the third category of situations that is of interest, what author Mark Walters referred to as *freestanding* principles,[8] with no textual anchoring to a constitutional or international document. Also relevant here are the situations in the second category, what author Charles Black called *structural* principles,[9] but only those where the inference is tenuous, merely deriving from the spirit of the constitutional or conventional instrument.[10] Accordingly, for the sake of clarity – and in spite of various terminology in legal literature (eg underlying, implied, hidden, invisible, extra-textual[11]) – the expression

[4] Interestingly, there are arguments highlighting the illusion (even uselessness) of legal principles. See Larry Alexander, 'Legal Objectivity and the Illusion of Legal Principles' in Matthias Klatt (ed), *Institutionalized Reason: The Jurisprudence of Robert Alexy* (Oxford, Oxford University Press, 2012) 115.

[5] For the present purposes, it is unnecessary to distinguish between rules and principles, which classic formulation (though there are others) comes from Ronald Dworkin's work. Ronald Dworkin, *Taking Rights Seriously* (Cambridge, Harvard University Press, 1977); and Ronald Dworkin, *Law's Empire* (London, Fontana, 1986).

[6] This conceptualisation was well summarised, recently, by my University of Montreal colleague Han-Ru Zhou, 'Legal Principles, Constitutional Principles, and Judicial Review' (2019) 67 *American Journal of Comparative Law* 889.

[7] On material constitution, as opposed to formal constitution, see Julian Arato, 'Constitutionality and Constitutionalism beyond the State: Two Perspectives on the Material Constitution of the United Nations' (2012) 10 *New York University International Journal of Constitutional Law* 627.

[8] Mark D Walters, 'The Common Law Constitution in Canada: Return of *Lex non Scripta* as Fundamental Law' (2001) 51 *University of Toronto Law Journal* 91. See also, in general, Lawrence H Tribe, *The Invisible Constitution* (Oxford, Oxford University Press, 2008); and David A Strauss, *The Living Constitution* (Oxford, Oxford University Press, 2010).

[9] Charles L Black Jr, *Structure and Relationship in Constitutional Law* (Baton Rouge, Louisiana State University Press, 1969). See also, in general, Thomas C Grey, 'Do We Have an Unwritten Constitution?' (1975) 27 *Stanford Law Review* 703; and Jack M Balkin, *Living Originalism* (Cambridge, Harvard University Press, 2011). In the Canadian context, for instance, one author has recently enumerated the numerous foundations of unwritten constitutional principles: '[T]heir source [is found] in "the general object and purpose of the Constitution", the preambles of the *Constitution Act, 1867* and *1982*, the operative provisions of the Constitution, the Constitution's architecture, the United Kingdom's and Canada's constitutional history, the common law, practice, and logic' [footnotes omitted]. See Vanessa A MacDonnel, 'Rethinking the Invisible Constitution: How Unwritten Constitutional Principles Shape Political Decision-Making' (2019) 65 *McGill Law Journal* 175, 179.

[10] Using the terminology of '*principes non-écrits*' (ie unwritten principles), French theorist Jean Boulanger had early on linked them to the *spirit* underlying the letter of the law. See Jean Boulanger, 'Principes généraux du droit et droit positif' in *Le droit privé français au milieu du XXe siècle: Études offertes à Georges Ripert*, vol 1 (Paris, Pichon and Durand-Auzias, 1950) 51, 67.

[11] See Rosalind Dixon and Adrienne Stone, 'The Invisible Constitution in Comparative Perspective' in Dixon and Stone (eds), *The Invisible Constitution in Comparative Perspective* (Cambridge, Cambridge University Press, 2018) 3.

unwritten principles shall be employed as encompassing freestanding principles, as well as (tenuously) structural principles, at the end of the sliding scale, with no, or almost no connection with constitutional or international texts.[12]

Another important preliminary point, with a view to providing focus in this chapter, is the relationship between international normativity and (constitutional) domestic law,[13] what I like to call *interlegality*.[14] Professor André Nollkaemper of the University of Amsterdam, who has written extensively on the subject,[15] has aptly suggested that beyond the theories known as monism and dualism, the national use of international law calls upon diversity of approaches to overcome and bridge the 'divide' between these two spheres.[16] I have myself suggested that, at least in the Anglo-Saxon tradition, the prevalent understanding continues to see, a priori, the international and the national legal realities as separate and distinct, forming non-intersecting sets,[17] the relationships of which are guided by a web of practices that are specific to every state.[18]

As I have written elsewhere,[19] it remains true in most, if not in all common law countries – Canada, Australia, UK, etc – that it is if, and actually only to the extent that national rules of reception allow international law to be part of domestic law, be it through a monist or dualist-type of reasoning, that international norms may have a direct legal effect in regard to domestic law. It follows that international law per se does not, in fact cannot be binding on domestic judges, who form part of the national judiciary and, indeed, are mandated by the Constitution to interpret and apply the law of the land (not international law).[20] In short, be it conventional

[12] On the different types of gaps and silences in constitutional texts, see Martin Loughlin, 'The Silences of Constitutions' (2018) 16 *New York University International Journal of Constitutional Law* 922.

[13] See eg Dinah Shelton (ed), *International Law and Domestic Legal Systems – Incorporation, Transformation, and Persuasion* (Oxford, Oxford University Press, 2011); and David Sloss (ed), *The Role of Domestic Courts in Treaty Enforcement: A Comparative Study* (Cambridge, Cambridge University Press, 2009).

[14] See Stéphane Beaulac, 'Constitutional Interpretation: On Issues of Ontology and of Interlegality' in Peter Oliver, Patrick Macklem and Nathalie Des Rosiers (eds), *The Oxford Handbook of the Canadian Constitution* (Oxford, Oxford University Press, 2017) 867; and Stéphane Beaulac, 'Interlégalité et réception du droit international en droit interne canadien et québécois' in Stéphane Beaulac and Jean-François Gaudreault-DesBiens (eds), *JurisClasseur Québec (coll. Droit public), Droit constitutionnel* (Montreal, LexisNexis Canada, 2022) ch 23.

[15] For instance, see André Nollkaemper and August Reinisch (eds), *International Law in Domestic Courts: A Casebook* (Oxford, Oxford University Press, 2018).

[16] See the introduction of the collective book: Janne Jijman and André Nollkaemper (eds), *New Perspective on the Divide between National and International Law* (Oxford, Oxford University Press, 2007).

[17] University of Toronto Professor Karen Knop notoriously explained that, 'domestic law is "here" and international is "there"'; see 'Here and There: International Law in Domestic Courts' (2000) 32 *New York University Journal of International Law and Policy* 501, 504.

[18] See Stéphane Beaulac, 'National Application of International Law: The Statutory Interpretation Perspective' (2003) 41 *Canadian Yearbook of International Law* 225. See also Charles-Emmanuel Côté, 'La réception du droit international en droit canadien' (2010) 52 *Supreme Court Law Review (2d)* 483.

[19] See Stéphane Beaulac, 'L'interprétation de la Charte: reconsidération de l'approche téléologique et réévaluation du rôle du droit international' (2005) 27 *Supreme Court Law Review (2d)* 1, 34–35.

[20] See Stéphane Beaulac, 'La mise en œuvre judiciaire des obligations internationales du Canada en matière de droits humains – Obstacles et embûches' in Oonagh E Fitzgerald, Valerie Hughes and Mark Jewett (eds), *Reflections on Canada's Past, Present and Future in International Law* (Waterloo, Centre for International Governance Innovation, 2018) 31.

or customary, international law cannot but be merely persuasive,[21] not binding, within the domestic legal order of a state.[22]

A third and last groundwork matter relevant to this chapter relates to the canon of interpretation – the very theme of the present collective book – namely *conforming legal interpretation*, and it concerns methodology, essentially. When considering this type of construction, be it in general or for specific applications, it is useful to distinguish between two things: the source of the normativity of reference (constitution, treaty), on the one hand, and the actual law (ordinary, domestic) to be interpreted in conformity with these fundamentals, on the other hand. Put another way, when one interprets 'in conformity with', there are two groups of norms at play, those deemed the reference point, the reference normativity, which will have an impact on the interpretation of the other set of normativity, which is the one actually applicable in a situation, ie positive law.

Hence, both the presumption of constitutionality and the presumption of conformity with international law necessarily rely on a comparison of two elements: the constitution or an international law source (treaty, customs) is first considered; then, sequentially, the ordinary domestic law ('presumed' to be in line with it) is construed accordingly, unless it is not possible. The main point here is that conforming legal interpretation, as it were,[23] acts at both these steps of the analysis, ie initially, on the construction of the constitution or the international treaty, and ultimately, on the interpretation of the normative content of the positive law at issue, presumably complying with such fundamentals.

This chapter focuses on the presumption of conformity with international law,[24] which I now turn to.

[21] As one author succinctly explained, *persuasive authority* is a source, 'regarded as relevant to the decision which has to be made by the judge, but not binding on the judge under the hierarchical rules of the national system determining authoritative sources'; see Christopher McCrudden, 'Common Law of Human Rights?: Transnational Judicial Conversations on Constitutional Rights' (2000) 40 *Oxford Journal of Legal Studies* 499, 502–503.

[22] This is the approach adopted by the Supreme Court of Canada in a recent case, *Quebec (Attorney General) v 9147-0732 Québec inc.*, 2020 SCC 32, where in a 5-4 split decision, the majority realigned the analysis of interlegality issues and corrected a trend in case law, as of late then, that allowed for an exaggerated role for international law. Referring to my writings on statutory interpretation and interlegality (paras 3 and 22), the majority of the Court wrote (para 22): 'While this Court has generally accepted that international norms *can* be considered when interpreting domestic norms, they have typically played a limited role of providing *support* or *confirmation* for the result reached by way of purposive interpretation'. See also Stéphane Beaulac, 'Arrêtons de dire que les tribunaux au Canada sont "liés" par le droit international' (2004) 38 *Revue juridique Thémis* 359.

[23] On this, see Danielle Pinard, 'Le principe d'interprétation issu de la présomption de constitutionnalité et la *Charte canadienne des droits et libertés*' (2004) 35 *McGill Law Journal* 305, 313–14.

[24] Some of the material used in this paper draws from Stéphane Beaulac, '"L'égalité des armes" – une phrase bénie? – en droit processuel au Québec: Le rôle du droit international' (2022) 52 *Revue générale de droit* 269.

II. Conforming Legal Interpretation Based on International Law

Although the rationales[25] underlying conforming legal interpretation may vary depending on whether one resorts to constitutional law or international law, we just saw that the same interpretative technique is at play. The idea is relatively simple and can be put thus: when judges consider legal rules, like a provision of domestic legislation (but it could also be judge-made-law, just the same), they should opt for an interpretation that allows it to be in line, to comply with the normativity of reference based either on constitutional law or on international law.[26] Put another way, faced with two possible meanings when reading the applicable domestic law, one that would be in breach of constitutional law or international obligations, and another that would be compliant with them, the latter ought to be favoured as much as possible.[27]

The presumption of conformity with international law, as I have explained elsewhere,[28] is basically one of the two techniques, within the methodology of legal interpretation, for a national judge to operationalise such norms in domestic law. The other one, to mention it without going in any detail,[29] is based on contextual interpretation.[30] It allows us to take into account norms based on

[25] On the rationales (legal certainty, legal coherence) for CCI, see Paul Daly, 'Canada. Legal Coherence versus Legal Certainty' in Matthias Klatt (ed), *Constitutionally Conforming Interpretation – Comparative Perspectives Volume 1: National Reports* (Oxford, Hart Publishing, 2023) s I. On the international plane, I shall come back to these rationales in my concluding remarks.

[26] See eg Pierre-André Côté, Stéphane Beaulac and Mathieu Devinat, *The Interpretation of Legislation in Canada*, 4th edn (Toronto, Carswell, 2011), ss 1398–1401. For a critical view of these presumptions, see Thomas A Cromwell, Siena Anstis and Thomas Touchie, 'Revisiting the Role of Presumptions of Legislative Intent in Statutory Interpretation' (2017) 95 *Canadian Bar Review* 297.

[27] For classic expositions of the presumption of constitutionality, in the USA, see Véase Note, 'Supreme Court Interpretation of Statutes to Avoid Constitutional Decision' (1953) 53 *Columbia Law Review* 633, 642ff; and in Canada, see François Chevrette and Herbert Marx, *Droit constitutionnel* (Montreal, Presses de l'Université de Montréal, 1981) 310ff. For more contemporary analysis of the situation in the US, see Fred Schauer's chapter in volume 1 of the present collective work: Frederick Schauer, 'United States: Constitutional Avoidance as Constitutional Conformation' in Klatt (n 25).

[28] See Stéphane Beaulac, 'International Law and Statutory Interpretation: Up with Context, Down with Presumption' in Oonagh E Fitzgerald et al (eds), *The Globalized Rule of Law – Relationships between International and Domestic Law* (Toronto, Irwin Law, 2006) 331.

[29] For more detail, see Stéphane Beaulac, 'Thinking Outside the "Westphalian Box": Dualism, Legal Interpretation and the Contextual Argument' in Christoffer C Eriksen and Marius Emberland (eds), *The New International Law – An Anthology* (Leiden, Brill Publishers, 2010) 17; and Stéphane Beaulac, 'Le droit international comme élément contextuel en interpretation des lois' (2004) 6 *Canadian International Lawyer* 1.

[30] In an important decision of the Supreme Court of Canada, *Baker v Canada (Minister of Citizenship and Immigration)* [1999] 2 SCR 817, the contextual argument of interpretation was used in order to make it possible to resort to *unimplemented* treaty norms, in spite of the dualist logic requiring the incorporation for conventions to have legal effects domestically. For the majority of seven judges (two wrote a concurring opinion), Justice L'Heureux-Dubé relied (para 70) on the author Ruth Sullivan, *Driedger on the Construction of Statutes*, 3rd edn (Toronto, Butterworth, 1994) 330, who wrote: '[T]he legislature

international treaty or on customary law – the two core formal sources pursuant to section 38(1) of the Statute of the International Court of Justice – as elements of legislative context, which may be relied upon with a view to ascertaining the normative substance of the domestic legal rule.[31]

Concentrating on the other operationalisation technique – what is known in the USA as the 'Charming Betsy Rule'[32] – the presumption of conformity with international law was originally developed in Great Britain, of course.[33] Author Peter Maxwell: '[E]very statute is to be so interpreted and applied, as far as its language admits, as not to be inconsistent with the comity of nations, or with the established rules of international law'.[34] A classic exposition of the canon was offered by Diplock LJ (later Lord Diplock):

> [T]here is a prima facie presumption that Parliament does not intend to act in breach of international law, including therein specific treaty obligations; and if one of the meanings which can reasonably be ascribed to the legislation is consonant with the treaty obligations and another or others are not, the meaning which is consonant is to be preferred.[35]

Another major case applying this technique of conforming legal interpretation in Great Britain was *R. v Lyons*[36] in 2002, a House of Lord decision which, in turn, was resorted to by the High Court of Justice in the Brexit legal challenge, the 2016 *Miller* case.[37]

Recently, the United Kingdom Supreme Court relied on the presumption of conformity with international law in the *Reference on Scottish Referendum*,[38] a judgment handed down in November 2022. In addressing the international law arguments based on self-determination and the right of secession – which saw the

is presumed to respect the values and principles enshrined in international law, both customary and conventional. These constitute a part of the legal context in which legislation is enacted and read'.

[31] In a recent case, handed down on 15 July 2022, the Supreme Court of Canada reiterated how context may be used as gateway for international law – see *Society of Composers, Authors and Music Publishers of Canada v Entertainment Software Association*, 2022 SCC 30, para 45: 'The modern approach to statutory interpretation requires interpreting the statute's text in its "entire context". The statute's context includes any relevant international obligations'. See also Stéphane Beaulac, 'International Law Gateway to Domestic Law: Hart's "Open Texture", Legal Language and the Canadian Charter' (2012) 46 *Revue juridique Thémis* 443.

[32] From the case *Murray v The Charming Betsy*, 6 U.S. 64 (1804).

[33] See Gerald L Neuman, 'International Law as a Resource in Constitutional Interpretation' (2006) 30 *Harvard Journal of Law and Public Policy* 177.

[34] Peter B Maxwell, *On the Interpretation of Statutes* (London, Sweet and Maxwell, 1896) 173. See also on this, the celebrated international legal scholar Hersch Lauterpacht, 'Is International Law a Part of the Law of England?' (1930) *Transactions Grotius Society* 51.

[35] *Salomon v Commissioners of Customs and Excise* [1967] 2 QB 116, 143.

[36] *R. v Lyons* [2002] UKHL 44, [2003] AC 976, paras 27–28. See also *Assange v Swedish Prosecution Authority* [2012] UKSC 22, [2012] AC 471, para 122.

[37] *R. (Miller) v Secretary of State for Exiting the European Union* [2016] EWHC 2768, para 33; judgment upheld by the Supreme Court of the United Kingdom in a final judgment, [2017] UKSC 5, 24 January 2017.

[38] *Reference by Lord Advocate of Devolution Issues under Paragraph 34 of Schedule 6 to the Scotland Act 1998* [2022] UKSC 31.

UK top Court cite at length the Supreme Court of Canada's reasons in the 1998 Reference on Quebec Secession[39] – the issue was addressed as follows:

> The strong presumption in favour of interpreting our domestic law in a way which does not place the United Kingdom in breach of its obligations in international law is well established. […] If there is ambiguity in a statutory provision operating in a field where the United Kingdom is bound by a treaty obligation, the presumption of conformity with international law will apply to the interpretation of that statutory provision […]. This presumption of compatibility extends to international treaty obligations whether or not they have been implemented into domestic law within the United Kingdom […]. However, the presumption will only be a permissible aid to interpretation if the statutory provision is not clear on its face […].[40]

Beside Great Britain,[41] Canada provides other examples of how to resort to conforming legal interpretation based on international law. The Supreme Court of Canada explained the presumptive reasoning as follows in 1998: 'In choosing among possible interpretation of a statute, the court should avoid interpretations that would put Canada in breach of such obligations'.[42] In the 2007 *Hape* case, the main reasons for judgment by LeBel J provided insights that are worth citing in full:

> The presumption of conformity is based on the rule of judicial policy that, as a matter of law, courts will strive to avoid constructions of domestic law pursuant to which the state would be in violation of its international obligations, unless the wording of the statute clearly compels that result. […] [T]he presumption has two aspects. First, the legislature is presumed to act in compliance with Canada's obligations as a signatory of international treaties and as a member of the international community. In deciding between possible interpretations, courts will avoid a construction that would place Canada in breach of those obligations. The second aspect is that the legislature is presumed to comply with the values and principles of customary and conventional international law. Those values and principles form part of the context in which statutes are enacted, and courts will therefore prefer a construction that reflects them.[43]

Thus, in Canada, like in the UK, not only binding international law like treaty obligations as such, but 'values and principles of customary and conventional international law' may trigger, just the same, conforming legal interpretation.[44]

[39] *Reference re Secession of Quebec* [1998] 2 SCR 217; the UK Supreme Court referred to paras 138 and 154 of the Canadian decision, quoting them in full (see para 88 of the UK judgment, ibid).

[40] *Reference on Scottish Referendum* (n 38) para 87 [references omitted].

[41] For more British references, see Shaheed Fatima, 'The Domestic Application of International Law in British Courts' in Curtis A Bradley (ed), *The Oxford Handbook of Comparative Foreign Relations Law* (Oxford, Oxford University Press, 2019) 485.

[42] *Ordon Estate v Grail* [1998] 3 SCR 437, para 137 [reference omitted].

[43] *R. v Hape* [2007] 2 SCR 292, para 53 [underlines added] [references omitted].

[44] To be complete, in the Canadian context, with regard to the interpretation of the *Canadian Charter*, a recent 5-4 split decision saw the majority make a surprising nuance – see *Québec inc.* (n 22) paras 32–35. In a somewhat unclear fashion, Brown and Rowe JJ suggest that the presumption of conformity may be triggered, in providing support and confirmation in *Canadian Charter* interpretation, but only with regard to international law that is 'binding' on the country (as opposed to non-binding international law, I suppose). It remains to be seen whether this novel position will be followed in subsequent cases, which is doubtful.

A further point made by LeBel J in the *Hape* decision – which was also highlighted by the UK Supreme Court in the *Reference on Scottish Referendum*[45] – is, of course, that the presumption of conformity is rebuttable: 'Parliamentary sovereignty requires courts to give effect to a statute that demonstrates an unequivocal legislative intent to default on an international obligation'.[46] This is uncontroversial in case law and was further explicated as follows by Canada's top Court:

> International law cannot be used to support an interpretation that is not permitted by the words of the statute. Likewise, the presumption of conformity does not overthrow clear legislative intent (see S. Beaulac, '"*Texture ouverte*", *droit international et interprétation de la Charte canadienne*', in E. Mendes and S. Beaulac, eds., *Canadian Charter of Rights and Freedoms* (5th ed. 2013), at pp. 231-35). Indeed, the presumption that legislation will conform to international law remains just that – merely a presumption. This Court has cautioned that the presumption can be rebutted by the clear words of the statute under consideration.[47]

Interestingly, a last quote from the Supreme Court of Canada, from a 2015 case, suggests that there is indeed universality in conforming legal interpretation: 'This interpretive presumption is not peculiar to Canada. It is a feature of legal interpretation around the world'.[48]

To recap, before proceeding with a case study, the principal point to highlight as regards the presumption of conformity with international law, considering it through the lens (or epistemology) of Anglo-Saxon interlegality analysis, is this: although the weight given may vary depending on the circumstances, there seems to be no objection to the use of unwritten principles coming from the international legal order as an aid to the construction of domestic law (including constitutional law) by means of conforming legal interpretation. On the contrary, in light of the UK's and Canada's experiences, no matter the source of law and, more importantly, no matter the actual nature or type of normativity – be it specific treaty and customary obligations or unwritten principles with no (or almost no) connection with these formal sources – the interpretative canon favouring compatibility between the international and the national legal realities shall be employed, whenever possible and appropriate.

III. Case Study: The Unwritten Procedural Principle of Equality of Arms

Be that as it may, the verification of the hypothesis according to which conforming legal interpretation based on international law allows domestic judges to rely on an

[45] See *Reference by Lord Advocate of Devolution Issues under Paragraph 34 of Schedule 6 to the Scotland Act 1998* (n 38).

[46] *Hape* (n 43) para 53.

[47] *Kazemi Estate v Islamic Republic of Iran* [2014] 3 SCR 704, para 60 [underlines added] [case law reference omitted]. See also *Society of Composers* (n 31) para 48.

[48] *B010 v Canada (Citizenship and Immigration)* [2015] 3 SCR 704, para 48 [reference omitted].

'unwritten principle' of this legal order is certainly not an easy task to undertake. The main reason why involves, arguably, the very sources of international law, the two core ones being international treaties and customary rules.[49] For the sake of brevity, let us agree that customary international rules being already unwritten – *as per* state practice and *opinio juris*[50] – it is in relation to treaties that issues of unwritten principles arise.

Indeed, unlike customs, conventional international law provides for written rules that have been laid down in treaty documents, the conclusion of which is governed by the Vienna Convention on the Law of Treaties.[51] The definition in section 2(a) is explicit in that regard: '"[T]reaty" means an international agreement concluded between States <u>in written form</u> and governed by international law, whether embodied in a single instrument or in two or more related instrument and whatever its particular designation'.[52] Hence, when it comes to unwritten principles from the international legal order in the following discussion, they shall be considered in connection to written rules of conventional law, a formal source under section 38(1)(a) of the Statute of the International Court of Justice.

The question then becomes whether and, if so, how these fundamental principles found in international conventional law – be them freestanding or (tenuously) connected with the treaty, in spirit only[53] – may be relied upon by a domestic judge in a case. Put another way, are there examples where the canon of conforming legal interpretation was used to give effect at the national level to unwritten international principles deemed fundamental pursuant to a conventional regime? A prime illustration, as it were, seems to come from international human rights law, with the important principle of procedural law known as 'equality of arms'.

A. Equality of Arms as an Unwritten Principle Based on International Law

The expression 'equality of arms' finds an equivalent in many other European languages: '*[É]galité des armes*' or '*égalité des moyens*' in French, '*uguaglianza delle armi*' in Italian, '*Waffengleichheit*' in German, to name a few. It reflects that the

[49] On the sources of international law, in general, see Stéphane Beaulac and Miriam Cohen, *Précis de droit international public – Théorie, sources, interlégalité, sujets*, 3rd edn (Montreal, LexisNexis Canada, 2021) 81ff.

[50] See the classic formulation of the two constituting elements of international custom, a formal source of international law pursuant to s 38(1)(b) of the Statute of the International Court of Justice, from the case, *North Sea Continental Shelf*, Judgment, ICJ Reports 1969 3, 33, para 77: '[T]wo conditions must be fulfilled. Not only must the acts concerned amount to a settled practice, but they must also be such, or be carried out in such a way, as to be evidence of a belief that this practice is rendered obligatory by the existence of a rule of law requiring it. The need for such a belief, ie, the existence of a subjective element, is implicit in the very notion of the *opinio juris sive necessitatis*.'

[51] See, in particular, arts 6 to 17 of the Vienna Convention 1969.

[52] [Underlines added].

[53] See section I of this chapter, on preliminary matters.

principle exists in many jurisdictions, be it in penal, civil or administrative procedures, predominantly in Continental Europe.

To identify the origins of equality or arms, one needs to look at the European level, especially at international human rights law. Although the European Commission was the first one to refer to the principle in the 1959 *Szwabowicz* case,[54] the initial classic articulation is credited to the European Court of Human Rights, in the *Delcourt* case: '[A] trial would not be fair if it took place in such conditions as to put the accused unfairly at a disadvantage',[55] the Strasbourg court wrote in 1970.

These statements cut across other important values underlying procedural schemes, be they in criminal or civil law. For example, in addition to fair trial, there would be the idea of adversarial hearing, the right to be heard, as well as values relating to impartial decisions, to making a full answer and defence, and to fairness in the debates. In the Anglo-Saxon tradition, one could add the ideas of due process and of level playing field: one has to make sure, not that each party has the same chances to win the case on the merits, but rather that the rules of the game are not such that a participant is put at a disadvantage during the procedure. At a higher level, equality of arms contributes to serving justice and, as importantly, to assuring that there appears to be justice rendered.

Having said that, to put it in terms relevant to our discussion on unwritten principles, it is crucial to highlight that the actual terminology of *equality of arms* is nowhere to be found in the binding international law instruments. Instead, it constitutes a typical freestanding principle, or at least one with a remote (ie tenuous) connection with the text of the human rights law instruments. One of them, surely enjoying cardinal authority, is the Universal Declaration of Human Rights,[56] which provides at Article 10:

> **10.** Everyone is entitled in full equality to a fair and public hearing by an independent and impartial tribunal, in the termination of his rights and obligations and of any criminal charge against him. [underlines added]

It is noteworthy that, although the word 'equality' is found expressly, the expression 'in full equality' is somewhat remotely linked to the principle of equality of arms. No doubt, it could be deemed structural to Article 10, though indeed instrumental to the *spirit* of the right to a fair and public hearing.

[54] *Szwabowicz v Sweden* (application no. 434/58), ECommHR, 30 June 1959, Annuaire II para 535 (quote found in French only): 'Le droit à un procès équitable implique que toute partie à une action civile et *a fortiori* à une action pénale doit avoir une possibilité raisonnable d'exposer sa cause au tribunal dans des conditions qui ne le désavantagent pas d'une manière appréciable par rapport à la partie adverse'.

[55] *Delcourt v Belgium* (application no. 2689/65), ECtHR, 17 January 1970, (1970) Series A no. 11, para 34.

[56] On the domestic role of the Universal Declaration of Human Rights, in general, see William A Schabas and Stéphane Beaulac, *International Human Rights and Canadian Law – Legal Commitment, Implementation and the Charter*, 3rd edn (Toronto, Thomson Carswell, 2007).

It is mainly on the basis of the European Convention on Human Rights that the unwritten principle of equality of arms has been articulated internationally. Albeit not in explicit terms either, it is deemed linked to the text of Article 6(1), which reads:

> **6(1).** In the determination of his civil rights and obligations or of any criminal charge against him, everyone is entitled to a fair and public hearing within a reasonable time by an independent and impartial tribunal established by law [...]
>
> [The second part of the provision relates to *in camera* procedures, not relevant for our purposes]

Applicable to both civil and criminal procedures,[57] equality of arms and Article 6(1) was utilised by the European Court of Human Rights in numerous cases,[58] some of which will be examined in a moment.

Also relevant, from the universal regime of human rights protection, is the International Covenant on Civil and Political Rights. Similar to the provision found in the European regional instrument, Article 14(1) of the 1966 Covenant is written in vague and broad terms, none of which, however, explicitly provide for equality of arms. Only the first two sentences, materially significant, are to be cited here:

> **14(1).** All persons shall be equal before the courts and tribunals. In the determination of any criminal charge against him, or of his rights and obligations in a suit at law, everyone shall be entitled to a fair and public hearing by a competent, independent and impartial tribunal established by law. [...]

Similar to the European Convention, the Covenant provides for hard law which, under the rules of the Vienna Convention,[59] is binding in international law. Accordingly, it may also be used domestically, and with much persuasive force, including by means of the conforming legal interpretation canon.

More explicit than Article 14(1) of the Covenant, as regards equality of arms, is the soft law instrument derived from it, namely General Comment no. 32.[60] Adopted in 2007 by the UN Human Rights Committee, it dwells upon the different universal procedural rights and refers to our principle by name, at sections 8 and 13:

> **8.** The right to equality before courts and tribunals, in general terms, guarantees, in addition to the principles mentioned in the second sentence of Article 14(1), those of equal access and equality of arms, and ensures that the parties to the proceedings in question are treated without any discrimination. [underlines added]
>
> [...]

[57] See *Feldbrugge v The Netherlands* (application no. 8562/79), ECtHR, 26 May 1986, Series A no. 99.

[58] See European Court of Human Rights, *Guide on Article 6 of the European Convention on Human Rights – Right to a fair trial (civil limb)*, available at rm.coe.int/1680700aaf. In particular, see the section on equality of arms 90ff.

[59] See Vienna Convention on the Law of Treaty, art 26, codifying the principle of *pacta sunt servanda*.

[60] United Nations, Human Rights Committee, *General Comment No. 32, Article 14: Right to Equality before Courts and Tribunals and to a Fair Trial*, U.N. Doc. N.U. CCPR/C/GC/32 (23 August 2007).

> **13.** The right to equality before courts and tribunals also ensures equality of arms. This means that the same procedural rights are to be provided to all the parties unless distinctions are based on law and can be justified on objective and reasonable grounds, not entailing actual disadvantage or other unfairness to the defendant. There is no equality of arms if, for instance, only the prosecutor, but not the defendant, is allowed to appeal a certain decision. The principle of equality between parties applies also to civil proceedings, and demands, inter alia, that each side be given the opportunity to contest all the arguments and evidence adduced by the other party. In exceptional cases, it also might require that the free assistance of an interpreter be provided where otherwise an indigent party could not participate in the proceedings on equal terms or witnesses produced by it be examined. [underlines added] [footnotes omitted]

This being so, such an express reference to equality of arms could hardly mean that the principle becomes more than unwritten. Indeed, the General Comment provides for soft law, not hard law, and given that the present analysis is rooted in positivism, as well as the formal sources under section 38(1) of the Statute of the International Court of Justice, equality of arms remains very much an unwritten principle, no doubt. Besides, for our purposes, it is generally true that the presumption of conformity with international law is not triggered when dealing with soft law instruments, but only when resorting to treaty obligations (or to customary international law) that are binding on states.[61]

To be complete, the last conventional instrument to be included in our review comes from the European Union regime, dealing with economic and political integration.[62] Since 2009, the EU enjoys the benefits of a formal protection of human rights for situations falling under the jurisdiction of the Court of Justice of the European Union, in Luxembourg. In Article 47 of the Charter of Fundamental Rights of the European Union,[63] one can read:

> **47.** Everyone whose rights and freedoms guaranteed by the law of the Union are violated has the right to an effective remedy before a tribunal in compliance with the conditions laid down in this Article.
>
> Everyone is entitled to a fair and public hearing within a reasonable time by an independent and impartial tribunal previously established by law. Everyone shall have the possibility of being advised, defended and represented. [...]

These first two paragraphs of Article 47, one will notice, are formulated very similarly to Article 6(1) of the European Convention on Human Rights; it is worth noting as well that, between the Strasbourg and the Luxembourg courts, there can

[61] See, on this point, John H Currie, *Public International Law*, 2nd edn (Toronto, Irwin Law, 2008) 262.

[62] See eg Paul Craig and Gráinne de Búrca, *EU Law – Text, Cases, and Materials*, 7th edn (Oxford, Oxford University Press, 2020).

[63] The instrument was proclaimed on 7 December 2000, but without direct legal effect, and only later entered into force as binding for the EU Member States, with the adoption of the Treaty of the European Union (or Treaty of Lisbon) on 1 December 2009 – Official Journal of the European Union, C 326.

sometimes be conflicts of jurisdictions.[64] More to the point, without providing for it expressly, the EU Charter of Fundamental Rights is also deemed to include the procedural principle of equality of arms, an unwritten principle developed in case law, the study of which we now turn to.

The European Court of Human Rights and the EU Court of Justice – interpreting the European Convention on Human Rights and the EU Charter of Fundamental Rights, respectively – have articulated the unwritten principle of equality on the basis of their international conventional instruments. Examining how the said principle may apply to criminal, civil and administrative matters, the discussion will focus on three cases.

First, the *Gryaznov*[65] case in 2012 concerned a Russian national who argued, referring to the right to a fair and public hearing in Article 6(1) of the European Convention, that the Russian Federation's Penal Code and Code of Civil Procedure violated the principle of equality of arms. The legislative provisions allowed for judicial audience without the accused present and, as a result, prevented him from making a full answer and defence in the proceedings. The First Section of the Court agreed and ordered compensation for the applicant, holding that domestic courts and tribunals in Russia needed to make sure that an accused was present during the proceedings in order for him to give his version of the facts, including here to testify on his personal experience of the alleged ill-treatments.

Other elements were considered in violation of Article 6(1) of the European Convention, namely the failure to serve documents on the applicant and the refusal to call a witness. All these procedural shortcomings, the Strasbourg court held, concern not only the right to a fair and public hearing, but also the adversarial principle and, most relevant for our purposes, the unwritten principle of equality of arms. Here are some short excerpts of the decision:

> 45. Article 6 of the Convention does not guarantee a right to personal presence before a civil court, but rather a more general right to present one's case effectively before the court and to enjoy equality of arms with the opposing side. Article 6 §1 leaves to the State a free choice of the means to be used in guaranteeing litigants these rights [case law reference omitted].
>
> [...]

[64] For comparisons of case law, see Hanneke Senden, *Interpretation of Fundamental Rights in a Multilevel Legal System – An Analysis of the European Court of Human Rights and the Court of Justice of the European Union* (Cambridge, Intersentia, 2011); and in criminal context, Sabine Gless and Jeannine Martin, 'The Comparative Method in European Courts: A Comparison between the CJEU and ECtHR?' (2013) 1 *Bergen Journal of Criminal Law and Criminal Justice* 36. On issues of conflict between the Strasbourg and the Luxembourg courts, see Mattias Kumm, 'The Jurisprudence of Constitutional Conflict' (2005) 11 *European Law Journal* 262; and Matthias Klatt, 'Balancing Competences: How Institutional Cosmopolitanism can Manage Jurisdictional Conflicts' (2015) 4 *Global Constitutionalism* 195.

[65] *Gryaznov v Russia* (application no. 19673/03), ECtHR, 12 June 2012.

> 51. In these circumstances, the Court finds that the principle of equality of arms was breached, owing to the domestic courts' refusal to secure the applicant's attendance at the hearing.
>
> [...]
>
> 53. The Court reiterates that the principle of adversarial proceedings and equality of arms, which is one of the elements of the broader concept of fair hearing, requires that each party be given a reasonable opportunity to have knowledge of and comment on the observations made or evidence adduced by the other party and to present its case under conditions that do not place it at a substantial disadvantage *vis-à-vis* its opponent [case law references omitted].
>
> [...]
>
> 57. Article 6 of the Convention does not explicitly guarantee the right to have witnesses called or other evidence admitted by a court in civil proceedings. Nevertheless, any restriction imposed on the right of a party to civil proceedings to call witnesses and to adduce other evidence in support of his case must be consistent with the requirements of a fair trial within the meaning of paragraph 1 of that Article, including the principle of equality of arms. Equality of arms implies that each party must be afforded a reasonable opportunity to present his case – including his evidence – under conditions that do not place him at a substantial disadvantage *vis-à-vis* his opponent [case law reference omitted].
>
> [underlines added]

Also in 2012, this time the EU Court of Justice examined such procedural issues in a case requiring a preliminary ruling on the interpretation of some conventional and regulatory provisions relating to competition law, and whether it was valid under Article 47 of the EU Charter. It concerned proceedings alleging anti-trust practices by companies in the business of elevators and escalators, brought before national courts of an EU member. The European Commission was to participate in the proceedings, which was challenged on the ground that it would play to the disadvantage of the defendant companies, given the situation of this EU organ in a previous case, where it adjudicated on the allegations. Beside the principle that no one should be a judge in their own cause (ie *nemo judex in sua causa*), the defendants argued judicial independence and equality of arms.

In the *Europese Gemeenschap*[66] case then, the Grand Chamber of the EU Court of Justice dwelled upon this unwritten principle, although in the end the arguments based on Article 47 of the EU Charter were insufficient. The Court did agree, however, that equality arms requires that there be a certain parity among the parties involved in judicial proceedings under a legal scheme of the European Union. The following passages of the judgment are on point, as they highlight the unwritten nature of this principle:

> 71. The principle of equality of arms, which is a corollary of the very concept of a fair hearing [case law reference omitted], implies that each party must be afforded a

[66] *Europese Gemeenschap v Otis NV et al.*, 6 November 2012, no. C-199/11.

> reasonable opportunity to present his case, including his evidence, under conditions that do not place him at a substantial disadvantage vis-à-vis his opponent.
>
> 72. As the Advocate General has observed [...], the aim of equality of arms is to ensure a balance between the parties to proceedings, guaranteeing that any document submitted to the court may be examined and challenged by any party to the proceedings. Conversely, the harm which a lack of balance will be likely to cause must, as a rule, be proved by the person who has suffered it.
>
> [underlines added]

A third illustration of how equality of arms constitutes an unwritten principle connected in spirit to conventional international human rights law comes again from the European Court of Human Rights in the 2017 *Regner*[67] case. The applicant was challenging the validity of an administrative procedure that led to ending his position at the Department of National Defense in the Czech Republic, on the basis of some alleged malfeasances. The problem was that the proceedings allowed for confidential evidence to be kept from the accused, information that was however made available for the tribunal to consider. In a 10-7 split decision, the motion was dismissed, the majority of justices holding that the restrictions on the European Convention rights, 'were offset in such a manner that the fair balance between the parties was not affected to such an extent as to impair the very essence of the applicant's right to a fair trial'.[68]

Many procedural rights were invoked and argued pursuant to Article 6(1) of the European Convention, including in regard to the unwritten principle of equality of arms, which was said to derive from the fundamental right to a fair hearing:

> 146. The Court reiterates that the adversarial principle and the principle of equality of arms, which are closely linked, are fundamental components of the concept of a 'fair hearing' within the meaning of Article 6 §1 of the Convention. They require a 'fair balance' between the parties: each party must be afforded a reasonable opportunity to present his case under conditions that do not place him at a substantial disadvantage vis-à-vis his opponent or opponents [case law reference omitted].
>
> [underlines added]

This excerpt from the main opinion of the Court, that is to say 7 of the 17 judges of the Grand Chamber, is not the only one relevant for our purposes. Indeed, a separate opinion by Justice Georigios Serghides (dissenting in part) includes very material passages on equality of arms. His analysis recalled the origins and the content of the right to a fair hearing and, relevant to the point in question, dwelled upon the numerous ramifications of this unwritten principle, as it applies to criminal, civil and administrative matters. He wrote the following: 'The right to a fair hearing incorporates a number of aspects of the due process of law, the

[67] *Regner v Czech Republic* (application no. 35289/11), ECtHR, 19 September 2017.
[68] ibid 38, para 161.

most fundamental of which are: (a) access to court, (b) equality of arms (*égalité des armes*), (c) adversarial proceedings, and (d) a reasoned judgment'.[69]

To recap, what comes out of this short review of the three main cases from the European regimes of international human rights law is how equality of arms was articulated around the idea of fair hearing, which is a right expressly provided for in conventional texts. The principle is said to be derived from the provisions of these treaties, extrapolated from the specific human rights. As such, equality of arms provides a good example of an unwritten principle of conventional international law, which now will be examined insofar as it may be used domestically.

B. Conforming Legal Interpretation and Equality of Arms in Domestic Law

With a view to verifying the hypothesis that conforming legal interpretation allows for recourse to unwritten principles based on international law and after fleshing out equality of arms as a top example of such a principle remotely connected to conventional human rights law, the next step is to examine the situation at the domestic level. Of course, there are many national jurisdictions, especially in Europe, that would provide interesting case studies on substantial issues of the right to a fair hearing and equality of arms. However, to make sure that, in methodological terms, the discussion brings out the dimension of interlegality and, more specifically, the judicial reasoning based on the presumption of conformity with international law, the choice was made to stay away from the somewhat hybrid (*sui generis*) legal reality in Europe, involving regional regimes of human rights.

A case study from a state that is viewed as traditional on these issues of interlegality, at least from an Anglo-Saxon common law legal tradition,[70] would seem more appropriate. Accordingly, Canada – which I happen to know best[71] – and, in particular, the provincial jurisdiction of Quebec, shall be examined below. The purpose, to put it most clearly, is to see how equality of arms, as an unwritten principle based on international law, has been used domestically in the interpretation and application of the province's procedural law, a word on which is now necessary.

Briefly, the law of civil procedure (criminal procedure is complex in Canada, with dual competence of the Federal and provincial legislatures,[72] and need not be addressed for the present purposes[73]) within the jurisdiction of Quebec is governed

[69] ibid 53, para 15 [underlines added].

[70] See Stéphane Beaulac and John H Currie, 'Canada' in Shelton (n 13) 116.

[71] See Stéphane Beaulac, 'Canada' in Fulvio M Palombino (ed), *Duelling for Supremacy: International Law vs. National Fundamental Principles* (Cambridge, Cambridge University Press, 2018) 21.

[72] See eg Marie-Eve Sylvestre, 'Droit criminel, droit pénal et droits individuels' in Beaulac and Gaudreault-DesBiens (n 14) ch 14.

[73] As regards the principle of equality of arms in the context of international criminal law, see Elise Groulx, '"Equality of arms": Challenges Confronting the Legal Profession in the Emerging International Criminal Justice System' (2010 – special issue) *Quebec Journal of International Law* 21.

by the Code of Civil Procedure, which was, incidentally, completely revamped in 2018.[74] Under the heading 'Guiding principles of procedure', section 17 of the Code provides as follows:

> **17.** The court cannot rule on an application, or take a measure on its own initiative, which affects the rights of a party unless the party has been heard or duly called.
>
> In any contentious matter, the court, even on its own initiative, must uphold the adversarial principle and see that it is adhered to until the judgment and during execution of the judgment. It cannot base its decision on grounds the parties have not had the opportunity to debate.

As important (if not more) a quasi-constitutional instrument in the province imposes some minimum requirements in terms of procedural law. The Quebec Charter of Human Rights and Freedoms, specifically section 23(1), reads as follows:

> **23.** Every person has a right to a full and equal, public and fair hearing by an independent and impartial tribunal, for the determination of his rights and obligations or of the merits of any charge brought against him.
>
> [underlines added]

Of course, the first striking thing upon reading section 23 is how the wording employed in this domestic law is similar to that of Article 10 of the Universal Declaration of Human Rights, which we saw before.[75] This feature was highlighted, among other things, in case law on the principle of equality of arms under the Quebec Charter, which we now turn to.

There are only a handful of cases from the province of Quebec that have invoked equality of arms as a principle of procedural law. One of them, in 2017, comes from Frédéric Bachand J (now at the Court of Appeal), who wrote the following in a Superior Court judgment: '[T]he [contractual] clause does not sit well with the general principle of equality of arms, which is a key component of natural justice and which finds expression in the first paragraph of section 23 of the Charter of Human Rights and Freedom.'[76] There are even fewer instances where a Quebec court resorted to international law to shed light on it. The two cases examined below were chosen because they show how, indeed, it was by means of a reasoning rooted in conforming legal interpretation that this unwritten principle based on international law was used domestically.

[74] See eg Catherine Piché, 'Le 'dialogue' des parties et la vérité plurielle comme nouveau paradigme de la procédure civile québécoise' (2017) 62 *McGill Law Journal* 901.

[75] See Schabas and Beaulac (n 56) and accompanying text.

[76] *Banque de Nouvelle-Écosse v Davidovit*, 2018 QCCS 5097, para 38 [underlines added] [references omitted]. Note that this first instance decision was overturned on appeal – see 2021 QCCA 551 – which included a rebuke of the argument based on equality of arms (para 25): 'The so-called "inequality of arms" infringement of the spirit of the right to a fair trial protected by section 23 of the *Charter* is simply without merit. […] Section 23 essentially refers to procedural rights, such as the right to be heard' [footnotes omitted].

The first one, from the Quebec Court of Appeal in 2015, concerned the special legislative scheme enacted to facilitate law suits against tobacco companies,[77] including as regards evidence and limitation periods. It was thus argued in *Imperial Tobacco*[78] that these new rules were unfair and, more to the point, violated equality of arms as between parties in a proceeding. In that context, the quasi-constitutional section 23 of the Quebec Charter was considered:

> [53] And what of the expression '*en pleine égalité*' (full and equal) in section 23?
>
> [54] The appellants maintain that, because of the objectives of the *Quebec Charter* and the rules governing the internal consistency of statutes, the expression '*en pleine égalité*' (full and equal) must be interpreted to include the principle of equality of arms, an interpretation that is in their view reinforced by the external case law cited, particularly that of the European Court of Human Rights [...].

In the end, the argument under section 23 of the Quebec Charter and the idea of equality of arms did not make a difference in this case, as the Court of Appeal concluded that the special rules for evidence and limitation periods could validly apply in law suits against tobacco companies. Having said that, as far as this unwritten principle is concerned, its origins in conventional law and the many references to such international normativity by the Quebec domestic courts are the most important features of the case, for our purposes. In her reasons for judgment, Justice Geneviève Marcotte further wrote thus:

> [56] It is true that the legislative history of the *Quebec Charter* reveals that it was enacted <u>to harmonize Quebec with the international obligations</u> set out in the 1948 *Universal Declaration of Human Rights* and the 1966 *International Covenant on Civil and Political Rights*, and that some of its expressions or concepts reiterate those of the [European] *Convention for the Protection of Human Rights and Fundamental Freedoms*. While these international instruments may prove useful when interpreting *Quebec Charter* provisions given the <u>similarity between section 23 of the *Quebec Charter* and Article 10 of the *Universal Declaration of Human Rights*</u>, international instruments and foreign law do not, however, support the interpretation of section 23 of the *Quebec Charter* proposed by the appellants, which moreover diverges from that developed in Quebec case law.
>
> [underlines added] [footnotes omitted]

'Harmonising' Quebec law, as the Court of Appeal wrote, with international obligations based on conventional law, including the unwritten principle of equality of law, this is no doubt a variation in language of the canon of conforming legal interpretation. Put another way, by means of a reasoning founded on an interpretative presumption, Marcotte J tried to read section 23 of the Quebec Charter, inasmuch as possible, in a way compatible with the relevant conventional documents – the Universal Declaration and the International Covenant – with which (remotely or

[77] See *Tobacco-related Damages and Health Care Costs Recovery Act*, C.Q.L.R. c. R-2.2.0.0.1.

[78] *Imperial Tobacco Canada Ltd. v Quebec (Attorney General)*, 2015 QCCA 1554, which upheld the first instance judgment by the Superior Court, see 2014 QCCS 842.

in spirit, at least) the unwritten principle of equality of arms is linked, as articulated in the case law of international courts.

The second judgment in Quebec, itself referring at length to the Court of Appeal reasons in *Imperial Tobacco*, is the Superior Court decision in the *Sanimax*[79] case, handed down in 2019. Decided after the reform of the Quebec Code of Civil Procedure, in 2018, one interesting thing Judge Lukasz Granosik does in his judgment is to make the connection between the guiding principles of procedure (sections 17ff of the Code) and section 23 of the Quebec Charter, explaining how important it is to interpret and to apply the former in light of the latter quasi-constitutional provision.[80] He then formulated the issue thus: 'Accordingly, the analysis must centre on the expression "*balance*", "*fairness in debates*" and "*full and equal*" [hearing] in the context of the present file'.[81]

In terms of international law, after referring to passages from the *Imperial Tobacco* case and connecting them with equality of arms in section 23 of the Quebec Charter, Judge Granosik referred to and quoted from the 2012 *Europese Gemeenschap* case, which was examined before.[82] He understood from the EU Court of Justice decision that equality of arms in a judicial proceeding 'constitutes a fundamental principle, which is included in the notion of fair trial and assures a balance between the parties'.[83] The Judge then relied on excerpts from legal writings (ie *doctrine*) before reaching his conclusion, which in the end read down the extraordinary powers given to city inspectors under the enabling legislation at issue.

A more expansive construction of the public powers was rejected by the Court because it would be, 'at odds with the principles of "*fairness in debates*" and the "*balance*" between the parties in court, which in turn require that "*equality of arms*" be respected'.[84] Clearly then, among the principles deemed material here, equality of arms was front and centre. More significant for our discussion, pursuant to both the Quebec Civil Code of Procedure (section 17ff) and the Quebec Charter (section 23), the domestic interpretation given to equality of arms was compatible with this unwritten principle of conventional law, as articulated by international case law (cf European Court of Human Rights, EU Court of Justice).

In sum, the canon of legal interpretation known as the presumption of conformity with international law – though maybe not in name, but surely the essence of it – was

[79] *Ville de Montréal v Sanimax Lom inc.*, 2019 QCCS 303 [no English translation is provided by the Court].

[80] ibid, paras 20–21.

[81] ibid, para 22, my translation. Translation of the French: 'Il s'agit donc d'analyser ce que signifient les expressions "*équilibre*", "*débat loyal*" et "*en pleine égalité*" dans le contexte du présent dossier'.

[82] See *Europese Gemeenschap v Otis NV et al.* (n 66) and accompanying text.

[83] *Sanimax* (n 79) para 25 [foonote omitted]. Translation of the French: '[C]onstitue un principe fondamental, compris dans la notion de procès équitable et assurant l'équilibre entre les parties' [footnote omitted].

[84] ibid, para 28 [foonote omitted]. Translation of the French: '[E]n porte-à-faux avec les principes du "*débat loyal*" et de l'"*équilibre*" des parties devant un tribunal, lesquels exigent le respect de "*l'égalité des armes*"' [footnote omitted].

at play in the two Quebec judgments that resorted to the procedural principle of equality of arms. It will be interesting to see how later domestic case law will continue building upon this jurisprudence and, more importantly, how conforming legal interpretation is likely to continue to be the means by which this unwritten legal principle based on international law helps interpret and apply Quebec's procedural law.

IV. Concluding Remarks

In a celebrated paper in 2004, titled 'The Unwritten Constitution and the Rule of Law',[85] legal theorist David Dyzenhaus engaged with Antonin Scalia[86] and argued that the late Justice of the US Supreme Court and his textualism/originalism were directed at resisting common law value-laden types of interpretation when ascertaining the content of written law, both statutory text and (even more so) constitutional documents.[87] Interestingly, such concerns are behind Scalia J's objections to both the idea of a living constitution and the domestic use of foreign and international law, including by means of what they call in the USA the 'Charming Betsy Rule',[88] the presumption of conformity with international law.

Dyzenhaus expressed the view that, 'the terrain of the unwritten constitution', that is of constitutional (and international) values, is 'important to the theme of the legitimacy of these modes of interpretation'.[89] Showing much realism, the Canadian author made the following suggestion: 'If interpretation of constitutional values [and international ones] were an activity which judges could not avoid, then it might seem that what they are doing when they interpret is also legitimate'.[90] Giving a warning not to confuse necessity with legitimacy, however, he rooted the justification to resorting to unwritten principles with the meta-principle of the rule of law: '[J]udges must – <u>if they are to be faithful to their duty to uphold the rule of law</u> – interpret

[85] David Dyzenhaus, 'The Unwritten Constitution and the Rule of Law' in Grant Huscroft and Ian Brodie (eds), *Constitutionalism in the Charter Era* (Toronto, LexisNexis, 2004) 383.

[86] See Antonin Scalia, *A Matter of Interpretation: Federal Court and the Law* (Princeton, Princeton University Press, 1997); and Antonin Scalia, 'Originalism: The Lesser Evil' (1989) 57 *University of Cincinnati Law Review* 849. For a criticism of Scalia J's take on originalism, see Randy E Barnett, 'Scalia's Infidelity: A Critique of "Faint-Hearted" Originalism' (2006) 75 *University of Cincinnati Law Review* 7.

[87] On originalism in general, among the vast literature on the subject, see the following particularly interesting texts: Jack N Rakove, *Original Meanings – Politics and Ideas in the Making of the Constitution* (New York, Vintage, 1997); Laurence B Solum, 'Originalist Methodology' (2017) 84 *University of Chicago Law Review* 269; and Randy E Barnett and Evan D. Bernick, 'The Letter and the Spirit: A Unified Theory of Originalism' (2018) 107 *Georgetown Law Journal* 1.

[88] See, on the American version of this type of interpretation, Curtis A Bradley, 'The Charming Betsy Canon and Separation of Powers: Rethinking the Interpretative Role of International Law' (1998) 86 *Georgetown Law Journal* 479.

[89] Dyzenhaus (n 85) 383.

[90] ibid.

the positive law of a [domestic] legal order in light of their understanding of unwritten constitutional values [and international ones]'.[91]

On the international plane, especially when dealing with conventional law – be it directly or with a remote connection, such as unwritten principles (as we saw) – the rule of law is very much intertwined with *pacta sunt servanda*, codified in the Vienna Convention of the Law of Treaties.[92] Acting similarly to the basic notions of consent and constituent power in constitutional and international legal theory,[93] the idea that a 'treaty in force is binding upon the parties to it', which means that these obligations 'must be performed by them in good faith',[94] is at the heart of the whole international legal structure founded on the positivist theory of voluntarism,[95] in the so-called Westphalian system of international relations,[96] which undoubtedly remains the dominant epistemology to help apprehend and rationalise this normative order.[97]

The rule of law[98] in its international version, which has been dwelled upon extensively in scholarship as of late,[99] has an important dimension relating to

[91] ibid 384 [underlines added]. See also, on the same theme of values in constitutional interpretation, Mark C Power and Darius Bossé, 'Une tentative de clarification de la présomption de respect des valeurs de la *Charte canadienne des droits et libertés*' (2014) 55 *Cahiers de droit* 775.

[92] See art 26 of the Vienna Convention 1969.

[93] For some reference works on this topic, from an American perspective: see Bruce Ackerman, *We the People – Foundations* (Cambridge, Harvard University Press, 1991); from a European perspective: Martin Loughlin and Neil Walker (eds), *The Paradox of Constitutionalism – Constituent Power and Constitutional Form* (Oxford, Oxford University Press, 2007); from an international perspective: Mattias Kumm, 'Constituent Power, Cosmopolitan Constitutionalism, and Post-positivist Law' (2016) 14 *International Journal of Constitutional Law* 697; Thomas Franck, *The Power of Legitimacy among Nations* (New York, Oxford University Press, 1990); and from a post-conflict transitional perspective: Simon Chesterman, *You, The People – The United Nations, Transitional Administration, and State-Building* (Oxford, Oxford University Press, 2004). See also, in broader philosophical terms, Alan S Rosenbaum (ed), *Constitutionalism: The Philosophical Dimension* (New York, Greenwood Press, 1988); and Randy E Barnett, 'Constitutional Legitimacy' (2003) 103 *Columbia Law Review* 111.

[94] Of course, one recognises the very wording of art 26 of the Vienna Convention 1969.

[95] See Mónica Garcia-Salmones Rovira, *The Project of Positivism in International Law* (Oxford, Oxford University Press, 2013); and Oriol Casanovas, *Unity and Pluralism in Public International Law* (The Hague, Martinus Nijhoff, 2001) 6–11.

[96] See Stéphane Beaulac, *The Power of Language in the Making of International Law – The Word Sovereignty in Bodin and Vattel and the Myth of Westphalia* (Leiden, Martinus Nijhoff, 2004). See also Richard Joyce, 'Westphalia: Event, Memory, Myth' in Fleur Johns, Richard Joyce and Sundhya Pahuja (eds), *Events – The Force of International Law* (New York, Routledge, 2011) 55, especially at 57 and 64–67.

[97] See Patrick Daillier, Mathias Forteau and Alain Pellet, *Njuyen Quoc Dinh – Droit international public*, 8th edn (Paris, Librairie générale de droit et de jurisprudence, 2009) 111ff.

[98] For some classic works on the rule of law, see Lord Tom Bingham, *The Rule of Law* (London, Allen Lane, 2010); Brian Z Tamanaha, *On the Rule of Law – History, Politics, Theory* (Cambridge, Cambridge University Press, 2004); Jeremy Waldron, 'Is the Rule of Law an Essentially Contested Concept (in Florida)?' (2002) 21 *Law and Philosophy* 137; and, for recent literature going against the grain of its virtues, see Csaba Varga, 'Rule of Law, Contesting and Contested' (2021) 1 *Central European Journal of Comparative Law* 245.

[99] See Stéphane Beaulac, 'The Rule of Law in International Today' in Gianluigi Palombella and Neil Walker (eds), *Relocating the Rule of Law* (Oxford, Hart Publishing, 2009) 197. See also Arthur Watts, 'The International Rule of Law' (1993) 36 *German Yearbook of International Law* 15; Simon Chesterman, 'An International Rule of Law?' (2008) 56 *American Journal of Comparative Law* 331; Jeremy Waldron, 'Are Sovereigns Entitled to the Benefit of the International Rule of Law' (2011) 22 *European Journal of International Law* 315; Kenneth J Keith, 'The International Rule of Law' (2015)

interlegality, that is to say the domestic use of international law.[100] In 'International Law in National Courts: The International Rule of Law and the Limits of the Internationalist Model', Mattias Kumm wrote that, '[t]here is something intuitively attractive about the idea that the international rule of law requires national courts to enforce international law,' which would explain, 'why the international rule of law exerts such a strong moral pull in many quarters'.[101] Of course, he spent the bulk of the paper testing and challenging this view and, in the end, highlighted the limitations of the internationalist understanding of the rule of law.[102]

Where does that leave us when considering the canon of conforming legal interpretation based on international law? How is this presumptive reasoning favouring compatibility between the domestic and the international justified when relying on unwritten principles from the latter legal order, be them freestanding or remotely (even tenuously) connected to conventional law, be it at least in spirit? Does it bring the process of interpretation and application of national law closer to the values dear to the rule of law, in its traditional domestic version,[103] such as the ideas of legality, equal application of the law, as well as independent judicial decision-making? What about the international rule of law – with *pacta sunt servanda*, but also other underlying values of this legal order, as evidenced by state practice[104] – is it better or worse with an approach that favours conforming legal interpretation at the domestic level using unwritten principles based on international law?

28 *Leiden Journal of International Law* 403; Robert McCorquodale, 'Defining the International Rule of Law: Defying Gravity?' (2016) 65 *International and Comparative Law Quarterly* 277; and Kostiantyn Gorobets, 'The International Rule of Law and the Idea of Normative Authority' (2020) 12 *Hague Journal on the Rule of Law* 227.

[100] See André Nollkaemper, *National Courts and the International Rule of Law* (Oxford, Oxford University Press, 2012); André Nollkaemper, Edda Kristjánsdóttir and Cedric Ryngaert (eds), *International Law in Domestic Courts – Rule of Law Reform in Post-Conflict States* (Antwerp, Intersentia, 2012); and Machiko Kanetake and André Nollkaemper (eds), *The Rule of Law at the National and International Levels – Contestations and Deference* (Oxford, Hart Publishing, 2016).

[101] Mattias Kumm, 'International Law in National Courts: The International Rule of Law and the Limits of the Internationalist Model' (2003) 44 *Virginia Journal of International Law* 19, 21.

[102] In his conclusion, ibid 32, Kumm wrote: 'This discussion of the international rule of law has yielded two propositions. First, there are morally attractive features about the idea of the international rule of law that provide *prima facie* support for the claim that courts have a role to play in the enforcement of international law, even absent specific endorsement from the political branches. Second, beyond furthering the international rule of law, there are countervailing considerations [reciprocity and flexibility concerns] that may limit the role of national courts as enforcers of international law'.

[103] For the archetype articulation of the principle of the rule of law, in the Anglo-Saxon legal tradition, of course see Albert Venn Dicey, *Introduction to the Study of the Law of the Constitution* (London, Macmillan, 1885) 188ff. For similar formulations, or at least which overlap substantially with Dicey's, see also Friedrich Hayek, *The Road to Serfdom* (London, Routledge, 1944) 54ff; Lon Fuller, *The Morality of Law*, 2nd edn (New Haven, Yale University Press, 1969) 38ff; John Finnis, *Natural Law and Natural Rights* (Oxford, Clarendon Press, 1980) 270ff; and Joseph Raz, *Ethics in the Public Domain: Essays on the Morality of Law and Politics* (Oxford, Clarendon Press, 1994) 373ff.

[104] See Noora Arajärvi, 'The Core Requirements of International Rule of Law in the Practice of States' (2021) 13 *Hague Journal on the Rule of Law* 173, who, based on an empirical study of the statements of governments at the UN, identified three such values as minimum requirements for the international rule of law, namely: (i) non-arbitrariness, (ii) consistency, and (iii) predictability.

All of these questions, which are more rooted in legal theory than anything this chapter (that ended up being quite applied, even empirical indeed) actually accomplished, will have to wait for another day, especially given that I am already treading dangerously close to the word limit for contributions to this collective book. To be continued, then.

PART II

Critical Perspectives

5

There is No Such Thing as the Duty to Save a Statute

VIRGÍLIO AFONSO DA SILVA

I. Introduction

The duty to interpret ordinary legislation in accordance with the constitution seems to be part of the daily routine of courts in several countries. The national reports in the first volume of this work demonstrate it.[1] However, those reports also seem to show that the meaning of the so-called constitutionally conforming interpretation (hereafter CCI) varies considerably across jurisdictions. While this might be a problem in itself, it is not the issue that will be analysed here. What I intend to show is that CCI is based either (a) on trivial premises, (b) on mistaken premises, or (c) on premises that are not confirmed by the outcomes of the interpretive process.

To this end, this chapter has the following structure. In the next section (II), I will analyse the theoretical premises of CCI (presumption of constitutionality, unity of the legal system, and deference to the legislature). As already mentioned, I will try to demonstrate that these premises are either trivial or mistaken; moreover, I will argue that in most cases, they play no role at all, and the outcomes of the CCI are often at odds with them. In the following section (III), I use two concrete cases to illustrate the conclusions drawn in section II. Section IV is dedicated to analysing the relationship between CCI and judicial review of legislation. I intend to show that this relationship is more complex than is often assumed and that this complexity is only perceptible if differences in institutional design are considered. In the conclusion (V), I intend not only to summarise the findings of this chapter but also to emphasise that the objections to CCI do not imply in any way a denial of the radiating effects of constitutional provisions in the process of interpreting ordinary legislation.

[1] See Matthias Klatt (ed), *Constitutionally Conforming Interpretation: Comparative Perspectives Volume 1: National Reports* (Oxford, Hart Publishing, 2023).

II. The Premises

Despite cross-country variations,[2] in more theoretical debates there is a certain convergence towards the existence of three assumptions that justify the use of CCI: (1) the presumption of constitutionality of laws, (2) the unity of the legal system, and (3) respect for the separation of powers (frequently summarised within the idea of *favor legis*).[3] In the following sections, I will demonstrate that these assumptions are either too trivial to be useful or are plainly mistaken. Moreover, irrespective of whether they are banal or mistaken, I will also show that the assumptions do not play any relevant role in the interpretation of ordinary law in accordance with the constitution.

A. Presumption of Constitutionality[4]

In legal argumentation, presumptions often play an important role. Presuming something to be true under given circumstances – above all when it is difficult or impossible to know the truth – is a strategy that has been used in legal argumentation and legal decisions for centuries. Presumptions are usually defined as:

(1) the acceptance of something as true;
(2) given certain conditions;
(3) unless there is proof to the contrary.[5]

Although the concept of presumption may be fairly straightforward in many legal disciplines, its applicability to constitutional argumentation – under the label 'presumption of constitutionality' – entails several formal problems, above all those concerned with the relationships between presumption and time, between presumption and conditions, and between presumption and proof. In this chapter, I will address only the last two of these problems.[6]

[2] See ibid.

[3] See Matthias Klatt, 'The Legitimacy of Constitutionally Conforming Interpretation' in Klatt (n 1) s III.

[4] This section uses ideas and excerpts from Virgílio Afonso da Silva, 'Legal argumentation, constitutional interpretation, and presumption of constitutionality' in Frans H van Eemeren et al (eds), *Proceedings of the Sixth Conference of the International Society for the Study of Argumentation* (Amsterdam, Sic Sat, 2007) 1291–94.

[5] In many legal systems, it is common to speak of two kinds of presumptions: *iuris tantum* and *iuris et de iure*. The scheme presented above corresponds to the presumption *iuris tantum*, ie presumptions that may be defeated (as expressed by the third element of the definition). See, for instance, Daniel Mendonca, 'Presumptions' (1998) 11 *Ratio Juris* 399, 410–11.

[6] For an assessment of the relationship between presumption and time, see da Silva (n 4). See also Gonçalo de Almeida Ribeiro, 'Portugal. The Conundrum of Constitutionally Conforming Interpretation' in Klatt (n 1) s I fn 3; Isabel Lifante-Vidal, 'Spain. Constitutionally Conforming Interpretation and Interpretative Judgements in the Spanish Constitutional Court' in Klatt (n 1) s V.

i. Conditions

As mentioned above, legal presumptions usually establish conditions or circumstances under which something should be presumed as true (meaning that under other conditions or circumstances, the presumption does not hold). For example, a civil code may contain a provision establishing that a child born *at least 180 days after wedlock* is presumably legitimate or that if husband and wife die *in the same car (or plane, or train) accident*, the deaths were presumably simultaneous. Such presumptions hold only if the stipulated conditions also hold. These conditions are expressed as a 'given-clause' (given that 'the child was born at least 180 days after wedlock', given that 'husband and wife die in the same car (or plane, or train) accident' etc.).

However, the idea of a presumption of constitutionality cannot be based on the same rationale because it is impossible to define under which conditions or circumstances a statute should be presumed constitutional and under which conditions it should not. Indeed, if there were any reason to believe in a presumption of constitutionality, one should believe in it *in every case*. The 'given-clause' is simply absent. There is no 'given that the child was born at least 180 days after wedlock …' (and not 179 days or fewer) or 'given that husband and wife were in the same plane that crashed …' (and not in different planes), but only 'given that a law was enacted', which states no real condition or circumstance.

Hence, to state that a law is always presumably constitutional is tantamount to saying that every law *is* constitutional unless someone (a constitutional court, for instance) declares otherwise. But such reasoning not only does not express a presumption, it is also superfluous.

ii. Proof

A legal presumption (*iuris tantum*[7]) presupposes the possibility of proving that the presumed fact is not true, therefore defeating the presumption. In the case of the examples mentioned above, it is possible, by means of a DNA test, for instance, to prove that a child is not legitimate, even if they were born more than 180 days after wedlock. However, this kind of rebuttal is impossible in a presumption of constitutionality because constitutionality and unconstitutionality are not subject to proof. 'Being' constitutional or unconstitutional are not inherent features of laws. The process of constitutional review of legislation is not a kind of search for a 'genetic code' – congenital to the enacted law – waiting to be discovered by 'legal scientists'.[8]

[7] See n 5 above.

[8] To be sure, one could argue that whenever legal scholars and practitioners argue that a statute cannot be declared unconstitutional unless it is provably unconstitutional, they are not making reference to a factual presumption (like those I used as examples above), but to an argumentative presumption. An argumentative presumption, even though not subject to rebuttal with factual proof or evidence, may still be rebutted: by means of arguments. However, in this case what role does the

B. The Unity of the Legal System

The duty to perform CCI has often been assumed to be a necessary consequence of conceptualising the legal system as a hierarchically stepped construction, at the top of which lies the constitution. According to this view, the CCI is a tool for preserving the unity of such a hierarchical system. As Hesse put it, this canon 'finds its root [...] in the principle of the unity of the legal order: for the sake of this unity, laws [...] must be interpreted in accordance with the constitution'.[9] In the first volume of this project, references to the unity of the legal system (employing this name or not) as a premise for CCI were made, for instance, by Klatt, Ondřejek, Bezemek and Gosch, Barczentewicz and Matczak, and Lifante-Vidal.[10]

However, having the constitution as an interpretative parameter does not necessarily entail the duty to give priority to the interpretation that maintains the constitutionality of an ordinary law.[11] The difference between these two ideas becomes clearer if one bears in mind that proceeding in exactly the opposite way to what the CCI proposes, ie striking down an ordinary law in the context of judicial review of legislation, preserves the unity of the legal system to the same extent. Thus, if the same reasoning – having the constitution as a parameter for the interpretation of ordinary law – is the justification not only for CCI (and therefore for upholding a piece of ordinary legislation) but also for its opposite (for striking down that piece of legislation), then the unity of the legal system cannot be a sufficient condition for CCI. Klatt acknowledges this:

> It must be noted that these considerations justify CCI only as a necessary condition. The unity of the legal system does not represent a sufficient condition for the canon because derogating the lower-ranked norm could alternatively resolve the norm conflict. A fully-fledged justification of CCI has to state sufficient conditions, not merely necessary ones. Therefore, we must supplement the unity of the legal system with further arguments. Additional arguments must demonstrate that the unity of the legal system should be protected by interpreting all rules constitutionally conforming and not by the alternative means of nullification. The principle of *favor legis* provides precisely this.[12]

presumption play? It seems that in such situations, it would make more sense to speak of a *default*, not a presumption.

[9] See Konrad Hesse, *Grundzüge des Verfassungsrechts der Bundesrepublik Deutschland*, 19th edn (Heidelberg, CF Müller, 1993) para 81 (my translation); similarly, see Ulrich Häfelin and Walter Haller, *Schweizerisches Bundesstaatsrecht*, 4th edn (Zürich, Schulthess, 1998) para 127.

[10] See Klatt (n 3) s III(B); Pavel Ondřejek, 'Czech Republic. Insights from the Constitutional Court's Post-Transition Practice of Constitutionally Conforming Interpretation' in Klatt (n 1) s I; Chiara Valentini, 'Italy. Constitutionally Conforming Interpretation and Judicial Dialogue' in Klatt (n 1) s II(A); Christoph Bezemek and Daniel Gosch, 'Austria. Embracing Tradition: Constitutionally Conforming Interpretation's Edge in Reconciling Statutory and Constitutional Law' in Klatt (n 1) s III; Mikołaj Barczentewicz and Marcin Matczak, 'Poland. Constitutionally Conforming Interpretation in Times of Constitutional Crisis' in Klatt (n 1) s II; Lifante-Vidal (n 6) s I.

[11] See Frederick Schauer, 'United States. Constitutional Avoidance As Constitutional Conformation' in Klatt (n 1).

[12] Klatt (n 3) s III(B).

However, this is the equivalent of saying that the unity of the legal system does not really play a relevant role in the justification of CCI. It only establishes that contradictions must be avoided and that ordinary legislation must be compatible with constitutional provisions. But it says nothing about what to do when contradictions arise. The whole job is done by the principle of *favor legis*. If *favor legis* fails, CCI – as we know it – also fails. One could of course argue that this is precisely the meaning of a necessary condition (as Klatt puts it). If the condition does not hold, something does not take place. But speaking of conditions (sufficient or necessary) is misleading in this context. As will become clear in the next section, *favor legis* stipulates an aim rather a condition.

C. Favor Legis

Favor legis has been defined as the duty to preserve a legal provision if there is any possibility of doing so. It therefore implies an alleged duty to avoid striking down a piece of legislation unless there is no other way to preserve the unity of the legal system. It is a 'duty to save the law'.[13] According to some authors, this is a corollary of the principle of the separation of powers.[14] As the German Constitutional Court puts it: 'The respect judges must pay to the legislature demands that the will of the legislature must be accommodated as much as possible within the frame of what the constitution permits.'[15]

References to the 'will of the legislature' are as such almost always problematic because they presuppose that it is possible to define what the legislature actually wanted. Frequently, the only thing that is certain when a parliamentary majority passes a law is that the majority wanted to pass that law. It is often not possible to know why those who voted in favour of the law did so or what meaning they attach to the law. There is therefore an important difference between respecting the will of the legislature and not striking down a piece of legislation. And this difference has relevant effects on the separation of powers. When a court does not strike down a piece of legislation, it upholds a *legal document* and attributes a meaning to it. Whether this meaning has anything to do with what the majority in parliament wanted is frequently difficult (or impossible) to assess.

Therefore, I argue that deference to the will of the legislature and respect for the separation of powers are only catchphrases. A court that resorts to CCI actually gives *its own* interpretation to an enacted law to make it compatible with the

[13] In the national reports, references to this duty (without necessarily endorsing it) may be found in Diego W Arguelhes and Rafael B Lima, 'Brazil. From Restraint to Preemption?' in Klatt (n 1) s II(A); Ondřejek (n 10) s II; Valentini (n 10) s III(A); Schauer (n 11) s IV; Richard Stacey, 'South Africa. The Siren Call of Constitutionally Conforming Interpretation: Statutory Validity at The Expense of Constitutional Values' in Klatt (n 1) s IV(B); Lael K Weis, 'Australia. Techniques of Developing Legislation and the Common Law to Align with Constitutional Legal Norms' in Klatt (n 1) fn 58.

[14] See Klatt (n 3) s III(C).

[15] BVerfGE 110, 226 (267) (my translation).

constitution *as interpreted by the same court*. There is nothing necessarily wrong with this; after all, it is the task of a court in the context of constitutional adjudication to interpret legal provisions and to assess whether they are compatible with the constitution (as interpreted by the same court).

Why then do so many courts resort to CCI? Irrespective of what constitutional courts or supreme courts actually do, they frequently claim that they cannot legislate, in the sense of doing what the legislature supposedly should have done (but did not do). In the context of constitutional adjudication, courts often see themselves as 'negative legislator', ie a court may strike down a statute because of nonconformity with the constitution, but it cannot create new law.[16] In this context, CCI can play a convenient role, which is to enable courts to remain faithful, at least on the surface, to the dogma of negative legislation and at the same time to correct, restrict or extend the work of the legislature.

Thus, when Klatt states that, 'unlike what critics argue, parliament is always free to make new enactments', and therefore, 'there is no difference between declaring a statute void and interpreting it in a constitutionally conforming manner',[17] this is not quite accurate. There is a difference: to admit what is being done. When a court strikes down a statute, it does not replace it with anything else; it is up to the legislature to reframe and reenact the statute as it sees fit. In contrast, when the court performs CCI, it may surreptitiously replace what the legislature had done with what the court wants; the court proudly announces a deferent stance when in fact there may be no deference at all. Speaking of *favor legis*, deference, or respect for the legislature and the separation of powers is just an unconvincing disguise.[18]

D. Results: Trivial or Unsound (or Both)

As I mentioned at the beginning of this chapter, the premises that have usually been put forward for justifying CCI – the presumption of constitutionality of laws, the unity of the legal system, and the respect for the separation of powers (*favor legis*) – are either trivial or based on unsound premises (or both). Let me summarise these claims here.

A *strong* reading of these premises reveals either that they cannot be justified or that the outcomes of CCI frequently clash with those premises. The presumption of constitutionality is actually not a presumption, among other things because it does not contain a 'given-clause' and because it is not rebuttable in the manner in which legal presumptions are rebuttable. The idea of the unity of the legal system

[16] For the concept of negative legislation, see Hans Kelsen, 'Wesen und Entwicklung der Staatsgerichtsbarkeit' (1929) 5 *Veröffentlichungen der Vereinigung der Deutschen Staatsrechtslehrer* 31, 34–35. See also Bezemek and Gosch (n 10) s II; Mathieu Carpentier, 'France. The Dynamics of "Interpretative Reservations" in the Jurisprudence of the French Constitutional Council' in Klatt (n 1) s III(D).

[17] Klatt (n 3) s V(C).

[18] Similarly, see Arguelhes and Lima (n 14) s III; Schauer (n 11) s V. See also Carpentier (n 17) s I.

assumes that legal systems are hierarchical and stepped constructions. As such, it demands that lower norms comply with higher norms. However, it does not give guidance when a lower norm is not in accordance with a higher one. Mutually exclusive solutions are possible: to strike down the lower norm or to adapt it until it becomes compatible with the higher one. Finally, *favor legis* is supposed to express a judicial deference towards the legislature,[19] while it may actually imply the contrary.

It is possible to avoid these problems by means of a *weak* reading of those premises. This reading would go as follows: (1) the presumption of constitutionality means that laws passed by the legislature are compatible with the constitution unless a court decides otherwise; (2) the unity of the legal system entails that the constitution is the apex of a hierarchical system, whose norms should therefore be interpreted in accordance with constitutional provisions; and (3) *favor legis* means that courts should take legislation seriously, but only if legislation is in accordance with the constitution.

Although the problems mentioned earlier are indeed avoided by means of this weak reading, the premises become so trivial that probably no one would ever deny them. There is no alternative to them because supposing their opposite makes no sense at all. As a consequence, any theory of constitutional adjudication is compatible with them.

III. Two Exercises

In the following two subsections, I will explore two instances of application of CCI to briefly show how it may not live up to its assumptions and how its outcomes may be incompatible with its aims.

A. What if the Text is Not Ambiguous?

Suppose there is a statute that aims to regulate the freedom of assembly (hereafter: Freedom of Assembly Act). This statute contains the following two provisions:

> § X. Anyone who intends to organise a public open-air assembly shall notify the competent authority at least 48 hours before the announcement, stating the subject of the assembly.
>
> § Y. Conducting a public open-air assembly without prior notification (pursuant to the provisions of § X) shall be punishable by imprisonment of up to one year or a fine.

These provisions are challenged before the constitutional court. The plaintiff argues that they unduly restrict the freedom of assembly protected by the constitution,

[19] See Ondřejek (n 10) s II.

among other things, because they make urgent and spontaneous assemblies illegal and punishable by imprisonment or fine. Suppose that the court acknowledges that urgent and spontaneous assemblies are indeed protected by the constitutional right of freedom of assembly and that therefore forbidding them is not compatible with the constitution. How should the court decide?

The court may strike down both provisions. However, this would perhaps be too strong a remedy, since it would revoke the duty to notify the authorities of *any* (ie, also non-urgent and non-spontaneous) assembly. This duty is an important element for the protection of the freedom of assembly[20] because if the authorities are not previously informed about an assembly that ultimately takes place, their ability to protect the participants, third parties and the community as a whole is undermined. It seems thus that striking down the provisions is not a good choice.

CCI could be a better choice. The court could issue a decision based on the following reasoning:

> § X of the Freedom of Assembly Act is constitutional if interpreted in conformity with the constitution. In principle, the duty to notify the authorities about open-air assemblies prior to their announcement does not violate the freedom of assembly guaranteed by the constitution. The purpose of such a duty is to provide the authorities with the information they need to be able to take precautions to ensure that the event runs smoothly and to protect the interests of third parties or the community as a whole. Therefore, for ordinary situations, the notification period of 48 hours before the announcement of the assembly, provided for in § X of the Freedom of Assembly Act, is not incompatible with the constitution.
>
> However, § X of the Freedom of Assembly Act requires a restriction. According to its wording, the duty to communicate with the authorities applies indiscriminately to all open-air assemblies. This would have the consequence that urgent meetings would be inadmissible from the outset. This conclusion would be incompatible with the fundamental right to freedom of assembly.
>
> The specific nature of urgent assemblies must be taken into account, and the notification period should be shortened. A constitutionally conforming interpretation of § X of the Freedom of Assembly Act leads to the conclusion that the realisation of urgent meetings must be reported to the authorities *as soon as possible*. As a rule, this will be at about the same time as the decision to organise the assembly, and at the latest, when it is announced.

This seems to be a much more reasonable decision than (a) to strike down §§ X and Y of the Freedom of Assembly Act or (b) to interpret them strictly, ie forbidding any unannounced open-air assembly. Both (a) and (b) would lead to results that would be at odds with the freedom of assembly.

The hypothetical decision suggested above is a translation – with rather minimal adaptations – of a decision of the German Constitutional Court,[21] and §§ X

[20] In some countries, the constitution itself provides for the duty to notify the authorities of open-air assemblies.

[21] See BVerfGE 85, 69 (74–75) (my translation).

and Y of the Freedom of Assembly Act are translations of §§ 14(1) and 26(2) of the German Assembly Act. What is interesting in this decision is that although CCI was employed by the German Constitutional Court, one of its most basic tenets is not present: the challenged provisions are not at all ambiguous.[22] They are actually very clear: assemblies without previous notification are not allowed, and conducting an assembly without proper notification of the authorities is punishable. Thus, the issue here cannot be ambiguity, but the fact that treating ordinary and urgent meetings in the same way would be unconstitutional. Therefore, what was at stake was not to choose between two possible *interpretations* of a legal provision but between two possible *solutions* for a given problem. In principle, choosing among possible solutions for a problem is a task for the legislature, not for the court. The problem is that the legislature – aware or unaware of all its implications – chose a solution (not to differentiate between regular assemblies and urgent assemblies) that was considered incompatible with the constitution. To make things worse, striking down the provisions would have led to a problematic situation (the absence of a clear rule on how and when to communicate the realisation of an assembly).

The court's decision was probably the best thing to do. However, we should not pretend that the court was choosing between possible interpretations of a text. To come up with a decision that could solve the problem without striking down the provisions (the supposed duty to save the law), it was necessary to read an unwritten exception into the written rule.[23] It may surely be claimed that this exception is compatible with the rule. Moreover, one could even assume that, if confronted with this question, the legislature could agree with this exception. But this is hardly a matter of pure interpretation of the text, as required by the assumptions of CCI.

B. Deferent, but not to the Legislature

Suppose that a constitution provides that 'everyone is equal before the law'. Suppose further that there exists a Marriage Act that, in all but one of its provisions, refers generally to 'persons', 'spouses', or 'parties'. The only provision in which more specific terms are employed is § Z:

> § Z. During the solemnisation of marriage each party must say to the other 'I AB [or CD], take thee CD [or AB], to be my wife [or husband]', or words to that effect.

The reference to wife and husband in this provision has always been interpreted as a ban on same-sex marriage. In addition, everything suggests that the intention of

[22] For ambiguity as a precondition for CCI, see Klatt (n 3) s II(A). According to him, this is accepted in several countries, such as Canada, New Zealand, Taiwan, Poland, Portugal, and the US (see the references in Klatt (n 3) fn 45).

[23] As Friedman puts it, in such cases the central condition for the judicial intervention is not ambiguity, but generality (Nick Friedman, 'United Kingdom. In the Shadow of Parliamentary Sovereignty: The Human Rights Act and the Principle of Legality' in Klatt (n 1) s IV(C)(i)).

the legislature was not different. However, § Z is eventually challenged before the constitutional court. The court acknowledges that preventing same-sex couples from marrying is incompatible with the equal protection clause provided for in the constitution. It argues further that although the terms 'wife' and 'husband' have traditionally been understood as 'woman' and 'man', they are not necessarily synonymous.

The court thus decides to perform CCI. As a consequence, the most literal and intent-bound interpretation of § Z – according to which the expression 'wife or husband' can only mean 'woman or man' – is marked as unconstitutional. But there is not only one but at least two alternative interpretations that, although less compatible with the traditional understanding of the meaning and the function of the terms 'wife' and 'husband' in § Z, are nevertheless more compatible with the constitutional provision according to which everyone is equal before the law.

According to the first alternative interpretation, which is also fairly literal, § Z does not preclude the possibility of *both* parties saying the same thing. Therefore, same-sex couples could marry and freely choose what to say in the solemnisation of the marriage. Both parties might say to each other 'to be my wife' (or 'to be my husband') or one might say 'to be my wife' and the other 'to be my husband', irrespective of the sex or gender of the parties.

However, a second alternative interpretation is also possible, according to which more than two persons may get married. If there is no definition of marriage as the union of only two persons, the formulation used in the solemnisation of the marriage, which is limited to only two persons (AB and CD), can be expanded if necessary.

Both alternative interpretations realise the constitutional provision 'everyone is equal before the law' better than the literal and intent-bound interpretation. One could even argue that the interpretation according to which marriages are not limited to the union of only two persons realises the equal protection clause even better. How should the constitutional court decide? Some argue that a constitutional court engaging in CCI should not decide which is the best interpretation of a provision of ordinary legislation. Ordinary courts should do this. The task of the constitutional court is only to exclude the interpretations that are incompatible with the constitution.[24] But what should be considered marriage then? May ordinary courts pick any definition they deem fit? May an ordinary court decide that three (or more) persons can marry? May two different ordinary courts decide differently?

One could of course argue that even if the constitutional court does not answer the question of which should be the preferred definition of marriage, a superior court (a court of appeals, for instance) will eventually do it. Legal uncertainty will disappear, and the competence of both courts (constitutional court and superior court of appeals) will thus be preserved.

[24] See Klatt (n 3) s IV(C)(ii).

However, since the constitutional court cannot decide which is the best interpretation of the legal provision – it can only sort out and block unconstitutional interpretations – one has to accept that the interpretation that will ultimately prevail will be established neither by the legislature nor by the constitutional court itself but by a court of appeal. As a consequence, the prevailing interpretation may be one that nobody in parliament would have approved.

One could argue that such a situation is ubiquitous in law, ie ordinary courts (and not the legislature or the constitutional court) ultimately decide what the provisions of ordinary law mean and how to enforce them. Otherwise, the competence of ordinary courts would be completely undermined, and every legal issue would potentially become a constitutional issue to be decided by the constitutional court. This would lead to an overconstitutionalisation of the legal system. This is an ongoing debate, and it is not necessary to take sides here. What is relevant is to note that one of the main justifications of CCI – deference vis-à-vis the legislature – should in such situations actually be better understood as a deference *to ordinary courts*.

IV. Constitutionally Conforming Interpretation as Judicial Review of Legislation

An important issue in the debate on CCI, not directly linked to what has been analysed thus far, is its relationship with judicial review of legislation. In the debate on this matter, there seem to be two entrenched camps. On the one hand, there are those who claim that CCI is judicial review of legislation and therefore cannot be performed by ordinary courts; on the other hand, there are those who suppose that the only way to allow ordinary courts to perform CCI is by arguing that CCI is merely statutory interpretation and not judicial review of legislation. However, this debate is perhaps more nuanced than it seems at first sight. It involves not only a conceptual but also an institutional dimension that deserve to be briefly analysed here.

The apparently clear difference between judicial review of legislation and CCI seems to stem from a specific institutional arrangement – present in only a few European countries – and from its theoretical assumptions. This arrangement and these assumptions seem to indicate that judicial review of legislation is something essentially different from CCI because the former implies the declaration of a legal provision as null and void, while the latter only blocks certain interpretations of a legal provision without affecting its validity.

However, this distinction does not hold in all legal systems. Declaring a law unconstitutional does not necessarily or in every place entail repealing it from the legal system. In many constitutional systems, judicial review of legislation does not necessarily imply declaring a legal provision null and void. The clearest examples are those jurisdictions that adopt some weak form of judicial review. However, even in jurisdictions that adopt a strong form of judicial review, the status of the provision declared unconstitutional may vary.

In countries where there is some form of diffuse judicial review, any court and any judge can perform judicial review, even though they cannot declare statutes null and void or repeal them. In these countries, therefore, the difference between CCI and judicial review of legislation is much less clear. In either case, what a judge does is refrain from enforcing a legal norm. The difference between CCI and judicial review thus ceases to be qualitative and becomes quantitative. That is, the difference becomes only the quantity of possible interpretations of a legal provision and the count of how many of these interpretations are compatible with the constitution and how many are not. In this context, to argue that CCI and judicial review are of different natures would require arguing that courts perform judicial review of legislation only when they refrain from enforcing *all* possible interpretations of a given legal provision; whenever they refrain from enforcing only one or a few, they are doing something completely different.

The strict distinction between judicial review (refraining from enforcing *all* possible interpretations) and CCI (refraining from enforcing *one* or *some* possible interpretations) becomes even more difficult to justify if one considers the following. When the best interpretation of a legal provision is also compatible with the constitution, there is no need to resort to CCI. In the rare cases where two interpretations can be considered equivalent in all respects but one is certainly better from a constitutional point of view, there is no need to resort to CCI either; after all, we must prefer the best interpretation to the worst. Courts often resort to CCI in a very specific situation: when the best interpretation of a statute – questions of constitutional interpretation aside, ie from a purely semantic, systematic, purposive, and historical point of view – is incompatible with the constitution. In this context, CCI aims to block the best interpretation and give precedence to suboptimal interpretations.[25] With this in mind, the differences between CCI and judicial review become even more blurred,[26] as it becomes a difference between blocking *all* interpretations and blocking *the best of all* interpretations.

It seems undeniable that this is not merely a conceptual issue; it also has an institutional dimension. There is not only one answer to the question 'which court may perform CCI?', just as there is no single answer to the question 'which court may perform judicial review of legislation?'. It varies across jurisdictions; it depends on the country.

[25] Similarly, see Schauer (n 11) s III.

[26] Similarly, see Ribeiro (n 6) s I: 'it is very hard if at all possible to draw a line between CCI and judicial review of constitutionality'.

V. Conclusion

Irrespective of institutional design, courts interpret ordinary legislation and the constitution all the time. Even in those jurisdictions in which only a constitutional court can declare a piece of legislation null and void, ordinary courts cannot avoid interpreting the constitution as well. Indeed, constitutions have been understood – even though to different degrees – as one of the most important parameters in the interpretation of ordinary legislation. Starting from this assumption, Klatt is surprised that CCI is so contested. As he puts it: 'While it is thus a standard view that we must interpret laws constitutionally conformingly, quite surprisingly, the legitimacy of this canon is a highly contested issue'.[27]

What I argue is that this should be no surprise, from a *theoretical* vantage point, because CCI is based on assumptions that are either unsound or do not always support its outcomes. It has been claimed that CCI is based on the presumption of constitutionality of laws and on respect for the separation of powers, but CCI aims mainly at adapting the meaning of those laws by means of an interpretive procedure within which that presumption and that respect play no role whatsoever. And it must be stressed that this mismatch between assumptions and outcomes is not caused by a mistaken application of CCI. Its canonical application itself potentially leads to such a mismatch. Furthermore, CCI gives rise to a 'duty to save ordinary statutes' that will almost never be compatible with the idea of deference towards the legislature, because either what the statute 'says' (or the legislature 'wants') is compatible with the constitution (and in this case there is no room for CCI), or it is not compatible with the constitution (and in this case performing CCI will most likely make the statute 'say' what it is neither written nor wanted).

From an *institutional* point of view, the debate on CCI is limited because the literature on the matter falls short of considering variations in institutional design that may affect the standard responses to criticisms of the similarities of CCI to judicial review of legislation. The answer to the question of which courts may perform CCI depends on institutional design.

At this point, it is legitimate to ask whether CCI is able to play any relevant role in the interpretation of ordinary legislation. The answer is a 'yes, but …'. There is nothing wrong with having the constitution as an interpretive parameter. Indeed, this is a duty anywhere where the constitution is considered the supreme law of the land, with which all other laws must comply. However, accepting the radiating effect of constitutional norms does not give rise to a duty to save an ordinary statute from being considered unconstitutional and struck down.

Whenever a court concludes that a given legal provision can be interpreted in (at least) two different ways, that these interpretations are equivalent (questions of constitutional interpretation aside), and that adducing constitutional reasons makes one interpretation incompatible with the constitution, there seems to be no

[27] Klatt (n 3) s I.

controversy at all: the interpretation in conformity with the constitution should prevail. If CCI were limited to this scenario, there would be nothing to discuss. In such cases, CCI is trivial.

However, as already pointed out above, CCI is usually employed in a different context and with a different aim: the best interpretation (constitutional reasoning aside) is discarded, and the interpretation that prevails is less (or not at all) compatible with the canons of statutory interpretation. The aim is to correct what the legislature has done, usually by restricting or expanding the scope of the legal provision. A court may have very good reasons to do so in some contexts (the two cases referred to in section III are good examples thereof). But in those cases, the basic assumptions of CCI (presumption of constitutionality, respect for the separation of powers, deference to the legislature) play no role whatsoever. In those cases, speaking of CCI is insincere (or simply wrong).

6

Constitutionally Conforming Interpretation and the Invisible Constitution

EOIN CAROLAN

I. Introduction and Scope

This chapter considers the relevance to constitutionally conforming interpretative (CCI) methods of the concept of the 'Invisible Constitution'.[1] While they operate in somewhat different contexts, both CCI and the invisible constitution are, at their core, addressed to situations where the resolution of a legal question cannot be determined – or, perhaps more precisely, might not *solely* be determined – by the text of the constitution itself. Whether they occur by reason of an omission or ambiguity in the text or an asserted absurdity of outcome, these are occasions where recourse to non-textual sources of constitutional meaning may (depending on one's view) be permissible, appropriate or even necessary. Both concepts are thus fundamentally concerned with how best to deal with situations of legal uncertainty – and, by extension – they thereby and inevitably engage the considerations of certainty, legal coherence and the separation of powers that underlie such scenarios.

The meaning and scope of each concept is also, however, highly contested. Volume 1 of this collection highlighted the diversity of ways in which constitutionally conforming interpretive methods are understood and applied across a range of different jurisdictions. The metaphor of the invisible constitution has also been subject to challenge.[2] It may, accordingly, be appropriate at the outset to try and clarify the sense in which the terms are being used in the remainder of this chapter.

[1] Laurence Tribe, *The Invisible Constitution* (Oxford, Oxford University Press, 2008).

[2] Eric Segall, 'Lost in Space: Laurence Tribe's Invisible Constitution' (2009) 103 *Northwestern University Law Review* 434. See the broader range of discussions of the concept in Rosalind Dixon and Adrienne Stone (eds), *The Invisible Constitution in Comparative Perspective* (Cambridge, Cambridge University Press, 2018).

This is necessary not only to assist the reader but also to make clear the limits of any claims or arguments that will be advanced below.

It is, perhaps, most important to emphasise that the definitions being used have been chosen as most relevant to the brief for this chapter, as indicated by the editorial team. That is, the understanding of both CCI and of the invisible constitution being discussed are those that appear to offer the most fruitful opportunities for inter-analysis. Their use in this chapter does not in any way indicate a judgement on the merits of the varying positions adopted by different theorists in the rich and extensive conceptual literature on the meaning and scope of these terms.

To look first at the invisible constitution, this is used here to refer to the factors outside the written text of a constitution that may shape constitutional meaning. This is not invisibility in the sense of a legal system, like the United Kingdom, that lacks a written master text. It is rather referring to that commonly acknowledged feature of any system with a written constitutional text whereby the meaning and application of its terms will necessarily be influenced by extra-textual considerations.

Turning then to the notion of a CCI, this is understood here to refer to 'a set of approaches whereby courts develop the content of non-constitutional legal norms in a manner that aligns with constitutional legal norms'.[3] Professor Klatt has highlighted how the classical 'German approach' to CCI presupposes that it satisfies the following four conditions:[4]

i. The interpreted legal statement must be ambiguous.
ii. At least one interpretation must violate the Constitution.
iii. At least one interpretation must conform to the Constitution.
iv. CCI 'must not wholly rewrite the normative content of the interpreted norm'.[5]

This approach, and others in the broader CCI family, is commonly stated to derive from or embody a presumption of constitutionality that, simultaneously assumes and promotes the unity and coherence of the relevant legal system. By presuming the conformity of all legal instruments within a given order with the constitutional master text, it makes permissible an interpretive juxtaposition (and, arguably, subordination) of lower-order provisions with the constitutional text, which thereby helps to preserves the supreme authority of that text. This, in turn, supports the unity of the legal system as a whole by mitigating the kind of 'conflict

[3] Lael K Weis, 'Australia. Techniques of Developing Legislation and the Common Law to Align with Constitutional Legal Norms' in Matthias Klatt (ed), *Constitutionally Conforming Interpretation: Comparative Perspectives Volume 1: National Reports* (Oxford, Hart Publishing, 2023).

[4] See Matthias Klatt, 'The Legitimacy of Constitutionally Conforming Interpretation' in Klatt (n 3).

[5] See Alfonso Garcia Figueroa, 'Constitutionally Conforming Argumentation and Legalism' in this volume s I, citing Matthias Klatt, 'The Legitimacy of Constitutionally Conforming Interpretation' in Klatt (n 3).

of norms [which] compromises the consistency of a legal system and … endangers the rule of law and its clarity, foreseeability and guiding function.'[6]

As this summary shows, however, there are two distinct aspects to this presumption of constitutionality.

The first is a general and overarching presumption that actions and actors within a legal system act, and intend to act, in a manner that comports with the constitutional order. This broad presumption can manifest itself in different ways which may speak not only to legal interpretation but also executive decision-making, the exercise of administrative discretion or, on its most expansive understanding, the legitimacy and limits of political discourse. The idea that all actors and actions are purposively constitution-compatible can, for example, be argued to justify the pursuit of 'of judicial restraint through deference than through 'interpretative' models of restraint' that are, in practice, anything but.[7]

The second, albeit related, version of the presumption is the one which is generally most discussed in this volume, and which is most familiar to legal practitioners. This is the understanding of the presumption that, while presuming that other actors intend to act constitutionally, tends to favour (even if only impliedly in some cases) the role of the courts as primary (or exclusive) interpreters of constitutional meaning. On this account, the assumed intention of other actors to act constitutionally is employed, in effect, as the justification for the courts' entitlement in its role as constitutional arbiter to identify the intention-as-constitutional-outcome.

Even when confined to this latter formally legal context, the presumption can take different forms. The role with which most of the contributions in these volumes are concerned is as a tool of interpretation. It is worth noting, however, that it can also fulfil other roles in public law litigation such as, for example, a rule of evidence that, in effect, imposes the burden of proof on the party seeking to assert that a particular measure or decision is unconstitutional.

While the logic and utility of such a presumption has been contested,[8] it has the potential to have a real-world impact on the practice of constitutional litigation. It may, for example, in rare cases permit a court to dismiss a challenge *in limine* where the claim as advanced does not discharge the legal burden of demonstrating that a statute is potentially unconstitutional. It may also have an influence on the form which litigation takes, especially in matters of evidence. The Irish Supreme Court has, for example, recently cited the presumption in support of its holding that there is no obligation on the state in any case where the unconstitutionality of a statute is alleged to positively prove the legitimacy of the pertinent legislative policy by adducing scientific or other evidence.[9]

[6] Klatt (n 4) s III(B).

[7] Brian Foley, 'Interpretative and Deference Based Models of Judicial Restraint in the Irish Constitution' (2006) 6 (1) *Hibernian Law Journal* 65, 68.

[8] See Virgílio Afonso da Silva, 'There is no such thing as the duty to save a statute' in this volume.

[9] *O'Doherty & Waters v Minister for Health* [2022] IESC 32.

This chapter is, as already indicated however, concerned with a related but narrower application of that presumption of constitutionality: namely, the approach under which a court is permitted when interpreting a statutory provision to choose from amongst the available meanings the one which best conforms to the constitution. As the Irish courts have observed, this double construction rule[10] derives from the presumption of constitutionality but operates in a more specific and constrained manner:

> One practical effect of this presumption is that if in respect of any provision or provisions of the Act, two or more constructions are reasonably open, one of them constitutional and the other is unconstitutional, it must be presumed that the Oireachtas (Parliament) intended only the constitutional construction.[11]

The presumption that Parliament intended its actions to conform to the Constitution may also support a variant of CCI under which a confirming construction is also applied to the exercise of the powers conferred by legislation. In the same decision, the Supreme Court went on to observe that it must also be presumed that:

> the Oireachtas intended that proceedings, procedures, discretions and adjudications which are permitted, provided for, or prescribed by an Act of the Oireachtas are to be conducted in accordance with the principles of constitutional justice.[12]

Thus, for the purposes of this chapter, CCI refers to the narrower context of the deployment by courts of the interpretive presumption that Parliament intended its legislation to comply with the constitution. It includes its use in situations of ambiguity (where the court may be asked to make a constitutionally-influenced choice amongst available meanings); and ones of omission (where a court may be urged to read-in a meaning or procedure that remedies the potential defect identified). It does not refer to the application of the presumption to matters of evidence or legal burden.

This chapter is also concerned only with the relationship between CCI and the invisible constitution in jurisdictions where there is a written constitutional text. Constitutional systems which operate without a specific master text are considered elsewhere in this volume.[13]

[10] As it is commonly known in Ireland.

[11] *East Donegal Co-Operative Livestock Mart Ltd v AG* [1970] IR 317.

[12] *East Donegal Co-Operative Livestock Mart Ltd v AG* [1970] IR 317, 341.

[13] See Stéphane Beaulac, 'Conforming Legal Interpretation Based on International Law: The Use of Unwritten Principles, the Example of Equality of Arms' s I, IV in this volume; Oran Doyle, 'Partly Laws Common to all Judge-Kind: The Commonality and Divergence of Constitutionally Conforming Interpretation' s IV(B) in this volume; Hanna Wilberg, 'Aotearoa New Zealand. Legislators' Understanding as a Constraint on Interpretive Presumptions' in Klatt (n 3); Nick Friedman, 'United Kingdom. In the Shadow of Parliamentary Sovereignty: The Human Rights Act and the Principle of Legality' in Klatt (n 3).

II. The Implications of an Invisible Constitution

A. How does the Invisible Constitution Affect Constitutionally Conforming Interpretations Claim to Certainty or Coherence?

Considered in this sense, CCI is fundamentally a tool of interpretation. It may derive from a presumption that Parliament intends to act constitutionally but it does so as a maxim rather than as a claim or assessment about the behaviour of legislators. As with other maxims of statutory interpretation, it may not factually be the case that Parliament, whether collectively or at the level of individual members, held actual knowledge of the nuances of the current state of the law; or engaged in any conscious contemplation of the measure's constitutional conformity. While the probability of such matter having happened may say something important about the state of either political culture or institutional process in a given polity, it does not really matter for interpretive purposes whether or not they actually occurred. The value of a statutory maxim is to promote legal certainty by ensuring a degree of predictability in how a court will come to construe a provision. Maxims, on this view, are important supports to the process of interpreting a legal text: a process which differs from other forms of purposive communication by reason of the non-availability of a speaker to clarify the intention that underlay or animated their expression. This exclusion of the speaker post-expression is, as Maxwell Cameron has pointed out, the distinctive feature and value of legal and constitutional text as a form of social communication.[14] Maxims represent a partial response to the one-sided character of legal text as communicated order:

> All the pragmatic maxims for statutes are justified in the same way. It is reasonable that a legislature should act in accordance with them; they are among the characteristics of rationality in legislation. From the point of view of the "hearer" – the reader of a statute – the propriety of the maxims is a precondition to the possibility of sensibly understanding, making use of, and guiding behavior by legislative speech. Being pragmatic constraints, they in fact may be violated on occasion, but the entire enterprise of legislation would fail if they were to be generally disregarded.[15]

Indeed, the maxim of CCI takes this further by pursuing an overarching coherence and consistency across the legal order. As Klatt summarised the case for the idea of a CCI in Volume 1:

> The unity of the legal system builds upon two elements: consistency and coherence. A legal system is consistent if its elements are not in logical contradiction with each other.

[14] Maxwell Cameron, *Strong Constitutions: Social-Cognitive Origins of the Separation of Powers* (Oxford, Oxford University Press, 2013).

[15] Michael Sinclair, 'Law and Language: The Role of Pragmatics in Statutory Interpretation' (1985) 46 *University of Pittsburgh Law Review* 373.

> Any conflict of norms compromises the consistency of a legal system, and it endangers the rule of law and its clarity, foreseeability, and guiding function.[16]

The foreseeability and consistency that these principles promote are also said to support the separation of powers by ensuring that the courts, when faced with situations in which there may be an ambiguity, absurdity or omission in a positive legal document, can resolve them with the guidance (and constraint) of established maxims and methods. This, it might be argued, respects the institutional dimension to any interpretive exercise by taking due account of the roles and competences that have been assigned by the constitutional order to the bodies or officials involved. While there may be a variety of justifications offered for such an assignation – democratic pedigree, public responsiveness, publicity of process, differing expertise, or so on – the point is that the specific separation of powers that any constitutional order has established reflects at least in part a normative assessment on the part of its designers about the primacy of one institution's competence in a given area relative to others. The claim for CCI as an instrument of the separation of powers is thus that it respects the relative authority of the courts and legislature by ensuring that cases of legal omission, ambiguity or absurdity are addressed by referring (at least in the first instance) to the presumed intention of Parliament rather than the preferences of the court.

Of course, the claim that CCI promotes certainty, consistency and the separation of powers has been challenged, including by some of the contributors to this volume. Mathieu Carpentier has, for example, drawn attention to how the use of CCI in France has been criticised as having just the opposite effect on judicial power to that asserted by its advocates. '[F]ar from being hailed as a way to exercise judicial restraint on the part of the Constitutional Council, conforming interpretation is often decried as an illegitimate way to re-write what the legislature intended.'[17] The Irish Supreme Court has expressed similar reservations about the permissible scope of CCI, having rejected its application in a number of recent cases on the basis that it would be contrary to the separation of powers for the courts to, in effect, legislate-by-CCI.

> It is one thing to save a legislative provision from invalidity by, for example, implying fair procedures (as in Dellway and ors. v. National Asset Management Agency and ors. [2011] IESC 14, [2011] 4 IR 1) or by reading down a provision so as to limit its apparent scope (as happened in Re National Irish Bank Ltd. No. 1 [1999] IESC 18, [1999] 3 IR 145), but quite another to use the rule to fundamentally re-orientate the structure and direction of a legislative scheme by changing an essential feature of that regime …. The double construction rule allows the adjustment of a single statutory provision so as to align it with constitutional requirements, it does not thereby permit the imposition of an entirely new legislative regime.[18]

[16] Klatt (n 4) s (II)(B).

[17] Mathieu Carpentier, France. The Dynamics of "Interpretative Reservations" in the Jurisprudence of the French Constitutional Council in Klatt (n 3).

[18] *A, B and C v Minister for Foreign Affairs and Trade* [2023] IESC 10, para 92. See also *DPP v Quirke* [2023] IESC 5.

Professor da Silva has meanwhile argued that the constitutionally conforming method is trivial, mistaken or plays no significant role. Without addressing these arguments in detail, it is at the very least correct to observe – as he does – that the maxim rests on number of underlying premises; and that these warrant further scrutiny.

Moreover (and most critically for the purposes of this chapter) the doubts and concerns that scholars like da Silva have raised are arguably exacerbated by the idea of the invisible constitution. The notion of an invisible constitution draws attention to the fact that constitutional meaning may be influenced by an array of factors outside the text of the constitution itself. These factors may, depending on the understanding of invisibility, range far beyond formal legal methods to include considerations of social, political, or historical context. As Laurence Tribe, one of the most prominent proponents of the concept, has summarised it:

> [T]he visible Constitution necessarily floats in a vast and deep – and, crucially, invisible – ocean of ideas, propositions, recovered memories, and imagined experiences that the Constitution as a whole puts us in a position to glimpse.[19]

This image of the constitution as comprising a vast and partially invisible array of culturally- and contextually-contingent attitudes poses obvious challenges to the prospects of a CCI of lower-order legal texts. One might recall here the point made by Professor Beaulac elsewhere in this volume about the bilateral and relational character of constitutional conformity.

> When considering this type of construction, be it in general or for specific applications, it is useful to distinguish between two things: the source of the normativity of reference (constitution, treaty), on the one hand, and the actual law (ordinary, domestic) to be interpreted in conformity with these fundamentals, on the other hand. Put another way, when one interprets 'in conformity with', there are two groups of norms at play, those deemed the reference point, the reference normativity, which will have an impact on the interpretation of the other set of normativity, which is the one actually applicable in a situation, i.e. positive law.[20]

The underlying premise of a CCI is arguably that there is a point of reference – the constitution – that can be reliably invoked and applied as a criterion of conformity. The method assumes that this constitution (whatever that is) is capable of operating as the yardstick that supplies the stability and constancy that the lower-order text appears to lack. An interpretive choice can permissibly be made by reference to the state of being (more) 'constitutional'. That necessarily assumes, however, that there is a coherent and stable understanding of what it means to 'be constitutional'. That (may) seem relatively unobjectionable where the criterion being applied is

[19] Tribe (n 1) 9.

[20] Stéphane Beaulac, 'Conforming Legal Interpretation Based On International Law: The Use Of Unwritten Principles, The Example Of Equality Of Arms' in this volume.

that of the constitutional text.[21] It may appear more problematic, however, where the yardstick of constitutional conformity is, itself, drawn from other sources of constitutional meaning or value. That applies, *a fortiori*, where the source can, in some respect, be characterised as unwritten or invisible. In that scenario, an interpretive issue arising from the absence of a sufficiently express provision in one legal document is determined by applying principles that are, themselves, not expressed in the constitution. To put it crudely, one textual gap is filled with another.

B. The Invisible Constitution in Action: Judicial Independence as an Unwritten Norm

The previous section outlined how the case for a CCI is complicated where the criteria of constitutional conformity are themselves derived from a source outside the written text. The key issue here is that the move to extra-textual meaning may weaken the basic case for CCI: that the application of what all relevant parties have pre-acknowledged as a constitutional standard offers a relatively neutral, objective and coherent approach to resolving situations of legal uncertainty. Even if parliamentarians did not actually direct their minds to that standard, its constitutional status suggests that it is something to which they might reasonably be expected to have had some regard; a standard to which they thus can, in turn, legitimately be held to.

However, while it does not necessarily destroy the case for CCI, the argument becomes a little less clear-cut where the constitutional status of the standards being used is itself contestable. In that scenario, the argument that legislators either factually might or constitutionally should have had regard to the standard is somewhat weaker. Moreover, the assumed neutrality or objective of the standard being applied is also open to question. Applying an extra-textual source in support of a CCI requires the courts to identify meaning at both stages of the interpretive exercise: first, as to the meaning of the standard being applied; and second, the meaning of the legislation that is being held to that judicially-identified standard. This, clearly, allows greater scope for interpretive subjectivity; for the application of contestable meaning or standards; and, relatedly, for doubt as to whether the legal outcomes identified are, fundamentally, those of the judges rather than legislators (or, indeed, the constitution).

This is analogous to the concerns that have been expressed in Canada and elsewhere about the use of unwritten or invisible constitutional principles as a criterion of unconstitutionality: '[h]ere, the question is what happens when the Court is released from the rigours of the analysis provided by individual sections

[21] Although this obviously assumes a level of objectivity in the reading of a legal text that is itself contestable.

of the Constitution and instead may strike down legislation based on its inconsistency with a far less defined unwritten constitutional principle.'[22] As the scope for judicial discretion expands, so too may concerns about the extent of judicial power within the constitutional system of separated powers.

A recent Irish decision on judicial appointments in *Re Article 26 and the Judicial Appointments Commission Bill 2023*[23] may help to illustrate the point. This is, of course, a particularly fraught issue for courts because of their direct interest in the legislation at issue. It is because of that directness of interest, however, that the subject may be a useful one for these purposes. By engaging judicial interests directly, the issue poses a greater challenge to the notions of neutrality, objectivity or judicial restraint that CCI is said to promote. It is, thus, a particularly testing context in which to apply a constitutionally confirming interpretation that is itself informed by an unwritten or invisible constitution.

Before examining the decision in any detail, it is worth noting that the question of judicial appointments has been the subject of considerable controversy and inter-branch tension in Ireland over the last decade. Ireland's traditional system of judicial appointments since independence has been that judges were chosen by the Government on a relatively discretionary basis. Formally speaking, judges in Ireland are appointed by the President but this is done on the advice of Government. Minor legislative reforms in the mid-1990s had created a statutory body with the power to send a list of suitable candidates to Government. There was no obligation on Government, however, to choose any person from this list; and the lists themselves tended to be very lengthy and lack any internal ranking.[24]

The publication of initial proposals for a new appointment system in 2017 led the then Chief Justice, Ms Justice Denham, together with the Presidents of each of the other courts in Ireland, to write a joint letter to the Taoiseach (Prime Minister) expressing concern about the Bill's 'serious implications for the administration of justice'.[25] The Association of Judges in Ireland also released a statement which pointed out that the judiciary had made a submission in 2014 calling for changes to the traditional system but which criticised the Bill produced as 'seriously flawed'.[26] A change of government led to amended proposals being put forward but these, again, were the subject of partial criticism from the Chief Justice. Nonetheless, the core of the proposals ultimately passed by the Houses of the Oireachtas in 2023 were consistent with submissions and comments made by the judiciary. In particular, the legislation contained two elements which senior judges had

[22] Vanessa MacDonnell, 'Rethinking The Invisible Constitution: How Unwritten Constitutional Principles Shape Political Decision-Making' (2019) 65 (2) *McGill Law Journal* 175, 190.

[23] [2023] IESC 34.

[24] For more detail, see Jennifer Carroll MacNeill, *The Politics of Judicial Selection in Ireland* (Dublin, Four Courts Press, 2016).

[25] Niamh Lyons, 'Chief Justice Susan Denham writes to Leo Varadkar in protest at legal reforms' *The Times* (27 June 2017).

[26] Association of Judges of Ireland, *Judicial Appointments Commission Bill* (Press Release, 26 June 2017), available at aji.ie/press-release-26-june-2017/.

publicly advocated: first, the introduction of merit as the criterion for appointment; and, second, the involvement of an independent body to screen candidates and provide the Government with a shortlist of those deemed most meritorious. The new Judicial Appointments Commission was to be given responsibility for the process by which persons interested in judicial office would apply and be assessed. The Government retained the power to select judges for appointment but were limited in so doing to those persons on a list of recommendations prepared by the Commission.

Following the passage of the Bill through the Houses, the legislation was then referred by the President of Ireland to the Supreme Court in order to consider its constitutionality on an ex ante basis – notably, specifically on parts of the Bill that had been welcomed by the Chief Justice. This referral procedure is provided for by Article 26 of the Constitution of Ireland. It is rarely used, with the last such reference having occurred in 2004. The argument advanced both in public and political commentary on the Bill, and by counsel before the Court, was that this was contrary to the separation of powers envisaged by the Constitution of Ireland and, in particular, the powers conferred on the executive branch by it.

What this meant, however, was that the Court was being asked to decide that legislation which directly affected the judicial branch; which was consistent in important respects with the publicly-expressed views of judicial representatives; and which replaced a prior proposal which had been the subject of unprecedented public criticism from senior judges; could not come into force. Moreover, it was being asked to do so on the basis that the traditional system of political appointments – one which judicial figures had suggested be replaced with precisely the kind of merit-based system envisaged by the legislation – was constitutionally entrenched. This necessarily placed the Court in a somewhat awkward position, as was starkly illustrated by the Chief Justice's recusal of himself from the case by reason of his prior public comments on the legislation.

Given the contentious and highly political backdrop to the decision, it is of some note, therefore, that these issues of merit and restraint on political appointment were resolved in part by reading words into the legislation. The key provision of the Bill in this context was section 51. This stated that:

> In advising the President in relation to the appointment of a person to a judicial office in the State the Government shall only consider for appointment those persons who have been recommended by the Commission to the Minister under section 47.

The Court was required to consider both the constitutionality and the correct interpretation of this section. It did so by reference to a variety of considerations. Some of these were clearly stated in the constitutional text. Others – the rule of law, the separation of powers, a broader principle of judicial independence – were implied, unwritten or invisible. The Court held ultimately that, while not expressly stipulated by the legislature, section 51 should be interpreted as preserving a right on the part of Government to decline to appoint any of the persons on the list of recommendations provided to it by the Judicial Appointments Commission. This outcome, it explained, was consistent with the constitutional principles of judicial independence and the separation of powers.

> In this context, one such highly relevant consideration, the status and importance of which cannot be disputed, is the necessity to protect and enhance the independence of the judiciary. By enhancing judicial independence, the Bill seeks to reinforce the most critically important aspect of the constitutional separation of powers, namely the separation between the judicial branch on the one hand and the political branches on the other. It would not be open to the Oireachtas to create a process or procedure which compromised or undermined the principle and reality of judicial independence. On the assumption – since, as explained, we do not consider it necessary to decide the issue – that the ultimate authority of the Government to make the final decision as to who to appoint as a judge must also be preserved, the question is whether this measure is such an extension of the acknowledged right and duty to legislate for eligibility as to constitute an impermissible constraint on the Government's freedom of choice. In our view it is not, in that it preserves for the Government a real and meaningful choice as to the acceptance or rejection of a list, the freedom not to nominate a person when it so wishes, and choice within the list.[27]

It is important to note that the Court referred to a variety of sources as part of its reasoning, many of which had a clear and prior basis in caselaw, reports or international instruments. This is not a case where the Court resolved the issue by reference to a principle derived (or made visible) from the constitutional ether for the first time. It is one, however, where the Court resolved an issue of meaning on which it had an evident (and expressed) self-interest by invoking at least some extra-textual principles. Yet, in building (or bootstrapping) legislative meaning from a judicially-identified meaning, the court is inevitably exposed to potential scepticism as to whether the intent to which effect is ultimately given is judicial or parliamentary in its origins – doubts which may, in turn, extend to the larger question of whether CCI-via-the-invisible-constitution is an instrument of judicial restraint or judicial power.[28]

In this regard, it is worth bearing in mind the implications which the application of CCI in this manner may have for future legislative activity. In general, the focus of most commentary on either the application of a constitutionally conforming method or any analysis thereof tends to be on the impact of the court's choices on the statute at issue. In many instances, however, the reasoning of the court will impose constraints on the legislature's future freedom of action. Where a court comes to choose between potential meanings of a statutory provision, and bases that choice on its assessment that one or more of the potential meanings would be unconstitutional, that – in effect – indicates that legislation which contained a provision with that express meaning would, for that reason, be constitutionally invalid. This is, in terms of the legislature's capacity to 'respond' to a judicial ruling,

[27] *In Re Article 26 and the Judicial Appointments Commission Bill 2023* [2023] IESC 34, para 287.

[28] See Frederick Schauer, 'United States. Constitutional Avoidance As Constitutional Conformation' in Klatt (n 3) s III.

not that dissimilar to the effect of a finding of constitutional invalidity. With a finding of invalidity, there is a legal gap which the legislature may or may not choose to fill. If it does so, it will be limited by a need to stay within the parameters of constitutionality identified in the decision to strike down the offending provision. With CCI, the court avoids the gap by giving a meaning to the provision which is constitutionally conforming but which not be the obvious, natural or intended meaning of the words. The legislature may wish to respond – but its capacity to do so is similarly constrained if the court has already effectively found that its preferred meaning would be unconstitutional.

To use a more concrete example, consider the Canadian cases which – like the Irish one above – review and interpret legislation affecting the judiciary by reference to unwritten or invisible constitutional values. In the *Reference re Remuneration of Judges of the Prov. Court of P.E.I*,[29] the Supreme Court of Canada ruled that the textual guarantees contained in the Constitution Act 1867 regarding judicial independence were 'not an exhaustive and definitive written code for the protection of judicial independence in Canada'.[30] The Court, citing earlier decisions such as *Valente v R*[31] and *Beauregard v R*[32] (decisions which, notably, were cited also by the Irish Supreme Court in its Article 26 reference) instead relied on the unwritten norm of judicial independence to 'fill … gaps in the express terms of the constitutional text'.[33] In the majority's view, '[t]he only way to explain the interpretation of [the written constitutional provisions dealing with judges], in fact, is by reference to a deeper set of <u>unwritten</u> understandings which are not found on the face of the document itself'.[34] Applying these broad and unwritten conception of judicial independence, the Court held that various state regulations regarding potential reductions in judicial remuneration were unconstitutional. The Court stipulated that judicial remuneration could only be reduced where that was recommended by an independent body such as a commission which could be interposed between the judiciary and the other branches of government. The majority stated that 'the depoliticization of th[e] relationship [between the legislature and executive on the one hand and the judiciary on the other] is so fundamental to the separation of powers, and hence to the Canadian Constitution, that the provisions of the Constitution … must be interpreted in such a manner as to protect this principle'.[35] 'The majority accordingly provided a detailed account of what would be required to ensure conformity with this unwritten constitutional requirement of "depoliticisation".'

> [T]he imperative of protecting the courts from political interference through economic manipulation requires that an independent body – a judicial compensation

[29] [1997] 3 SCR 3.
[30] [1997] 3 SCR 3, para 109.
[31] [1985] 2 SCR 673.
[32] [1986] 2 SCR 56.
[33] [1997] 3 SCR 3, para 95.
[34] [1997] 3 SCR 3, para 89. Emphasis contained in the original.
[35] [1997] 3 SCR 3, para 142.

> commission – be interposed between the judiciary and the other branches of government. The constitutional function of this body would be to depoliticize the process of determining changes to or freezes in judicial remuneration. This objective would be achieved by setting that body the specific task of issuing a report on the salaries and benefits of judges to the executive and the legislature, responding to the particular proposals made by the government. As well, in order to guard against the possibility that government inaction could be used as a means of economic manipulation by allowing judges' real salaries to fall because of inflation, and also to protect against the possibility that judges' salaries will drop below the adequate minimum required by judicial independence, the commission must convene if a fixed period of time (eg three to five years) has elapsed since its last report, in order to consider the adequacy of judges' salaries in light of the cost of living and other relevant factors.[36]

Once such a body was established '[a]ny changes to or freezes in judicial remuneration made without prior recourse to the body are unconstitutional'. Furthermore, the Court also reserved the right to review any decisions to depart from the recommendations of such independent bodies. In its view,

> Although the recommendations of the body are non-binding they should not be set aside lightly. If the executive or legislature chooses to depart from them, it has to justify its decision according to a standard of simple rationality – if need be, in a court of law.

As Vanessa MacDonnell has pointed out in her work on the invisible constitution in Canada, 'this decision has proven to be very controversial, given the inevitable perception of self-dealing'.[37] The Court relied on unwritten norms in an area of clear self-interest to invalidate provincial legislation. More relevant for this chapter, however, is that portion of the ruling in which the majority then proceeded to outline in detail what was required for any future legislation to conform to these unwritten constitutional principles. This comes arguably close to a form of *ex ante* CCI given that it effectively excludes the possibility of certain interpretive outcomes in advance. At the very least, it highlights that there may be a finer line between a determination of constitutional invalidity and a CCI than is sometimes appreciated – at least where the meaning found by applying CCI departs from the more obvious or optimal meaning of the provision. This is a particular issue if, as da Silva suggests, CCI is most 'usually employed' in situations where 'the best interpretation (constitutional reasoning aside) is discarded, and the interpretation that prevails is less (or not at all) compatible with the canons of statutory interpretation.'[38]

In that situation, the result of both a finding of invalidity and an application of CCI is an outcome different from that intended by the legislature. In both

[36] [1997] 3 SCR 3, para 147.

[37] Vanessa MacDonnell, 'Rethinking The Invisible Constitution: How Unwritten Constitutional Principles Shape Political Decision-Making' (2019) 65 (2) *McGill Law Journal* 175, 182, citing Jean Leclair, 'Canada's Unfathomable Unwritten Constitutional Principles' (2002) 27 (2) *Queen's Law Journal* 389, 420–24 and Mark Carter, 'The Rule of Law, Legal Rights in the Charter, and the Supreme Court's New Positivism' (2008) 33 (2) *Queen's Law Journal* 453, 460–61, 468.

[38] Virgílio Afonso da Silva, 'There is no such thing as the duty to save a statute' in this volume.

instances, the legislature's capacity to respond may be constrained by the fact that the court's reasoning has found certain interpretations or outcomes to be inconsistent with the constitution. In situations of strained meaning, the primary difference between the two approaches may lie in the remedy ordered. Yet, it is at least arguable that the retention of legislation based on a judicially-substituted meaning is no less disruptive of legislative intent than the striking down of a statute. From a government or legislator's perspective, remedial restraint may not always be preferable to interpretive expansion. Certainly, the Canadian authorities on judicial independence and remuneration provide a real-world example of where a court's specification of constitutionally conformity based on unwritten principles has proved highly controversial. That this assessment of constitutional conformity occurred *ex ante* rather than the more familiar reading-down or reading-in[39] of an existing statute does not detract from the more fundamental point about the risks associated with the interpretive invocation of unwritten or invisible norms.

III. A Spectrum of (In)visibility? The Implication for Constitutionally Conforming Interpretation

The previous section provided an example of how the application of non-textual standards could be seen to detract from the values of neutrality, consistency and judicial restraint that are often associated with constitutionally conforming methods of interpretation. This has potentially adverse implications for the capacity of CCI to promote certainty, consistency or the separation of powers. It is one thing to claim that constitutionally conforming interpretations promote certainty or coherence when they involve the direct application of a constitutional master text. There can be no doubt in such cases – whether for draftspersons, parliamentarians, citizens or lawyers – that the provisions in question (or the exercise of powers conferred thereunder) will in principle be susceptible to being read in a manner that secures conformity with any relevant constitutional provision. The prospect of that evaluation is foreseeable; the content of it is confined by the words of the constitutional provision; both of which, in theory at least, ensures that the outcome of any such interpretation is somewhat predictable. This serves at least some conceptions of the separation of powers by providing a legitimate and, to some extent, constrained basis for a judicial decision to prefer one interpretation over available alternatives.

The paradigm of CCI may be imperilled, however, if the constitutional standard by which a statute is evaluated is, itself, ambiguous. There are clearly significant differences in the nature and putative legitimacy of a constitutionally conforming

[39] Richard Stacey, 'South Africa. The Siren Call of Constitutionally Confirming Interpretation: Statutory Validity at the Expense of Constitutional Values' in Klatt (n 3) s I.

interpretation carried out on the basis of the constitutional text on the one hand; and one based on a court's derivation of values, norms or principles from an invisible or shadow[40] constitution on the other. In the latter case, the court must first identify and define the relevant standard before considering how it applies to the particular issue before it. This necessarily increases the number of decisions required of a court. Moreover, these additional decisions are more likely to require the consideration by the court of non-written or less formal sources of potential legal meaning. Each step thereby increases the scope for judicial discretion, with all of the consequent implications of this for CCI's ostensible commitment to certainty or the separation of powers.

This is the core of the case against using unwritten norms in the CCI method. It is argued hereafter, however, that the case is – at the very least – an unduly simplified one. In principle, it is certainly true that the application of standards or principles that are clearly delineated in the constitutional text is less open to challenge, whether on the grounds of legitimacy, objectivity, or systemic coherence. In practice, however, the extent to which either the CCI method or the use of invisible principles or unwritten norms may give increase uncertainty or judicial power is more complex to assess.

This depends, of course, in part on how these methods or principles are applied. But event leaving that aside, it would be a mistake to assume that more ostensibly textually driven methods of resolving legal questions are inevitably preference. Very few would suggest that either legal meaning or legislative intent can or should be solely derived from clear statements in the constitutional master text. There are several reasons why this is so, none of which are likely to appear surprising to anyone with even a passing familiarity with public law.

First, the constitutional text may itself be somewhat ambiguous as to the precise meaning or import of its terms. Even if it is not always as extreme as case, as Larry Simon has argued in an American context, that 'the language of a great many [of the provisions of the Constitution] is so vague, ambiguous and open-textured that they might be understood to mean almost anything',[41] it is certainly generally true that 'constitutions tend to be open-textured'.[42] This is an enduring challenge for constitutional lawyers which should not be overlooked in debates about whether, and to what extent, courts can permissibly look to considerations or sources outside the text. Frederick Schauer's point that we must always bear in mind the ambiguity of the text itself remains pertinent decades on:

[40] Ullrich Gerhard, *The Law of the International Civil Service* (Berlin, Duncker and Humblot, 2018). Gerhard is describing here a potentially narrower context under which conceptions of legality may be influenced by asset of beliefs, norms and values held by bureaucrats. It seems, however, correct to see this as a variant of the same phenomenon whereby legal meaning is shaped by extra-textual values.

[41] Lary Simon, 'The Authority of the Constitution and its Meaning: A Preface to a Theory of Constitutional Interpretation' (1985) 58 *Southern California Law Review* 603.

[42] Samuel Issacharoff, 'The Elusive Search for Constitutional Integrity: A Memorial for John Hart Ely' (2004) 57 (3) *Stanford Law Review* 727.

> [B]efore we can argue intelligently about whether to go outside of the [constitutional' txt, we ought to explore the meaning of the words inside the text. Only then will we know what counts as going outside and until then, it is not clear that there even is an outside because 'inside' and 'outside' are relative terms.[43]

That a question of legal judgment may involve degrees of ambiguity, or admit of more than one possible meaning or outcome, is thus true of both the textual and non-textual elements of a constitutional order. Of itself, therefore, the presence of ambiguity cannot be regarded as a decisive marker of interpretive illegitimacy.

Second, any assumed reservation about looking outside the constitution is complicated by the fact that there are in most jurisdictions several established and written sources of constitutional meaning outside the basic provisions of that master text. In the Irish ruling summarised in the previous section, for example, the Court's consideration of the relationship between judicial independence, the rule of law, and the statutory scheme was informed by a variety of domestic and international sources including prior decisions of the Irish courts and reports from the Council of Europe's Group of States Against Corruption and caselaw from the Court of Justice of the European Union, the European Court of Human Rights, and the Canadian Supreme Court. While there may be a separate question about whether reference to external sources – and especially foreign legal materials[44] – may also allow judges a wider discretion about how to approach and resolve legal problems, it is generally the case in most legal systems that a select and specific range of written materials are repeatedly cited as authoritative sources of constitutional meaning.

Third, the use of non-textual sources of meaning is in many respects a familiar and established part of any act of judicial interpretation of a statute. Even the most basic canons or maxims that guide that process will rarely be articulated in the constitutional text itself. That does not mean, however, that they are not legitimate sources of interpretive meaning. Indeed, it is at least plausible that such commonly known principles may in fact have been taken into account in the drafting or enactment of any legislation under consideration: which is, of course, part of the logic of the constitutionally conforming method.

None of these reasons may, of themselves, makes the case for the use of CCI as a permissible or appropriate method of statutory interpretation. They do, however, highlight that the case does not depend on, and cannot realistically be confined to, a search for statutory meanings that conform to the written text of the constitution. Constitutional meaning is neither self-executing nor solely textual. It will regularly – and in many non-CCI situations – depend upon broader considerations of context. The invisible constitution, in this sense, is unavoidable.

[43] Frederick Schauer, 'An Essay on Constitutional Language' (1981–1982) 29 *UCLA Law Review* 797, 797.

[44] This debate has been most prolonged in US constitutional circles including, notably, on the Supreme Court. For a flavour of judicial views on this, see Norman Dorsen, 'The relevance of foreign legal materials in U.S. constitutional cases: A conversation between Justice Antonin Scalia and Justice Stephen Breyer' (2005) 3(4) *International Journal of Constitutional Law* 519.

Nonetheless, the point remains that the further from the master text that a constitutionally conforming meaning is derived, the greater is the interpretive burden on the court. Where a court is required to first, identify the constitutional meaning, and then choose the statutory meaning that best conforms to it, the court is, in practice, likely to be operating in a world of wider interpretive possibilities. If there is an increase in what might 'be constitutional' at this first point of interpretation, it is reasonable to expect that there will be an associated increase in the number of possible outcomes at the second point of statutory interpretation.

This suggests that there may be merit to distinguishing between some kinds of 'constitutional invisibility'. While invisibility may, to some extent, be unavoidable, it equally seems correct to observe that there are differences between, for example, the written and established precedents of the superior or constitutional courts on the one hand; and vague or ill-defined notions of constitutional culture on the other. The reality is that there are differing degrees of stability – and thus visibility – between different potential sources of legal meaning.

It is worth, accordingly, considering in some more detail what, precisely, the 'invisible constitution' might entail. Laurence Tribe's depiction of the concept as a somewhat amorphous miasma of potential meanings has already been outlined above. Perhaps more usefully for our purposes here, Larry Solum has endeavoured to offer a more specific account of what can be said to fall within the scope of the invisible constitution He argues that that there are six categories of invisible (or, more precisely, extra-textual) sources to which a court might plausibly look for contextual guidance on the meaning of a legal provision:

> (i) One category consists of foundational documents other than the Constitution of the United States; examples include the Declaration of Independence, the Treaty of Paris, and the Articles of Confederation.
> (ii) Another category consists of documents and records that relate to the Framing and ratification of the original Constitution and its amendments; examples include The Federalist Papers, Madison's notes of the Philadelphia Convention
> (iii) A third category of possible sources consists of moral and political values.
> (iv) The fourth category is social norms and values – the content of these norms may correspond to true propositions of political morality, but this need not be the case. The fourth category refers to what is sometimes called "ethos" – the positive morality of a particular political culture.
> (v) The fifth category is institutional practice. One particularly salient member of this category consists of judicial decisions and opinions – that is, "precedent." But the practices of nonjudicial actors could also serve as a source of constitutional norms; sometimes the term "historical practice" is used to describe a subset of this category.
> (vi) Finally, the logical space of extratextual sources includes the idea that constitutional law might simply be "made up" by an official; judges come to mind.[45]

[45] Lawrence B Solum, 'Originalism and the Unwritten Constitution' (2013) *University of Illinois Law Review* 1935.

Even allowing for the fact that some of these sources may be more or less readily ascertainable in particular cultural or historical contexts, there are clear differences in their relative specificity, and thus in the degree of interpretive autonomy which they demand of, or leave to, a court.

This variability in the availability and clarity of such extra-textual sources also points, however, to a broader and more basic requirement when examining the relationship between CCI and the invisible constitution: namely, to consider and define what is connoted by invisibility in this context. It is arguable that, while they do not form part of the authoritative master text, some of Solum's sources of potential meaning can scarcely be described as 'invisible', at least in the sense of being difficult to identify. The Articles of Confederation, or Federalist Papers, for example, are not just written texts but are widely known and acknowledged as authoritative sources of potential insight even outside specialist legal circles. The same could arguably be said about judicial precedents, at least insofar as they have been articulated and applied over a considerable period of time. The 'basic structure' doctrine in India, the principle of the separation of powers in Canada,[46] or the principle of proportionality in Ireland[47] are all features of the respective constitutional orders that do not appear in the written text of the constitution but are as familiar to first year law students as to experienced practitioners or jurists.

By contrast, Solum's third and fourth categories seem potentially more difficult to operationalise in a manner that would be consistent with the ideas of interpretive reliability and rigour that the CCI method is intended to promote. That is not to say that these kinds of broader social, moral or political values may not impact on constitutional meaning. In fact, there has been a long-standing recognition in the field that the enduring nature of constitutional systems tends to mean that the social and political context in which a given constitution operates is likely to change and evolve over time.[48] Indeed, Martin Loughlin has argued that one of the functions of a constitutional system is to provide a language and process by which these social changes can be managed and integrated into the system anew,[49] a view which is echoed in the literature on the use of social movements to effect constitutional change.[50] Yet, the very fluidity of values and meaning that is of interest to scholars working in these more sociologically-oriented areas of study poses a particular and obvious challenge for the CCI method: if constitutional meaning is socially-situated and thereby responsive to changes in social norms and attitudes,

[46] *Reference re Remuneration of Judges of the Provincial Court of PEI* [1997] 3 SCR 3, 150 DLR (4th) 577; *Newfoundland (Treasury Board) v NAPE*, 2004 SCC 66.

[47] See the discussion in *O'Doherty & Waters v Minister for Health* [2022] IESC 32.

[48] Karl Llewellyn, 'The Constitution as an Institution' 34 *Columbia Law Review* 1 (1934).

[49] Martin Loughlin, 'Constitutional law: the third order of the political' in Nicholas Bamforth and Peter Leyland (eds), *Public Law in a Multi-Layered Constitution* (Oxford, Hart Publishing, 2003); See also Martin Loughlin, 'The Constitutional Imagination' (2015) 78 (1) *Modern Law Review* 1.

[50] Reva B Siegel, 'Text in Contest: Gender and the Constitution from a Social Movement Perspective' (2001) 150 *University of Pennsylvania Law Review* 297; Doug NeJaime, 'Constitutional Change, Courts, and Social Movements' (2013) 113 *Michigan Law Review* 877; Scott Cummings, 'The Puzzle of Social Movements in American Legal Theory' (2017) 64 *UCLA Law Review* 1552.

can it provide the certainty, stability and foreseeability that is the object of the method?

One of the challenges in thinking about how these social values may be integrated into the CCI method is that the scholarship on both is primarily concerned with different aspects of the constitutional enterprise. In her comprehensive and perceptive account of the myriad ways in which the label 'constitutional culture' appears in the field, Tanja Herklotz has argued that there is a necessity for a more precise and developed understanding of what culture means in this context.[51]

In that regard, it should be noted that Solum's categories three and four appear directed to the influence of broader social norms on constitutional meaning rather the 'internal' culture of officials such as judges with which much of the 'constitutional culture' literature is concerned. If we look at these aspects of the 'invisible constitution', there is a legitimate question for CCI as to how the recognition that social values may shape constitutional meaning in the long run might influence the determination of a question in the very-short-run of actual litigation. Fundamentally, these are different questions that arise in different contexts. The influence of social changes on constitutional meaning may be important but it is also a process which is opaque, likely uneven, and often only clear after the event. What the application of the constitutionally conforming method requires, on the other hand, is a standard that is established enough within that society and system to be plausibly constitutional; and precise enough to resolve a formal legal dispute. One process is fluid, multi-faceted and without particular limitations of scope or time; the other is formal, fixed in scope, and focused on finality. To put another way, there are sizeable differences in time, scope and application between a constitutional imaginary and a CCI. They are concerned with, and doing, quite different things.

Moreover, any efforts at bridging that gap are complicated by the fact that much of the literature on the sociological dimensions to the constitution can, themselves, be challenging to operationalise. While the emergence of a specific group of scholars working on 'sociological constitutionalism' has brought increasing conceptual and methodological sophistication to efforts to integrate sociology with constitutional studies, the literature remains predominantly, theoretical or historical in character.[52] Blokker has observed a tendency in much work in the field to draw conclusions from universalist assumptions of rational public reason: a 'line of reasoning [that leads] to the end when constitutional sociology itself seems to lose its sociological line of thinking'. This, in a practical sense, makes the prospect of looking to these social sources of meaning more distant.

[51] See Tanja Herklotz, 'Legal Cultures' (2023) *Max Planck Encyclopaedia of Comparative Constitutional Law*.

[52] Paul Blokker, 'Politics and the Political in Sociological Constitutionalism' in Paul Blokker and Christopher Thornhill (eds), *Sociological Constitutionalism* (Cambridge, Cambridge University Press, 2017) 203.

IV. Conclusion

For CCI, what all of this points to, perhaps, is the necessity to distinguish between different degrees of visibility when considering potential sources of constitutional meaning. While it seems correct to say that social, political and moral norms may shape constitutional meaning, that does not automatically signify that they ought to play a role within the narrower context of CCI. Certainly, for the court to take account of such broader social norms in identifying a constitutional meaning by which a statutory meaning would then be assessed would – to repeat the point made earlier in section II – be far away from the classic CCI case of a provision being read to conform to the constitutional master text, of which all were aware, and which the legislature could (and, in principle, should) have taken into account. That problem seems particularly pronounced if the values are to be derived from what might, broadly speaking, be regarded as sociological rather than legal sources. In addition to the issues of uncertainty, consistency and judicial restraint already identified, requiring the courts to look to social sources of meaning risks introducing further concerns around how such evidence might be obtained; and about the disciplinary competence of courts to engage with or evaluate it.

This suggests that there may be merit in considering a working distinction between written and unwritten sources of extra-constitutional meaning. The invisible constitution may, as Tribe suggests, be out there and all around us – but legal disputes cannot be reliably addressed in the ether. In seeking to ensure the consistency and foreseeability that are central to the rule of law, there is arguably a balance to be struck between, on the one hand, seeking constitutional meaning in a single master text and, on the other, looking to 'invisible' social norms.

Nor should a distinction between written and unwritten sources be thought of as simply a matter of pragmatism. One consequence of the fluidity that allows for changes in constitutional meaning over time is that there may, at any given point, be present in the system a variety of alternative or competing norms or narratives. There is no guarantee that any or all of them will ultimately become accepted as a core element of the constitutional order. Such status is arguably only possible through the kinds of formal mechanisms by which legal authority is ultimately conferred: be that reports, papers or legislation from Parliament; confirmation by a court; an amendment to the constitution; or other kinds of formal institutional process. Obviously, there may be scope for differences of opinion or approaches as to what should constitute a formal institutional process for these purposes. A strict approach may confine the permissible sources to those that enjoy formal constitutional status. A less strict approach could allow a court to search for meaning in parliamentary debates or official reports from other public bodies. This reflects the possibility of a spectrum of constitutional (in)visibility: and, relatedly, a continuum along which the use of extra-constitutional norms in CCI may be more or less contentious.

7

Constitutionally Conforming Argumentation and Legalism

ALFONSO GARCÍA FIGUEROA*

I. Constitutionally Conforming Interpretation as an Epiphenomenon

The requirement of constitutionally conforming interpretation (CCI) has been considered in Germany as a specific 'principle of constitutional interpretation'.[1] This principle imposes on judges the duty to discard unconstitutional interpretations in favour of those that are constitutional.

CCI is controversial. Some say that CCI is not 'constitutional' and some others argue that CCI is no 'interpretation' at all. On the one hand, some say that CCI is not 'constitutional' because, at first glance, CCI is not an interpretation of the constitution, but rather a statutory interpretation, ie the interpretation of infraconstitutional legal provisions. However, since the interpretation of statutes ought to be developed according to the (interpretation of the) constitution, CCI necessarily involves both infraconstitutional and constitutional interpretation.[2] On the other hand, some say that CCI is not 'interpretation', by arguing that CCI would simply amount to a priority rule. In this case, CCI would be a metanorm giving priority to the constitutionally conforming norm resulting from interpretation.[3]

Be it as it may, in this chapter, I will assume that CCI means much more than a method or principle of constitutional interpretation. Brian Bix points out that we cannot expect that questions of statutory interpretation – such as those involved

* I am grateful to professors Javier Díaz Revorio, Matthias Klatt, Leonor Moral, Eva Nieto, Miguel Ángel Pacheco and Luis Prieto for their comments on the earlier drafts of this chapter. Obviously, the responsibility for all mistakes is exclusively mine.

[1] See eg Peter Häberle, 'Métodos y principios de la interpretación constitucional. Un catálogo de problemas' in Ferrer MacGregor (ed), *Interpretación constitucional*, vol 1 (Francisco Balaguer Callejón tr, México, Porrúa, 2005) 696.

[2] See Virgílio Afonso da Silva, 'Interpretação constitucional e sincretismo metodologico' in Afonso da Silva (ed), *Interpretação constitucional* (São Paulo, Malheros, 2005) 132f.

[3] See Xabier Arzoz Santisteban, 'Aproximación a la interpretación conforme como técnica de coordinación normativa' (2021) 4 *Revista de Derecho Público: Teoría y método* 67, 80ff.

in CCI – 'will be resolved by reference to statements about the nature of law',[4] because those questions basically involve political controversies. However, I will assume here that the converse is true instead: CCI can serve as a touchstone for a better understanding of our concept of law, for CCI represents an epiphenomenon,[5] that provides us with an insight into the very nature of law and legal interpretation, particularly in constitutional states.

We all know that 'law' and 'interpretation'[6] are extremely controversial concepts. Paul Daly has outlined the 'intractable disagreement' on legal interpretation between two types of lawyers: 'Type A lawyers', who are in favour of legal certainty and textualism, and 'Type B lawyers', who stress the value of coherence and principles. In his own words: 'Type A lawyers seek the authentic meaning of statutes as authoritative legislative commands. Type B lawyers prefer to view the judicial role as weaving statutes into the timeless tapestry of the common law, rich with values and principles (of which constitutional norms are just a few)'.[7] Daly concludes that unless and until this disagreement is resolved, the debate on CCI will continue, and there is no reason to expect that this disagreement will be ever resolved shortly.[8] After all, could anybody realistically expect a final agreement between, say, Robert Bork, who was a Type A lawyer, and Ronald Dworkin,[9] who was a typical Type B?

My contribution intends to be that of a Type B lawyer. However, I will not deal with the nature of law, but more modestly, with the conception of law underlying the officials' practice and the evolution of such a conception of law instilled in judges. Particularly in Spain, ordinary judges' discomfort with CCI unveils deeper problems concerning the limits of objectivity in legal interpretation, the very nature of law, the role of judges in a democratic society, and the convenience of a concentrated model of constitutionality control.

To cope with such complex questions, we need a clear concept of CCI. According to the classical 'German approach',[10] genuine CCI meets four conditions:

i. The interpreted legal statement must be ambiguous.
ii. At least one interpretation must violate the Constitution.
iii. At least one interpretation must conform to the Constitution.

[4] Brian Bix, *Jurisprudence: Theory and Context*, 4th edn (London, Thomson/Sweet & Maxwell, 2006) 151.

[5] Giusi Sorrenti, 'La interpretación conforme a la Constitución en el ordenamiento italiano: estado de la cuestión' (2014) 2 *InDret* 1, 6, available at indret.com/wp-content/themes/indret/pdf/1047__es_.pdf.

[6] See below s II(B).

[7] Paul Daly, 'Canada. Legal Coherence versus Legal Certainty' in Matthias Klatt (ed), *Constitutionally Conforming Interpretation – Comparative Perspectives Volume 1: National Reports* (Oxford, Hart Publishing, 2023) s V(F).

[8] ibid.

[9] See on such disagreement eg Ronald Dworkin, *Freedom's Law. The Moral Reading of the American Constitution* (Oxford, Oxford University Press, 1996) 261ff.

[10] See Matthias Klatt, 'The Legitimacy of Constitutionally Conforming Interpretation' in Klatt (n 7) s II(A).

iv. CCI 'must not wholly rewrite the normative content of the interpreted norm'.[11] This means that CCI must respect the wording of the legal statement, in the sense that the result of CCI must be recognisable by its author, the legislature.[12]

However, this final requirement (iv) turns out to be particularly controversial in a constitutional state. After all, the German Federal Constitutional Court (FCC) itself justifies the need for CCI in the following terms:

> For the Basic Law, as the supreme domestic law, is not only the standard for assessing the validity of legal norms from domestic legal sources; each of these norms must also be interpreted substantively in harmony with the Basic Law. Accordingly, the text of each legal norm receives, as needed, a supplementary sense or, when the other preconditions are met, each must be developed in harmony with the Basic Law. The Basic Law, too, is part of the comprehensive legal order, which must be understood as a totality of meaning and must underlie every interpretation of domestic law.[13]

If 'the text of each legal norm receives, as needed, a supplementary sense', then it is impossible not to 'rewrite' such a legal statement, when performing CCI. *A fortiori*, when that legal statement was enacted by a non-democratic preconstitutional legislator, very often it should be mandatory to display CCI by rewriting such a text entirely to make it fit into the constitutional framework and felicitously make it unrecognisable for its author. Similarly, when a new Constitution is enacted with a deep transformative spirit, then the postconstitutional legislation might need that CCI especially involves an à la Dworkin 'moral reading of the Constitution'. Bearing both pre- and postconstitutional scenarios in mind, I am going to stress the complex relashionship between CCI and the legalistic culture of judges by focusing on the CCI of a preconstitutional norm (the widower case) and the CCI of a postconstitutional norm (the same-sex marriage case). Finally, I will deal with some objections to the concentrated control of constitutionality coherently raised by the full acceptance of the underlying principles that support CCI.

II. The Widower Case

A. Preconstitutional Norms for Postconstitutional Widowers

A statute enacted during the General Franco regime stated that, in case a (male) worker died, his widow would be entitled to receive a pension from the State:

[11] ibid.
[12] ibid.
[13] BVerfGE 51, 304, 323 (1979), *apud* Matthias Jestaedt, 'The Karlsruhe Phenomenon. What Makes the Court What It Is' in Jestaedt et al (eds), *The German Federal Constitutional Court. The Court Without Limits* (Jeff Seitzer tr, Oxford, Oxford University Press, 2020) 62f.

LS1: The National Fund for Old-Age and Disability Insurance of the National Welfare Institute will grant, charged to its funds, a pension to the widows of the workers who are beneficiaries of the aforementioned insurance.[14]

For the sake of simplicity, let us rephrase legal statement LS1 as follows:

N1: Workers' widows have the right to a pension.

In 1984, Antonio Tomé's wife died, and Mr. Tomé applied for a pension. After all, his wife had been a worker. However, both the Spanish National Institute of Social Security and the ordinary courts dismissed the case, since LS1 exclusively referred to 'widows' ('viudas') and not 'widowers' ('viudos'). So they interpreted LS1 literally, ie in a manner that was fully recognisable by the Francoist authors of that norm:

N1': Only workers' widows (not widowers) have the right to a pension.

Mr. Tomé brought his claim to the Spanish Constitutional Court (*Tribunal Constitucional*) by means of a constitutional complaint ('recurso de amparo'[15]). Then the *Tribunal Constitucional* (TC) did recognise Mr. Tomé's right to a pension,[16] by virtue of a so-called 'additive court ruling' ('sentencia aditiva'), which assumes that LS1 can be constitutionally valid, if and only if the words 'and widowers' were 'read in'[17] on legal statement LS1:

N1": Workers' widows *and widowers* have the right to a pension.

Obviously, such an interpretive 'jump'[18] from LS1 to N1" by means of CCI would have been based on a constitutional norm, namely Article 14 of the Spanish Constitution (CE), which reads as follows:

[14] Art 3, Decreto-ley de 2 de septiembre de 1955, dealing with the so-called 'Seguro obligatorio de vejez e invalidez' ('SOVI'), a compulsory disability and old age insurance in favour of workers. The original text in Spanish reads as follows: 'La Caja Nacional del Seguro de Vejez e Invalidez del Instituto Nacional de Previsión concederá con cargo a sus fondos una prestación a las viudas de los trabajadores beneficiarios del expresado seguro'.

[15] The so-called 'recurso de amparo' amounts to the German *Urteilsverfassungsbeschwerde*. For more details on the Spanish legal system, see Isabel Lifante-Vidal, 'Spain. Constitutionally Conforming Interpretation and Interpretative Judgements in the Spanish Constitutional Court' in Klatt (n 7).

[16] Spanish Constitutional Court Ruling (STC) 253/1988 de 20 de diciembre.

[17] The Spanish decision amounts to a French 'constructive reservation' (Matthieu Carpentier, 'France. The Dynamics of "Interpretative Reservations' in the Jurisprudence of the French Constitutional Council' in Klatt (n 7), s III(C)) or a 'sentenza additiva di regola', an expression coined by the Italian legal science when the Italian *corte costituzionale* states that one norm is constitutional if and only if something is added to N1. Therefore, N1 ('Workers' widows have the right to a pension') is constitutional if and only if it is interpreted as N1": 'Workers' widows *and workers' widowers* are entitled to a pension'. Interestingly, this is a case where the pressumption of the constitutionality of LS1 hardly applies since LS1 was enacted in 1955, long before the enactment of the Spanish Constitution of 1978. Obviously, the democratic principle (usually underlying the presumption of constitutionality of legal norms) cannot apply to norms enacted under a non-democratic regime such as Franco's. Consequently, the principle *in dubbio pro legislatore* seems more adequate to support CCI here (see on the difference between both justifying principles of CCI: Lucio Cabrales, *El principio de interpretación conforme en la justicia constitucional* (México, Porrúa, 2015) s I(3)).

[18] Aulis Aarnio, Robert Alexy and Aleksander Peczenik, 'The Foundations of Legal Reasoning'(1981) 12 *Rechtstheorie* 133, 137.

> Spaniards are equal before the law and may not in any way be discriminated against on account of birth, race, *sex*, religion, opinion or any other personal or social condition or circumstance (emphasis added).

It is important to note that the Spanish Constitution had come into force in 1978 and the whole Spanish legal order had to be interpreted in light of the new Constitution ever since. So, the underlying argument in favour of the TC's decision was that CCI is compulsory for ordinary judges. Since the contents of the Spanish Constitution must *pervade* or 'irradiate' every single norm of the legal system (including preconstitutional norms), ordinary judges should have interpreted LS1 by applying CCI.[19] This counterfactual about what ordinary courts should have done makes clear two points. First, it shows why this kind of so-called 'interpretive decisions' (ie Italian 'sentenze interpretative') made by constitutional courts are 'macroscopic examples'[20] of ordinary judges' CCI. Second, this also shows that, with regards to the constitutional court's (over)activity, ordinary judges' CCI might well work as a sort of 'filter'[21] easing the excess of work assigned to the TC.

B. Is Constitutionally Conforming Interpretation Just Interpretation or Something Else?

Since CCI involves constitutional interpretation, the concept of constitutional interpretation needs further clarification. Due to multiple reasons, constitutional interpretation looks peculiar, but it is not essentially different from any other kind of legal interpretation.[22] Therefore, some remarks on general interpretation may suffice here. *Sensu largo*, we ambiguously call 'interpretation' both the activity and the result of attributing a meaning to a signifier (ie a linguistic formulation). Interpreting the statement 'S', 'the cat is on the mat', is a complex task, by means of which a proposition P (true or false) is attributed to a statement S:

> I^1: 'S' means P

Where 'S' is a signifier, a linguistic formulation, and P is a proposition expressing the meaning of 'S'. Therefore, each element lies on different linguistic levels, but they are not ontologically different. After all, no matter our metaphysical

[19] See para 4 of the aforementioned STC 253/1988 de 20 de diciembre.

[20] Riccardo Guastini, *Interpretar y argumentar* (Silvina Álvarez tr, Madrid, CEPC, 2014) 296.

[21] Riccardo Guastini, *Estudios sobre la interpretación jurídica* (Marina Gascón and Miguel Carbonell trs, México, UNAM, 1999) 809.

[22] See eg Paolo Comanducci, 'Modelos e interpretación de la Constitución' in MacGregor (n 1) 469–99; Marina Gascón, 'Particularidades de la interpretación constitucional' in Gascón (ed), *Argumentación jurídica* (Valencia, Tirant lo Blanch, 2014) 285ff.; Riccardo Guastini, 'Peculiaridades de la interpretación constitucional' in MacGregor (n 1) 653–72; Rafael Hernández Marín, *Interpretación, subsunción y aplicación del Derecho* (Madrid, Marcial Pons, 1999) 117; Luis Prieto, 'Notas sobre la interpretación constitucional' (1991) 9 *Revista del Centro de Estudios Constitucionales* 175, 175–98.

assumptions on the existence of meanings,[23] both elements ('S' and P) retain in practice their linguistic nature.[24] From this point of view, interpretation and translation are 'congener'.[25] Actually, interpretation somehow amounts to an 'intralinguistic' translation[26] or an 'accurate lexicographic exercise'.[27] The fact that legal interpretation is usually intralinguistic (eg English-English) apparently makes things more simple in terms of legal certainty, for interlinguistic translation is infradetermined.[28]

So in practice, we can express I^1 more properly like this:

I^2: 'S' means 'P'

Such isomorphism between signifiers and meanings may cause a *regressus in infinitum*, for every meaning is expressed by means of signifiers, which can, in turn, be interpreted along a virtually infinite chain of interpretations:

I^3: 'S' means 'P1'

I^4: 'P1' means 'P2'

I^5: 'P2' means 'P3'

I^6: 'P3' means 'P4'

…

Legal statements are usually normative. For example, the statement 'Stop' (on a traffic sign) means that you ought to stop. The statement 'Stop' is a legal statement (LS2) and its meaning (if I may say so[29]) is not properly a (either true or false) proposition, but a norm (N2), which is neither true nor false. Actually, N2 can express the sense of a normative speech act, the meaning of which can be

[23] See a Quinean skeptic approach in Hernández Marín (n 22) 116: 'It is possible to state that statements have meaning (sense) without stating the existence of the meanings of the statements, without stating the existence of propositions'. Quine states that specifically, the indetermination of translation shows that the very notion of proposition (meaning) is unacceptable (Willard VO Quine, *Pursuit of Truth* (Cambridge, Harvard University Press, 1990) para 43).

[24] See Riccardo Guastini, *Dalle fonti alle norme* (Torino, Giappichelli, 1992) 18; and Riccardo Guastini, 'Introduzione allo studio del linguaggio normativo' in Castignone et al (eds), *Introduzione teorica allo studio del diritto. Prime lezioni* (Genova, ECIG, 1984) 39.

[25] Guastini, *Estudios sobre la interpretación jurídica* (n 21) 5f.

[26] Guastini, *Interpretar y argumentar* (n 20) 35.

[27] Hernández Marín, *Interpretación, subsunción y aplicación del Derecho* (n 22) 113ff. Then, according to Quine, interpreting is providing a synonym, and an interpreter is a qualified lexicographer.

[28] See Quine (n 23) s 18.

[29] Here it suffices to state 'meaning' *sensu latissimo*. Carlos E Alchourrón and Eugenio Bulygin used to distinguish between two main conceptions on norms: The hyletic and the expressive conceptions of norms. The hyletic conception of norms holds that norms somehow have a meaning. The traffic sign 'Stop' can be rerpresented as Op (obligatory pull over). According to the expressive conception of norms, norms do not express a semantic unity of information. Rather, a norm is a specific *mode* of using a semantic piece of information. Consequently, 'Stop' can be represented as '!p', where '!' represents the illocutionary force applied to the proposition p (stopped vehicle) (Carlos E Alchourrón and Eugenio Bulying, 'The Expressive Conception of Norms' in Risto Hilpinen (ed), *New Essays in Deontic Logic* (Dordrecht, Reidel, 1981) 95–124).

justified[30] on semantic and/or normative rules. Therefore, judges might express the following opinions in a debate in Court:

I[7]: 'LS2' means 'N2'

I[8]: 'N2' means 'N3'

I[9]: 'N3' means 'N4'

…

In semantic terms, the ultimate controversy on interpretation is not about the obvious ambiguity of legal statements ('LS2' might mean: 'N2', 'N3', 'N4', etc.). The point is rather whether 'the set of meanings of a legal statement is either finite or infinite'.[31] Were this set of meanings infinite, then the thesis of the radical indetermination of law would somehow be right, as extreme legal realism states.[32] Were this set of (acceptable) meanings just one, then the well-known Ronald Dworkin's 'one right answer thesis' would be right. But we can assume instead that, despite the impossibility of *finding* a single right abstract interpretation of a legal statement for good (the so-called 'eternal interpretation'), we can rationally define in every concrete case a range of 'discursively possible'[33] solutions for legal and practical problems. In other words, the opposite of the Dworkinian one right answer thesis is not necessarily that the right answer may be anyone. So here I will assume that rationality and discretion may be compatible when applying the law. A case can have a range of discursively possible results.

Now let us assume that 'LS2' has two basic acceptable meanings: 'N2' and 'N3'. Let us also assume that 'N4' is by no means an acceptable interpretation of 'LS2' according to the most elementary semantic rules. In this scenario, Riccardo Guastini classifies interpretation into three basic classes:[34]

i. Cognitive interpretation, which merely lists the acceptable meanings of 'LS2'. A cognitive interpretation of LS2 would read as follows: 'LS2' may mean: 'N2' and 'N3'. Cognitive interpretation of law is alledgely a purely descriptive (lexicographic) activity typically developed by legal science.
ii. *Adjudicative interpretation*, which selects only one meaning. In our case, an adjudicative interpretation might be: 'LS2' means 'N3' and not 'N2'. From this

[30] 'Justified' *sensu largo*, for it also refers to the (semantic and not semantic) *reasons* why a meaning can be assigned to a statement.

[31] In Becchi's opinion, *apud* Victoria Iturralde, *Interpretación literal y significado convencional. Una reflexión sobre los límites de la interpretación jurídica* (Madrid, Marcial Pons, 2014) 32.

[32] Radical realism ignores that a provisional (end) meaning is possible because our communicative practices are based on 'prima facie entitlements' in Brandom's terms (see Matthias Klatt, 'Semantic Normativity and the Objectivity of Legal Argumentation' (2004) 90 *ARSP* 51, 57). This explains why extreme skepticism looks counterintuitive. Under no *acceptable* interpretation, could someone ever state that LS2 may mean, say, 'row, row, row your boat gently down the stream'?

[33] Robert Alexy, 'Eine Theorie des praktischen Diskurses' in Willi Oelmüller (ed), *Normenbegründung Normendurchsetzung* (Padeborn, Schöningh, 1978) 22, 52.

[34] Guastini, *Interpretar y argumentar* (n 20) 45ff.

point of view, adjudicative interpretation is an 'adscriptive' activity[35] usually performed by judges. So CCI is usually supposed to be a typical adjudicative interpretation.

iii. *Creative interpretation*, which would state in our example: 'LS2' means 'N4'. It is creative, inasmuch as 'N4' is not an 'acceptable' meaning of 'LS2' in semantic terms, and it might not be 'recognisable by the legislature'. Seemingly, CCI is sometimes quite creative, as the widowers case shows.

Interestingly, Riccardo Guastini states that creative interpretation is quite rare. In his opinion, the real and usual operation is not creative interpretation but pure creation, ie *principle-based legal construction*. So in hard cases, it seems to me that we could describe judges' activity not as a *creative interpretation* but more properly as an *interpretive creation* of *a new norm* (eg N1"). Namely, CCI usually seems to be a principle-based legal construction. Strictly speaking, it is a matter of *argumentation* rather than proper *interpretation*. Certainly, according to the aforementioned 'German approach', such a creative operation cannot be considered CCI anymore. However, the difference between interpretation and argumentation, between what I call 'creative interpretation' and 'interpretive creation' is too subtle. In Elisabetta Lamarque's words, 'it is (…) very difficult, or impossible, to determine, in each concrete case, whether a statutory reading in the light of the Constitution made by an ordinary judge is a *genuine interpretation* or a *correction* of that statute'.[36] In order for us to distinguish between *interpretation* and *correction* (ie creation, *construction*, *Rechtsfortbildung*) of legal statements, we should have at our disposal a clear criterion to determine at least two sets of interpretations: a range of *acceptable* interpretations and a range of unacceptable interpretations of any legal statement. But, apparently, no such clear criterion is available, and this is a problem for the 'German approach' to CCI.[37]

[35] Guastini (ibid 53, fn 62) states that adjudicative interpretation is adscriptive but not properly prescriptive. The adscriptive function of interpretation is related to the performative function of language as opposed to the constative function of language in the well-known J.L. Austin's theory. However, eg Hernández Marín states that interpretation is always assertive or constative, since it provides us with either a true or false description.

[36] Elisabetta Lamarque, 'Interpreting statutes in conformity with the constitution: the role of the constitutional court and ordinary judge' (2010) 1 *Italian Journal of Public Law* 87, 89, my italics. This point is very relevant when we address the four conditions of CCI according to the 'German approach' to CCI. The limits between CCI and other methods such as the 'further development of law' are not clear, especially with regards to condition four. Klatt himself (n 10, s V(A)) assumes that CCI is not an all-or-nothing question but a balancing of competences. For instance, the evolution of Brazilian jurisprudence from the 'German approach' to a more creative or constructive conception of CCI illustrates this point. See on this evolution: Diego W Arguelhes and Rafael B de Lima, 'Brazil. From Restraint to Preemption?' in Klatt (n 7). Of course, this point is quite controversial. See Victoria Iturralde, *Interpretación literal y significado convencional* (Madrid, Marcial Pons, 2014).

[37] I am well aware of the relevance of the 'limits of the wording (*Wortlautgrenze*)' theory in Germany. Matthias Klatt's defence of this theory is extremely stimulant and persuasive. However, my approach will be slightly different. It is impossible for me to make it explicit now, but I hope that my arguments in this chapter will do. See Matthias Klatt, *Hacer el derecho explícito: Normatividad semántica en la argumentación jurídica* (Francisco J. Campos Zamora tr., Madrid, Marcial Pons, Filosofía y derecho, 2017, 289 ff.). I recommend the Spanish edition, which is more complete than the English one.

Back to the widower case: What makes the difference between 'LS1 means N1" and only N1", because it is the constitutionally correct interpretation' (ie creative interpretation) and 'LS1 does not mean N1", but it should belong to the legal order' (ie norm creation)? Some would reply that only N1 (and maybe N1') is the right interpretation of LS1. If so, the widower case is simply irrelevant with regards to LS1. Accordingly, N1" would not really be a (semantically) acceptable interpretation of LS1, but a *creation of a brand new norm* that had nothing to do with LS1. It would read as follows:

N5: *Workers' widowers* have the right to a pension.

Apparently, between the literal observation of the wording allegedly expressing the will of the legislator and the pure interpretive creation of a new norm challenging the democratic principle, we can find a range of adjudicative and creative interpretations. This is the range of discursive possibilities of argumentation.

C. Systematic Co-Text and Social Context in Legal Interpretation

Now, some legal philosophers would probably insist on saying that N5 never can be an interpretation of LS1, because LS1 is a text, and LS1 being unchanged, its meaning cannot change even in the case that a new Constitution is enacted. For example, Rafael Hernández Marín argues that the meaning of Aristotle's works cannot change over the centuries and that their meaning cannot depend on the particular circumstances of every single moment. I guess this perspective might be shared by 'textualist' authors such as, eg Justice Antonin Scalia.[38] But of course, this conclusion might be misleading. After all, the meaning of every single text is closely connected to a system of knowledge and its social context.

Now it is quite tempting to illustrate the point with a short story, 'Pierre Menard, Author of Don Quixote',[39] where Jorge Luis Borges takes to the extreme the idea that the very same text, keeping its wording unchanged, might change its meaning over the years. The story may be resumed as follows: Pierre Menard is a French writer who literally rewrites several chapters of *Don Quijote*. Where Cervantes writes this:[40]

[38] See eg Frederick Schauer, 'United States. Constitutional Avoidance As Constitutional Conformation' in Klatt (n 7), s III.

[39] Jorge L Borges, 'Pierre Menard, autor del Quijote' in Borges, *Narraciones* (Madrid, Cátedra, 1981) 81–92.

[40] Miguel de Cervantes, *Don Quijote de la Mancha* (Madrid, Real Academia Española/Alfaguara, 2004) 88. John Ormsby's English translation reads as follows: '(T)he truth, whose mother is history, rival of time, storehouse of deeds, witness for the past, example and counsel for the present, and warning for the future'.

> (…) la verdad cuya madre es la historia, émula del tiempo, depósito de las acciones, testigo de lo pasado, ejemplo y aviso de lo presente, advertencia de lo por venir.

Menard rewrites exactly the very same words for his own *Don Quijote*:

> (…) la verdad cuya madre es la historia, émula del tiempo, depósito de las acciones, testigo de lo pasado, ejemplo y aviso de lo presente, advertencia de lo por venir.

However, Borges notes that the same wording does not mean the same thing. The new text by Menard looks quite different from the original, due to the new context. After all, for the meaning of the text to be the same, Menard should 'speak Spanish, be Catholic, fight the Moors and forget about the European history between 1602 and 1918'.

The time factor is particularly relevant when it comes to law. Legal statements are probably more sensitive to context than Aristotle's and Cervantes' works because they belong to a normative discourse and to a legal system. Indeed, normative *co-text* and social context are particularly important because the meaning of every single legal statement depends on the meaning of other legal statements from the legal system, which is changing all the time, due to the plain fact that every day some norms get out of the legal order (ie they are repealed) and many others get into it (ie they are enacted). Furthermore, the changing social context is particularly important when interpreting terms regarding eg sexual morality.

i. The Importance of Legal Co-Text

In law, normative context (let us call it 'co-text'[41]) is overwhelmingly important because legal interpretation is systemic. Legal interpretation is systemic because the adscriptive interpretation is guided by other norms belonging to the same legal system (a system of legal statements). Certainly, in a broad sense, CCI is interpretation, since it aims at attributing meaning (norm) to a provision, but such interpretation is not supposed to be simply true or false, for this interpretation involves a *normative* aspect. It purports to state what a statement *ought to* mean according to some other norms. So such an interpretation does not simply state:

> I^{10}: 'LS1' means N1".

Actually, not every semantically right interpretation of a legal statement is normatively acceptable. The *duty* to choose the constitutionally right interpretation depends on further normative criteria that justifiy such a decision. Hence, the (adscriptive) interpretation is a *decision* based on interpretive directives *and values*.[42] For example, judges may openly hold the following CCIs:

[41] On the dichotomy of cotext/context, see Richard W Janney, 'Cotext as context: vague answers in court' (2002) 22/4 *Language and Communication* 457, 457–75.

[42] Jerzy Wróblewski, *Constitución y teoría general de la interpretación jurídica* (Arantxa Azurda tr, Madrid, Civitas, 1985) 65ff.

I^{11}: 'LS1' ought to mean N1" according to the Constitution.

I^{12}: 'LS1' ought not to mean N1 and N1' according to the Constitution.

And this might be the starting point of a constitutional debate since the reasons why 'LS1' *should* be understood as N1" (and not N1 and N1') are based on the Constitution. Then interpretation is no longer a mere descriptive or adscriptive activity but a *normative* activity, which involves two normative statements: the *interpreted* legal statement ('LS1') and the *interpreting* legal statement (Article 14 CE). This is relevant, because CCI necessary involves reducing the potential (semantic) range of meanings of LS1. Among the potential meanings of LS1, CCI compells us to choose the constitutional one (I^{11}) and rule out the rest (I^{12}) on *normative* (systemic and constitutional) grounds. If so, the underlying problem is not about the concept and extent of what is called 'interpretation', but something else. Somehow, the point might merely become a matter of names or labels. So, if we do not like the word 'interpetation' in CCI any more, we could simply talk about 'argumentation', say, 'constitutionally conforming argumentation'.

Alchourrón and Buygin[43] would probably argue that there was an 'axiological gap', which had to be solved specifically on equality grounds *ex* Article 14 CE. From this alternative point of view,[44] the widower case would have unveiled an 'axiological gap' in the legal system, which means that LS1 was constitutionally acceptable but the legal system lacked a norm, which was requested on (constitutional) normative grounds. From this perspective, no reasonable interpretation of LS1 is unconstitutional. Only the gap is, and N5 would be the new norm that fills in the gap. Under these circumstances, judges are actually requested to create a new norm by means of *analogia juris* (ie principle-based creation). In this case, judges would fill in the gap by directly applying the Constitution as the guiding principle of such a creation.

At the end of the day, the point is our very concept of legal system. Legal interpretation is time-dependent in the sense that (dynamic) normative systems change every day as soon as new norms are enacted and others are repealed. Strictly speaking, as soon as a new norm is enacted, a whole brand-new legal system arises. In fact, one single change can modify the content of many other norms, and when the new norm is a Constitution, changes are particularly dramatic. This is the reason why Alchourrón and Bulygin would probably define the Spanish law not as a genuine 'legal system' (an axiomatic system of legal statements), but rather as a 'sequence of legal systems' (ie what they call a 'legal order').[45] So, the Spanish law is a *legal order* encompassing a sequence of *legal systems*, and the interpretation of each legal system depends on a new broader context and co-text each time a new

[43] Carlos E Alchourrón and Eugenio Bulyin, *Introducción a la metodología de las ciencias jurídicas y sociales* (Buenos Aires, Astrea, 1993) 161ff.

[44] See eg Guastini, 'Peculiaridades de la interpretación constitucional' (n 22) 671.

[45] Carlos E Alchourrón and Eugenio Bulying, 'Sobre el concepto de orden jurídico' in *Análisis lógico y Derecho* (Madrid, CEC, 1991) 393–407.

system arises. Therefore, the interpretation of a legal statement is changing all the time, and the value of its wording gets quite relative.[46]

Indeed, since in a constitutional state no provision can be an island, legal systems need to be reconstructed so as to be applied in a very concrete case. Reconstructing the whole legal system axiomatically is not feasible. Reconstructing the part of it that is applicable to a case is the judges' task instead. After all, when applying the law, judges are required to rebuild a limited normative system *ad casum*. In order to illustrate this task, let us get back to the widower case again. In this case, we can built an *ad casum* little normative system upon two relevant legal statements: LS1 and Article 14 CE. They can be respectively interpreted as N1 and N6. *Once interpreted*, then we can rationally operate with them and find out that, after all, N5 is a part of the relevant legal system in this case:

Signifiers (explicit norms):	LS1 (art. 3, Decreto-ley de 2 de septiembre de 1955); art 14 CE
Meanings and implicit statements:	N1: Widows have the right to a pension; N6: Women and men have equal rights
	Def1: Widows are women and widowers are men
	N7 (ex N6 and Def 1): Widows and widowers have equal rights
	N8 (ex N1 and N7): If widows have the right to a pension, then widowers have the right to a pension
CCI:	N1": Workers' widows and widowers have the right to a pension
Applicable CCI:	N5: Workers' widowers have the right to a pension
Aplication by subsumption	Fact: Mr. Antonio Tomé is a (worker's) widower Conclusion: Mr. Antonio Tomé has the right to a pension

Apparently, *no pure creation of law* is needed to solve this case, despite the fact that a new *ad casum* legal system is created. Under these circumstances, N1" and N5 necessarily belong to this legal system by implication. In other words, it seems *rational* that N1" and N5 belong to this *ad casum* legal system, as long as the set of explicit (N1 and N6) and implicit (N7 and N8) legal statements belong to the legal system and Def 1 is lexically accepted.

[46] Pavel Ondřejek quotes a widow's case too: A widow's prisoner during the Nazi persecution was not provided with the legal one-off pecuniary compensation to relatives, because the prisoner died probably on 8 May 1945 (ie after the legal term, on 4 May 1945). The Constitutional Court stated against the wording of the law that '(t)he concept that an aggrieved person could lose this status as a result of prolongation of their incarceration after 4 May 1945 is absurd and contrary to the sense of the law' (Judgment of the Czeck Constitutional Court of 7 May 1997, File No. Pl. ÚS 23/96, *apud* Pavel Ondřejek, 'Czech Republic. Insights from the Constitutional Court's Post-Transition Practice of Constitutionally Conforming Interpretation' in Klatt (n 7) s II).

However, given that N5 belongs to the *ad casum* normative system on *argumentative* grounds too, such a membership can be discussed. Apparently, in the widower case, the CCI *jump* from LS1 to N1" does not reduce the content of the *literal* interpretation (N1). Rather, N1" *adds* by means of CCI (somehow an *additive* decision) a new content ('a supplementary sense', in FCC words) that the preconstitutional Parliament originally did not enact. Judges do so to preserve the constitutionality of the entire system. Yet, such a decision possibly does *curtail* the legal system and the democratic will; for, *ex hypothesi*, the (current) Parliament could have wished to prevent widowers from receiving a pension on, say, eg affirmative action measures in favour of women and not men. In this case, the Parliament could have not considered necessary to say something on this matter by assuming that TC takes condition (iv) of the 'German approach' to CCI seriously. If so, CCI made by ordinary judges may clearly preclude potential alternative regulations that Legislators might have liked to decide otherwise. So, in principle, it seems quite reasonable that the respect for the democratic legislator's will instilled in the very wording of the text could restrict the scope of CCI to some extent. CCI needs to be nuanced by pointing out a range of discursive possibility.

ii. The Scope of Constitutionally Conforming Interpretation and Laws Aging

The widower case dramatically shows the importance of co-text. We can not always assume the presumption of constitutionality, ie the 'principle that it would be inadmissible to allege from the outset that the legislator intended the statutes they passed to be unconstitutional'.[47] In the widower case, we could expect the applicable norms to be unconstitutional from the very outset since the legislator was preconstitutional and non-democratic.[48] In other words, time becomes a very relevant factor in assessing the scope of CCI in cases such as the widower's. After all, in this case, it is particularly legitimate to question the original intent of the legislator reflected in the wording of the norm. Conversely, the very relevance of the 'age of a law' is a consistent reason to reduce the scope of CCI in recently enacted norms. In Lin's words, '(t)he general principle is that CCI tends to be an inappropriate interpretive method for newly enacted laws because, at least in theory, they reflect recent public opinion and enjoy considerable public support'.[49]

To sum up, the age of a legal text is an influential factor when considering the absoluteness of the condition (iv) of the German approach. Actually, it becomes a

[47] Christoph Bezemek and Daniel Gosch, 'Austria. Embracing Tradition: Constitutionally Confirming Interpretation's Edge in Reconciling Statutory and Constitutional Law' in Klatt (n 7), s II(B).

[48] This issue is particularly important in post-colonial states, where law does not completely break from the past. See Raeesa Vakil, 'India: The Ultimate Interpreter: Democracy and Constitutionality in the Indian Supreme Court' in Klatt (n 7), s IV.

[49] Chien-Chih Lin, 'Taiwan: Constitutionally Conforming Interpretation and Judicial Sleight of Hand' in Klatt (n 7), s II(D).

matter of degree in the following terms: The more ancient the norm, the less important the fact that CCI respects the recognisability of the legislative intent in the wording of the norms. *A fortiori*, the enactment of a new Constitution is extremely important when CCI takes place because preconstitutional norms prima facie lack the legitimacy that supports the wording of the norm as an expression of the legislator's will. Conversely, the more recent the norm, the more important it turns out to be the fact that CCI respects the recognisability of the legislative intent in the wording of the norms. We could ideally represent these circumstances as follows:

Figure 1 Area of discursive possibilities of the ordinary judges' acceptable creativity, when performing today CCI of past statutes

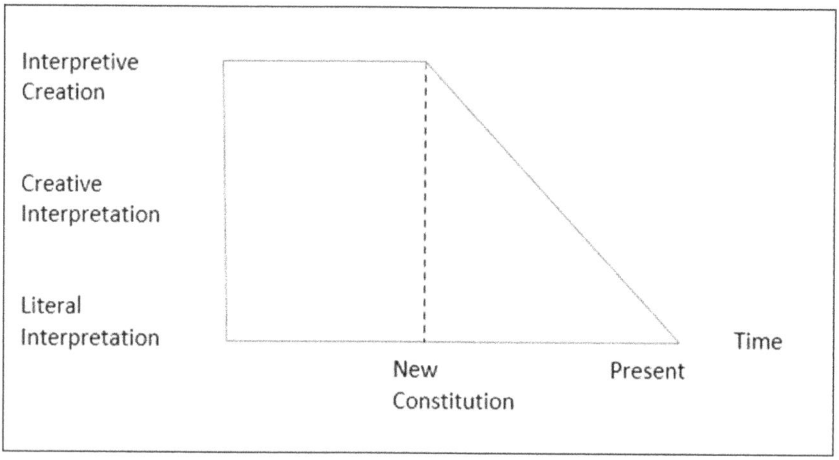

III. The Same-sex Marriage Case

A. Social Context and Transformative Constitutions

CCI is not only related to intrasystemic norms (normative co-text) but also to extrasystemic norms (social context). Neil MacCormick used to express this idea by stressing that the logic of justification in law is similar to that of natural science in two 'points of contact': 'legal decisions must make sense in the world, and they must also make sense in the context of a legal system'.[50] That is to say, the application of law is related to social context and legal co-text.

For example, in order to preserve it against constitutional challenges, India's courts 'read down' section 377 of the Indian Penal Code (1860), which

[50] Neil MacCormick, *Legal Reasoning and Legal Theory*, 2nd ed (Oxford, Oxford University Press, 1994) 103.

criminalised 'unnatural sex', supposed to be 'against the order of nature'. By means of such 'reading down', the Indian Supreme Court interpreted that this criminal norm (originally intended to punish homosexuality) exclusively applied to non-consensual acts involving all persons, thus decriminalising consensual sexual activity between non-heterosexual adults.[51] The 'unnatural sex' case shows not only that 'nature' is, if I may say so, quite an unnatural concept, but also that CCI may go beyond the original intention of the legislator and the wording of the text due to social changes in what the addressees of norms consider to be 'unnatural' when it comes to sexual morality. This factor is particularly important in states where the Constitution plays a transformative role.[52]

Therefore, interpretation may change, particularly according to extrasystemic normative concepts. The Spanish same-sex marriage case may be helpful to grasp this idea in detail.[53] When the Spanish Civil Code was modified so as to include same-sex unions in the concept of marriage, the Spanish TC deemed such a modification constitutional, despite the fact that the Spanish Constitution clearly stated that (legal) marriage was heterosexual: 'Men and women have the right to marry with full legal equality' (Article 32(1) CE).[54] So the Spanish TC argued that the 'concept of marriage' ('imagen del matrimonio') had somehow changed in our society between 1978 and 2012 and 'legal culture is built not only upon literal, systemic, or originalistic interpretation of legal texts but also (…) by means of the observation of the legally relevant social reality'.[55]

By following the well-known 'living tree doctrine', the Spanish TC based its decision on the 'evolutive interpretation' of *marriage* and stated that the very concept of marriage had changed over the years.[56] In his dissenting opinion,[57] Justice Andrés Ollero (who is a legal philosopher) argued against the well-known Dworkinian distinction between concepts and conceptions.[58] This distinction is implicitly held by the TC, for constitutional concepts such as *marriage* might reflect multiple conceptions over the years. Consequently, Ollero J. stated that the only way to constitutionally accept homosexual marriage in the Spanish legal order was the amendment of Article 32(1) CE, according to the complex

[51] See Vakil (n 48) s III(C).

[52] See Richard Stacey, 'South Africa. The Siren Call of Constitutionally Confirming Interpretation: Statutory Validity at the Expense of Constitutional Values' in Klatt (n 7).

[53] See STC 198/2012, de 6 de noviembre, in particular para 6. On the impact of CCI on the same-sex marriage regulation in Brazil, see Arguelhes and de Lima (n 36) s III.

[54] The original text in Spanish ('El hombre y la mujer tienen derecho a contraer matrimonio con plena igualdad jurídica') is particularly clear about the exclusively heterosexual nature of marriage in 1978 and along the procedure before the TC nobody hesitated that art 32(1) CE defined 'marriage' as an heterosexual union of a man *with* a woman.

[55] STC 198/2012 para 9.

[56] ibid.

[57] See Judge Ollero's dissenting opinion on STC 198/2012, para 4.

[58] Judge Ollero used a definite description for Ronald Dworkin: 'An argument due to a prestigious expert on the Northamerican constitutional case law'.

constitutional amendment procedure.[59] Otherwise, TC would be *legislating*, *creating* new norms, replacing the (positive) Legislature. Again, the difference between interpretation and creation could be quite subtle, but its consequences may be far-reaching.

B. Preconstitutional Widowers and Postconstitutional Same-sex Marriages

Unlike the widower case, the evolutive interpretation of 'marriage' needs something more than logical and argumentative skills. In its decision, the TC accordingly explores how the conception of marriage had changed over the years.

Figure 2 Legally discursive possibility of the constitutional interpretation by the TC according to the living tree doctrine

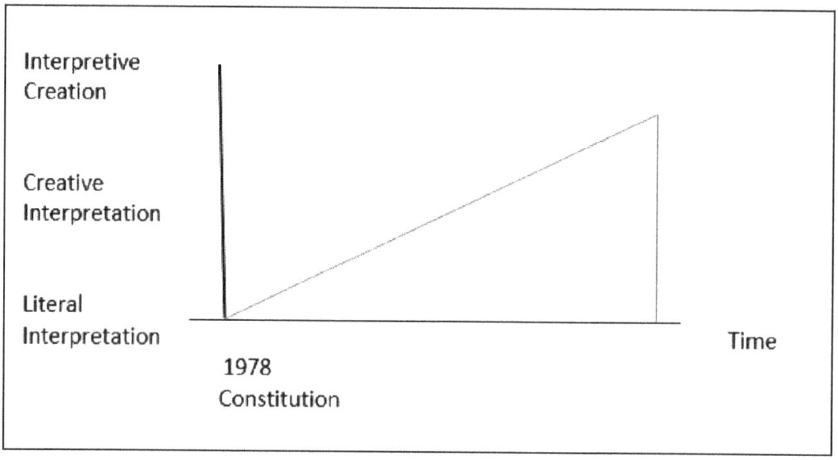

This sociological analysis becomes political when bereft of further empirical support. In fact, some critics have argued in political terms that TC delay in deciding the case was a political strategy because the more time went by, the more socially accepted same-sex marriages became, which increased the level of creative

[59] Art 167 CE reads as follows: '1. Bills on Constitutional amendment must be approved by a majority of three-fifths of the members of each House. If there is no agreement between the Houses, an effort to reach it shall be made by setting up a Joint Commission of Deputies and Senators, which shall submit a text to be voted on by the Congress and the Senate. 2. If approval is not obtained by means of the procedure outlined in the foregoing clause and provided that the text has been passed by an absolute majority of the members of the Senate, Congress may pass the amendment by a two-thirds vote in favour. 3. Once the amendment has been passed by the *Cortes Generales* (Parliament), it shall be submitted to ratification by referendum, if so requested by one tenth of the members of either House within fifteen days after its passage'.

interpretation, as Figure 2 suggests. Indeed, when TC becomes an interpreter of the social morality of the population, then the political dimension of TC arises. To some extent, this is precisely what constitutional courts have been required to do. After all, constitutional courts are distinctively legal-political bodies (*politische Akteure*) when they are asked to fullfil a 'coupling task' ('Kopplungsaufgabe') between law and politics.[60] This task has been successfully accomplished where constitutional courts have become particularly popular. Recently, the FCC has been described as an 'entgrenzte Gericht' ('court without borders'[61]). The borders that blur when constitutional courts fulfill their distinctive 'coupling task' are those between law and politics, law and morality, decision-making and legislation. Indeed, an 'isolated' Constitutional Court is aledgedly convenient because decentralised or 'diffuse' control (and interpretation) by any ordinary judge would amount to no control at all under the motto: 'fiat iustitia, pereat argumentum'.[62] Indeed, the consequences of such a situation would be even worse when any ordinary court performed CCI.

This might be true unless we consider that such a coupling task (between law and morality and between law and politics) is by no means an exclusive task of constitutional courts, but it is also performed to some extent by ordinary courts, particularly in constitutional states, because every legal reasoning is a special case of general practical reasoning, as Robert Alexy has famously stated.[63] If so, this might be an argument in favour of decentralised or diffuse constitutional control systems. As a result, the specific competence of constitutional courts is an argument in favour of the special case thesis, but the special case thesis can be an argument against some exclusive competences of constitutional courts on constitutional interpretation.

To sum up, under a constitutionalised legal order, we can regard CCI as the result of building up an *ad casum* normative (sub)system involving logical and hermeneutical operations. The logical aspect of constructive interpretation can be shown by using Alchourrón and Bulygin's normative systems theory. This might make a (quite subtle) difference between, say, creative interpretation of norms within the legal system (widowers case) and interpretive creation of norms (same-sex marriage case). Apparently, CCI by ordinary judges applies to the former, but TC's constitutional interpretation involving certain creation (coupling task between politics and law) is needed for the latter. In both cases, the differences seem too subtle.

[60] See eg Möllers, 'Legality, Legitimacy, and Legitimation of the Federal Constitutional Court' in Jeastedt et al (n 13) 143ff.

[61] ibid.

[62] Juan A García Amado, 'Interpretar, argumentar, decidir', in Faustino Gutiérrez-Alviz and Javier Martínez Lázaro (eds), *El juez y la cultura jurídica contemporánea. Vol. III: La función y los poderes del juez en una sociedad democrática* (Madrid, Consejo General del Poder Judicial, 2009) 123.

[63] Robert Alexy, 'The Special Case Thesis' (2008) 12/4 *Ratio Juris* 374, 374–84.

IV. Constitutionally Conforming Interpretation and Legalism

A. Constitutionally Conforming Interpretation and Judicial Referral

As stated, despite the fact that CCI is not *primarily* an interpretation of the Constitution, such a statutory interpretation always involves constitutional interpretation to some extent. What is more, if we take the CCI principle seriously, why should not every single statutory interpretation involve CCI after all? At this point, it is worth recalling the well-known Wróblewski's distinction between interpretation *sensu largo* and *sensu stricto*,[64] because the lack of attention to this distinction obscures the real scope of CCI in the routine activity of ordinary judges.

Sensu largo, interpretation is simply the activity (and its result) of assigning a meaning to a (legal) statement. *Sensu stricto*, interpretation is the activity and result of attributing meaning to a legal statement just *in hard cases*.[65] So, no matter how hard or easy a case may be, every CCI requires that ordinary judges perform constitutional interpretation[66] *sensu largo*. This happens even in the case that ordinary judges aim at avoiding (the responsibility for) CCI (*sensu stricto*) by bringing before the constitutional court a judicial referral (Spanish 'cuestión de constitucionalidad'[67]). A judicial referral is a request for clarification of constitutionality that judges *may* address to the TC, when a legal statement such as LS1 has to be applied and might be unconstitutional in a particular case:

> If a judicial body considers, in some action, that a regulation with the status of law which is applicable thereto and upon the validity of which the judgment depends, may be contrary to the Constitution, it *may* bring the matter before the Constitutional Court in the circumstances, manner, and subject to the consequences to be laid down by law, which shall in no case be suspensive (Article 163 CE, emphasis added).

Hence, CCI (*sensu largo*) paradoxically is the previous necessary step for ordinary judges to avoid CCI (*sensu stricto*) and defer this operation to the constitutional court.[68] This is a natural consequence of the fact that every single statutory

[64] Wróblewski adds a sense of interpretation (*sensu largissimo*) meaning the activity and result of attributing meaning to any cultural object (eg a sculpture, a picture, and a piece of rock on the floor of an ancient Greek temple).

[65] Unlike Interpretation *sensu largo* (which is always needed), interpretation *sensu stricto* is only needed in hard cases. Therefore, the old saying 'in claris non fit interpretatio' makes sense when it comes to *sensu stricto* interpretation (but not *sensu largo*). See Wróblewski, *Constitución y teoría general de la interpretación jurídica* (n 42) 21ff.

[66] Guastini, *Estudios sobre la interpretación jurídica* (n 21) 80.

[67] On the new *question prioritaire de constitutionnalité* in France, see Carpentier, 'Constitutionally Conforming Interpretation in France' (n 17) s II(A).

[68] This paradox takes place in the so-called 'avoidance canon' in the United States too. According to this canon, in the case of two potential interpretations, judges should take the one which does not

interpretation implicitly involves constitutional interpretation to some extent, for the Constitution pervades the meaning of every single norm of the legal system (ie the so-called *Austrahlungswirkung*). Let us recall that this very idea underlies the justification of CCI by the FCC: 'The Basic Law, too, is part of the comprehensive legal order, which must be understood as a totality of meaning and must underlie every interpretation of domestic law'.

Therefore, we need to qualify the term 'interpretation' in 'CCI' so as to understand the apparent contradictions that the application of CCI involves: (constitutionally) hard cases require CCI (*sensu stricto*), because *a routine* CCI (*sensu largo*) had previously shown that CCI (*sensu stricto*) is needed. In other words, CCI (*sensu largo*) is usually required and legitimate, but it only gets explicit in some cases (CCI *sensu stricto*). This certainly explains some perplexities, but it also shows how our *taking Constitutions seriously* blurs the difference between constitutional and non-constitutional interpretation. After all, in Gonçalo de Almeida Ribeiro's words, '(a)ll legal reasoning is, in a broad sense, constitutionally conformed'.[69]

To sum up, when a certain legal statement has at least two meanings, then ordinary judges must choose the interpretation that is in accordance to the Constitution (eg N1"), and reject the interpretation (eg N1'), that is not (CCI *sensu stricto*). As a consequence, statutes should not be declared invalid as long as CCI is possible, and judges should accordingly apply CCI in hard cases.

However, as stated, the Spanish legal system allows judges to bring a judicial referral before the constitutional court. In practice, in hard cases, judges can always defer CCI (*sensu stricto*) towards the TC, for they are allowed to do so when the result of the decision depends on the controversial provision (eg LS1) and they have doubts about its constitutionality. *A fortiori*, they are obliged to do so in the event that no potential interpretation of the norm is constitutionally conform.

B. Legalistic Resistence to Constitutionally Conforming Interpretation

Back to the widower case, LS1 (N1) can have at least two interpretations: N1' and N1". Thus, ordinary courts had had three available solutions:

i. *The legalistic decision* (made by ordinary courts and administrative bodies), ie applying N1' literally, which was constitutionally unacceptable in terms of Article 14 CE: no pension allowed to widowers.

involve constitutional interpretation. However, in Frederick Schauer's words, 'the avoidance is an illusion. In order to decide whether constitutional avoidance is appropriate, a court must decide and not avoid the constitutional question' (Schauer, 'Constitutional Avoidance As Constitutional Conformation: The Case of the United States' (n 38)).

[69] Gonçalo de Almeida Ribeiro, 'Portugal: The Conundrum of Constitutionally Conforming Interpretation' in Klatt (n 7), s II.

ii. CCI by ordinary judges, who should have applied N1" (constitutionally acceptable in terms of Article 14 CE): pension allowed to widowers.
iii. *The deferent solution*, ie bringing before the TC a judicial referral (*via* Article163 CE).

Now, since the CCI principle excludes (i), only solutions (ii) and (iii) look acceptable. In favour of (ii), the *legal-political justification* of CCI is based on a complex chain of principles allegedly justifying CCI: equality before the law, unity of the legal order, presupposition of legal norms constitutionality, *in dubbio pro legislatore*, and, above all, Constitution supremacy.[70] Specifically, the supremacy of the Constitution justifies that every judge applies the Constitution, and this is at the very core of what Carlos S Nino called 'Marshall's logic'. This 'logic' (famously underlying Marbury v. Madison) boils down in the reasoning sketched by Carlos S. Nino[71] as follows:

Premise 1	It is the Judiciary's duty to apply laws.
Premise 2	When two laws are contradictory, we can apply one and reject the other.
Premise 3	The Constitution is the supreme law and defines which other norms are laws.
Premise 4	The Constitution's supremacy entails that in the event of a conflict between the Constitution and a law enacted by the Congress, the latter ceases to be a valid law.
Premise 5	Denying premise 4 would mean that the Congress may modify the Constitution by enacting an ordinary law, and therefore the Constitution would no longer be operational to limit the Congress.
Premise 6	The Congress is limited by the Constitution.
Premise 7	If a norm is not valid, it does not have obligatory force.
Conclusion:	A law contrary to the Constitution ought not to be applied by the Judiciary.

'Marshall's logic' obviously underlies CCI in constitutional states, but, as stated, many ordinary judges usually *aim* at avoiding CCI by means of a judicial referral under a *key justification*: respect for democracy and legal certainty. This is relevant because very often CCI is not applied in Spain with full extension by ordinary judges. When applying CCI, they somehow *feel* like invading someone else's turf, and they usually exhibit a deferent attitude towards the TC.[72] Furthermore,

[70] Cabrales, *El principio de interpretación conforme en la justicia constitucional* (n 17) s 1.3.
[71] Carlos S Nino, 'Los fundamentos del control judicial de constitucionalidad' in *Fundamentos y Alcances del Control Judicial de Constitucionalidad* (Madrid, CEC, 1991) 100ff.
[72] See Xabier Arzoz Santisteban, 'Aproximación a la interpretación conforme como técnica de coordinación normativa' (n 3) 69.

ordinary judges are allowed to do so because, *in practice*, they can defer to the TC the responsibilitity of performing CCI. As stated, judges are *allowed* to ask about the constitutionality of a statute, except when no CCI of the statute is available, in which case asking the TC for a CCI is *compulsory*.[73] Since something compulsory is also something permitted, *in hard cases* (ie the relevant ones), Spanish judges may easily avoid CCI (*sensu stricto*) by deferring this task to the TC.

Certainly, the Spanish TC does not admit such a judicial referral in the absence of relevance. This means that TC only accepts judicial referrals if and only if the statute likely to be unconstitutional is relevant to the point of the specific case. And of course, it is when the statute is relevant for the decision that judges need CCI (*sensu stricto*). As a result, in practice, whenever a judicial body has doubts about the constitutionality of any statute, it may bring the judicial referral before the TC.[74] This circumstance displays three scenarios in Spain:[75]

i. *CCI*: In principle, judicial bodies can perform CCI in hard cases.
ii. *Permitted Judicial referral*: In case of *doubts* about which is the right CCI, they *may* request clarification before the TC.
iii. *Compulsory Judicial referral*: In the event that CCI is *impossible* because no potential interpretation of the norm is compatible with the Constitution, then it is *compulsory* for judicial bodies to request clarification of constitutionality before the TC.

In Xabier Arzoz's opinion, the reasons that explain the asymetry between the high legal value of CCI in theory and its limited use in judiciary practice (particularly in Spanish Administrative law practice) are twofold: strategic and institutional.

The strategic reason is, as stated, that, in general terms, judges feel *more comfortable* when using the judicial referral. The closely connected institutional reason that, at the same time, explains why judges avoid CCI is that judges *feel* that CCI involves a sort of interference of judges in other state bodies competences, namely the democratic legislator and the TC.[76] More specifically, judges feel that by reducing the content of a norm on constitutional grounds, CCI amounts to a partial declaration of unconstitutionality.[77] Indeed, inasmuch as ordinary courts could make material decisions on the constitutionality of statutes, somehow they would behave as 'little constitutional courts' – 'kleine Verfassungsgerichte', as Alexy[78] puts it – and every ordinary judge might 'become a "dominus" of the law,

[73] See arts 35ff Spanish Constitutional Court Organic Law (LOTC).

[74] See art 163 CE, very similar to art 100 German Constitution (GG).

[75] See Javier Díaz Revorio, *Las sentencias interpretativas del Tribunal Constitucional* (Valladolid, Lex Nova, 2001) 233.

[76] See Arzoz Santisteban, 'Aproximación a la interpretación conforme como técnica de coordinación normativa' (n 3) 92.

[77] ibid 95.

[78] Robert Alexy, 'Verfassungsrecht und einfaches Recht – Verfassungsgerichtbarkeit und Fachgerichtsbarkeit' in Alexy et al, *Veröffentlichungen der Vereinigung der Deutschen Staatsrechtsleher* (Berlin, de Gruyter, 2002) 29.

with the excuse of the Constitution'.[79] This would entail uncertainty (and even arbitrariness), because, in Sorrenti's words, we 'slowly go down a way that leads either to the cancellation of the legislative bases of the rule of law or the dissolution of law due to casuistry'.[80] However, such a conclusion sounds misleading, for uncertainty is precisely what CCI is meant to dispel. After all, certain *horror vacui* explains why CCI is required. Since gaps in law cause uncertainty (eg: what to do when widowers claim for a pension after 1978?) and it obviously takes time for Legislators to fill in the gaps as unconstitutional norms are declared invalid by TC, CCI might be the straightest and quickest relief to the thread of such a *horror vacui*.[81]

To sum up, in order to avoid CCI, Spanish judges have a justification (respect for democracy), an institutional instrument (judicial referral), and we have one probable explanation thereof: the legalistic legal culture of ordinary judges. At this point, Giussi Sorrenti raises a good question when she asks, 'Is it the fault of a cultural backwardness that the judges do not look up to the Constitution but still interpret according to the old rules of a legalistic formalism?'.[82] I think the answer in Spain is yes. After all, ordinary judges' reluctance to CCI is a question of mentality. A certain nostalgia for legalism and its underlying values[83] would explain judges' lack of commitment to CCI. CCI will not be applied to its full extent as long as a legalistic conception of the law application keeps pervading the activity of judges. At the end of the day, it is all about the 'software of legal culture'[84] and such a formalism reflects what Matthieu Carpentier names, *à la* Montesquieu, the 'mouthpiece ideology'.[85] As an epiphenomenon, CCI is a key notion to understand the evolution of our legal culture, by making explicit two problems, namely: the analytical problem of the nature of interpretation and the normative problem of the justification of the application of CCI by ordinary judges in states, where the constitutional control is specifically assigned to a constitutional court, such as the Spanish TC, the German FCC and other European 'isolated' constitutional courts following the Austrian model.

[79] Javier Jiménez Campo, 'Analogía "secundum constitutionem"' (1992) 13 *Revista del Centro de Estudios Constitucionales* 9, 12.

[80] Giusi Sorrenti, 'Corte costituzionale, giudici e interpretazione ovvero l'insostenibile leggerezza della legge' in Antonio Ruggeri (ed), *La ridefinizione della forma di governo attraverso la giurisprudenza costituzionale* (Napoli, Edizioni Scientifiche Italiane, 2006) 468ff, 494–96; *apud* Roberto Romboli, 'La interpretación de la ley a la luz de la Constitución. La llamada "interpretación conforme" en las relaciones entre la Corte Costituzionale y los jueces ordinarios en Italia' (2007) 60 *Derecho PUCP: Revista de la Facultad de Derecho* 123, 162.

[81] See Francisco Fernández Segado, 'Reflexiones en torno a la interpretación de la Constitución' in MacGregor (n 1) 518.

[82] Sorrenti, 'La interpretación conforme a la Constitución en el ordenamiento italiano: estado de la cuestión' (n 5) 12.

[83] Andrés Ollero, *La justicia en el escaparate* (Valencia, Tirant lo Blanch, 2022) 20ff.

[84] Jestaedt, 'The Karlsruhe Phenomenon. What Makes the Court What It Is' (n 13) 68.

[85] Carpentier, 'Constitutionally Conforming Interpretation in France' (n 17) s III(D). Carpentier refers to the well-known idea of the judge as the 'bouche de la loi'.

V. Conclusions and Consequences

Originally, CCI was meant to be a judicial restraining instrument that prevented judges from going beyond the limits of the wording expressing the democratic legislator's will. However, the evolution of CCI shows a certain detachment from the 'German approach' to CCI and its implicit linguistic essentialism. History tells us that a good deal of progress in legal thinking comes with the rejection of such language essencialism, which regards words as Platonic essences – it is tempting to recall the well-known episode of the *Gaii Institutiones*, when a judge dismissed the plaintiff's claim because he did not pronounce in court the words 'arbora' (trees) but 'viniae' (vineyards). Legalistic approaches usually ignore that CCI is not only a matter of words but real interpretation, which may involve creative interpretation and interpretive creation according to the legal co-text (widower case) and the social context (same-sex marriage case). As a result, the difference between constitutional interpretation and CCI tends to blur, as does the very justification of the concentrated control of constitutionality.

At this point, the epiphenomenon of CCI gives us the opportunity to think beyond this precise interpretative operation because it somehow shows that 'Marshall's logic' gets clumsy when constitutional control is assigned to a centralised constitutional court and ordinary judges have to perform CCI at the same time. Indeed, once we accept CCI and the underlying Marshall's logic to their full extent, we may wonder why we need a centralised, *isolated* constitutionality control by a constitutional court, given that every judge is required to develop constitutional interpretations. Furthermore, when the constitutional court and the ordinary judges are put on the same level by virtue of CCI, we run the risk that the specifics of each body's tasks can get overlooked and blurred. In other words, the charm of the Austrian model can vanish,[86] which is probably the case yet.

In Spain, the evolution from Franco's regime to the current constitutional regime has prompted the constitutionalisation of the legal system but not the full constitutionalisation of judges' (legalistic) culture. Maybe the very existence of a TC is in itself an obstacle to overcome ordinary judges' legalism implicit in the deference to TC, while the Spanish TC is playing an increasingly politicised role. Christoph Schönberger has outlined a circumstance that is worth mentioning here: 'The great success in exporting German constitutional law and constitutional review since the 1970s, extending from Spain to South Africa, was due not least of all to similarly complex relationships with a non-democratic, dictatorial past'.[87] Certainly, *in illo tempore*, an 'isolated' constitutional court separated from the rest of specialised judges had been a remedy against the legalistic worship of authority remaining among ordinary judges after the collapse of dictatorships.[88] Today,

[86] See eg Jestaedt (n 13) 46f.

[87] Christoph Schönberger, 'Karlsruhe. Notes on a Court' in Jestaedt et al, *The German Federal Constitutional Court* (n 13) 20f.

[88] Ollero, *La justicia en el escaparate* (n 83) 20ff.

such a worship of a non-democratic authority has been left behind. However, as stated, legalism still seems to stay alive among ordinary judges.[89] Almost fifty years after Franco's death, Spain is a full democracy that no longer needs to protect itself from ordinary judges' worship of the norms of a past non-democratic legal order, but it probably does need protection from the current overpolitisation of TC. If so, the very existence of an isolated constitutional court avoiding a fluent CCI by ordinary judges might be regarded as an obstacle to the full constitutionalisation of the Spanish legal order. If we additionally consider the increasing politisation of the TC, then the very legitimacy of the TC seems to be at stake.

Luis Prieto[90] has convincingly stressed that the Spanish Constitution should no longer be 'highjacked' by a body such as the TC. Prieto plainly argues that the current Spanish TC should dissappear and ordinary judges should assume control of constitutionality by following the above mentioned 'Marshall's logic'. Prieto's main argument is that concentrated constitutional control models, such as the Spanish TC or the German FCC, are 'foreign bodies' ('cuerpos extraños') in the current constitutional systems.[91] After all, the Kelsenian centralised model of constitutional control was born when Constitutions were merely formal and procedural and did not include contents such as fundamental and social rights, which are more abstract, vague, and controversial. In other words, in the past, constitutions used to point out *who* was allowed to make norms and *how* to make them, but not *which* norms should or should not be made or how to interpret them. The so-called 'Rematerialisierung des Verfassungsrechts' (the introduction of dense material contents, such as fundamental rights, in the Constitution) came later. As a result, particularly when a Kelsenian constitutional court is required to decide constitutional complaints due to the infringement of fundamental rights (*Urteilsverfassungsbeschwerde, recurso de amparo*), this body looks like a sort of foreign body ('cuerpo extraño') instilled in the very Kelsenian model.

Such a 'foreign body argument' takes to the extreme the principle of CCI and confirms that 'a constitutional State tends to be a Judiciary State',[92] while the increasing politisation of the TC announces the effective decay of this constitutional body. The Polish case is particularly revealing. In Mikolaj Barczentewicz and Marcin Matczak's opinion, the justification for the exclusive competence of the Constitutional Tribunal is rendered obsolete under the ongoing constitutional crisis, where CCI by ordinary judges works as a sort of remedy against the

[89] And not only in Spain. See eg, Eszter Bodnár, 'Hungary: Conflicts Over Competence' in Klatt (n 7), s IV(B), who provides us with some numbers, and Chiara Vallenti, 'Italy: Constitutionally Conforming Interpretation and Judicial Dialogue' in Klatt (n 7), s III.

[90] Luis Prieto, 'Presupuestos neoconstitucionalistas de la teoría de la argumentación jurídica' in Gascón (ed), *Argumentación jurídica* (n 22) 23, 28.

[91] Luis Prieto, *El constitucionalismo de los derechos. Ensayos de filosofía jurídica* (Madrid, Trotta, 2013) 170; and Marina Gascón, 'La justicia constitucional: Entre legislación y jurisdicción' (1994) 41 *Revista Española de Derecho Constitucional* 63, 63–87.

[92] Sorrenti, 'La interpretación conforme a la Constitución en el ordenamiento italiano: estado de la cuestión' (n 5) 18.

'spectre of a dysfunctional Constitutional Tribunal'.[93] Meanwhile, in Germany, some are suggesting the German FCC to 'practise one of the most difficult arts: the art of retreat'.[94] Similary, Prieto's criticism naturally leads in Spain to Baltasar Gracián's good piece of advice, which might well be addressed to the Spanish TC: 'Do not wait till you are a sinking sun'[95] ('No esperar a ser sol que se pone').

[93] Mikolaj Barczentewicz and Marcin Matczak, 'Poland: Constitutionally Conforming Interpretation in Times of Constitutional Crisis' in Klatt (n 7) s IV.

[94] Hans M Enzensberger, 'Die Helden des Rückzugs. Brouillon zu einer politischen Moral der Macht' (1989) 9 *Frankfurter Allgemeine Zeitung*, *apud* Schönberger (n 87) 31.

[95] Baltasar Gracián, *The Art of Worldly Wisdom* (Joseph Jacobs tr, London, MacMillan, 1904) 63.

8

What is the 'Doomsday Weapon' – Annulment or Interpretation? A Critical Perspective on Constitutionally Conforming Interpretation in Israel

HILLEL SOMMER AND YANIV ROZNAI*

I. Introduction

There is a general accepted method in constitutional review according to which every interpretive effort must be made to reconcile laws with protected constitutional rights and principles before such law is held unconstitutional. This is the German method of 'interpretation in conformity with the Constitution' (*Verfassungskonforme Auslegung*), that exists one way or another in different jurisdictions.[1] In the US, the famous *Ashwander* case provided various principles for a restraint judicial review, called the 'Avoidance Doctrine'.[2] The relevant principles for our matter are those of:

> 4. The Court will not pass upon a constitutional question [...] if there is also present some other ground upon which the case may be disposed of [...] Thus, if a case can be decided on either of two grounds, one involving a constitutional question, the other a question of statutory construction or general law, the Court will decide only the latter.[3]

* The authors would like to thank Shani Abodi and Emanuel Broza for extremely useful research assistance.

[1] See Matthias Klatt (ed), *Constitutionally Conforming Interpretation – Comparative Perspectives, Volume 1: National Reports* (Oxford, Hart Publishing, 2023).

[2] *Ashwander v Tennessee Valley Authority*, 297 U.S. 288 (1936).

[3] ibid 347.

And:

> 7. When the validity of an act of the Congress is drawn in question, and even if a serious doubt of constitutionality is raised, it is a cardinal principle that this Court will first ascertain whether a construction of the statute is fairly possible by which the question may be avoided.[4]

Using such an interpretive method of 'constitutional avoidance',[5] courts may choose the interpretation of a law that is compatible with the constitution rather than annulling the legislation under review. This is another 'line of defence' of the constitution, which avoids the remedy of annulment.[6]

However, we critically argue that often, interpretation in contrast with the explicit statutory text and/or legislative intent, even if conforming with the constitution, may be more violative of separation of powers. In other words, from the perspective of the principle of separation of powers, in certain cases it is preferable for the court to invalidate unconstitutional laws rather than to interpret them in accordance with the constitution, if such interpretation amounts to re-writing the law. Accordingly, interpretation is not always the more 'conservative' judicial method and may be more 'activist' than striking down legislation, as paradoxical as it may sound.

In order to support our claim, this chapter uses Israel as an example. Allegedly, constitutionally conforming interpretation (CCI) is an accepted doctrine in Israeli jurisprudence. Before the 'constitutional revolution', the court used the doctrine in the form of 'rights conforming interpretation' to justify the broadening of rights protection without constitutional supremacy. After the constitutional revolution, the court expanded the doctrine, using the form of 'basic laws conforming interpretation'. Israeli courts have held that 'constitutional review – the "doomsday weapon" shall be a last resort and used only when all other means have failed.'[7] Even at the constitutional level, the interpretation of basic laws is subject to conforming interpretation, this time to the fundamental values of the state as a Jewish and Democratic state and seeking harmony between the various basic laws. However, as we shall argue, conforming interpretation is not always a symbol of judicial restraint but rather of judicial activism. In other words, sometimes invalidation of a statute is less intrusive than interpretation that is contrary to the explicit wording

[4] ibid 348.

[5] On the resemblance of this American 'avoidance' practice to the constitutional conforming principle, see Frederick Schauer, 'United States. Constitutional Avoidance as Constitutional Conformation' in Klatt (n 1) 267–81.

[6] Ernst Livneh, 'Basic Laws and Ordinary Legislation' (1978) 13 *Israel Law Review* 251, 255.

[7] HCJ 3267/97 *Rubinstein v Minister of Defence*, PD 52(2), 441, 524 (1988) ('The Court circumvents possible delegation problems by making a narrow interpretation of statutory language, thus using the delegation doctrine as an Ashwander like principle. [...] The Courts in Germany adopted a similar approach. [...] We, too, have followed this approach, incorporating the law established in *Ashwander v Tennessee Valley Authority* (1936). Accordingly, all legitimate interpretative efforts must be made to avoid a law's invalidation.'). The English translation is available at versa.cardozo.yu.edu/opinions/rubinstein-v-minister-defense. For a critical overview of the application of this doctrine in Israel, see also Gideon Sapir, 'The Presumption of Conformity – Outlines of Its Character' (unpublished manuscript, on file with authors, 2025) (Hebrew).

of the statute and the clear intent of the legislature. In this chapter we illustrate this argument by focusing on the Israeli case study.

This chapter proceeds as follows. Section II provides a brief history of Israeli constitutional law which is necessary to place the constitutionally conforming doctrine in context, and describes how the courts established and used the doctrine. Sections III and IV describe the development of the doctrine in Israeli case law before and after the 'constitutional revolution' of the 1990s. Section III describes how the Israeli Supreme Court used the principle of 'CCI' prior to the constitutional revolution, and section IV describes the more extensive use of doctrine as part of the constitutional revolution. Section V takes the doctrine to a specific Israeli expansion – using it at the constitutional level, in the context of unconstitutional constitutional amendment challenges. Recent Israeli case law had to consider that issue and whether the doctrine could be used to resolve it. In section VI we argue and demonstrate that often, using the doctrine with an interpretation of the laws in question that is completely contradictory to the legislature's intent or to the text, may be more intrusive in nature than invaliding the statute.

II. A Brief History of Israeli Constitutional Law

Israel's constitutional status is quite unique. For historical and political reasons, Israel does not have one document entitled 'Constitution' or 'Bill of Rights' as most countries do. Israel does have a series of so called 'basic laws' which regulate many (but not all) matters of a constitutional nature. The Israeli Supreme Court held that these basic laws are superior to ordinary laws and allow judicial review of The Knesset's (Israeli Parliament) ordinary legislation in case of conflict of such legislation with the basic laws. This section provides a brief summary of the structure of Israeli constitutional law, essential for a better understanding of the way the courts established and used the principle of CCI.

Israel was established in 1948, following United Nations General Assembly Resolution 181.[8] That resolution held, with respect to the Jewish and the Arab states it aimed to form, that 'The Constituent Assembly of each State shall draft a democratic constitution for its State […]'. The resolution further provided for the inclusion of specific provisions in the future constitution of the two states. These dictated provisions included those regarding the form of government,[9] and a short list of civil rights to be guaranteed to all persons.[10]

[8] G.A. Res. 181 (II) (Nov. 29, 1947), available at www.gov.il/en/Departments/General/un-general-assembly-resolution-181.

[9] Establishing a legislative body elected by universal suffrage and by secret ballot on the basis of proportional representation, and an executive body responsible to the legislature.

[10] The resolution required 'Guaranteeing to all persons equal and non-discriminatory rights in civil, political, economic and religious matters and the enjoyment of human rights and fundamental freedoms, including freedom of religion, language, speech and publication, education, assembly and

Israel's Declaration of Independence[11] followed Resolution 181 so as to rely on the international recognition. The Declaration thus anticipated a formal constitution-making process, and stated that a constituent assembly was to be elected shortly with the goal of adopting a constitution for the new state. The Declaration also established temporary authorities (legislative and executive) and regarding human rights, held that:

> The State of Israel [...] will foster the development of the country for the benefit of all its inhabitants; it will be based on freedom, justice and peace as envisaged by the prophets of Israel; it will ensure complete equality of social and political rights to all its inhabitants irrespective of religion, race or sex; it will guarantee freedom of religion, conscience, language, education and culture; it will safeguard the Holy Places of all religions; and it will be faithful to the principles of the Charter of the United Nations.

A Constituent Assembly was indeed elected.[12] But for political and historical reasons the 'original intent' of creating a constitution never fully materialised.[13] Soon after its formation, on 16 February 1949, the Constituent Assembly – established to promulgate Israel's constitution – declared itself Israel's legislature by enacting the Transition Law, which provided that the legislative body shall be named 'the Knesset' and the Constituent Assembly shall be called 'the First Knesset'. That decision meant that the Constituent Assembly assumed dual capacity – being the legislative and constitutive body in one. That dual capacity has been held by the Israeli parliament until now.

In 1950, it became clear that because of disagreements over core values, the prospect of reaching a widely-acceptable constitution was not feasible in the near

association; Preserving freedom of transit and visit for all residents and citizens of the other State in Palestine and the City of Jerusalem, subject to considerations of national security, provided that each State shall control residence within its borders.'

[11] Formally entitled The Declaration of The Establishment of The State of Israel, available at www.gov.il/en/Departments/General/declaration-of-establishment-state-of-israel. On the history of the declaration, see Yoram Shachar, 'Jefferson Goes East: The American Origins of the Israeli Declaration of Independence' (2009) 10 *Theoretical Inquires in Law* 589.

[12] The Elections were held on 25 January 1959, even though the Declaration of Independence called for the elections to be no later than 1 October 1948. The elections were delayed because of the war of independence caused by the rejection by the Arab states surrounding Israel of the two-state solution envisioned by Resolution 181.

[13] For a more detailed account, see Nir Kedar, *David Ben-Gurion and the Foundation of Israeli Democracy* (Bloomington, Indiana University Press, 2021); Daphne Barak-Erez, 'From an Unwritten to a Written Constitution: The Israeli Challenge in American Perspective' (1995) 26 *Columbia Human Right Law Review* 309, 312; Amos Shapira, 'Why Israel Has No Constitution, but Should, and Likely Will, Have One' (1993) 37 *St. Louis University Law Journal* 283, 285; Tamar Hostovsky Brandes, 'Israel's Legal System – Institutions, Principles and Challenges' in Guy Ben-Porat et al (eds), *Routledge Handbook on Contemporary Israel* (London, Routledge, 2022) and the Knesset's own account 'The Knesset as a constitutive authority: Constitution and basic laws', available at main.knesset.gov.il/EN/activity/pages/BasicLawsAndConstitution.aspx.

future.[14] The Knesset subsequently adopted a resolution,[15] which abandoned, at least temporarily, the effort to reach a single-document constitution. Instead, the Knesset decided to enact separate 'Basic Laws'. Each of these would arrange a different constitutional subject and be enacted as a separate act of Parliament in its capacity as the Constituent Authority. The Knesset decided that upon the future completion of the process, all Basic Laws would be combined into a single-document Constitution.[16]

Since 1950 the Knesset has enacted 13 Basic Laws,[17] yet until 1992 all Basic Laws were structural in nature – regulating the branches of government and other State institutions.[18] Basic Laws protecting civil rights were not enacted until 1992, primarily because it was hard to overcome the wide differences of opinions on human rights issues in the Israeli polity.

The absence of a written constitution or bill of rights did not prevent the young Israeli Supreme Court from protecting civil rights. The Court declared and strongly protected by way of case law most civil and human rights usually stated in written constitutions.[19] The freedom of expression, freedom of movement, freedom of religion, equality and many other rights were recognised as fundamental rights, and enforced by the Israeli Court. In the absence of a written constitution and without any statutory authority to do so,[20] the Court found the legal basis for upholding these rights as arising from the 'nature of Israel as a freedom-seeking democratic state'.[21] As one commentator notes, CCI is an important addition to

[14] See Gary Jeffrey Jacobsohn, *Apple of Gold: Constitutionalism in Israel and the United States* (New Jersey, Princeton University Press, 1993) 3–18.

[15] The 'Harari Resolution', adopted 13 June 1950: 'The First Knesset charges the Constitution, Legislative and Judicial Committee [of the Knesset] with the duty to prepare a draft Constitution for the State. The Constitution will be comprised of several Chapters, and each of the said Chapters shall in itself constitute a Basic Law. Each of the several chapters shall be brought before the Knesset as soon as the said Committee completes its work and all Chapters (already adopted) shall form the State's Constitution.' Cited in Eliahu Likhovski, 'Can the Knesset Adopt a Constitution that Will Be the Supreme Law of the Land?' (1969) *Israel Law Review* 61, 63.

[16] See Suzie Navot, *Constitutional Law in Israel*, 2nd edn (Philadelphia, Wolters Kluwer, 2016) 21–23, 35–38. On the Israeli incremental constitution-making, see also Hanna Lerner, *Making Constitutions in Deeply Divided Societies* (Cambridge, Cambridge University Press, 2011) 51–108.

[17] For a list of the Basic Laws, summaries and full text in English see main.knesset.gov.il/EN/activity/Pages/BasicLaws.aspx.

[18] The structural Basic Laws included Basic Law: The Knesset; Basic Law: Israel Lands; Basic Law: The President of the State; Basic Law: The Government; Basic Law: The State Economy; Basic Law: The Army; Basic Law: Jerusalem, the Capital of Israel; Basic Law: The Judiciary; and Basic Law: The State Comptroller. In 2014, the Knesset added another structural basic law – Basic Law: Referendum. In 2018 the Knesset passed Basic Law: Israel the Nation State of the Jewish People, discussed in s V below.

[19] Amos Shapira, 'The Status of Fundamental Individual Rights in the Absence of a Written Constitution' (1974) 9 *Israel Law Review* 497; Asher Maoz, 'Defending Civil Liberties Without A Constitution – The Israeli Experience' (1987) 16 *Melbourne University Law Review* 815.

[20] Initially the Supreme Court held that the Declaration of Independence had no binding legal authority. For a critical assessment, see Michal Tamir, 'The Declaration of Independence as a Transitional Constitution: The Case of Israel' (2016) 8(1) *Middle East Law and Governance* 57.

[21] HCJ 25/53, *Kol Ha'am Ltd. v Minister of the Interior*, 7(1) PD 165 (1953), English translation available at versa.cardozo.yu.edu/opinions/kol-haam-co-ltd-v-minister-interior; HCJ 243/62 *Film Studios Israel v Levi Geri*, 16 PD 2407 (1962).

the contribution of the Israeli Supreme Court to the creation of human rights in Israel, as the Supreme Court:

> [N]ot only developed the norm that such basic values exist, but also developed the principle that statutes should be interpreted to avoid impairing these values. The Court reads statutes in such a way as not to violate the rights it has recognized. The Court also uses the values when reviewing the validity of administrative actions. Administrative actions that violate the basic values are held invalid.[22]

In 1992 the Knesset started discussing several Basic Laws bills relating to civil rights. Two of these bills – Basic Law: Human Dignity and Liberty[23] and Basic Law: Freedom of Vocation[24] passed and became Basic Laws. Basic Law: Human Dignity and Liberty lists a series of enumerated constitutional rights, which include the protection of life, physical integrity and most important for our current discussion – human dignity (Articles 2 and 4), the protection of property (Article 3), personal liberty,[25] (Article 5) the external freedom of movement (Article 6) and the right of privacy (Article 7).

Article 8 of Basic Law: Human Dignity and Liberty, often referred to as the Limitation Clause, allows the violation of rights 'under this Basic Law' only by 'a law befitting the values of the State of Israel, enacted for a proper purpose and to an extent no greater than is required.'[26] This section served the Supreme Court shortly thereafter in 1995, to hand down the Israeli equivalent of *Marbury v Madison*[27] – the *Bank Hamizrahi* case.[28] In *Bank Hamizrahi* the Court held that the two Basic Laws of 1992 are constitutional, in the sense that no ordinary legislation can contradict or limit the rights enumerated in them except to the extent permitted by them, most notably in the aforementioned Article 8. In this way the Court interpreted that it has the power of constitutional review, ie the power to strike

[22] Marcia Gelpe, 'Constraints on Supreme Court Authority in Israel and the United States: Phenomenal Cosmic Powers; Itty Bitty Living Space' (1999) 13 *Emory International Law Review* 493, 508; see also Barak-Erez (n 13).

[23] Basic Law: Human Dignity and Liberty.

[24] Basic Law: Freedom of Vocation. This Basic Law is often referred to as Basic Law: Freedom of Occupation. Given the current political situation in the Middle-East, we prefer the name 'Freedom of Vocation'.

[25] 'Personal liberty' is probably to be interpreted only in the physical sense, as the law reads: 'There shall be no deprivation or restriction of the liberty of a person by imprisonment, arrest, extradition or otherwise.' Basic Law: Human Dignity and Liberty.

[26] See Navot (n 16) 217–18. A similar provision is included in art 4 of Basic Law: Freedom of Vocation.

[27] *Marbury v Madison*, 5 U.S. 137 (1803). This is the classic American case announcing that the Supreme Court has the power of judicial-constitutional review. See Yoram Rabin and Arnon Gutfeld, 'Marbury v. Madison and Its Impact on Israeli Constitutional Law' (2007) 15(2) *University of Miami International Law and Comparative Law Review* 303.

[28] CA 6821/93, *United Bank Mizrahi v Migdal*, 49(4) PD 221 (1995). For a detailed description of the case, see Barak Cohen, 'Empowering Constitutionalism with Text from an Israeli Perspective' (2003) 18 *American University International Law Review* 585, 641–48; Suzie Navot, 'Mizrahi Bank Case (Isr)' in *Max Planck Encyclopedia of Comparative Constitutional Law*, available at oxcon.ouplaw.com/view/10.1093/law-mpeccol/law-mpeccol-e597?rskey=9d8OP8andresult=32andprd=MPECCOL.

down a statute which infringes a right included in Basic Law: Human Dignity and Freedom if that statute does not hold to the standards of Article 8.[29]

Since *Bank Hamizrahi*, in 30 years, the Israeli Supreme Court has declared 24 Knesset Statutes partially unconstitutional and thus invalid.[30] This drew sharp criticism from politicians, one result being that the Knesset has slowed down the enactment of additional Basic Laws.[31] As a result, several very important rights have not yet been incorporated into Basic Laws. These include freedom of expression, the freedom of association, freedom of religion and from religion, and the principle of equal protection (the right to equality). The practical solution, once again, was court activism, resulting in still more controversy.

In a series of cases since 1994, the Supreme Court has used the protection of human dignity in Basic Law: Human Dignity and Liberty as a springboard for upholding other civil rights normally found in other bills of rights but not included in that basic law. A simplified explanation of the general form of these cases is this: one cannot have human dignity to its fullest without having freedom of expression/equal protection etc, hence the right to human dignity includes these non-enumerated rights.[32] In this manner, the Supreme Court may invalidate a statute for unduly infringing a right which was not elevated to constitutional status in the slow piecemeal legislative process, simply by viewing this right as a part of human dignity. Thus, the right to dignity, a right with very little presence in the US legal system,[33] became the cornerstone of the Israeli partial bill of rights. Interpreted broadly, it became a major tool for Israeli judicial review of legislation and administrative actions.[34]

[29] For further analysis, see generally Joshua Segev, 'Who Needs a Constitution – In Defense of the Non-Decision Constitution-Making Tactic in Israel' (2006–2007) 70 *Albany Law Review* 409; Aharon Barak, 'A Constitutional Revolution: Israel's Basic Laws' (1993) 4 *Constitutional Forum* 83; Gideon Sapir, *The Israeli Constitution: From Evolution to Revolution* (Oxford, Oxford University Press, 2018).

[30] See eg HCJ 1715/97 *Association of Investment Managers in Israel v Minister of Treasury* 41(4) PD 367 (1997); HCJ 6055/95 *Zemach v Minister of Defense* 43(5) PD 241 (1999); HCJ 1030/99 *Oron v Speaker of the Knesset* 56(3) PD 640 (2002). A Magistrates' (first tier) Court declared another statutory section unconstitutional, holding that any court in Israel has the power to do so. CrimC (TA) 4696/01 *State of Israel v Hendelman, PM* (unpublished, 2003). See also Guy Lurie and Yuval Shany, 'Invalidations of Laws in Israel in a Comparative Perspective' (2019) 49 *Israel Yearbook on Human Rights* 261.

[31] In 2003, the Knesset's Law, Constitution, and Justice Commission launched an effort to complete the constitution 'by a wide consensus' that did not succeed. The only exceptions were the Basic Law: Referendum, which was passed in 2014 and Basic Law: Israel the Nation State of the Jewish People passed in 2018.

[32] Gary J Jacobsohn and Yaniv Roznai, *Constitutional Revolution* (New Haven, Yale University Press, 2020) 208–11. For a broader description and analysis, see Tamar Hostovsky Brandes, 'Human Dignity as a Central Pillar in Constitutional Rights Jurisprudence in Israel: Definitions and Parameters' in Gideon Sapir, Daphne Barak-Erez and Aharon Barak (eds), *Israeli Constitutional Law in the Making* (Oxford, Hart Publishing, 2013) 267, 269–83; and Izhak Englard, 'Human Dignity: From Antiquity to Modern Israel's Constitutional Framework' (2000) 21 *Cardozo Law Review* 1903, 1925.

[33] On human dignity and US law, see eg Vicki C Jackson, 'Constitutional Dialogue and Human Dignity: States and Transnational Constitutional Discourse' (2004) 65 *Montana Law Review* 15; Rex D Glensy, 'The Right to Dignity' (2011) 43 *Columbia Human Rights Law Review* 65; and Maxine D Goodman, 'Human Dignity in Supreme Court Constitutional Jurisprudence' (2006) 84 *Nebraska Law Review* 740, 780.

[34] See Aharon Barak, *Human Dignity – The Constitutional Value and the Constitutional Right* (Cambridge, Cambridge University Press, 2015) 156–83.

III. Constitutionally Conforming Interpretation Prior to the Constitutional Revolution

This section describes the ways in which the Israeli Supreme Court used the principle of CCI prior to the Constitutional Revolution of the 1990s.

As described in the previous chapter, during this period human rights were not based on a constitution or even basic laws. It was the Supreme Court which advanced human rights upon appropriate cases. CCI was then used by choosing statutory interpretations that would broaden the scope of a human rights and limit the State's ability to infringe on them.

Aharon Barak, who was both an influential Justice (and then President) of the Israeli Supreme Court and a prolifc academic writer, wrote in his monumental treatise on interpretation: 'The Presumption is that every piece of legislation seeks to advance human rights and does not seek to infringe on them [...] Out of two possible interpretations, the choice should be that interpretation that upholds human and civil rights'.[35] One application of the rule was to favour interpretations that reduce the infringement on civil rights. In one case the Supreme Court held: 'When the authority has a material violation of a basic right of a citizen in a free society, we will not hesitate to hold in favour of the interpretation that reduces the damage to civil rights, because the presumption is that the legislator respects these rights.'[36]

A significant case in that respect is *Kol Ha'Am v Minister of the Interior*,[37] in which the Court held that freedom of speech could be derived (in the absence of a constitution or even legislation) from the very nature of the state as a democratic state, since freedom of speech is an inherent feature of democracy.[38] The Supreme Court went on to interpret a statute explicitly limiting freedom of speech in a very liberal interpretation that would protect the newly-declared right further.[39]

In the *Kol Ha'Am* case, the Court reviewed an order by the Minister of the Interior suspending the publication of two newspapers associated with the opposition's communist party for 10 and 15 days, respectively. The Minister (which inherited the authority of the British Mandate High Commissioner) had exercised his authority derived from the Press Ordinance, according to which the High Commissioner may suspend the publication of a newspaper 'if any matter

[35] Aharon Barak, *Interpretation in Law, Vol. II Statutory Interpretation* (Jerusalem, Nevo Publishing, 1993) 553.

[36] HCJ 124/70 *Shemesh v the Registrar of Companies*, PD 25(1) 505, 513 (1971).

[37] HCJ 73/53 *Kol Ha'Am v Minister of the Interior*, PD7 871(1953) English translation available at versa.cardozo.yu.edu/opinions/kol-haam-co-ltd-v-minister-interior and at supremedecisions.court.gov.il/Home/Download?path=EnglishVerdicts%5C53%5C730%5C000%5CZ01&fileName=53000730_Z01.txt&type=4.

[38] ibid; see Daniel J Rothstein, 'Adjudication of Freedom of Expression Cases under Israel's Unwritten Constitution' (1985) 18 *Cornell International Law Journal* 247, 261–72.

[39] HCJ 73/53 (n 37); see also Stephen Goldstein, 'Protection of Human Rights by Judges: The Israeli Experience' (1994) 38 *Saint Louis University Law Journal* 605, 611.

appearing in a newspaper is, in the opinion of the High Commissioner in Council, likely to endanger the public peace ….'[40]

The High Court of Justice was well aware of the precedential importance of the case.[41]

Accepting that the 'right to freedom of expression is not an absolute and unlimited right, but a relative right', the Court had to interpret what is the standard that would be 'likely to endanger the public peace', ie which degree of behaviour would justify the suspension of the newspapers.

The Court considered two possible approaches:

> According to one approach it is sufficient, in order to satisfy the condition stated in the section in question that the publication reveals only a tendency – even a slight or remote tendency – in the direction of one of the consequences that we included in the notion, "endangers the public peace"; while according to the other approach, the Minister of Interior must be convinced beforehand that there has been created, having regard to the circumstances in which it takes place, a link between the publication and the possibility of one of the said consequences occurring, which must lead to the inference that the occurrence of that consequence is probable.

The Court proceeded to state that Israel 'is indeed a state founded on democracy' and 'a freedom-loving State.' Despite previous case law that held that Israel's Declaration of Independence 'does not consist of any constitutional law laying down in first any rule regarding the maintaining or repeal of any ordinances or laws',[42] the Court held that insofar as it 'expresses the vision of the people and its credo […] we are bound to pay attention to the matters set forth in it when we come to interpret and give meaning to the laws of the State'.

The Court then concluded that this analysis leads to the conclusion 'that we must interpret the term "likely", when we read it together with the other matters stated in section 19(2)(a), in the sense of "probability" rather than in the spirit of the view which favours the doctrine of the "bad tendency" and "indirect causation"'. Bottom line: The authority of the Minister of Interior was severely limited by CCI.

Another application of the CCI rule was established in the area of delegated (or secondary) legislation. In *Mitrani v Minister of Transportation*,[43] the Minister exercised his authority to regulate automobiles' annual inspection to hold that only the car's owner or a licensed carshop worker may bring the car for inspection. The purpose of the regulation was to eliminate the 'service' of middlemen specialising in getting the cars to pass inspection even if they should not have. The purpose

[40] Section 19(2)(a) of the Press Ordinance.

[41] Simon Agranat J: 'From time to time, a case reaches this court which raises some fundamental problem, demanding the reconsideration of ancient and well-worn principles. The two cases in question here belong to that group.'

[42] For a background on Israel's declaration of independence see Suzie Navot, *The Constitution of Israel – A Contextual Analysis* (Oxford, Hart Publishing, 2014) 4–6, 12–15; Tamir (n 20).

[43] HCJ 337/81 *Mitrani v Minister of Transport*, PD 37(3) 337 (1983).

was to increase car safety, since the middlemen were considered detrimental to the inspection's purpose.

The middlemen petitioned to the High Court of Justice since the new regulation practically put them out of work.

The Court held the regulation illegal despite its important purpose because the statute granting the Minister's authority to regulate the annual inspection did not explicitly authorise the Minister to violate the freedom of vocation. The Court held that 'as a rule, a law will not be construed as violating or as granting power to violate the freedom of vocation unless it is explicitly determined therein.' The Court added that 'authorization for this purpose, means express authorization, and for my part, I refer exclusively to a case in which the primary legislator states clearly and expressly that he authorizes the secondary legislator to enact regulations that establish prohibitions or restrictions on occupation in a particular profession.'

The Mitrani Court again applied CCI with no written constitution and with respect to human rights which were developed by the Supreme Court.

However, until the constitutional revolution of the 1990s, the court was clear that CCI has its limits: the principle will not be used to overcome a law which explicitly and unequivocally limits human rights. The Court stated that 'when there is an explicit legal instruction of the Knesset that leaves no room for doubt, it must be followed, even if it is incompatible with the principles of the Declaration of Independence.'[44]

A special place was given to equality-conforming interpretations. Again, until the constitutional revolution of the 1990s the general right to equality was not founded in any basic law.[45] But given the Court's view on the importance of the right to equality, the Court used the conforming interpretation principle in many cases in varied fields. For example, in tax appeals the Court favoured interpretations that would increase equality between different taxpayers.[46] In a tort case, the Court held that immunity provisions need to be interpreted narrowly, again to favour equality.[47]

So, without a constitution, and with the Court developing a judicial bill of rights, before the constitutional revolution, the Court's approach was 'rights conforming interpretation'. This was developed to ensure a better protection of rights not in order to avoid striking down laws – because the Court lacked the authority to invalidate Knesset's legislation. Following the constitutional revolution in the mid-1990s, this method became similar to the CCI method.

[44] CA 450/70, *Rogozinsky v The State of Israel*, PD 26(1) 129 (1971). See Gideon Sapir, 'Constitutional Revolutions: Israel as a Case-Study' (2009) 5(4) *International Journal of Law in Context* 355.

[45] At that time only specific areas of equality were enacted into ordinary legislation. These include a prohibition to discriminate in the area of labour law, and gender equality. Basic Law: the Knesset includes a provision that required equality in elections.

[46] CA 527/76 *Kuperberg v Tax Collector Haifa*, PD 31(2) 138 (1977).

[47] CA 437/65 *Maurer v Regional Council High Gallilee*, PD 20(3) 645 (1966).

IV. Interpretation in Accordance with the Basic Laws after the Constitutional Revolution

Already in the famous *Bank Hamizrahi* case, in which the Supreme Court recognised its judicial review power, President Shamgar referred to the abovementioned *Ashwander* rules that have been shaped to serve the courts when deciding upon the invalidity of legislation on constitutional grounds in order to 'examine claims of unconstitutionality with caution and restraint.' President Shamgar noted that 'the fundamental approach expressed in the rules, and the spirit emerging from them are worthy of attention and thought, because the experience gathered in other places in the area under discussion here can assist us.'[48] As we shall demonstrate, the Israeli Supreme Court has generally taken this approach, but not always.[49]

In his book on constitutional interpretation, published in 1994, after the enactment of the two basic laws on human rights in 1992, Aharon Barak explained the aspiration for a normative harmony. Interpreting laws according to the constitution, he wrote, means the interpretation of laws in a manner that would be compatible with the constitution and not contradict it. So, between two possible interpretations, one has to choose the interpretation that results in an accordance between the law and the constitution and not the interpretation that results in a conflict resulting in an unconstitutional law. According to Barak, this conception is derived from the desire to ensure a normative harmony in the legal system. An interpretation that leads to a contrast between the constitution and laws creates an undesirable disharmony, hence the interpreter should aspire to make the laws conform with the constitution.[50]

Elsewhere, Barak explained that this rule of interpretation is not a constitutional remedy but rather part of the ordinary rules for statutory interpretation. It applies to all laws and not only to laws that do not correspond with the limitations of the constitution. In other words, this interpretive rule does not necessitate a judicial ruling that the law violates a constitutional right not in according with the limitation clause and is thus unconstitutional; on the contrary, this interpretation in accordance with the basic laws is meant to avoid the unconstitutionality of the law and the need to declare it as unconstitutional and void.[51]

The use of this method by the Court may be exemplified by various important constitutional cases, for example, by the *Zandberg v Broadcasting Authority* case, shortly after the constitutional revolution.[52] This case followed a series of court cases holding that the Broadcasting Authority charged citizens an excessive fee compared with the legal fee. Following this determination, the Knesset enacted

[48] CA 6821/93 (n 28), paras 88–90.

[49] Hillel Sommer, 'In Favor of Judicial Restraint in Constitutional Cases' (2012) 14 *IDC Law Review* (2012) 155, 178–80.

[50] Aahron Barak, *Constitutional Interpretation* (Jerusalem, Nevo Publishing, 1994) 116–17.

[51] Aharon Barak, 'On the Theory of Constitutional Remedies' (2017) 10 *Law and Business* 301, 311.

[52] HCJ 4562/92 *Zandberg v Broadcasting Authority IsrSc* 50(2) 793, 800 (1996).

a law that retroactively ratified the excessive fee as charged by the Broadcasting Authority. The petitioner accepted the payment of the fee itself (which was ratified by the retroactive law), but challenged the payments of fines for arrears and linkage differences, which he considered a violation of the right to property which is protected in Basic Law: Human Dignity and Liberty. In order to avoid the constitutional conflict and to avoid the need to invalidate a law for unconstitutionality, the Supreme Court chose to interpret the retroactive statute as not applicable to fines for arrears, even though arriving at this interpretation was not simple. In his ruling, President Barak wrote that the interpreter's ambition is to portray the law as consistent with the constitution:

> it is preferable to limit the scope of a law by means of interpretation rather than be required to reach that same limitation by way of the declaration of part of that law as nullified since it contradicts the provision of a Basic Law […] The reasonable interpretation of a law is preferable to a determination regarding its constitutionality.[53]

Thus, from two possible interpretations, the constitutionally-harmonious one must be chosen, as was done in this case.

The case of *Segal v Knesset Speaker*,[54] delivered a year later, raised another interesting constitutional question relating to the broadcasting fee – this time a fee specific to vehicle owners who paid the fee as part of their annual car licence fee. The petitioners, owners of a private car, were required to pay the annual broadcasting fee even though their car did not have a radio receiver installed, since the law held that 'the vehicle owner is obligated to pay the vehicle license fee in full regardless of the presence or absence of a radio receiver in the vehicle.'

The petitioners argued that imposing the fee on those who do not have a radio receiver installed in their car would violate their constitutional right to property and should be declared as unconstitutional. The majority rejected this argument. Justice Goldberg held that 'when the language of the norm is not vague, and the purpose of the legislation can be upheld, there is no justification for deviating from the linguistic meaning, which is consistent with the purpose of the legislation, in the name of the fundamental principles. Otherwise, the fear arises that we are not interpreting a norm but creating a norm to replace it.'[55] We shall return to such criticism in section VI. In any event, the majority opinion was that the infringement on the right is proportionate and accordingly the law is constitutional.[56] But the dissenting opinion of Justice Cheshin is of relevance to our matter.

Cheshin begins the dissenting opinion by citing the relevant *Ashwander* rules, claiming that these 'rules that we have brought are the sons of common sense, and it is appropriate that we adopt them. These rules have been applied to this day on secondary legislation – for example, the rule of *ut res magis valeat quam pereat*

[53] ibid 812.
[54] HCJ 5503/94 *Segal v Knesset Speaker*, IsrSC 51(4) 529 (1997).
[55] ibid 539.
[56] ibid 544.

(let the thing live and not perish) – and should apply, all the more so, on primary legislation.'[57] Accordingly, before considering constitutionality, one must examine the possibility of deciding the case by interpretation of the law.[58] This leads Justice Cheshin to hold that as long as the law does not explicitly state that the radio fee applies to car owners without a radio receiver, it should be interpreted to impose the radio fee only on car owners who have a radio receiver in their car, and not on car owners without one. This interpretation rests on basic legal principles, principles of fairness and justice.[59]

In the *Ganimat* case,[60] the principle of conforming interpretation of laws that were enacted prior to Basic Law: Human Dignity and Freedom arose. This was a challenging question because laws enacted prior to the enactment of Basic Law: Human Dignity and Freedom are protected from invalidation by a grandfathering clause holding that: 'This Basic Law shall not affect the validity of any law that existed prior to the inception of the Basic Law.'[61] Do the words 'affect the validity' refer only to invalidation of the law, ie so that the Court cannot strike down a pre-1992 law or does the grandfathering also prevent the new CCI of a pre-1992 law? In *Ganimat*, that centred on the interpretation of the law of arrest in light of the elevation of the right to personal liberty to constitutional right under Basic Law: Human Dignity and Freedom: the majority of the Supreme Court held that although the old arrest legislation is protected from judicial review given the grandfathering clause, the Court may allow the new constitutional right to change the interpretation of pre-1992 laws.[62] According to President Aharon Barak:

> It is here that the Basic Law performs its interpretive deed. Under its influence, different weights are likely to be assigned to the protected values and interests. Consequently, there is liable to be a change in the point of balance between the interests and the values that constitute the objective purpose of the law [...] The piece of legislation is no different, but its meaning is different. The validity of the existing law is preserved, however there is a change in the scope of its deployment.[63]

President Barak noted in his ruling that with the enactment of the basic laws the status of human rights has changed – human rights are given constitutional status. Rules of interpretation express the need to maintain a constitutional harmony that requires that the basic law also affects old legislation. And so, the interpretation in

[57] ibid 549–50.

[58] ibid 548–50.

[59] ibid 553–54, 560, 568–69. See also Aharon Barak, 'Statutory Interpretation: The Approach of Justice Mishael Cheshin' (2024) 26 *IDC Law Review* (forthcoming).

[60] CrimFH 2316/95 *Ganimat v State of Israel*, 49(4) PD 589, 654 (1995). An English translation is available in (1997) 15 *Israel Law Review* 754–63.

[61] Section 10 of Basic Law: Human Dignity and Freedom. For a general discussion, see Rivka Weill, 'Bills of Rights with Strings Attached: Protecting Death Penalty, Slavery, Discriminatory Religious Practices and the Past from Judicial Review' in Geoffrey Sigalet, Grégoire Webber and Rosalind Dixon (eds), *Constitutional Dialogue: Rights, Democracy, Institutions* (Cambridge, Cambridge University Press, 2019) 308.

[62] CrimFH 2316/95 (n 60).

[63] *Israel Law Review* (n 60) 762.

accordance with the basic laws applies not only to laws that are enacted after Basic Law: Human Dignity and Liberty but also to pre-1992 laws.

Thus, the Supreme Court's general approach, as pronounced in the *Hoffnung* case that dealt with the issue of equality in elections, is that: 'the court tends to interpret the law (and it does this even with regard to secondary legislation and even with regard to a contract) in a way that is compatible with the constitutional principles, and as a result it can be maintained and not annulled. In this way, the court can often cancel, or at least reduce, the possible infringement of a law on constitutional principles, such as human rights or equality in elections.'[64]

The method of interpretation in accordance with the basic laws has been applied not only to the basic laws on human rights, but also to institutional basic laws.

One example is the *Herut* case which dealt with the disqualification of a television commercial for elections of the 16th Knesset. The commercial included a jingle composed from the tune of the national anthem, combined with words of praise and congratulations to Yasser Arafat and a call for the deportation of Jews from Jaffa and Ramla. The Israeli flag was shown above the Knesset building turning into the Palestinian flag within seconds. The chairman of the central elections committee decided to disqualify the commercial holding that it caused severe damage to the honour of the flag and humiliated the national anthem.[65] The State Attorney argued that this decision was final and that the High Court of Justice lacks the authority to review it. The argument was based on section 137 of the Knesset Elections Law (Consolidated Version) 1969: 'Any complaint as to an act or omission under this Law shall be within the exclusive jurisdiction of the Central Committee, and, save as otherwise provided by this Law, *no court shall resort to an application for relief relating to any such act or omission or to any decision or direction* of the Central Committee, the Chairman and Vice-Chairman of the Committee [....]' (emphasis added). Prior to the constitutional revolution, this provision was interpreted as granting 'procedural immunity' from judicial review, even by the High Court of Justice. The Court rejected the previous decisions and highlighted that the authority of the High Court of Justice was anchored in Basic Law: The Judiciary which is a superior law which an ordinary law cannot modify. Accordingly, President Aharon Barak noted in his majority opinion:

> inasmuch as section 137 of the Elections Law – which states that 'no court' shall grant the remedies there stated – can be interpreted as negating the authority of the High Court of Justice, it is unconstitutional, and thus void regarding its application to the High Court of Justice. Of course, the law continues to apply to all other courts. This same conclusion may be reached – and I think more properly – by reinterpreting the phrase 'no court' as referring to all other courts besides the High Court of Justice. This

[64] HCJ 3434/96 *Hoffnung v The Speaker of the Knesset*, 50(3) PD 57, 68 (1996).

[65] HCJ 212/03 *Herut National Movement v Chairman of Central Elections Committee*, 57(1) PD 750 (2003). An English translation is available at supremedecisions.court.gov.il/Home/Download?path=EnglishVerdicts/03/120/002/A04&fileName=03002120_a04.txt&type=4.

> interpretation reflects the view that 'it is preferable to limit the scope of a law through interpretation, rather than achieve the same result by declaring a part of that law as being unconstitutional and void.' [...] As such, we find that we have the authority to consider the petition at hand.[66]

And so, a narrow interpretation which is contrary to the explicit wording of the law was given in order to avoid a declaration of unconstitutionality and invalidation of the law.

A somewhat similar battle over statutory text appeared in the *Ganis* case.[67] Here, the Knesset passed Amendment No. 5 of the Housing Loans Law that gave certain persons an entitlement to financial grants for the purchase or expansion of an apartment in Jerusalem. After the elections, about six weeks later, the Knesset suspended the grants by section 20 of the Arrangements Law, and included an explicit provision to the effect that the suspension of the grants was retroactive, from the date on which the grants originally came into effect. The petitioners challenged this retroactive suspension of the grants, on the grounds that they had relied on the grants and undertook to buy or expand an apartment in Jerusalem during the interim period, and therefore the retroactive suspension of the grants violated their protected right to property in Basic Law: Human Dignity and Freedom and was thus unconstitutional.[68]

The Supreme Court held unanimously that the Knesset had acted improperly when it retroactively suspended the grants, since it had not considered the possibility that some persons may have taken financial commitments upon themselves as a result of relying on the grants. However, the justices differed as to the proper approach that should be adopted to remedy the situation.

Albeit the explicit statutory text, the majority opinion opted for interpretation compatible with the constitution. It held that it was possible to construe the statute narrowly in such a way that the retroactive suspension would only apply to potentially entitled persons who had not relied on the statute during the interim period, but it would not apply to those entitled persons who did rely on the statute during the interim period. See, for example, Justice Cheshin, for the majority: 'for the purpose of determining the scope of the application of section 20, and relying on the basic presumption – which adopts the guise of a rule of interpretation – that tells us that the legislator will not act unjustly to an individual nor will he turn his back on persons who followed him and relied on promises and undertakings that he made, we will interpret section 20 as seeking to apply only to persons who did not rely on the legislator's promise and not to apply to persons who relied on the legislator's promise.'[69] In contrast, the minority opinion – to which we shall return

[66] ibid 755–56.

[67] HCJ 9098/01 *Ganis v Ministry of Building and Housing*, 59(4) PD 241 (2005). An English translation is available at versa.cardozo.yu.edu/sites/default/files/upload/opinions/Ganis%20v.%20Ministry%20of%20Building%20and%20Housing.pdf.

[68] ibid 257–58.

[69] ibid s 23 to Mishael Cheshin J's opinion.

in section VI – was that it was not possible to construe the statute narrowly as aforesaid, and therefore one cannot avoid the constitutionality examination according to which the retroactive suspension ought to be declared void.

In various other cases concerning constitutional protected rights, the Supreme Court has repeated the idea that statute should be interpreted in harmony with the constitutional system and with fundamental values in order to avoid annulling a law.[70]

The method of interpretation according to the Constitution has been applied by the Israeli Supreme Court not only to protect against infringement of constitutional rights or violations of basic laws, but more broadly to correspond with general legal principles. A recent example is the case of personalised law in local authorities' elections.[71] The petitions in this case challenged the validity of the Local Authorities Law (Elections) (Amendment No. 53), which amended section 7 of the 1965 Local Authorities Law (Elections). This amendment removed a limitation and allowed individuals who held caretaker mayor positions to run in subsequent local elections. The problem was that this law was designed to benefit a particular candidate in the local elections in Tiberius (a small city in Israel).

The judiciary's opinions on the law varied, yet there was a consensus that it should not influence the imminent local elections. Acting President of the Supreme Court Uzi Vogelman expressed reservations about the law, stating it undermined the neutrality and professionalism of caretaker appointed committees and unfairly altered the competitive landscape for local election candidates. He criticised the timing of the amendment's enactment, during an electoral period, and its being tailored to benefit one person's mayoral candidacy. Without reaching a clear conclusion on the right to vote and the right to be elected or the principle of equality in local elections, and avoiding these constitutional questions by citing the *Ashwander* rules, Justice Vogelman opted to interpret the timing of the law's implementation rather than assess its legality outright, in line with treating constitutional invalidation as a measure of last resort. He distinguished between the law's explicit, personal aim for quick application and its broader, objective purpose, advocating for the latter by highlighting the importance of stability in electoral rules and the general applicability of laws; thereby deciding that the amendment not be enforced in the upcoming electoral cycle: 'providing that the amendment shall not apply on the upcoming municipal electoral cycle is the interpretive alternative that its infringement upon the legal system's basic

[70] See eg CrimA 6659/06 *Doe v State of Israel*, 62(4) PD 329, 345 (2008); CrimApp 8823/07 *A v State of Israel*, 63(3) PD 500 (2009); HCJ 3809/08 *Association for Civil Rights in Israel v Israel Police*, pp 7, 27 (Nevo, 28 May 2012); HCJ 5113/12 *Friedman v The Knesset*, p 3, (Nevo, 7 August 2012); HCJ 7385/13 *Eitan – Israel's immigration policy v Government of Israel*, p 60, (Nevo, 22 September 2014); HCJ 5239/11 *Avnery v The Knesset*, p 17, (Nevo, 15 April 2015); HCJ 8665/14 *Desta v The Knesset*, 30, (Nevo, 11 August 2015); FHCJ 5026/16 *Gini v Chief Rabbinate of Israel*, p 4, (Nevo, 12 September 2017).

[71] HCJ 5119/23 *Anti-Corruption Movement v The Knesset* (Nevo, 26 October 2023).

principles is the more limited. The opposite interpretive stance means that in the delicate area of election law, the law of elections, during elections, was amended to benefit one person.'[72]

The use of CCI in this case raises a theoretical difficulty. As aforementioned, this rule is intended to prefer the interpretation that recognises the constitutionality of the law (and its validity) over the interpretation that leads to its unconstitutionality (and its invalidation). But this was not the case here. The existing flaws in Amendment No. 53 – the personal motive, the impairment of the functioning of called committees and a real-time change of the 'rules of the game' – do not constitute sufficient anchors for striking down a law due to unconstitutionality according to existing law. There is no explicit constitutional rule prohibiting 'personal legislation' and there is no explicit constitutional rule providing for equality in municipal elections. As Elad Gil wondered, even if these flaws are undesirable from policy point of view, if repeal is not on the agenda, it is not CCI.[73] Yet this case demonstrates how far the Court has taken the idea of conforming interpretation.

V. Interpretation According to the Constitution at the Constitutional Level

Finally, Israel presents another interesting case. As we explained, Israel has no rigid constitution and *a fortiori* no explicit unamendable provisions ('eternity clauses').[74] There are numerous basic laws which function as constitutional documents, superior to ordinary legislation and enforced by strong judicial review but peculiarly, the basic laws are enacted through precisely the same process as ordinary legislation.[75] In other words, in Israel, there are generally no procedural, substantive or temporal explicit limits on the Knesset's constituent power, and, with some very minor exceptions, basic laws can be enacted and amended very quickly and through a simple majority.[76] Does that mean that in exercising its constituent power, the Knesset is omnipotent? Not necessarily.

For many years, the Israeli Supreme Court has stated, in various *obiter dicta*, that there are basic constitutional principles, mainly the character of the state as

[72] ibid, para 62 Uzi Vogelman J.

[73] See Elad Gil, 'Interpretation empowers democracy: its applicability is rejected as an interpretive remedy, following the cases of the Law of Tiberias and the Law of Incapacitation' (*ICON-S-IL Blog*, 24 September 2023), available at israeliconstitutionalism.wordpress.com/2023/09/24/240923/.

[74] On eternity clauses, see Yaniv Roznai, *Unconstitutional Constitutional Amendments – The Limits of Amendment Powers* (Oxford, Oxford University Press, 2017); Silvia Suteu, *Eternity Clauses in Democratic Constitutionalism* (Oxford, Oxford University Press, 2021).

[75] See Rivka Weill, 'Hybrid Constitutionalism: The Israeli Case for Judicial Review and Why We Should Care' (2012) 30 *Berkeley Journal of International Law* 349.

[76] Suzie Navot, 'Israel' in Dawn Oliver and Carlo Fusaro (eds), *How Constitutions Change – A Comparative Study* (Oxford, Hart Publishing, 2011) 191.

Jewish and Democratic, that might limit even the Knesset's constituent power.[77] But such judicial statements were always voiced with due precaution and as non-binding *obiter dicta*. Until recently, there was no precedent regarding the limits to the Knesset's constituent authority, and *a fortiori* no basic law was ever invalidated for violating basic constitutional values.

The question received an interesting treatment in the dramatic judgment on Basic Law: Israel the Nation State of the Jewish People enacted on 19 July 2018. This Basic Law was meant to be another 'chapter' in the Israeli Constitution dealing with the Nation's identity. It established that Israel is the 'national home of the Jewish people', and dealt with state symbols like the flag and national anthem, the official language, national holidays, the Sabbath, Jerusalem as the capital, etc.[78]

Supporters of the Basic Law state that it is mainly declaratory and does not change the existing legal state of affairs. Opponents claim that because it mentions neither the democratic nature of the state nor the principle of equality, it allows discrimination against the non-Jewish minorities in Israel and aims to have the 'Jewish' feature of the state prevail over the 'democratic' feature. Moreover, the provisions regarding the 'exclusive' right to self-determination for the Jewish People (Article 2), the lowered status of the Arabic language from an official language to 'special status' and the provision stating that 'The state views the development of Jewish settlement as a national value and will act to encourage and promote its establishment and consolidation' (Article 7), are allegedly discriminatory towards non-Jews.

After the enactment of this Basic Law, multiple petitions were filed to the Hight Court of Justice asking that Basic Law: Israel as the Nation State of the Jewish People be declared null. The challenges against the 'constitutionality' of the Basic Law brought to the fore the question whether the HCJ possess the power to review basic laws, which have constitutional status.

On 8 July 2021, an eleven-judge panel rejected the petitions.[79] The 201-page decision has ten justices in the majority, each of whom wrote a separate opinion. It also includes the single minority opinion of Justice Kar'a, the only Arab judge in the Court, and the only justice who thought that several of the Basic Law's provisions should be invalidated for undermining the core democratic identity of the state and shaking the foundations of its constitutional structure.

[77] See, for elaboration, Sharon Weintal, 'The Challenge of Reconciling Constitutional Eternity Clauses with Popular Sovereignty: Toward Three-Track Democracy in Israel as a Universal Holistic Constitutional System and Theory' (2011) 44(3) *Israel Law Review* 449; Mazen Masri, 'Unamendability in Israel – A Critical Perspective' in Richard Albert and Bertil Emrah Oder (eds), *An Unconstitutional Constitution? Unamendability in Constitutional Democracies* (Berlin, Springer, 2018) 169; Suzie Navot and Yaniv Roznai, 'From Supra-Constitutional Principles to the Misuse of Constituent Power in Israel' (2019) 21(3) *European Journal of Law Reform* 403.

[78] For an English translation of the full text of the basic law, see main.knesset.gov.il/EN/activity/documents/BasicLawsPDF/BasicLawNationState.pdf.

[79] HCJ 5555/18 *Hasson v the Knesset* (rendered 8 July 2021).

The main opinion of the majority was written by President Hayut. Consistent with her approach in earlier cases,[80] President Hayut held that it was not the time to adopt a comprehensive doctrine regarding the constitutionality of constitutional amendments, because the constitution-making process is still ongoing.[81] Nevertheless, Hayut's ruling clearly stated that the Knesset's legislative power when enacting or amending Basic Laws is not unlimited: 'this does not necessarily mean that in the absence of such a comprehensive doctrine, the powers of the Constituent Assembly in Israel are unlimited.'[82] The Court declared that the constituent power of the Knesset is limited in the sense that 'The Knesset cannot deny in a basic law the very existence of Israel as a Jewish and democratic state.'[83] And for this matter, it was irrelevant for President Hayut and the Court that the constitution-making process is still ongoing: 'Indeed, our constitutional structure is incomplete and it is quite possible that floors and branches will be added along the way, but these two pillars – the Jewish pillar and the democratic pillar – have long been placed in it. Denial of any of them leads to the collapse of the entire structure.'[84]

Notwithstanding this decision, regarding the limited scope of the Knesset's constituent power, there was no clear statement as to whether the Court is empowered to repeal or invalidate a basic law that would undermine the core values of the state as Jewish and democratic. The majority ruled that there was no need to decide upon the power of the Court to invalidate basic laws, because, as President Hayut noted: 'Even if I assume for the purpose of this case that the Court is empowered to judicially review the content of basic laws, Basic Law: the Nation State does not negate the Jewish and democratic characteristics of the state in a manner that justifies interference with its content.'[85] In other words, instead of solving the constitutional difficulty through the doctrine of unconstitutional constitutional amendment, the Court solved them through interpretation.

The Court interpreted the 'problematic' provisions of the basic law narrowly, as compatible with the principles of democracy and equality. According to the Court, the basic law does not undermine the democratic nature of Israel because all the principles that are missing from the basic law (such as the principle of equality and the idea of a democratic state), exist anyway in the Israeli legal system, including in other basic laws. The Court stated, for example, that the impugned basic law does not negate the character of Israel as a democratic state, it does not give priority to the Jewish identity of Israel over the principle of democracy; it does not detract from or limit the status of equality in the legal system and it does not deny personal rights to members of minority groups. Those conclusions are reached following enabling or conforming interpretation, as well as a presumption of constitutional

[80] See eg HCJ 10214/16 *MK Yousef Jabareen v Knesset* (27 May 2018), para 25 of President Esther Hayut's opinion.

[81] HCJ 5555/18 (n 79), para 15 of President Esther Hayut's opinion.

[82] ibid, para 15 of President Esther Hayut's opinion.

[83] ibid, para 16 of President Esther Hayut's opinion.

[84] ibid, para 18 of President Esther Hayut's opinion.

[85] ibid, para 35 of President Esther Hayut's opinion.

harmony. As this basic law is only one chapter in the Israeli constitutional project, it ought to be read together with the other basic laws, and especially with Basic Law: Human Dignity and Liberty, which protects Israel's democratic identity and – due to the Court's decisions – also the right to equality as a non-enumerated right.

Accordingly, the Court assumes that the Knesset intended to protect equality among all citizens of the state and to preserve the democratic values of the state. It is this 'basic principles interpretation' that allows the Court to refrain from intervening in the provisions to reconcile Basic Law: The Nation State with Israel's democratic values, and to leave undecided the challenging question of its own authority to invalidate basic laws that violate the core values of the Jewish and democratic state.[86]

According to Rivka Weill, this interpretive move has crucial consequences. This, she writes:

> marked the first time that the Court applied this interpretation method to Basic Laws. Previously, it had only been applied to ordinary legislation, ensuring that it aligns with the Basic Laws, which are superior. However, now it has been applied to Basic Laws, where no hierarchy sets one Basic Law as superior to any other. […] Thus, we can see that, despite the Justices' claims, applying the constitutional avoidance doctrine, by its very nature, asserts that the Justices indeed have the authority to repeal the Basic Law, if the doctrine is not exercised to *de facto* modify its problematic nature. With this understanding in mind, we can appreciate the true revolutionary nature of the *Hasson* decision. In many ways, it is more radical than voiding *Basic Law: Nation State.* The Court had officially rejected the petitions, including their request that the Court rewrite this Basic Law and read democracy and the right for equality into it. However, by exercising constitutional avoidance, the Court has in fact done just that. It didn't wait for the Knesset to react. Rather, the Court remedied *Basic Law: Nation State* on its own. Now, because of the *Hasson* ruling, *Basic Law: Nation State* doesn't need to just be read in tandem with other Basic Laws which uphold democracy and the right for equality. Rather, the principle of democracy and the right for equality are now an intrinsic part of *Basic Law: Nation State* itself. Any other approach would undermine the Basic Law's validity and would leave it vulnerable to challenges in Court on grounds of unconstitutionality.[87]

The Court's approach corresponds with the general notion that before invalidation of amendments, 'every interpretive effort must be made to reconcile amendments with protected rights and basic constitutional principles',[88] yet this interpretative move, as Weill claims, may be no less 'activist' than striking down provisions of the basic law. We elaborate on this argument in the next section. But before that,

[86] See generally Rehan Abeyratne and Yaniv Roznai, 'Basic Structure Interpretation' in Catherine O'Regan, Carlos Bernal and Sujit Choudhry (eds), *Research Handbook on Constitutional Interpretation* (Cheltenham, Edward Elgar Publishing, forthcoming 2025).

[87] Rivka Weill, 'A Covert Constitutional Revolution? Is Basic Law: Israel – the Nation-State of the Jewish People Democratic?' *Balkinization* (19 December 2021), available at balkin.blogspot.com/2021/12/a-covert-constitutional-revolution-is.html.

[88] Roznai (n 74) 220.

two important constitutional cases which highlight the issue were delivered by the Supreme Court in early 2024.

The first case was the momentous judicial decision in *The Movement for Quality Government* case,[89] in which the High Court of Justice declared an unconstitutional part of the 'reform in the judicial system',[90] that removed the authority of all courts to review the 'reasonableness' of decisions of the Prime Minister, the Ministers or the Cabinet.[91]

The petition under consideration challenged Amendment No. 3 to Basic-Law: The Judiciary, focusing on the removal of courts authority to review the 'reasonableness' actions of the government and of ministers. It raised critical issues: the authority of the High Court of Justice to review basic laws and if the amendment constitutes an excessive overstep of the Knesset's constitutional boundaries, calling for its annulment. For the first time in its history, a full bench of all 15 justices heard the case.

On 1 January 2024, the High Court of Justice delivered its 738-page landmark judgment, which was the first case in the Court's history in which the Court invalidated a part of a basic law.

Lead by President Hayut, a majority of 12 to 3 asserted that the Court has the authority to review basic laws and strike them down when the Knesset appears to exceed its constitutional limits.[92] Against the backdrop of the absence of a formalised procedure for creating constitutional norms in Israel's system and concerns over the political misuse of basic laws for expedient ends, the majority emphasised the Supreme Court's crucial role in maintaining the constitutional structure. On the merits of the case, in a split decision of 8 to 7, the Court deemed the amendment invalid for significantly restricting scrutiny over governmental actions, a move seen as severely damaging to Israel's democratic fabric and especially the rule of law and separation of power.[93]

Notwithstanding the importance of this judgment, more relevant to our matter are the minority opinions. Justices Solberg and Mintz contested the Court's very authority to nullify a basic law, arguing against any perceived Knesset overreach in

[89] HCJ 5658/23 *The Movement for Quality Government in Israel v The Knesset* (Nevo, 1.1.2024). An English translation is available here versa.cardozo.yu.edu/opinions/movement-quality-government-v-knesset.

[90] Critics describe this reform as a 'judicial overhaul'. In this chapter we shall not expand on the judicial overhaul in Israel. For an overview, see the collection of arts in special symposiums of the (2024) 56 *Israel Law Review* 289–540; (2024) 39(1) *Israel Studies Review* 1–178 and (2023) 28(3) *Israel Studies* 1–49.

[91] On 24 July 2023, the Knesset adopted Basic Law: The Judiciary (Amendment No. 3), according to which: 'Notwithstanding what is stated in this Basic Law, a holder of judicial authority under law, including the Supreme Court sitting as the High Court of Justice, shall not address the reasonableness of a decision by the Government, the Prime Minister or a Government Minister, and will not issue an order in such a matter; in this section, "decision" means any decision, including in matters of appointments, or a decision to refrain from exercising authority.'

[92] See Yaniv Roznai and Shani Schnitzer, 'Navigating the Judicial Ship in Stormy Waters: President Esther Hayut and the Israeli Constitutional Crises, 2018–2023' (forthcoming) *International Journal of Constitutional Law*.

[93] HCJ 5658/23 (n 89).

this case, and Justice Elron argued for a cautious approach, suggesting it is premature to conclude the amendment's potential negative impact without a clear restrictive interpretation being applied. Relevant to our discussion, Justices Willner, Stein and Canfy-Steinitz called for a narrow interpretation of the amendment, thereby removing the need to invalidate it. For example, according to Justice Willner:

> the amendment can be interpreted as a sustaining interpretation, and there is no place anyway to order its invalidation. This is because it is a fundamental understanding that a sustaining interpretation of a basic law – if it is linguistically possible and compatible with its purposes – according to which it does not deny the core Jewish or democratic identity of the State of Israel, in the face of an interpretation which could lead to the opposite conclusion and therefore to its invalidation. […] I believe that the interpretation of the amendment in accordance with our customary rules of interpretation, leads to the conclusion that the term 'reasonableness' within the amendment, refers exclusively to the reasonableness grounds in the sense that was given to it following the High Court ruling 389/80 Yellow Pages Ltd. v. The Broadcasting Authority [ie balancing formula reasonableness and not extreme unreasonableness – Y.R and H.S] […] In my view, given this interpretation, the amendment – although one should be sorry that it was enacted – does not deny the core of the democratic identity of the State of Israel. […] there is no place to order invalidation of the amendment, and one must choose the possible interpretive route that upholds it.[94]

But, as aforementioned, this interpretive approach, to which we return in the next section, was rejected by the majority who opted for invalidation of the amendment, for the first time in the Court's history, making this judgment probably the most important judgment in the Supreme Court's history.

The second case, which is another example for conforming interpretation at the constitutional level was the case concerning the incapacitation of the Prime Minister. Amendment No. 12 to Basic-Law: The Government altered the criteria for declaring a prime minister's incapacity to 'physical or mental incapacity' and introduced a detailed and challenging process for such a declaration, contending it was specifically crafted to favour the existing Prime Minister. This amendment was challenged in the High Court of Justice on claims of abuse of constituent power.[95]

The High Court of Justice, with a majority of 6 out of 11 judges, decided to postpone the amendment's implementation until the next Knesset term, labelling it a clear personal amendment designed to protect the current Prime Minister from being deemed unfit due to legal proceedings against him. The majority highlighted the amendment's explicit purpose to advance the personal interests of the Prime Minister, noting its rapid introduction and passage in the Knesset following petitions for his impeachment and his direct comments post-approval as indicative of the amendment's personal intent. Concluding that the amendment's immediate enforcement would constitute a misuse of constitutional power, the majority opted for a constitutional remedy by postponing its effective date to the start of

[94] HCJ 5658/23 (n 89), para 8 to Yael Willner's opinion (our translation).
[95] HCJ 2412/23 The Movement for Quality Government in *Israel v The Knesset* (3 January 2024).

the next Knesset's term, addressing the issue without invalidating the amendment altogether.[96] This approach aimed to correct the legislation's personal bias, ensuring it would not impact the current Prime Minister's tenure. This is another instance of conforming interpretation aimed at correcting a constitutional flaw which might lead to invalidation.

VI. A Critical Perspective: Why Interpretation According to the Constitution may Often be More Intrusive than Invalidation

Traditionally, in Israeli jurisprudence, when considering constitutional remedies, invalidation of laws as unconstitutional is considered to be a means of last resort – the 'doomsday weapon'. This is understandable, because declaring a law (and all the more so a basic law) enacted by the legislature invalid is considered to be the ultimate intrusion at the will of the people and their elected representatives.

However, against the backdrop of the Israeli jurisprudence, we argue that often, an interpretation of laws that is completely opposite to the legislature's intent or the text, may be more intrusive – in terms of separation of powers – than invalidation.

Consider the *Ganis* case[97] and the *Herut* case[98] mentioned above. In the *Herut* case, when the Court interpreted the legislative text 'no court' to exclude the High Court of Justice thus preventing unconstitutionality and avoiding invalidation it actually rewrites the law in contrast with the clear wording of the legislative text and the legislative intent. Likewise, in the *Ganis* case, when the Court interprets an explicit retroactive law as to not apply to those who have relied upon it. Vice-President Mazza, in his dissenting opinion, was correct to argue that:

> it is not possible to interpret the suspending law as applicable only to whoever did not rely on the entitling law. Such an interpretation does not have a minimal foothold in the text. It constitutes, in practice, a change in the language of the statute, and as such it departs from the legitimate boundaries of interpretation. […] In such circumstances, we are obliged to examine the constitutionality of the retroactive application of the suspending law in accordance with the constitutional criteria set out in Basic Law: Human Dignity and Liberty. Indeed, I too accept that whenever it is possible to refrain from constitutional intervention in the validity of a statute by giving an interpretation – even a 'creative' interpretation – to a problematic statutory provision we are obliged to prefer this method. But even interpretation has its linguistic limits. We are not speaking of a choice between 'literal interpretation' and 'purposive interpretation', but of a choice between purposive interpretation that is based on the text and purposive interpretation that is detached from it.[99]

[96] ibid.
[97] HCJ 9098/01 (n 67).
[98] HCJ 212/03 (n 65).
[99] HCJ 9098/01 (n 67) Vice-President Eliahu Mazza, para 1 to his opinion.

And similarly, Justice Rivlin accepted the fundamental position:

> according to which we should turn to constitutional review – which can be described as a 'doomsday weapon' – only when we have exhausted all other avenues [...] But care must be taken so that excessive use is not made of this tool. [...] A provision should not be given an interpretation that is entirely in conflict with its language. The art of interpretation, although it is desirable and essential, has limits, beyond which the interpreter cannot pass; otherwise, he will find himself rewriting legislation. In the case before us, the interpretation proposed by the majority justices goes, in my opinion, beyond the confines of what is possible and what is permitted.[100]

We accept this approach and argue that sometimes, certain interpretations of a statute, which completely depart from the explicit language of the statute and the legislative intent, are more intrusive to the legislative realm than striking down the law as unconstitutional.[101] The results of an interpretation that differs significantly from the legislative intent, or is detached from the statute's wording, could be more severe than the act of annulment. Otto Pfersmann describes provisions that were given a different meaning from what they actually mean – because otherwise they would be invalidated by the Court – as 'norms without texts'.[102] Such application of interpretation may conflict with principles of legal certainty and separation of powers.[103] One may compare this with the theory of 'Falsification of the Constitution', which occurs when 'constitutional norms are given an interpretation and a sense different from those that they really possess: this is in reality an informal modification of the Constitution itself.'[104]

Returning to the Movement for Quality Government case,[105] this seems to be the rationale behind President's Hayut objection to the minority opinions suggesting resolving the constitutional difficulty through a narrow interpretation to the 'reasonableness' being removed from Court's authority. As she states:

> the fundamental principle in our system states that we are obligated to seek out an interpretive solution that will avoid the need to decide upon the validity of a piece of legislation [...] However, at times, the Court is forced to decide that no such interpretation is possible. This is particularly the case when such an interpretation is artificial and leads to emptying the legal arrangement of all content or leads, in practice, to rewriting the law [...] Such is the case before us. In my opinion, an interpretation that would narrowly construe the application of the amendment that abolishes the reasonableness

[100] ibid Eliezer Rivlin J, paras 2–3.

[101] Yaniv Roznai, 'Retroactivity – Not Only a Matter of Time! Thoughts on Analyzing Retroactive Legislation Following Genis' (2008) 9 *IDC Law Review* 395, 435 [Hebrew].

[102] Otto Pfersmann, 'Ontological and Epistemological Complexity in Comparative Constitutional Law' in Antonina Bakardjieva Engelbrekt and Joakim Nergelius (eds), *New Directions in Comparative Law* (Cheltenham, Edward Elgar Publishing, 2009) 81, 88.

[103] See references in Kerstin Tobisch, 'Public Procurement Law and Effective Legal Protection' (2011) *Vienna Journal on International Constitutional Law* 424, 427.

[104] Allan R Brewer-Carias, 'The Principle of Separation of Powers and Authoritarian Government in Venezuela' (2009) 47(4) *Duquesne Law Review* (2009) 813, 835.

[105] HCJ 5658/23 (n 89).

> standard in regard to the elected echelon only in its sense in Dapei Zahav would be a dubious interpretation that would effectively constitute a redrafting of the Amendment by the Court in a sense that would be completely different from that of the existing Amendment. This is all the more so because we are concerned with interpretation that touches upon the core of the constitutional arrangement and not its ancillary aspects, such as the time of its entry into force [...] For all the above reasons, I do not believe that we can adopt the distinction among the various meanings of the reasonableness standard proposed by the Knesset in regard to the application of the Amendment by means of interpretation. My conclusion is, therefore, that the Amendment should be interpreted in accordance with its plain meaning, i.e. as a provision that comprehensively abolishes judicial review on the basis of the reasonableness standard, in all its senses, as regards decisions by the Government, the Prime Minister, and the ministers.[106]

In this case, President Hayut held that 'the comprehensive, unqualified language of the Amendment is, indeed, "explicit and unequivocal". It lacks any foothold for the suggested narrow interpretation, and leaves "no room for doubt" as to the application of the Amendment to the reasonableness standard in its entirety.'[107] Not just that the constitutional text was implicit and making no distinctions as for the different meanings of 'reasonableness' but also throughout the legislative process the amendment's initiators have repeated time and again that the amendment applies to any decision, including decisions that are extremely unreasonable and implausible. Accepting a contradictory interpretation instead of invalidation would be an exercise more intrusive than striking down the amendment. Paradoxically, the interpretation of the minority judges – who are considered conservative – can be regarded as an activist exercise, while the invalidation of the amendment by the majority judges – who are considered activists – is the more conservative option.[108]

As Christine Landfried explains:

> A clear-cut invalidation of a law can give the legislature more room for political manoeuvring, in that a new law can be enacted. However, the declaration that only one particular interpretation of a law is constitutional often entails precise prescriptions and can quite easily result in law-making by the Constitutional Court.[109]

In the case of invalidation, the 'ball returns to the hands' of the political authority – the legislature, which can re-enact the law according to the Court's decision

[106] ibid, paras 135–36.

[107] ibid, para 125.

[108] See Yaniv Roznai, 'The Reasonableness Judgment – Not What You Thought! Conservativism, Activism and the Unconstitutional Constitutional Amendment' in Suzie Navot and Anat Thon-Ashkenazy (eds), *The Supreme Court Ruling on the Reasonableness Doctrine: Some Initial Analyses* (Jeruslaem, Israeli Democracy Institute, 2024), available at www.idi.org.il/media/24415/reasonableness-verdict-first-studies.pdf.

[109] Christine Landfried, 'Constitutional Review and Legislation in the Federal Republic of Germany' in Christine Landfried (ed), *Constitutional Review and Legislation: An International Comparison* (Baden-Baden, Nomos, 1988) 154.

or otherwise. In the case of judicial interpretation, if the legislature is not satisfied with the new meaning of the statute, it would have to annul it through the same legislative process, only this time, the 'ball has left the hands' of the political authorities. Until the enactment of the new law, the legal norm is now in the public sphere shaped by the judiciary until its abolishment or replacement with a new law. Therefore, often an acrobatic interpretation that significantly departs from the language of the law and the legislative intent may be regarded as more intrusive than invalidation.

VII. Conclusion

CCI is an accepted doctrine in Israeli jurisprudence. Before the constitutional revolution, it was part of the HCJ's development of a judicial bill of rights. Without constitutional supremacy, the Court used the doctrine in the form of 'rights conforming interpretation' to justify the broadening of human rights. Following the constitutional revolution, the HCJ expanded the already existing doctrine further, and used it in the form of 'basic laws conforming interpretation'. Even at the constitutional level, the interpretation of basic laws is subject to conforming interpretation, this time to the fundamental values of the state as a Jewish and Democratic and seeking harmony between the various basic laws and the core state values.

In this chapter, we use the Israeli jurisprudence as a case study in order to critically argue that often, interpretation in contrast with the explicit statutory text and legislative intent, even if conforming with the constitution, is more violative of separation of powers. In other words, from the perspective of the principle of separation of powers, in certain cases it is preferable for the Court to invalidate unconstitutional laws rather than interpreting them in according to the constitution, if such interpretation amounts to re-writing the law. Interpretation, therefore, is not always the more conservative judicial method and may be more activist than striking down legislation, as paradoxical as it may sound.

9

Constitutionally Conforming Interpretation and Constitutional Amendments

SILVIA SUTEU

I. Introduction

In the by now classic debates regarding the legitimacy of constitutional interpretation, which interpretive canon a judge chooses will be indicative of her judicial philosophy and determinative of the methodology for reaching her decision. The choice is not value-neutral, as it rests on the judge's understanding of the principle of the separation of powers and courts' place within it, of the principle of democracy and the elected representatives' role in giving effect to popular will, and of the judge's own role as guarantor of the Constitution and the limits of exercising it. These are complicated questions whose answer will depend on the particular constitutional dispensation the judge operates. They are rendered even more difficult to answer when the question of interpretive choice is applied not to ordinary legislation but to constitutional amendment.

As the first volume in this project has amply established, constitutionally conforming interpretation (CCI) is a canon of judicial interpretation that is ubiquitous across legal systems.[1] At its most basic, it establishes that '[w]henever the wording of a norm allows for more than one interpretation, the interpreter must give effect to the interpretation that is most harmonious with the Constitution.'[2] CCI is thus tantamount to a presumption of constitutionality that the courts extend to the legal acts they are tasked with reviewing. This in turn hinges on considerations of respect for the principle of the separation of powers in a constitutional democracy, which recognises the legislature and courts as engaged in a joint endeavour of constitutional interpretation and implementation. Underpinning

[1] Matthias Klatt (ed), *Constitutionally Conforming Interpretation: Comparative Perspectives Volume 1: National Reports* (Oxford, Hart Publishing, 2023).

[2] Matthias Klatt, 'The Legitimacy of Constitutionally Conforming Interpretation' in Klatt (n 1) 1.

CCI is also the presumption that the normative levels of the Constitution and ordinary laws can and should be unified via interpretation.[3]

Local variations of CCI have been documented across systems of both civil and common law, on all continents, and with very different models of judicial review in place. As a canon of interpretation, it may be viewed as a sub-type of systemic or holistic interpretation as has been developed in numerous jurisdictions across the world.[4] Some constitutions even explicitly mandate for the holistic interpretation of the constitution, in whole or in part. Article 39(2) of the South African Constitution, for example, stipulates this for the bill of rights. Several of the constitutions adopted after the so-called 'Arab Spring' also included provisions mandating holistic or coherent interpretation of the text, such as Article 146 of Tunisia's 2014 Constitution referring to the harmonious interpretation of the Constitution 'as an indissoluble whole' and Article 227 of Egypt's 2014 Constitution indicating that the constitutional text and the preamble are 'non-divisible' and the Constitution 'one coherent unity'.

The form CCI takes may differ significantly, and may at times not be immediately recognisable as an instantiation of the same interpretive tool. For example, the principle of legality deployed by UK courts when interpreting legislative acts sees them looking for clear and unambiguous statutory words when common law norms are to be ousted.[5] The principle of legality has been called a weak form of judicial control over legislation,[6] but is nevertheless an example of CCI central to a legal system centred on parliamentary sovereignty.[7] A different example is that of the United States, where a veritable 'judicial avoidance canon' has sprung up that sees courts able and even encouraged to avoid ruling on the constitutionality of an issue before them through creative interpretive techniques.[8] Whereas its defenders may see it as the interpretive embodiment of the call to judicial restraint, opting for judicial avoidance still requires courts to engage in statutory interpretation that may create more, rather than less, new statutory meaning.[9] As one study

[3] Chiara Valentini, 'Italy. Constitutionally Conforming Interpretation and Judicial Dialogue' in Klatt (n 1) 111.

[4] Klatt (n 1). See also Donald P Kommers, 'Germany: Balancing Rights and Duties' in Jeffrey Goldsworthy (ed), *Interpreting Constitutions: A Comparative Study* (Oxford, Oxford University Press, 2007) 161, 204; Vicki C Jackson, 'Holistic Interpretation: Fitzpatrick v. Bitzer and Our Bifurcated Constitution' (2001) 53(5) *Stanford Law Review* 1259; and Manoj Mate, 'Judicial Supremacy in Comparative Constitutional Law' (2017) 92(2) *Tulane Law Review* 393, 418.

[5] Jason NE Varuhas, 'The Principle of Legality' (2020) 79(3) *Cambridge Law Journal* 578.

[6] Hayley J Hooper, 'Legality, Legitimacy, and Legislation: The Role of Exceptional Circumstances in Common Law Judicial Review' (2021) 41(1) *Oxford Journal of Legal Studies* 142, 147.

[7] In addition, s 3 of the Human Rights Act requires UK courts to, so far as possible, read and give effect to primary and secondary legislation in a manner compatible with the European Convention on Human Rights. For a discussion of CCI in the UK, see Nick Friedman, 'United Kingdom. In the Shadow of Parliamentary Sovereignty: The Human Rights Act and the Principle of Legality' in Klatt (n 1) 197.

[8] Frederick Schauer, 'United States. Constitutional Avoidance as Constitutional Conformation' in Klatt (n 1) 267.

[9] ibid.

has shown, such avoidance tactics are certainly not unique to the US and courts engage in them for a variety of strategic reasons.[10]

Despite its ubiquity, CCI's legitimacy continues to be contested, with the grounds for this contestation differing from jurisdiction to jurisdiction.[11] The presumption in favour of the constitutionality of legislative acts comes under the fire of critics of the parliamentary deliberative and participatory process, who see no good reason to place faith on the product of such flawed processes. The very availability of judicial review may be taken as evidence of distrust in them. Another type of objection refers to the often missing constitutional basis for courts' embracing CCI and the availability of other, seemingly no less legitimate, canons of interpretation. Another still is that it would be wiser to adopt a presumption of *un*constitutionality, which is no less respectful of the principle of separation of powers than the presumption of constitutionality underpinning CCI.

All of the above relates primarily to the constitutional review of legislation. What of constitutional amendment review, however? As the recently exploding comparative constitutional literature on amendments has shown, legal systems vary greatly regarding whether constitutional courts have the competence to review formal amendments to the constitution, whether they can do so on procedural or also on substantive grounds, and whether and how far courts are actually willing to step in and deploy their powers of amendment review.[12] We have also come to understand that, even absent such expressly conferred competences, constitutional courts have often crafted their own judicial doctrines that allow them to review the conformity of constitutional amendments with explicit and even implicit limits to constitutional change.[13]

In this chapter, I am less interested in the normative, prescriptive analysis of the operation of CCI in the constitutional review of amendments. Instead, I seek to map how this canon of interpretation does or does not operate in this area, on what normative bases, and with what outcomes. As I will show, the normative

[10] Erin F Delaney, 'Analyzing Avoidance: Judicial Strategy in Comparative Perspective' (2016) 66(1) *Duke Law Journal* 1.

[11] For a good overview of these objections, see Klatt (n 1).

[12] See inter alia Mads Andenas (ed), *The Creation and Amendment of Constitutional Norms* (London, British Institute of International and Comparative Law, 2000); Dawn Oliver and Carlo Fusaro (eds), *How Constitutions Change: A Comparative Study* (Oxford, Hart Publishing, 2011); Xenophon Contiades (ed), *Engineering Constitutional Change: A Comparative Perspective on Europe, Canada and the USA* (London, Routledge, 2012); Richard Albert, Xenophon Contiades and Alkmene Fotiadou (eds), *The Foundations and Traditions of Constitutional Amendment* (Oxford, Hart Publishing, 2017); Richard Albert, *Constitutional Amendments: Making, Breaking, and Changing Constitutions* (Oxford, Oxford University Press, 2019); Xenophon Contiades and Alkmene Fotiadou (eds), *Routledge Handbook of Comparative Constitutional Change* (London, Routledge, 2020); Richard Albert (ed), *The Architecture of Constitutional Amendments: History, Law, Politics* (Oxford, Hart Publishing, 2023); Bui Ngoc Son and Mara Malagodi (eds), *Asian Comparative Constitutional Law, Volume 2: Constitutional Amendments* (Oxford, Hart Publishing, 2024).

[13] Yaniv Roznai, *Unconstitutional Constitutional Amendments: The Limits of Amendment Powers* (Oxford, Oxford University Press, 2017); Silvia Suteu, *Eternity Clauses in Democratic Constitutionalism* (Oxford, Oxford University Press, 2021); Rehan Abeyratne and Ngoc Son Bui (eds), *The Law and Politics of Unconstitutional Constitutional Amendments in Asia* (London, Routledge, 2021).

problems raised by constitutional amendment review overlap and at times diverge from those raised by the use of CCI vis-à-vis ordinary legislation. Because of the nature of the legal act under review, the normative justifications for its review, and the possibly upended presumption of constitutionality involved, the recourse to CCI in amendment review is not simply a matter of translating its application from the context of judicial review of ordinary legislation. Moreover, the arguably extreme case of substantive amendment review, taking the form of unconstitutional constitutional amendment doctrines, raises the stakes and complicates the picture when it comes to identifying the appropriate canon of constitutional interpretation. Finally, the blurry lines delineating formal constitutional change from informal or de facto amendment, either via legislation or via judicial review, further muddle the interpretive waters.

The chapter proceeds to unpack all of these issues sequentially. Section II delves into the specificity of constitutional amendments as compared to ordinary legislation. I focus on the different nature of the object of constitutional review (amendment versus legislative act) and the disparate normative justifications for this review. I also question whether amendment review, especially in its substantive form, actually upends the presumption of constitutionality on which CCI is founded. Section III then examines the thorny question of the substantive review of constitutional amendments, whether on the basis of a formal constitutional eternity clause or of implicit limits to constitutional change identified by the courts themselves. The section investigates normative accounts of judicial restraint in amendment review and documents empirical cases of both judicial overreach and underreach in this area. I thereby show the difficulties in calibrating the scope of interpretation in the domain of substantive constitutional amendment review. In section IV, I move beyond formal amendments to consider informal ones, whether in the form of statutes that are de facto amendments or judicial interpretations that alter constitutional meaning. I conclude by revisiting the normative foundations of CCI in light of what the analysis of its deployment in the amendment context reveals.

II. The Specificity of Constitutional Amendment Review

When it comes to constitutional interpretation and amendments, one of the most important questions for constitutional drafters and courts to answer is how far constitutional review of amendments is to go, if it is to happen at all. Constitutional texts the world over contain more or less detailed provisions on the procedures for and limits on their own change.[14] In terms of the legislative procedure involved, these range from simple majority voting to supermajorities and other forms of

[14] See inter alia Rosalind Dixon, 'Constitutional Amendment Rules: A Comparative Perspective' in Tom Ginsburg and Rosalind Dixon (eds), *Comparative Constitutional Law* (Cheltenham, Edward Elgar

escalating amendment difficulty. Some constitutions include mechanisms for popular participation from referendums and citizens' initiatives to new constituent assemblies. Some include temporal roadblocks such as passing the same amendment in successive legislatures. And some entirely set aside certain constitutional values, principles, and rights from the possibility of formal amendment in the form of eternity clauses. Germany's *Ewigkeitsklausel* contained in Article 79(3) is perhaps the most well-known, but is by far not the only constitutional eternity clause. Insofar as courts are formally empowered to review amendments at all, they may do so strictly limiting themselves to procedural review, certifying that the formal procedural steps have been met, or they may also engage in substantive review. The latter, especially in the guise of various types of unconstitutional constitutional amendment doctrines, has become widespread both as a doctrinal choice and as an object of scholarly study.[15] India's basic structure doctrine developed by its Supreme Court is the most famous but, again, not the only such doctrine of implicit amendment limits.

To the extent that CCI is justified on the basis of, on the one hand, respect for the constitutional hierarchy of norms and, on the other hand, separation of powers considerations, constitutional amendments complicate the picture significantly. I discuss several ways in which they do so.

A. The Nature of the Act under Review

CCI is said to be deployed to unify two normative levels: that of the Constitution and that of ordinary legislation.[16] The connection between them is hierarchical,[17] insofar as the constitutional norms are normatively superior by virtue of the constitution's supremacy. With unity of the legal system at stake, in case of ambiguity that may result in a conflict between the two levels it is the ordinary legislative norm that must yield and its interpretation that must adapt to the constitutional norm.[18] The role of the constitutional court as ultimate arbiter of constitutionality is paramount in this equation, even while different levels of concentration or diffusion of judicial review functions may empower the ordinary judge to engage in CCI herself to a higher or lesser degree.

This neat hierarchy cannot so neatly be mapped onto constitutional amendments. In most constitutional systems, whether initiated by the legislature, popularly, or by the executive branch, an amendment proposal will take the form of a legislative bill that must be adopted by Parliament according to whatever

Publishing, 2011) 96; Rosalind Dixon and David Landau, 'Tiered Constitutional Design' (2018) 86(2) *George Washington Law Review* 438; and Albert, Contiades and Fotiadou (n 12).

[15] See inter alia Roznai (n 13) and Suteu (n 13).

[16] Valentini (n 3) 111.

[17] ibid 113.

[18] ibid 114.

procedure the Constitution stipulates. In this form, one could envision an amendment remaining of sub-constitutional normative value until it is duly adopted and formally becomes part of the constitution. Constitutional review enters onto the scene where a constitutional court is mandated with (or arrogates for itself) powers of amendment review, whether as a type of abstract or concrete review. It is the former type that can stop the proposed amendment in its tracks. In some instances, courts are even able to rule on the constitutionality of initiatives to revise the Constitution *ex officio*.

An example of such powers in practice comes from the Romanian Constitution. It entrusts the Constitutional Court with amendment review powers, which the Court can also initiate ex officio (Article 146). For example, in the case of popularly-initiated amendments, the Romanian Constitutional Court has the opportunity to review the amendment bill twice: once when it is first introduced into Parliament and once when it has been adopted, with any modifications, by both houses of Parliament but before it has been ratified in a mandatory referendum. This review entails both procedural review, including checking that the onerous signature collection requirements have been met, and substantive review, evaluating whether the proposed changes come into conflict with the constitutional eternity clause in Article 152. The Court has engaged in a priori and ex officio amendment review on numerous occasions, both of large amendment packages as part of large-scale constitutional revision[19] and of discrete amendments to single constitutional provisions.[20] The Court has also clarified that a posteriori review of constitutional revisions is not within its competences.[21]

Whether constitutional amendments should be subsumed to ordinary law or not has been a question courts have grappled with in many jurisdictions, sometimes with far-reaching consequences. For example, the Indian Supreme Court had to consider precisely this question in the *Golakhnath* case, the precursor to its famous *Kesavananda* judgment which would announce the basic structure doctrine to the world.[22] In the former, at stake was the correct interpretation of Article 13(2) of the Indian Constitution, which states that: 'The State shall not make any law which takes away or abridges the rights conferred by this Part and any law made in contravention of this clause shall, to the extent of the contravention, be void.' Article 13(3) provided a non-exhaustive list of the types of legislative acts to be considered 'law', without explicitly including amendments. In the *Golakhnath* judgment, for the first time, the

[19] This was the case in 2003, the only time the Romanian Constitution was revised (Decision 148/2003, 16 April 2003), and subsequently eg Decision 80/2014, 16 February 2014 (when a politically-negotiated revision package was struck down).

[20] Decision 580/2016, 20 July 2016, declaring constitutional an amendment to the constitutional definition of family/marriage that would have restricted the institution to heterosexual couples only.

[21] Decision 356/2003, 30 September 2003. Constitutional commentators defended this position as respecting the primacy of the original constituent power (expressed through referendum approval of the revision) as compared to a derived power. See Ion Deleanu, 'Revizuirea Constitutiei' (2003) 5 *Dreptul* 5, 6.

[22] *Golaknath v State of Punjab*, AIR 1967 SC 1643 and *Kesavananda v State of Kerala* (1973) 4 SCC 225.

Indian Supreme Court ruled that constitutional amendments passed in conformity with Article 368 of the Indian Constitution (the amendment rule) did come under the purview of Article 13 and could thus be subject to constitutional review, including on the basis of implied limits. The decision was hotly contested.[23] It would be expressly overturned in 1971 by the Twenty-Fourth Amendment to the Indian Constitution, which sought to expressly eliminate amendments from the scope of both Articles 368 and 13. The *Kesavananda* judgment reiterating that there were substantive limits to constitutional amendments – which could not alter the constitution's basic structure – would come two years later.

B. The Normative Justifications for Amendment Review

Both in cases of eternity clauses and with regard to judicially created doctrines of constitutional unamendability, the justification for court review is similar: the potential for an abusive amendment is too great for courts to refrain from intervening. What David Landau has termed 'abusive constitutionalism' refers to 'the use of mechanisms of constitutional change to erode the democratic order.'[24] Using the examples of countries like Hungary, Egypt, and Venezuela, he has shown that, rather than opting for the military coups of the past, the autocrats of today use the tools of constitutional amendment and replacement to undermine democracy. Kim Lane Scheppele, herself focusing on the Hungarian case, has referred to this phenomenon as 'autocratic legalism' and has blamed precisely its legalistic focus for how difficult it is both to resist and to undo.[25] Richard Albert, in turn, has coined the term 'constitutional dismemberment' to similarly capture the abusive use of the constitutional amendment rule to subvert the constitution:

> A constitutional dismemberment can occur suddenly in a big-bang moment or gradually by erosion or accretion. It can occur to constitutions both codified and uncodified, and it can either enhance or deteriorate liberal democracy. These changes are often made using the ordinary rules of amendment, and they are commonly described as amendments or even sometimes as new constitutions. But they are amendments in name alone.[26]

He differentiates between a mere amendment and dismemberment on the basis of the scale and reach of the latter, arguing that it 'intends deliberately to disassemble one or more of a constitution's elemental parts. An amendment does not go nearly as far because, properly defined, it keeps the altered Constitution coherent with its pre-change identity, rights, and structure.'[27]

[23] Sudhir Krishnaswamy, *Democracy and Constitutionalism in India* (Oxford, Oxford University Press, 2009) 11–23.

[24] David Landau, 'Abusive Constitutionalism' (2013) 47 *UCD Law Review* 189.

[25] Kim Lane Scheppele, 'Autocratic Legalism' (2018) 85(2) *University of Chicago Law Review* 545.

[26] Albert (n 12) 84.

[27] ibid.

Both scholars and courts have sought to clarify the canons of constitutional interpretation to deploy in order to review and sanction such abusive constitutional change.[28] The task is not always easy, as the changes may be more subtle or incremental. The scenario in which an otherwise lawfully adopted constitutional amendment may actually be unconstitutional in substance poses difficult questions for advocates of CCI. The presumption of constitutionality on which CCI is based is in direct opposition to the sceptical view of drafter intent when it comes to potentially abusive amendments. In their case, we could well see a stronger case for what Christoph Bezemek and Daniel Gosch have termed 'the supremacy of abolition strategy'.[29] They contrast it to the 'supremacy of validity strategy' that would see it as inadmissible for constitutional interpretation to depart from the assumption that the legislator intended to breach the constitution.[30]

If we accept that the stakes are higher and the negative consequences of not striking down an abusive amendment may be more far-reaching, then it may be that the case for CCI is weaker. If nothing else, the generally higher threshold for adopting constitutional amendments means that mobilisation for constitutional amendment is difficult and resource-intensive. The democratic costs of striking down an otherwise procedurally compliant amendment are not to be taken lightly. Conversely, allowing an amendment to stand will typically mean it attains the same level of constitutional entrenchment as the rest of the constitution. Its undoing will therefore require a larger and more sustained popular effort than legislation tends to do.

As we will see in the examples discussed shortly, assessing the role of CCI in the constitutional review of amendments cannot be done in the abstract. We need deeper contextual familiarity with a given constitutional system and with constitutional amendment practice within it in order to assess how courts can walk the interpretive tightrope in amendment review. Moreover, contrary to the hierarchical, ordered, predictable constitutional hinterland presupposed by proponents of CCI, many real-world constitutions actually contain a hodgepodge of norms. These do not always sit together easily or coherently, and may even contradict each other. This may reflect incoherent compromises at the time of negotiating the constitution.[31] It may also reflect intentional exclusionary goals, for example of minorities or women, embedded at the heart of otherwise liberal democratic documents.[32] Writing about such semi-liberal constitutional systems, as she calls

[28] For one such attempt to lay out a formula for detecting abusive constitutional practices, see Jan Petrov, 'How to Detect Abusive Constitutional Practices' (2024) 20(1) *European Constitutional Law Review* (2024) 1.

[29] Christoph Bezemek and Daniel Gosch, 'Austria. Embracing Tradition: Constitutionally Conforming Interpretation's Edge in Reconciling Statutory and Constitutional Law' in Klatt (n 1) 35, 42.

[30] ibid.

[31] Donald P Horowitz, *Constitutional Processes and Democratic Commitment* (New Haven, Yale University Press, 2021) 72–73.

[32] I make this argument more extensively in Suteu (n 13) 110–13.

them, Gila Stopler has argued that 'the application of liberal rights reasoning in semi-liberal settings neglects the power differentials inherent in such systems and tends to overprotect the rights of some at the expense of the rights of others.'[33]

III. The Substantive Review of Constitutional Amendments and Unconstitutional Constitutional Amendment Doctrines

Courts in disparate jurisdictions have adopted very different approaches to operationalising substantive limits on constitutional amendment. In some cases, the Constitution itself may contain a formal eternity clause, but courts may nevertheless refuse to engage in substantive constitutional amendment review. This is the case in France, whose Constitution declares unamendable the republican form of government in Article 89. However, the *Conseil Constitutionnel* has refrained from reviewing constitutional amendments, despite several opportunities to do so, such as: De Gaulle's 1962 revision of the Constitution to make the president directly elected, the 1992 ratification of Maastricht Treaty, and decentralisation in 2003.[34] This is in line with the sceptical view of judges and judicial review in France, where they are meant to apply and not make the law, and where the fear of a *gouvernement des juges* has endured since the French Revolution. In this context, the *Conseil* performs the task of a railroad switch, simply redirecting constitutionally problematic statutes to the track to constitutional amendment instead.[35] France is not alone in resisting substantive amendment review, however. Other jurisdictions have done similarly, on account of strong traditions of formalism in constitutional interpretation and of reading popular sovereignty as precluding amendment review.[36]

Where substantive amendment review has been embraced, courts have developed unconstitutional constitutional amendment doctrines that centre either the constitutional eternity clause or, where one is not present in the text, implicit limits to constitutional change. In some contexts, the doctrines have done both. In Italy, for example, Article 139 of the Constitution declares the republican form of government unamendable, as the French one does. However,

[33] Gila Stopler, 'Semi-liberal Constitutionalism' (2019) 8(1) *Global Constitutionalism* 94.

[34] Decision No. 62-20DC, 6 November 1962; Decision No. 92-308DC, 9 April 1992; Decision No. 2003-469DC, 26 March 2003, respectively. See discussion in Denis Baranger, 'The Language of Eternity: Judicial Review of the Amending Power in France (or the Absence Thereof)' (2011) 44 *Israeli Law Review* 389, 391–98.

[35] It has happened on at least two occasions that constitutional amendments were passed to achieve goals that legislation could not achieve. See Mathieu Carpenter, 'France. The Dynamics of "Interpretative Reservations" in the Jurisprudence of the French Constitutional Council' in Klatt (n 1) 67, 81.

[36] Richard Albert, Malkhaz Nakashidze and Tarik Olcay, 'The Formalist Resistance to Unconstitutional Constitutional Amendments' (2019) 70 *Hastings Law Journal* 639.

the Italian Constitutional Court has gone beyond this textual hook in defining its amendment review powers. Already back in 1988, it explained that there are, in addition to the limits on constitutional revision expressly provided for in Article 139, additional, implicit ones, which 'belong to the essence of the supreme values on which the Italian Constitution is founded.'[37] Another permutation is where a judicially-created doctrine of unamendability was later placed on textual footing by incorporating substantive amendment limits in the constitution. This was the case of Bangladesh, where the Fifteenth Amendment Act of 2011 introduced the unamendable 'basic provisions of the constitution', now listed in Article 7(B), 20 years after the Supreme Court first embraced its own basic structure doctrine.[38]

In what follows, I propose to investigate aspects of unconstitutional constitutional amendment doctrines in practice that distinctly tie into CCI debates. They centre on the question of judicial restraint, ie whether courts can deploy such doctrines as a measure of last resort and thereby depart only in exceptional circumstances from a presumption of constitutionality of amendments.

A. Substantive Amendment Review and the Normative Bases for Judicial Restraint

Scholars disagree on whether unamendability review is a tool that courts can use sparingly and only in exceptional circumstances, or else one that necessarily leads to judicial self-aggrandisement.[39] Given how far-reaching the power to strike down otherwise procedurally proper constitutional amendments is, especially on the basis of implicit constitutional limits the courts themselves are solely mandated to identify, the question becomes: what are the limits to this power? What is to rein in the judicial guardians of the Constitution so that they do not exceed their constitutional mandate and do not simply substitute their own will for the lawfully expressed popular one?

Some scholars have answered this question by appealing to a higher normative order.[40] Rosalind Dixon and David Landau, for example, make a strong case that transnational values can curb any judicial overreach in the enforcement of substantive amendment limits. They even speak of 'an international democratic "minimum core"' which can be identified in the overlapping consensus among

[37] Sentenza n. 1146/1988, para 2.1.

[38] See discussion in Suteu (n 13) 138.

[39] For my own views, see Suteu (n 13).

[40] Lech Garlicki and Zofia A Garlicka, 'External Review of Constitutional Amendments? International Law as a Norm of Reference' (2011) 44 *Israel Law Review* 343; Rosalind Dixon and David Landau, 'Transnational Constitutionalism and a Limited Doctrine of Unconstitutional Constitutional Amendment' (2015) 13(3) *International Journal of Constitutional Law* 606; and Roznai (n 13) 71–102. See also Suteu (n 13) 186.

countries about what represents the minimum content of any 'basic structure' of democratic constitutions.[41]

If we think back to the contours of CCI, what such arguments do is introduce an additional normative level into the interpretive exercise. Whereas CCI is mainly concerned with the domestic order and ensuring the conformity of legislation to the normatively higher constitutional order, such an appeal to transnational norms essentially amounts to subjecting the constitutional order to a normatively superior supranational order of values. Leaving aside the possible indeterminacy of the latter, we are also faced with the fraught stance taken by many constitutional courts in cases involving apparent conflicts between national and supranational law. The rise of constitutional identity review across European constitutional systems in cases involving challenges to the primacy of European law is a case in point.[42] It illustrates that merely appealing to a transnational value order may be neither appealing nor easy for courts to do, and is a move that raises more questions of constitutional authority and democratic legitimacy.

There have also been attempts to find normative solutions endogenous to a given constitutional system, by way of interpretive canons that would engender judicial self-restraint in amendment review. Yaniv Roznai, for example, believes that the intensity of judicial scrutiny of amendments may be rendered more predictable if pinned to the popular characteristics of the amendment process: the more participatory and multi-stage the process, the less need for court supervision; the more executive-led, the more likely to be manipulated and as such the more need for court intervention.[43] The ideal scenario in general is for courts not to need to resort to amendment strike-down, which is a measure of last resort raising potentially grave democratic concerns. They would only do so in cases where the potential harm of the amendment under review is extreme.

Normatively, this sliding scale of intensity of review goes hand in hand with Roznai's delegation theory of amendment powers.[44] He differentiates between primary and secondary constituent power, the former attached to the foundational moment of constitution-making, with the latter corresponding to the amendment power.[45] The primary constituent power merely delegates amendment power to constitutional actors, who hold it in trust until such time as a constitutional revolution or new constitution-making moment arise. As a secondary, derived power, the power to amend the Constitution is naturally more limited than the power to

[41] Rosalind Dixon and David Landau, 'Competitive Democracy and the Constitutional Minimum Core' in Tom Ginsburg and Aziz Huq (eds), *Assessing Constitutional Performance* (Cambridge, Cambridge University Press, 2016) 268, 278.

[42] Delving deeper into this topic exceeds the aims of this chapter, but see discussion in Suteu (n 13) 113–23.

[43] Roznai (n 13) 219–20. See a full discussion in Suteu (n 13) 145–58.

[44] For a critique of the delegation theory of unamendability as practically deficient and internally inconsistent, see Mikael Ruotsi, 'A Doctrinal Approach to Unconstitutional Constitutional Amendments: Judicial Review of Constitutional Amendments in Sweden' (2024) 20(1) *European Constitutional Law Review* 1.

[45] Roznai (n 13) 158–75.

remake it entirely. The more the process of constitutional change approximates the foundational process of constitutional creation – so goes Roznai's argument – the stronger the incentive for courts to take a backseat and exercise self-restraint.

The presumption of constitutionality, then, is in favour of amendments, with courts invalidating them only in very exceptional circumstances. It has also been argued that, through skilful calibration, courts can ensure they deploy unconstitutional constitutional amendment doctrines sparingly and with a democracy-reinforcing effect.[46] As we will see in the following section, however, courts very often do not perform this calibration in a manner that is easily defensible on principled grounds and are frequently likely to overreach when identifying attacks on constitutional principles.

B. Substantive Amendment Review in Practice: The Threat of Judicial Overreach

When looking at the practical reality of courts enforcing unconstitutional constitutional amendment doctrines, we find them not always able to exercise such restraint. In some instances, we may be able to attribute judicial overreach to overzealous courts overextending the scope of the constitution's minimum core or basic structure to rights and principles that cannot reasonably be viewed as indispensable to constitutional democracy.

For example, the Colombian Constitutional Court has progressively expanded its constitutional replacement doctrine (*inconstitucionalidad por sustitución*), first developed in cases of presidential re-election to stop executive overstay. It relied on this doctrine when reviewing Constitutional Amendment Act 02 of 2009, which introduced into Article 49 of the Colombian Constitution the prohibition of drug possession in direct response to a prior judicial decriminalisation.[47] Another example is the Croatian Constitutional Court reviewing a popular initiative to block government plans to allow private entities to administer public roads. The Court found the entrepreneurial and market freedom (enshrined in Article 49 of the constitution) to be part of the constitutional identity of Croatia.[48] There may be good policy reasons for the measures reviewed in both instances. However, one wonders whether their constitutionalisation and the Courts' analysis under the aegis of unamendability and constitutional identity does not risk trivialising the unconstitutional constitutional amendment doctrine.

The risk of judicial overreach in amendment review is both higher and more difficult to assess in cases where judicial independence may be at stake. This is

[46] Rosalind Dixon, *Responsive Judicial Review* (Oxford, Oxford University Press, 2023) 122–27.

[47] Sentencia C-574/11.

[48] Decision U-viir-1158/2015 of 21 April 2015 cited in Jurij Toplak and Djordje Gardasevic, 'Concepts of National and Constitutional Identity in Croatian Constitutional Law' (2017) 42 *Review of Central and East European Law* 263, 286.

universally accepted as a core component of the rule of law and often also of the minimum core/basic structure of a functioning constitutional democracy. However, whether and when judicial independence has been compromised is not always straightforward to establish. Cases of political capture of courts or the outright ouster of judicial review will be clear instances of unconstitutional action. However, reforms of judicial appointments procedures and of court competences may be far less so.

One prominent case in which the Indian Supreme Court may have overreached in its application of the basic structure doctrine is the 2016 *National Judicial Appointments Commission (NJAC)* judgment.[49] The Court reviewed the Ninety-ninth Amendment to the Indian Constitution creating a new National Judicial Appointments Commission. The Commission was meant to replace a collegium system of high court appointments dominated by Supreme Court justices. The reform was justified on grounds of increased accountability and transparency, as while it retained the Chief Justice and two senior justices in the Commission, it would also include the union minister of law and civil society representatives.[50] An appointment could be vetoed by two members of the Commission.

Undoubtedly, the new system would make more room for political and civil society actors, though it was not unprecedented in comparative terms when looking at other models of judicial appointments worldwide. In fact, the Indian Constitution does not explicitly clarify the question of final say in judicial appointments and it was the cabinet that had retained it until 1993, when the system was changed in response to Supreme Court case law.[51] Nevertheless, the Supreme Court ruled the amendment unconstitutional as breaching the basic structure doctrine. Its reasoning was that, by removing the judicial supremacy previously existing in the judicial appointments process, judicial independence was under threat. Its interpretation thus turned the CCI presumption of constitutionality on its head. Even admitting that there might have been ambiguity in the formulation of the constitutional amendment, the Court interpreted the mere threat of encroachment on judicial independence as triggering a finding of unconstitutionality. It went even further than this, however, by also identifying a mandatory constitutional duty, grounded in Article 124(2) of the Indian constitution, of the president to consult with senior justices in judicial appointments. Judicial independence had been recognised as integral to the basic structure of the Constitution since the time of *Kesavananda*. Its *NJAC* reading, however, appears to depart quite significantly from the type of unconstitutionality it was originally envisioned to prevent.

[49] *Supreme Court Advocates-on-Record Association v Union of India* (2016) 4 SCC 1.

[50] Rehan Abeyratne, 'Upholding Judicial Supremacy in India: The NJAC Judgment in Comparative Perspective' (2017) 49 *George Washington International Law Review* 569.

[51] ibid 611.

Other courts have similarly embraced basic structure doctrines, and judicial independence as one of its central pillars. The Supreme Courts of Bangladesh and Pakistan, for example, have done so. The former embraced the basic structure doctrine in a case concerning diffusing judicial review and politically subordinating the judiciary during military rule.[52] When a judicial restructuring amendment came before it in 2016, the Bangladeshi Supreme Court struck it down even though the text of the amendment replicated verbatim an original constitutional provision.[53] The Court feared that it afforded Parliament too much say in judicial removals, although at the time of the judgment, the legislation on the precise details of judicial impeachment had not yet been passed. Moreover, the status quo the judgment preserved had itself been introduced during Bangladesh's period of martial rule.

The Pakistani Supreme Court for a time resisted embracing the doctrine and deploying it in order to strike down amendments. It initially took the intermediary step of adopting a structural method of interpretation that referred to the Constitution's basic structure,[54] while ruling that this did not imply the judicial power to review its possible breach.[55] Then in 2015, when reviewing the Eighth Amendment to the Constitution (largely seen as a conduit for the restoration of constitutional democracy following the rule of Pervez Musharraf), the Court reviewed the changes introduced that would remove judicial supremacy in judicial appointments.[56] This judicial supremacy in appointments had itself been a judicial creation.[57] Rather than striking it down, however, the Court issued an interim order that listed the problems with the proposed reforms.[58] Parliament adopted the Nineteenth Amendment in response, although it retained the shift of the final word on judicial appointments to a parliamentary committee. In turn, the Supreme Court declared the decisions of this committee justiciable, thereby reasserting its primacy in judicial appointments.[59]

Colombia's constitutional replacement doctrine has already been mentioned above. It, too, has been deployed in the context of attempted reform of the judicial appointments procedure. In 2016, the Colombian Constitutional Court struck

[52] *Anwar Hossain Chowdhury v Bangladesh*, 1989, 18 CLC (AD). For a discussion of the basic structure doctrine in Bangladesh, see Ridwanul Hoque, 'The Politics of Unconstitutional Amendments in Bangladesh' in Abeyratne and Son Bui (n 13) 210.

[53] *Advocate Asaduzzaman Siddiqui v Bangladesh*, Writ Petition No. 9989 of 2014, 5 May 2016. See discussion in Ridwanul Hoque, 'Developments in Bangladeshi Constitutional Law: The Year 2016 in Review' (12 October 2017) *ICONnect Blog*, available at www.iconnectblog.com/developments-in-bangladeshi-constitutional-law-the-year-2016-in-review/.

[54] *Al-Jehad Trust v Federation of Pakistan* PLD 1996 SC 324.

[55] *Wukala Mahaz Barai Tahafaz Dastoor v Federation of Pakistan* PLD 1998 SC 1263.

[56] *District Bar Association, Rawalpindi and others v Federation of Pakistan* PLD 2015 SC 401.

[57] *Al-Jehad Trust v Federation of Pakistan* PLD 1996 SC 324, also known as the 'Judges' case'. See Moeen H Cheema, 'The "Chaudhry Court": Deconstructing the "Judicialization of Politics" in Pakistan' (2016) 25(3) *Washington International Law Journal* 447, fn 45.

[58] *Nadeem Ahmad and Others v Federation of Pakistan*, PLD 2010 SC 1165.

[59] Moeen H Cheema, 'Two Steps Forward One Step Back: The Non-linear Expansion of Judicial Power in Pakistan' (2018) 16(2) *International Journal of Constitutional Law* 503, 520.

down two initiatives to create new institutions in the area of judicial governance and criminal and disciplinary proceedings of judges.[60] It rejected the stated aim of these reforms – increasing judicial accountability and efficiency – and instead found them to be in breach of the principles of judicial self-governance, judicial independence, and the separation of powers. This in spite of the two institutions proposed retaining a mixed composition, dominated by judicial appointees. It is at least in question whether the reforms might have been constitutionally compliant, yet the Court resolved this doubt in favour of strike-down.

A final example I will briefly discuss here is that of the Romanian Constitutional Court. As already noted, the Court is empowered to review constitutional amendments *in abstracto* and *ex officio*. In practice, this means reviewing both the constitutional revision *initiative*, meaning the amendment proposal as introduced by drafters, and the *law* adopted by Parliament containing the final version of the proposed amendment to be put to a referendum vote. Additionally, the law on the functioning of the Court was amended to expand its competences to include the review of decisions of either house of Parliament.[61] When a package of constitutional amendments attempted to alter its competences in 2014, removing one of the abstract reviews and this late expansion of competences, the Court ruled this to be an affront to the unamendable constitutional principle of access to constitutional justice.[62] In the eyes of the Court, any restriction of its competence – even those that sought to restore its original set of competences as envisioned at the time of its creation – amounted to an unconstitutional constitutional amendment.

C. Substantive Amendment Review in Practice: The Threat of Judicial Underreach

Cases discussed in the previous section highlight the threat of courts adopting an expansive interpretation of their powers of amendment review. This can lead both to over-inclusiveness in terms of principles deemed unamendable and to over-zealous strike-down of amendments that curtail judicial power, even where they might fall short of undermining judicial independence and access to justice. There is, however, also the mirror problem of judicial underreach when it comes to deploying doctrines of unconstitutional constitutional amendment. In such scenarios, it is not that courts are too active but that they remain passive or avoidant in the face of constitutional change that should be deemed in breach of constitutional minimum cores or basic structures. Let me provide two examples.

[60] Decision C-285 of June 1, 2016 and Decision C-373 of July 13, 2016. See discussion in Mario Alberto Cajas-Sarria, 'Judicial Review of Constitutional Amendments in Colombia: A Political and Historical Perspective, 1955–2016' (2017) 5(3) *The Theory and Practice of Legislation* 245.

[61] Law No. 177/2010 modifying Law No. 42/1992.

[62] Decision 80/2014.

In 2016, the Romanian Constitutional Court was called on to review the compatibility of an amendment born via citizen initiative to redefine the understanding of marriage in Article 48 of the Constitution as between a man and a woman.[63] The original text of the provision refers to equality between the spouses in neutral terms but, the drafters argued, this left too much ambiguity in the law and led to – in their view – pernicious consequences, not least of which the possible legal recognition of same-sex couples. This ignored the fact that the Romanian Civil Code had been amended explicitly to exclude same-sex couples from the legal understanding of the institution of marriage.[64] In its judgment, the Court did not engage in CCI. Instead, it relied on a – rather rudimentary, it should be said – textualist reading of the 1991 constitution, arguing that the constitution-makers had always envisioned a heterosexual understanding of marriage and the family. This ignored the gender-neutral language of both the Constitution and the civil code at the time of its adoption. While these elements do not amount to de facto legal recognition of same-sex marriage, of course, they do indicate that the constitutional text was far more capacious than the Court acknowledged in its 2016 ruling.[65] Moreover, by adopting its restrictive textualist interpretation, the Court operated a significant narrowing of constitutional meaning.

One might still, on this evidence, be tempted to think that even had it resorted to CCI, the Romanian Constitutional Court might have been on solid normative ground to allow the amendment initiative to stand. However, the constitutional eternity clause contained in Article 152 also includes a rights non-regression clause that would prevent the suppression of fundamental rights. A proper structural interpretation would have forced the Court to explain why an amendment seeking to pre-emptively ban the recognition of same-sex marriage, as well as to restrict the constitutional understanding of family to only heterosexual and married couples, did not constitute a suppression of constitutional rights to equality and private and family life. While the Court paid lip service to these rights, it simply asserted that, as the proposed amendment did not result in the suppression of the right to marry for same-sex couples (it could not have, since such a right was not recognised under Romanian law), the revision was not in breach of the prohibition of rights non-regression in Article 152(2). This judgment is not only a poor example of constitutional reasoning, but also exhibits the shortcomings of an overly formalistic approach to constitutional interpretation.[66]

The Indian Supreme Court provides the other example I wish to briefly mention here. While its basic structure doctrine has brought it much acclaim and has been emulated worldwide, we have recently also seen how it can remain a democratic

[63] Decision 580/2016.

[64] Art 277 of the Romanian Civil Code.

[65] Simina Elena Tanasescu, 'De l'initiative populaire au référendum constitutionnel en Roumanie' (2018) 1 *Romanian Journal of Comparative Law* 97, 107.

[66] I make this argument more fully in Silvia Suteu, 'Between Dialogue, Conflict, and Competition: The Limits of Responsive Judicial Review in the Case of the Romanian Constitutional Court' (2023) 48 (3/4) *Review of Central and East European Law* 519.

defence gun that refuses to fire. In the context of the Citizenship (Amendment) Act 2019 (CAA), the Court has yet to rule despite hundreds of petitions having been lodged before it to challenge the constitutionality of the act.[67] The CAA purported to facilitate the path to citizenship for illegal migrants escaping persecution, but did so on religious grounds that excluded certain religions (Islam and Judaism) and certain countries of origin (Sri Lanka). In conjunction with the Indian Government's planned roll out of the National Register of Citizens (NRC), the CAA's effects are potentially immense. The NRC would allow for the detention and deportation of so-called' doubtful citizens', ie those who cannot prove their citizenship status. The combined effects of the NRA and CAA would be potentially to increase the number of persons being rendered stateless by millions.[68]

There is a strong case to be made that the CAA breaches the constitutional protection of secularism, in addition to the constitutional guarantees of equality and non-discrimination.[69] Secularism has long been recognised by the Supreme Court as a pillar of its basic structure doctrine.[70] The Court has thus far opted not to rule on the constitutionality of the CAA, however. It initially postponed hearings in the case due to the pandemic. Five years after the passing of the act, however, we are nowhere nearer having the court's views on its constitutional compliance. It has been argued that the court's prevarication is everything but accidental and is instead an indirect form of support for Narendra Modi's exclusionary legal agenda, allowing it to become social fact before a legal ruling is issued.[71]

The CAA would have been a prime example of a case in which the Supreme Court might have engaged in CCI. As Raeesa Vakil has argued, however, the Court's reliance on CCI has been inconsistent and unpredictable, with the CAA an especially egregious example.[72] In response to a petitioner worried about the multiple petitions seeking the stay of execution of the act and about the Supreme Court's silence on the matter, the Chief Justice is quoted to have said that: '[t]here is anyway a presumption of constitutionality. You have been a student of law, you would know.'[73] This view is highly problematic: it means that the Court implicitly relies on the presumption of constitutionality of the CAA while it strategically chooses not to rule on the act. The normative force of the basic structure doctrine, in this instance, its protection of secularism as a constitutional principle, is thereby

[67] For a fuller discussion, see Silvia Suteu, 'Friends or Foes: Is Unamendability the Answer to Democratic Backsliding?' (2024) 16 *Hague Journal on the Rule of Law* 315.

[68] Adil Hasan Khan, 'India and Statelessness: An Introduction' (2021) 3(1) *Statelessness & Citizenship Review* 176, 178.

[69] Abhinav Chandrachud, 'Secularism and the Citizenship Amendment Act' (2020) 4(2) *Indian Law Review* 138.

[70] *S. R. Bommai v Union of India*, AIR 1975 1994 SC 1918.

[71] Nandini Sundar, 'The Supreme Court in Modi's India' (2023) 1(1) *Journal of Right-Wing Studies* 106, 133.

[72] Raeesa Vakil, 'India. The Ultimate Interpreter: Democracy and Constitutionality in the Indian Supreme Court' in Klatt (n 1) 281, 304.

[73] ibid.

severely curtailed.[74] As Vakil argues, the presumption of constitutionality therefore 'sometimes leads to reduced enforcement of rights and a greater burden on the petitioner, who approaches the Court for the protection of her freedoms.'[75]

IV. Informal (De Facto) Constitutional Amendments

The discussion hitherto has proceeded on a very formal understanding of constitutional amendments, as textual alterations to the Constitution enacted through the constitutionally prescribed procedure and recognised by constitutional actors as amendments in name and substance. However, the picture becomes more complicated when we expand the conceptual category of amendment and define it on the basis of whether constitutional change has been enacted, regardless of whether the formal amendment route has been pursued. Put differently, we may find ourselves faced with a change in constitutional meaning, even while the constitutional text has remained unaltered.

So defined, we would have to deal with at least two additional forms of constitutional amendment: amendment via sub-constitutional means, such as through ordinary legislation and other types of acts, and amendment via judicial review. Comparative constitutional history and practice suggests these forms of constitutional change may have an especially deleterious effect on the rule of law, and they have at times been called 'amendment by stealth'[76] to signal their departure from accepted norms of good amendment practice. I therefore proceed to discuss each of them in turn.

A. Sub-constitutional (Legislative) Amendments

When it comes to sub-constitutional amendments, we are faced with a scenario in which constitutional meaning is changed not through the constitutionally prescribed route, with its typically more onerous procedural hurdles, but usually through the ordinary legislative process. The most infamous example is that of the 1933 Enabling Act (*Ermächtigungsgesetz*) in Nazi Germany which empowered the executive to legislate, even departing from the Constitution (therefore effectively to amend it), so long as the institution of the Parliament formally remained in place. The road to the *Ermächtigungsgesetz* had been prepared in advance, however, with the National Socialists repeatedly adopting laws that amounted to non-explicit constitutional amendments:

[74] A significant problem in the Indian case is the fact that the Supreme Court judgments are issued by different benches of judges, in different permutations, which leads to further muddling of its jurisprudential coherence.

[75] Vakil (n 72) 305.

[76] Richard Albert, 'Constitutional Amendment by Stealth' (2015) 60(4) *McGill Law Journal* 673.

> This so-called breaking-through of the constitution (*Verfassungsdurchbrechung*) was often – deliberately – practiced and allowed for the adoption of the infamous *Ermächtigungsgesetz* of March 1933 which transferred practically all legislative powers of Parliament to the government under the new chancellor Adolf Hitler.[77]

The postwar Basic Law was designed in direct response to these experiences. On the one hand, a parliamentary system with a ceremonial president was put in place in order to prevent a similar decent into dictatorship. On the other hand, the amendment rule was also drafted so as to thwart 'revolutions under the mask of legality' from ever reoccurring.[78] The eternity clause (*Ewigkeitsklausel*) included in Article 79(3) of the Basic Law declares the inviolability of human dignity and of human rights, as well as of the democratic, federal, and social nature of the German state, the electoral nature of the German democracy, and the rule of law. It was meant as a legalistic solution to what was perceived as a legalistic problem – the subversion of the constitutional text through de facto amendments, obscured under the cover of legality – adopted in a highly legalistic culture.[79]

This way of attaining the semblance of legitimate authority through legalistic but abusive means has not remained confined to the National Socialists, nor to the distant past. If we look at the breakdown of the rule of law in Poland during the time in power of the Law and Justice Party (*Prawo i Sprawiedliwość* (PiS)) (2015–2023), no formal constitutional amendment was adopted. The amendment rule in the Polish Constitution would have required a two-thirds majority in the lower House and a majority in the upper House of Parliament for any amendment to be passed, which PiS did not have. Instead, the route it chose was that of ordinary legislation through which the independence of the Constitutional Tribunal and later the regular courts was severely curtailed, fundamental rights restricted, and accountability institutions such as the media regulator captured.[80]

Thus, Poland's situation was different to that in neighbouring Hungary where Viktor Orban has enjoyed repeated electoral wins with significant majorities in Parliament since 2010. The latter could proceed via the formal amendment route to change, then replace, then change again Hungary's Constitution so as to entrench an authoritarian populist political project. Wojciech Sadurski has raised the question of whether the Polish degradation of the rule of law is not, in fact, more damaging in the long-term:

> one may speculate that constitutional amendments via statutes along with simple breaches of the Constitution, Polish-style, are more destructive of the principles

[77] Werner Heun, *The Constitution of Germany: A Contextual Analysis* (Oxford, Hart Publishing, 2011) 19.

[78] Jens Woelk, 'Germany' in Oliver and Fusaro (n 12) 143, 144. See also Markus Kotzur, 'Constitutional Amendments and Constitutional Changes in Germany' in Contiades (n 12) 125, 129.

[79] Christoph Möllers, '"We Are (Afraid of) the People": Constituent Power in German Constitutionalism' in Martin Loughlin and Neil Walker (eds), *The Paradox of Constitutionalism: Constituent Power and Constitutional Form* (Oxford, Oxford University Press, 2008) 87.

[80] For a fuller account of these statutory changes, see Wojciech Sadurski, *Poland's Constitutional Breakdown* (Oxford, Oxford University Press, 2019).

> of constitutionalism and the rule of law. In Hungary, the disempowerment of the Constitutional Court was done *lege artis*; in Poland, it was more a demolition job than the restructuring of an institution, in full disregard of the constitutional provisions.[81]

This type of de facto, or sub-constitutional, amendment clearly raises problems for constitutional interpretation. On the one hand, such changes may escape constitutional review if the latter targets constitutional amendments. Their enactment through procedures otherwise reserved for ordinary statutes or even non-legislative means they may go undetected for longer, both because their importance may be missed and because their impact on the rule of law may be cumulative rather than discrete. These are the scenarios that proponents of unconstitutional constitutional amendments often have in mind when promoting judicial intervention to sanction incremental constitutional change that has a systemic negative effect, rather than a big bang abusive amendment.

On the other hand, however, one could see this as exactly the type of setup for which CCI would be best suited. These de facto amendments are, after all, statutes on whose constitutionality constitutional courts are typically competent to rule (according to the respective rules of each constitutional system). For amendment scholars, their sub-constitutional nature makes them hard to capture under formal amendment review. However, their legislative status should make them ripe for judicial sanction under normal rules of constitutional interpretation. CCI's propensity to lead to a systemic analysis of compliance between the norm under review and constitutional norms read holistically is here an asset.

Nevertheless, a possible hurdle remains. It is unclear whether legislative changes such as to judges' pension ages, judges' salaries, court structure, judicial disciplinary procedures etc (all changes adopted in both Hungary and Poland during their rule of law crises), especially when introduced piecemeal and at the start of a period of rule of law breakdown, would be read as excluding any constitutionally compliant interpretation. If the judge only has discrete laws before her when engaged in her interpretative practice, it is uncertain whether CCI would be the best canon of interpretation to allow her to strike them down for their insidious, cumulative, indirect effects. CCI thus has an uneasy relationship to abusive sub-constitutional amendments.

B. Informal Constitutional Amendments via Judicial Review

There is an additional sense in which we may speak of de facto or informal amendments: when constitutional change is achieved via judicial review. In other words, significant alterations to constitutional meaning may come at the hands of judges themselves deploying their interpretive tools. Scholarship abounds with studies on the normative contours within which judicial innovation is permissible, and

[81] ibid 18.

on identifying when judicial activism is welcome and justified as opposed to a hindrance and illegitimate.[82] More generally, while amendment rules have often been missing in the well-established debate on the legitimacy of judicial review, astute observers have in fact noted that the nature of the constitutional amendment provision is directly relevant to such debates.[83] Thus, it is not just through ordinary legislation that political branches may have the final word in a dispute with the judiciary; it may also be that the amendment route is open to entrench a constitutional solution different to that chosen by the court.

Returning to the idea of judicial amendments, they can be viewed in both a positive and a negative sense. Positively, judicial innovation amounting to de facto amendment may be defended where the age and difficulty of amending the existing Constitution leave little room for keeping the fundamental law in line with changing social reality *but* through creative judicial interpretation. The US Constitution is the typical example here, with the US Supreme Court's interventions – in cases such as racial desegregation, access to contraceptives and abortion, and the recognition of same-sex marriage – defended (at least until recently) as necessary in a constitutional system where formal constitutional change has become all but impossible.[84] The Canadian Constitution has similarly been viewed as so rigid as to make formal amendment unavailable,[85] and the country's Supreme Court has intervened to fill in the gaps, such as by identifying the novel constitutional rights to strike and to assisted dying.[86]

Those who view such judicial innovation positively do not necessarily deny the virtues of formalism. In fact, they may even defend going down the formal amendment route as ideal, as it is more transparent, conducive to legal certainty,[87] and signals to all constitutional actors 'the point at which a particular exercise in constitutional law-making comes to an end.'[88] Nevertheless, they believe that

[82] For overview accounts of the vast debate on judicial activism, see Luís Pereira Coutinho, Massimo La Torre, and Steven D Smith (eds), *Judicial Activism: An Interdisciplinary Approach to the American and European Experiences* (Berlin, Springer, 2015); Craig Green, 'An Intellectual History of Judicial Activism' (2009) 58(5) *Emory Law Journal* 1195. See also Susan D Carle, 'The Failed Idea of Judicial Restraint: A Brief Intellectual History' (2024) 49(1) *Law & Social Inquiry* 569.

[83] Rosalind Dixon and Adrienne Stone, 'Constitutional Amendment and Political Constitutionalism: A Philosophical and Comparative Reflection' in David Dyzenhaus and Malcolm Thorburn (eds), *Philosophical Foundations of Constitutional Law* (Oxford, Oxford University Press, 2016) 95.

[84] On the US described as having a de facto unamendable Constitution because of the near-zero likelihood of the art V amendment route to be followed, see Richard Albert, 'Constructive Unamendability in Canada and the United States' (2014) 67 *Supreme Court Law Review* 181. For an opposing view, see Vicki Jackson, 'The (Myth of Un)amendability of the US Constitution and the Democratic Component of Constitutionalism' (2015) 13(3) *International Journal of Constitutional Law* 575.

[85] Albert (n 84).

[86] For a critical view of taking the judicial route in these matters, see Grégoire Webber, 'The Remaking of the Constitution of Canada' (1 July 2015) *UK Constitutional Law Blog*, available at ukconstitutionallaw.org/2015/07/01/gregoire-webber-the-remaking-of-the-constitution-of-canada/.

[87] Walter Dellinger, 'The Legitimacy of Constitutional Change: Rethinking the Amendment Process' (1983) 97(2) *Harvard Law Review* 386, 389.

[88] Bruce Ackerman, 'Higher Lawmaking' in Sanford Levinson (ed), *Responding to Imperfection: The Theory and Practice of Constitutional Amendment* (Princeton, Princeton University Press, 1995) 63, 84.

where the formal amendment route is unavailable (typically for reasons of political stalemate or polarisation), informal alternatives may be legitimate. The latter can be no less responsive to popular will and changing social realities than a constitutional amendment would. In the US context, this position is defended by scholars such as Akhil Reed Amar and Bruce Ackerman, who have long argued that the constitutional provision regulating amendment, Article V of the US Constitution, is not exhaustive of legitimate channels of constitutional change.[89] For the latter, innovative constitutional interpretation may be a no less legitimate way to achieve constitutional change that ensures the Constitution is a living document. For others, like Frederick Schauer, all constitutions not just the American one rest on both written and unwritten foundations, so it is unavoidable and even necessary that these change constantly, both according to the prescribed written amendment rule and beyond it.[90]

Unsurprisingly, not all agree with such a view. The progressive legislation and judgments adopted during the civil rights era in the US, perhaps the most exalted period in the life of the US Supreme Court, were not unanimously accepted as legitimate. For example, during the 1964 general election, Barry Goldwater argued that the Civil Rights Act and other such laws would have required Article V amendments.[91] Justice Black dissented in *Harper v Virginia Board of Elections*, the 1966 case in which the US Supreme Court ruled that the Fourteenth Amendment prohibited states from requiring citizens to pay a fee or tax to obtain access to polls.[92] He opined that such departure from the text and prior interpretation would have required formal amendment:

> when a 'political theory' embodied in our Constitution becomes outdated, it seems to me that a majority of the nine members of this Court are not only without constitutional power, but are far less qualified, to choose a new constitutional political theory than the people of this country proceeding in the manner provided by Article V.[93]

These objections receded from public consciousness in time and the Warren Court era soon became lionised in the American constitutional imaginary. However, as the aftermath of the repeal of the *Roe v Wade* decision granting a federal right to abortion has shown,[94] de facto amendments via judicial interpretation are vulnerable to changing judicial winds.

[89] Akhil Reed Amar, 'Consent of the Governed: Constitutional Amendment outside Article V' (1994) 94 *Columbia Law Review* 457; Bruce Ackerman, *We the People Volume 2: Transformations* (Cambridge, Harvard University Press, 1998).

[90] Frederick Schauer, 'The Unwritten Foundations of (All) Written Constitutions' in Richard Albert, Ryan C Williams and Yaniv Roznai (eds), *Amending America's Unwritten Constitution* (Cambridge, Cambridge University Press, 2022) 217.

[91] Bruce Ackerman, *We the People Volume 3: The Civil Rights Revolution* (Cambridge, Harvard University Press, 2014) 118.

[92] *Harper v Virginia Board of Elections*, 383 U.S. 663 (1966).

[93] ibid 678.

[94] *Dobbs v Jackson Women's Health Organization*, 597 U.S. 215 (2022).

In terms of constitutional interpretive canons, the contours of this debate in the US are usually circumscribed by very entrenched camps of originalists versus those who believe in more evolutive readings of the US Constitution. The peculiarities of the US Constitution, among which we may include its age, difficulty of formal amendment, and the lack of a clear textual basis for judicial review, have a direct bearing on the interpretive tools used by the US Supreme Court. As Schauer has shown, the pervasive preference for judicial avoidance by the Court is actually more similar to CCI than might initially appear.[95] He argues persuasively that such avoidance is not a vehicle for judicial restraint, as its application requires constitutional analysis and may well lead to the creation of statutory meaning going beyond that intended by the legislature.[96] Instances that might be characterised as de facto judicial amendments may simply represent the pinnacle of this endeavour.

Looking beyond the US context, we find many more negative understandings of the idea of judges changing constitutional meaning. Courts themselves have been said to engage in constitutional change deemed unconstitutional[97] or abusive.[98] As Rosalind Dixon and David Landau have argued, in contexts of democratic backsliding, there may be complex incentives for political actors to retain a certain degree of judicial independence and then proceed to use courts to their advantage. Thus, for instance, when formal avenues for constitutional amendment are unavailable, informal change may be channelled through the courts.[99] We have discussed legislative de facto amendments in Poland in the previous section. However, Poland during the PiS era may also be seen as an example here, insofar as the captured Constitutional Tribunal legitimised government legislation eroding judicial independence on the basis of constitutional interpretation that stretched into amendment territory.[100]

We need not reach the threshold of a rule of law crisis and a captured court to find dubious instances of informal amendment by courts, of course. In contexts where the constitutional court is embroiled in political tugs of war between the other branches, the chances that its interventions are perceived as illegitimately stretching constitutional meaning beyond the constitutional text increase. Take again the Romanian Constitutional Court, whose power has gradually expanded over the years and became most consequential during periods of high political conflict.[101] In such periods, such as during tense cohabitation between the president and prime minister, the Court's purported clarifications of issues such as the competences of

[95] Schauer (n 8).

[96] ibid 277.

[97] Yaniv Roznai, 'Unconstitutional Constitutional Change by Courts' (2017) 51 *New England Law Review* 557.

[98] Rosalind Dixon and David Landau, *Abusive Constitutional Borrowing: Legal Globalization and the Subversion of Liberal Democracy* (Oxford, Oxford University Press, 2021).

[99] ibid 112.

[100] Agnieszka Bień-Kacała, 'Informal Constitutional Change. The Case of Poland' (2017) 40(6) *Przegląd Prawa Konstytucyjnego* 199.

[101] Bianca Selejan-Gutan, 'The Constitutional Court and Others in Romanian Constitutionalism – 25 Years After' (2017) 11(4) *Vienna Journal of International Constitutional Law* 565.

political actors, the legal nature of national referendums, and its very own competences have been deemed to amount to informal constitutional changes.[102]

Here then is a potential subversion of the logic of CCI. The trigger for courts relying on CCI at all is the vagueness or ambiguity of the constitutional text.[103] However, that same condition may allow the interpretive exercise to stretch beyond the limits of interpretation and into the realm of amendment. In the Romanian example above, the Constitutional Court's interventions were not mere gap-filling or clarification exercises – they amounted instead to informal constitutional amendment facilitated by a vague constitutional text.[104]

V. Conclusion

This chapter has set out to map the different ways in which CCI as a canon of interpretation comes into play in the judicial review of constitutional amendments. It has first discussed the special nature of constitutional amendments and their differences as compared to ordinary legislation. Insofar as they remain at the stage of legislative proposals, court review may be more legitimate, especially where the constitutional text itself mandates abstract review. Once adopted, however, constitutional amendments become integral parts of the constitutional text and their normative level changes. A posteriori review of constitutional amendments therefore raises deeper legitimacy problems. Any court review in such instances necessarily relegates all post-foundational constitutional change to a lower, derived, secondary level to that of the original constitution, a proposition that is not universally accepted across constitutional systems.

The specificity of the amendment context raises the stakes of findings of unconstitutionality in other ways as well. Insofar as constitutional change is designed to be difficult and to require a higher threshold of both political and popular agreement (such as via supermajority votes and referendum approvals), amendment strike-down has different consequences to legislation strike-down. On balance of probabilities, revised statutes will be easier to pass so as to address court concerns, whereas mobilisation for constitutional amendment may well be more difficult to achieve repeatedly. While this is in itself not reason to expect constitutional courts simply to waive through problematic amendments, it does mean that the impetus for judicial restraint may be stronger in the case of amendment review.

The chapter then proceeded to discuss the case for judicial restraint in the substantive review of constitutional amendment, the scenario in which court oversight raises most legitimacy concerns. I analysed various normative arguments in

[102] Simina-Elena Tanasescu and Bianca Selejan-Gutan, 'Formal and Informal Constitutional Amendment: Report on Romania' (2018) 9 *Romanian Journal of Comparative Law* 389, 410–16.
[103] Klatt (n 2) 5.
[104] Tanasescu and Selejan-Gutan (n 102) 410.

favour of courts developing unconstitutional constitutional amendment doctrines cautiously and deploying them as a last resort. These included both an appeal to transnational norms as an additional normative level to which constitutional interpretation is to be subjected and the development of a sliding scale of judicial review intensity depending on the participatory nature of the amendment procedure. I then examined a variety of empirical examples to highlight that, in practice, even well-intentioned courts have a hard time calibrating their unconstitutional constitutional amendment doctrines. In certain cases, such as when they fear that judicial independence is at stake, they may overreach and slip into a presumption of unconstitutionality contrary to the ethos of CCI. In others, where they are navigating highly polarised societal and political waters, they may instead underreach and not sanction unconstitutionality precisely where the rights of vulnerable minorities are at stake.

Finally, the chapter moved beyond formal amendments and considered informal or de facto amendments. In the case of sub-constitutional or legislative amendments, ie constitutional change stealthily packaged as ordinary legislation, the positive role of CCI might be greatest. In concrete democratic backsliding scenarios, however, we have seen courts struggle to sanction this type of legislative unconstitutionality as the pernicious effect was achieved incrementally. Thus, while the discrete piece of legislation for review before the court (such as on judicial pensions, salaries, or disciplinary proceedings) may individually seem unproblematic, their cumulative effect may amount to the erosion of judicial independence. The problem is, however, that by the time this outcome is evident, it is too late.

A final type of informal amendment discussed is that achieved via judicial interpretation. Here, the scenario flips and the risk of illegitimacy is posed by constitutional interpretation itself. The same conditions that trigger the reliance on CCI, in particular the presence of ambiguity in constitutional meaning, lead to another type of court overreach, which stretches into constitutional amendment.

I have not set out to either assess or take a stand on the normative question of the desirability of CCI in amendment review. Instead, I hope to have illuminated some of the differences and similarities between its deployment in ordinary judicial review as compared to amendment review. As we have seen, the higher stakes in constitutional amendment invalidation strengthen the case for the exercise of judicial restraint. At the same time, the potentially far-reaching consequences of overt or covert constitutional amendments make court supervision more rather than less important. In many scenarios, especially in the context of democratic backsliding and attacks on the rule of law, we have seen the normative foundations of CCI called into question. The presumption of constitutionality, the comity between the judiciary and political branches, and the very unity and systemic coherence of the constitutional order have been revealed to be more vulnerable than proponents of CCI might have thought. Constitutional amendment review is merely one of the arenas in which these battles have been fought.

PART III

Comparison and Analysis

10

Partly Laws Common to All Judge-Kind: The Commonality and Divergence of Constitutionally Conforming Interpretation

ORAN DOYLE*

I. Introduction

Doctrines of constitutionally conforming interpretation (CCI) require that a court should, where more than one reading of a statutory provision is open, adopt the interpretation that saves the provision from constitutional invalidity. CCI itself is indifferent to the norms that a constitution contains. Its sole injunction is that any declaration of unconstitutionality that would be reached following the accepted norms of interpretation for a given constitutional system should be avoided through the adoption of a constitutionally consistent statutory interpretation, *where possible*. The 19 jurisdictions analysed in Volume 1 show CCI emerging in remarkably similar form across very different constitutional contexts: old and new constitutional systems; consolidated and partial democracies; dispersed and centralised constitutional review. The commonality of CCI across constitutional systems is accompanied, however, by significant divergence within and between systems over the import of that *where possible* caveat: to what extent can CCI legitimately be pushed to protect a statutory provision from a finding of invalidity? For some judges, CCI remains a largely technical device for minimising the disruption of constitutional review to settled legal expectations. But CCI frequently evolves into a more far-reaching suffusion of constitutional standards and constitutional

* I am grateful to all who commented on a draft of this chapter at the Taipei Comparative Constitutional Law Roundtable on 12 June 2023 and to a Faculty Research Workshop at Academia Sinica Taiwan on 16 January 2024, and to Conor Casey, Paul Daly, and Daniel Gosch who read subsequent drafts.

thinking throughout the entire legal system. Adapting Waldron, CCI is a constitutional doctrine only partly common to all judge-kind.[1]

This chapter addresses the intriguing puzzle raised by the national reports. Why is there such commonality in the adoption of CCI yet such divergence over its application? Answering these essentially empirical questions requires one to read the national reports in a subtly different way from how they are written. For the most part, the national reports are written from the participant's perspective, providing a *legal* analysis of the legitimate use of CCI within each constitutional system. Some reports adopt this perspective exclusively.[2] Others, perhaps reflecting different cultures of legal scholarship, present both the participant's perspective and external explanations of that perspective that could not be advanced – at least not without embarrassing self-reference and regress – by the participants themselves.[3] Each mode of scholarship is legitimate and makes a valuable contribution to our understanding of CCI. But this chapter, addressing empirical questions about 19 constitutional systems, cannot be written from the participant's perspective: there is no such participant and, even if there were, the norms of valid legal argumentation might compel them to justify their actions in ways that did not reveal their motivations for action.

The national reports, however, provide the evidence base on which this chapter addresses the empirical questions. In sections II and III, I draw on the national reports to provide a picture of how CCI emerges and is practised across jurisdictions. The intensification of CCI over time, I argue, is best understood as an interaction of four dimensions: suffusion of the legal system with constitutional values; semantic stretching of statutes; pre-emption of legislative choices; dispersing authority for constitutional interpretation. Each of these dimensions admits of degrees; even one judgment may vary in its intensity on different dimensions. To address the question of *why* CCI emerges and develops in this way, section IV takes two different approaches. It first takes the participant's perspective seriously, repurposing the legal, conceptual and normative arguments canvassed in the national reports as potential motivations for judicial decisions. It then explores the strategic reasons in the form of bureaucratic incentives that might motivate judges to adopt CCI. In section V, I review the interaction of these motivations and suggest that CCI is a legal doctrine partly common to all judge-kind because there are multiple motivations for its adoption but those motivations have different implications for the extent to which it should intensify.

[1] Jeremy Waldron, *'Partly Laws Common to All Mankind': Foreign Law in American Courts* (New Haven, Yale University Press, 2012).

[2] See for instance Christoph Bezemek and Daniel Gosch, 'Austria. Embracing Tradition: Constitutionally Conforming Interpretation's Edge in Reconciling Statutory and Constitutional Law' in Matthias Klatt (ed), *Constitutionally Conforming Interpretation – Comparative Perspectives Volume 1: National Reports* (Oxford, Hart Publishing, 2023).

[3] As we shall see below, Daly attributes a difference in Canadian approaches to differences between Type A and Type B judges. The explanation is illuminating, but it is not open to a judge to say they adopt a particular approach *because* they are a Type A/B judge; the judge must explain why they are *correct* to adopt that approach. Paul Daly, 'Canada. Legal Coherence versus Legal Certainty' in Klatt (n 2).

This analysis has four implications for our assessment of CCI and the development of judicial doctrine more generally. First, the intensification framework allows for a more nuanced account of the extent to which CCI increases judicial power at the expense of the legislature, a critical element both for the assessment of CCI's normative legitimacy and for any cross-jurisdictional or cross-temporal comparison. Second, because CCI is common across constitutional systems but is almost exclusively a judicial artifact, it provides a unique case study of the factors that drive judicial expansion of judicial power. Third, because CCI is indifferent to the substantive constitutional values at stake and because it is largely common across constitutional systems with different values, its development highlights the strategic rather than attitudinal factors that may motivate judicial expansion of judicial power. Fourth, while the national reports provide ample evidence for the relevance of bureaucratic self-interest to judicial motivation, the commonality and divergence of CCI cannot be explained solely on these terms, suggesting that judges remain – to some extent – ideationally motivated actors, emphasising the importance of participants' perspectives even to empirical questions of the type explored in this chapter.

II. The Commonality of Constitutionally Conforming Interpretation

CCI is practised in the 19 jurisdictions addressed in Volume 1. Of course, a selection bias is at play: countries were not included for consideration if CCI was not practised; CCI is not universal.[4] Nevertheless, there is remarkable similarity in the emergence, formulation and evolution of the doctrine. CCI typically emerges early in the development of a constitutional system, on the basis of judicial reasoning, with little or no cross-reference to other constitutional systems. With the exception of South Africa, CCI has emerged through judicial decision-making rather than explicit textual authorisation.[5] Eight of the National Reports specifically mention that CCI was adopted at or close to the beginning of their country's constitutional governance.[6] With the exception of Taiwan and Brazil, where German case law and scholarship have been cited,[7] there are few references in the National Reports

[4] Shanil Wijensinha informs me that CCI is not practised in Sri Lanka.

[5] Stacey writes that South Africa's interim Constitution (1993) expressly mandated courts to interpret legislation to conform to the Constitution, including legislation that appeared on its face to limit constitutional rights, as long as the text of the statute in question was 'reasonably capable of a more restricted interpretation' that did not limit rights. This precise direction did not reappear in the Constitution ultimately adopted, but the courts continued with the approach of CCI. Richard Stacey, 'South Africa. The Siren Call of Constitutionally Confirming Interpretation: Statutory Validity at the Expense of Constitutional Values' in Klatt (n 2) s I.

[6] The Czech Republic, Hungary, Italy, Brazil, India, Indonesia, South Africa, Australia.

[7] Chien-Chih Lin, 'Taiwan: Constitutionally Conforming Interpretation and Judicial Sleight of Hand' in Klatt (n 2) s I; Diego W Arguelhes and Rafael B De Lima, 'Brazil. From Restraint to Preemption?' in Klatt (n 2) s II(B).

to transnational judicial influences, still less explicit borrowing. Notwithstanding the paucity of explicit cross-reference, the formulation of CCI across jurisdictions is strikingly similar. To take two examples, in 1996 the Czech Constitutional Court stated:

> If a certain provision of a legal regulation allows for two different ways of interpretation, one of which conforms to constitutional laws … and the other contradicts them, there is no reason to invalidate this provision. It is up to the courts to interpret and apply the given provision in a manner conforming to the Constitution.[8]

In 1992, the Canadian Supreme Court expressed CCI in these terms:

> if there are two possible interpretations of a statutory provision, one of which embodies the Charter values and the other does not, that which embodies the Charter values should be adopted.[9]

CCI is initially presented as almost axiomatic, an obvious and uncontroversial truth about constitutional and statutory interpretation. In this regard, CCI differs markedly from, for example, the practice of suspended declarations of unconstitutionality, where academic commentary assisted the migration of a constitutional idea that challenged embedded conceptions of the judicial role in declaring legislation unconstitutional.[10] In contrast, CCI is taken to need little by way of textual grounding or extra-textual justification.

Judicial convergence on the axiomatic character of CCI is all the more striking because it occurs across constitutional systems that diverge in highly salient respects. CCI has markedly different implications depending on whether the same court is vested with the power both to interpret statutes and consider whether statutes are constitutional. Where constitutional review is vested in a constitutional court while ordinary courts retain the power of statutory interpretation, CCI raises institutional difficulties: either the constitutional court must get involved in statutory interpretation, or the ordinary courts must get involved in constitutional interpretation, or both. Similar issues could arise in a federal system, depending on whether the national apex court has the jurisdiction to interpret provincial or state-level statutes. No such issue arises in a non-federal system where a general apex court is vested with the power of both constitutional review and statutory interpretation. Yet CCI arises across all these systems without any obvious difference. Of further significance in this regard is that CCI is not confined to countries with a mastertext constitution. In both the UK and New Zealand, we see a principle

[8] Judgment of the Constitutional Court of 26 March 1996, File No. Pl. ÚS 48/95 (on the condition of conformity of a statute with the constitutional order) (author's translation). See Pavel Ondřejek, 'Czech Republic. Insights from the Constitutional Court's Post-Transition Practice of Constitutionally Conforming Interpretation' in Klatt (n 2) s II.

[9] *R v Nova Scotia Pharmaceutical Society* [1992] 2 SCR 606, 660. See Daly (n 3) s IV(A). Daly adverts to important but nuanced differences in formulation in different Canadian cases but this qualification does not detract from the core point here about the similarity of expression across different systems.

[10] See Robert Leckey, 'Remedial Practice Beyond Constitutional Text' (2016) 64 *The American Journal of Comparative Law* 1.

of legality, operating as an interpretative presumption that the legislature does not intend powers conferred in general terms to authorise the doing of acts that adversely affect the legal rights of the citizen or the basic principles of the law.[11]

CCI thus emerges as an axiom of judicial practice, without textual authorisation, irrespective of any commitment to legal-constitutional supremacy and despite significantly different implications for the extent of judicial power. Notwithstanding this core commonality, however, practices of CCI begin to diverge – within systems as much as between systems – as judges adopt differing views on the extent to which CCI should intensify. CCI involves a reshaping of legislative directives. In the simplest case, the legislature has used an objectively ambiguous phrase and the court must choose between two equally plausible meanings. But, as we shall see in the next section, the reshaping of legislative directives frequently goes beyond this bare minimum. We can best capture the variation in CCI by focusing on its *intensity*, ie the amount of norm-reshaping carried out under the rubric of CCI. *Intensification* characterises not the extent of normative change introduced by CCI but rather the activity of norm-reshaping itself. That activity can be more or less intense along several dimensions: whether its orientation is limited to situations where a declaration of unconstitutionality would otherwise ensue or more broadly aims at the infusion of constitutional values through the legal system; the extent to which the apparent semantic meaning of words can be stretched; the degree to which future legislative choices are pre-empted; and the range of actors that can engage in norm-reshaping. The concept of intensification allows us to assess the capacity for norm-reshaping under each dimension and the cumulative level across dimensions, as a precursor to comparing different judges, courts, jurisdictions, and/or periods.

III. Intensification of Constitutionally Conforming Interpretation

A. The Trend of Evolution

A recurring theme in the National Reports is that CCI is almost always initially presented as a modest interpretative approach but frequently develops into something far more intense. Two typical statements of initial application can be seen in Hungary and South Africa. Bodnár describes the interpretative limits of

[11] Nick Friedman, 'United Kingdom. In the Shadow of Parliamentary Sovereignty: The Human Rights Act and the Principle of Legality' in Klatt (n 2) s IV; Hanna Wilberg, 'Aotearoa New Zealand. Legislators' Understanding as a Constraint on Interpretive Presumptions' in Klatt (n 2) s II(B)(iii). In Australia, the principle of legality operates as a free-standing doctrine, independent of the supremacy of the mastertext constitution. Lael K Weis, 'Australia: Techniques of Developing Legislation and the Common Law to Align with Constitutional Legal Norms' in Klatt (n 2) s IV. In this chapter, however, I focus on the UK and New Zealand as the clearer examples of the potential independence of CCI from notions of constitutional supremacy.

the Hungarian approach in the following terms: 'The limit of the constitutional requirement is that the Constitutional Court cannot give an interpretation to a norm that cannot be read into it, because in this instance, the Court would eliminate the lawmaker's competence, and the Court cannot override the lawmaker's own authentic interpretation.'[12] Stacey notes that the South African Constitutional Court 'has emphasised in just about every case where a CCI is urged upon it, that courts can prefer a CCI only where the text of the statute reasonably accommodates it. The CCI must not "unduly strain" statutory language.'[13]

But courts routinely push at these boundaries. Assessing the approach of the Spanish Constitutional Court, Lifante-Vidal writes that despite the declarations on the boundaries of CCI, 'numerous Constitutional Court judgments seem to have clearly exceeded these limits'.[14] Arguelhes and de Lima provide a detailed account of how the Brazilian Supreme Court has expanded CCI. They recount Judge Moreira Alves delivering a majority opinion in 1987, concluding that CCI 'cannot go against the rule's meaning, including when it derives from its unequivocal legislative origins, because this Court cannot act as a positive legislator, that is, one that creates news rules'.[15] They summarise later approaches of the Court, however, in the following terms:

> [The Court] reads into the law many elements that might have not been deliberated upon and decided at all by legislators and policymakers. The court is not saying that a particular path taken by the legislator is unconstitutional, but rather that any statute on that topic could only be constitutional if it included a set of specific elements. In doing so, the [Court] uses CCI to directly raise and answer questions that have not yet been asked, foreclosing future legislative discussions that a more restrained judicial stance would instead keep open.[16]

The transition in Brazil is a particularly acute example of a trend common across many of the national reports: over time, courts apply CCI with increasing intensity. What starts as an anodyne mechanism for selecting between permissible interpretation variants becomes a tool for reshaping legislation in very specific ways, often quite at odds with any plausible account of what the legislature might have intended.

The National Reports frequently analyse CCI and its evolution in terms of whether a court has shifted from negative to positive legislating. This approach reflects the Kelsenian idea of a constitutional court as negative legislator, substantively repealing laws but not amending them.[17] In striking down a law, a

[12] Eszter Bodnár, 'Hungary. Conflicts Over Competence' in Klatt (n 2) s IV(A).

[13] Stacey (n 5) s I.

[14] Isabel Lifante-Vidal, 'Spain. Constitutionally Conforming Interpretation and Interpretative Judgements in the Spanish Constitutional Court' in Klatt (n 2) s V.

[15] BRASIL. Supremo Tribunal Federal (Pleno). Representação 1417. Relator: Min: Moreira Alves, 09 de dezembro de 1987, available at stf.jusbrasil.com.br/jurisprudencia/2803880/representacao-rp-1417-df. Arguelhes and De Lima (n 7) s II(B).

[16] ibid s I.

[17] Simon Butt, 'Indonesia. "Conditional" Decisions in the Constitutional Court' in Klatt (n 2) s IV.

constitutional court permissibly acts as a negative legislator but it cannot extend this power to the enactment of new laws. One challenge to the legitimacy of CCI – particularly as it intensifies – is that the statutory reinterpretation demanded by CCI is tantamount to the enactment of new legislation. In other words, it involves the court impermissibly acting as a positive legislator. Assessing challenges in Austria to the legitimacy of CCI, Bezemek and Gosch defend CCI as consistent with the Constitutional Court's role as a negative legislator, implicitly endorsing the positive/negative legislator distinction as the relevant heuristic for legitimacy.[18] The Spanish Constitutional Court grounds its inability to reconstruct a statutory norm 'in a way that is contrary to its obvious meaning' on the basis that such would amount to positive legislation beyond the scope of its powers.[19]

The distinction between positive and negative legislation does not, however, provide a helpful framework for grappling with the intensification of CCI. While a declaration of unconstitutionality can be formally understood as negative legislation – a statutory provision is removed from the statute book – CCI can never formally amount to either positive or negative legislation: the law on the statute book remains in the same form irrespective of any CCI. If we shift our focus from formal legal status to substantive legal effect, however, we see that every CCI has implications for people's legal obligations. CCI will nearly always require that the Court adopt a statutory interpretation that it otherwise would not have. In the most minimal case theoretically possible, CCI still renders mandatory a statutory interpretation that was previously only optional, itself an alteration of people's rights and obligations. Even if we accept, which is far from obvious, that substantive alteration of people's legal rights and obligations is tantamount to legislation, there are no criteria to divide CCIs into positive and negative legislation. We could perhaps attach the label of 'positive legislation' to a CCI that we consider excessive, but any such judgment of excess depends on a prior assessment of how intrusive or activist that CCI is.

To ground such assessments, the remainder of this section outlines a framework that captures the four different dimensions along which CCI can become more intense: whether the courts view the constitution as a control on the content of the legal system or a repository of values to suffuse the legal system; the extent to which the courts are prepared to stretch semantic constraints; the extent to which the courts are prepared to pre-empt legislative decision-making; the extent to which bodies other than courts are empowered and required to adopt and act on CCIs. There is no necessary correlation between intensity levels on the different dimensions, although some contingent correlations are likely. I label the phenomenon 'intensification' to capture how the cumulative effect across different dimensions is at least as salient as where a particular CCI lies on one dimension. Having analysed each dimension in turn, the section concludes with a consideration of their possible interactions.

[18] Bezemek and Gosch (n 2) s III.
[19] Lifante-Vidal (n 14) s V.

B. Constitutional Control versus Constitutional Suffusion

Constitutional standards can be understood as a control on legislative measures, setting outer boundaries for permissible content, or as a repository of values that should suffuse the entire legal system. This distinction runs through the National Reports and is explicitly called out in several. Barczentewicz and Matczak follow Polish legal theory in distinguishing between CCI as 'interpretation of statutes in conformity with the Constitution' and CCI as 'pro-constitutional interpretation'. Interpretation in conformity with the constitution uses the constitution to rule out certain interpretations as impermissible or identify the interpretation that most supports constitutional values. Pro-constitutional interpretation, in contrast, 'realizes the postulate that constitutional values and constitutional axiology should "saturate" the entire system of laws. It consists in using particular substantive rights in interpreting and applying legal regulations and can be understood as the co-application of the Constitution and other legal acts.'[20]

Stacey identifies two different approaches of the South African Constitutional Court to CCI.[21] One treats CCI as meaning 'that courts should always prefer a statutory interpretation that does not limit a right protected in the Bill of Rights. As long as the court can find such an interpretation, it does not need to make a declaration that the statute or parts of it are invalid.' The other suggests that 'avoiding statutory invalidity is not the primary objective of CCI. Rather, courts should favour whatever result promotes the spirit, purport and objects of the Bill of Rights, even if this means finding that a statutory provision is unconstitutional.' The Polish and South African distinctions do not map precisely onto each other: a crucial implication of the second approach, for Stacey, is that courts should reject CCI where a declaration of unconstitutionality would better promote constitutional values. But each envisages a form of CCI that does not merely control legislative provisions for unconstitutional content but rather seeks actively to promote constitutional values.

Daly articulates a similar distinction but framed as an attitude on the part of lawyers to the law, rather than as an objective property of the doctrine.[22] Type A lawyers place a premium on legal certainty and only apply CCI where statutory meaning is ambiguous. Type B lawyers 'believe that statutory language must be woven into the fabric of the constitutional order, in a way which contributes to the ongoing creation and maintenance of a coherent pattern in the common law tradition.' While there is more to Daly's distinction between Type A and Type B lawyers (see further below), these elements point to the distinction between a controlling and suffusion approach. Type A lawyers approach CCI – and constitutional enforcement generally – as a minimal exercise, with remedies to be deployed only to the extent necessary to prevent a discrete constitutional infringement. Type B lawyers,

[20] See Mikolaj Barczentewicz and Marcin Matczak, 'Poland. Constitutionally Conforming Interpretation in Times of Constitutional Crisis' in Klatt (n 2) s I (references omitted).

[21] Stacey (n 5) s I.

[22] Daly (n 3) s IV(B).

in contrast, use CCI to suffuse legislation with constitutional values, even where there is no clear case of a definitive unconstitutionality. CCI under a suffusion model is more intense because it reduces the scope for independent legislative action.

C. Semantic Stretching

The second dimension of intensification involves the extent to which courts are prepared to stretch the semantic meaning of words to accommodate a CCI. While it is conceptually possible for CCI to act simply as a tiebreaker between two equally plausible statutory interpretations, we are unlikely ever to perceive a CCI without some degree of semantic stretching. The UK House of Lords decision in *Ghaidan v Godin-Mendoza* provides an instructive debate on the extent of semantic stretching.[23] *Ghaidan* involved a challenge to a provision of the Rent Act 1977, which allowed surviving spouses to succeed to the tenancy of the original tenant only if they were 'living with the original tenant as his or her wife or husband' before that tenant's death. All five members of the House of Lords agreed that this provision unjustifiably violated the Article 8 and 14 ECHR rights of same-sex couples, but there was significant disagreement over whether it fell within the bounds of CCI to extend the scope of the section to include same-sex couples.[24] The majority viewed their interpretative obligation under section 3 of the Human Rights Act 1998 as being 'of an unusual and far-reaching character … [which] may require a court to depart from the unambiguous meaning [of] the legislation'. Lord Nicholls held that courts could not be too bound by 'the particular form of words adopted by the parliamentary draftsman in the statutory provision', which 'would make the application of section 3 something of a semantic lottery.' Lord Millett in dissent agreed that section 3 permitted courts to 'do considerable violence to the language and stretch it almost (but not quite) to breaking point.' That breaking point, as Lord Nicholls put it, was that courts cannot 'adopt a meaning inconsistent with a fundamental feature of legislation'; their interpretation 'must be compatible with the underlying thrust of the legislation'. The disagreement between the majority and minority reduced to the question of whether the proposed CCI would be inconsistent with a fundamental feature of the Act. For the majority, the underlying legislative policy was a broad one of protecting couples who share each other's life and make a home together; for the minority, protection of specifically opposite-sex couples was an essential feature of the statute.

In Taiwan, Justice Hsu has repeatedly criticised majority judgments of the Taiwan Constitutional Court that deployed CCI.[25] In Interpretation No 585 (2004), the Court considered a statute – enacted by the opposition-controlled legislature – that established an independent commission to investigate controversial events,

[23] [2004] UKHL 30.
[24] Friedman (n 11) s III(B).
[25] Lin (n 7) s III(B).

including an assassination attempt, surrounding the President's re-election. The Court upheld the constitutionality of the commission on the grounds that it served to assist the legislature in exercising its constitutionally granted investigative powers. Justice Hsu considered that this CCI distorted the intention of the Act's supporters, who had intended the commission to be independent of the organs of government. The majority's CCI, in his view, distorted legislative intent and imposed the judges' understanding of the law.

Daly's distinction between Type A and Type B lawyers also captures the extent to which judges are prepared to engage in semantic stretching.[26] For Type A lawyers, statutes owe their authoritative force to the status of the body that enacted them. Ascertaining statutory intent is therefore critical and CCI should only be permissible where the statute truly is ambiguous. For Type B lawyers, the capacity of a statutory provision to bind depends on its place in a coherent normative pattern; given the open texture of language, statutory provisions can better acquire authoritative force through their place in a coherent scheme of principles informed by constitutional values.

D. Prescription and Legislative Pre-Emption

The third dimension of CCI's intensity concerns the extent to which the CCI makes detailed prescriptions about what is constitutionally permissible, thereby pre-empting legislative action. In some senses, every CCI makes these sorts of prescriptions: it provides a legally binding interpretation of a statutory provision that helps resolve the case before the court. Nevertheless, there seems to be a distinction – at least in intensity if not in kind – between a judicial decision that can be understood as a choice between two or more interpretations of a statutory phrase and a judicial decision that can only be understood as the court interpolating new text into the statutory provision. This roughly follows the South African distinction, noted by Stacey, between reading down and reading in.[27] In South Africa, however, only reading down is understood to be CCI. If a CCI is insufficient, the court must declare the legislation invalid and then decide whether to read words out (severance) or read words in. In other jurisdictions, 'reading out' is entailed by the declaration of unconstitutionality, while reading down and reading in are both available as forms of CCI that can avoid a declaration of unconstitutionality. In this regard, Lin draws a distinction between traditional CCI, which 'requires courts, when interpreting a law, to choose a single interpretation that is most harmonious with the constitution and to exclude unconstitutional interpretations' and a second type of CCI where 'courts read in several words that do not exist in the text' as the only means of upholding the statute.[28]

[26] Daly (n 3) s IV(B).
[27] Stacey (n 5) s III.
[28] Lin (n 7) s II(A).

A brief diversion into Irish constitutional law helps to illustrate these points. The first Irish example of CCI involved an extensive reading in, prescribing how a statutory process ought to be conducted and pre-empting the freedom of the legislature to choose alternative approaches. In *McDonald v Bord na gCon*, the Supreme Court considered the constitutionality of provisions of the Greyhound Industry Act 1958 that allowed the Greyhound Board effectively to exclude persons from participating in the industry.[29] Walsh J provided a formulation of CCI very similar to those we considered in section II:

> The Greyhound Industry Act of 1958, being an Act of the Oireachtas, is presumed to be constitutional until the contrary is clearly established. One practical effect of this presumption is that if in respect of any provision or provisions of the Act two or more constructions are reasonably open, one of which is constitutional and the other or others are unconstitutional, it must be presumed that the Oireachtas intended only the constitutional construction and a Court called upon to adjudicate upon the constitutionality of the statutory provision should uphold the constitutional construction. It is only when there is no construction reasonably open which is not repugnant to the Constitution that the provision should be held to be repugnant.[30]

To ensure that the legislation could be held constitutional, Walsh J read in provisions to the effect that a proper investigation with natural justice – respecting the rights of *audi alteram partem* and *nemo iudex in causa sua* – would be carried out before an exclusion order was made:

> The wording of the provisions of sections 43 and 44 does not exclude the application of the principles of natural justice to these investigations. While the Board may determine the manner in which the investigation shall be carried out the clear words or necessary implication which would be required to exclude the principles of natural justice from such investigation are not present in the sections.[31]

The Court did not spell out the textual additions to the Act that were constitutionally necessitated, but it effectively stipulated in considerable detail the process that the Greyhound Board would have to follow in Mr McDonald's case.[32] The Court read provisions into the Act rather than interpreted words that were already there, thereby prescribing legislative content. Moreover, the Court effectively put the legislature on notice that any future statute that failed to respect the requirements

[29] [1965] IR 217.
[30] [1965] IR 217, 239.
[31] [1965] IR 217, 243.
[32] An alternative characterisation of this case is Daly's constitutionally conforming administration, which I will discuss further in sub-section E. In this characterisation, the Court was holding that administrative bodies – such as the Greyhound Board – had a constitutional obligation to exercise their discretion in a manner that complied with natural justice, without mediating that constitutional requirement through a CCI. While this characterisation is open, it does make it more difficult for us to perceive a crucially different element of CCA, where state agencies are under an obligation to apply the constitution themselves even if this involves beaching their statutory obligations. This is the focus of sub-section E.

of natural justice would be reinterpreted to include those requirements, thereby pre-empting future legislative choices.

Similarly but with greater prescriptiveness, the Taiwan Constitutional Court upheld the constitutionality of a provision authorising police inspections or traffic stops at public places to question suspicious people, but only on reading the following conditions into the law: the requirement of a reasonable belief that the person might cause harm; a requirement to inform the person of the reason for the search and identify themselves as police officers; an obligation to conduct the search on the spot; a prohibition on asking the person to go to the police station; a freedom for the person, having confirmed their identification, to leave immediately unless they were suspected of crimes that would be followed up by criminal procedures.[33]

The Brazil National Report provides the most extreme example of this sort of prescriptiveness and pre-emption.[34] In 2008, the Brazilian Supreme Court considered the constitutionality of a statute that authorised the use of surplus human embryos from *in vitro* reproduction processes in research on the therapeutic potential of embryonic stem cells. While a narrow majority of 6:5 upheld the law without resort to CCI, the five dissenting judges would have read conditions into the law to ensure its constitutionality. These conditions included narrowing the definition of *in vitro fertilisation*, providing for public authority assessment of proposals for research on embryonic stem cells, and determining the composition of future oversight bodies and their relationship with the Ministry of Health. The minority judges accepted that this was a creative decision, since the statute made no provision for public oversight of private research projects, but nevertheless considered it within the bounds of CCI. For Arguelhes and Lima, pre-emptive decisions of this type lie beyond both any idea of interpretation and any conceivable account of judicial restraint. Judges were both methodologically and institutionally going beyond the text and reaching into the future. Had the minority position prevailed, the legislature would have been pre-empted from considering the issue on a clean slate because the Supreme Court had prescribed in such detail the scope of constitutionally permissible legislation.

E. The Locus of Interpretative Authority

Which actors within a legal system are responsible and authorised to provide constitutionally conforming interpretations? Daly suggests a concept of constitutionally conforming administration, where public agencies must exercise their powers in a constitutionally conforming manner.[35] Requiring public agencies to conform to judicial mandated CCIs – as in the Irish *McDonald* case considered in the previous section – is not a significant extension. But might agencies

[33] Lin (n 7) s III(C).
[34] Arguelhes and De Lima (n 7) s IV.
[35] Daly (n 3) s IV.

themselves be empowered to adopt a constitutionally conforming interpretation that runs counter to what would ordinarily be the most plausible interpretation of a statute? Klatt convincingly addresses the potential objection that only a body that can declare legislation unconstitutional can adopt a CCI. Writing in the German context, he rejects the argument that ordinary courts should not, because they lack the power to declare statutes unconstitutional, be empowered to adopt CCI. He argues that interpretation variants cannot be void; they can only be more or less convincing. Rejection of one interpretation variant in favour of another does not imply a finding that the rejected variant is void and so does not depend on a competence to declare laws void. Klatt's argument opens up space for the suggestion that all public agencies, not just courts, should be vested with the power of CCI, ie to exercise their powers – subject always to subsequent judicial correction – on the basis of a CCI that they adopt rather than the most obvious 'normal' reading of a statute. It appears from the National Reports that this potential has been realised in several jurisdictions.

Writing about the Czech Republic, Ondřejek states that CCI is used as a general method of interpretation by public authorities, who are required to apply the constitution in their decision-making under all circumstances. The Constitutional Court has specifically held that 'it is the task of all governmental authorities to interpret any given provision in a constitutionally conforming manner'.[36] Writing of Poland, Barczentewicz and Matczak state 'CCI, as a purposive interpretation, ensures that interpretative results at the bottom of the legal system (eg the interpretations of administrative agencies and courts in their decisions vis-à-vis individuals) realise those values'.[37] Specifically, the Constitutional Tribunal encourages all organs applying the law to choose from competing interpretations the one that is consistent with constitutional norms and values.[38] Writing about Taiwan, Lin comments, 'CCI is a method of constitutional interpretation, which means that, in a constitutional state, all law-enforcement officials in the broadest sense of the term, ranging from police officers and prosecutors to politicians, may apply CCI when necessary because they are all bound, in their professional duties, by the Constitution.'[39]

This development intensifies CCI by removing the sort of scrutiny that is generated by court processes. It does not necessarily follow from the desirability of state agencies conforming to the constitution that those agencies should be empowered to adopt CCIs that expand or restrict their apparent legal powers and obligations. Where CCI occurs in the context of a court case, there will be an opportunity for those affected by the CCI to argue why it should or should not be adopted. There will also be publicity for the fact that a CCI has been adopted, so affected parties will know that a statutory provision has been reinterpreted in a way that alters their legal obligations. Consider, in contrast, a parking regulator who impounds

[36] Ondřejek (n 8) ss I and III.
[37] Barczentewicz and Matczak (n 20) s II.
[38] ibid s III.
[39] Lin (n 7) s II.

cars based on a sincere belief that the constitution, properly understood, protects the rights of nature which are infringed by driving cars. Or a police officer who decides that the constitution's references to the common good vest them with a power of detention to protect against crime, without any of the commonly understood procedural safeguards. Such CCIs would be open to correction by a court, but there might be no record of a CCI ever being adopted, correction could take time, and irreparable harm might have been done by the time of correction. Of course, constitutionally conforming administration could be qualified in some ways to address these concerns. In Canada, it appears to be limited to administrative tribunals – rather than all agents of the state – and confined to 'the kind of remedy that the legislature intended would fit within the statutory framework of the particular tribunal'.[40] Some take an optimistic view of diversifying the *loci* of interpretative authority.[41] In many African countries, there are explicit and wide-ranging obligations on citizens, state agencies and others to ensure observance of the constitution, perhaps suggesting that the *loci* of constitutional interpretation are necessarily diversified.[42] Whether there are good normative or textual grounds for diversifying the *loci* of constitutional interpretation, such diversification intensifies the practice of CCI.

F. Cumulative Intensification

Each dimension of intensification allows for differences of degree, not differences of kind. The distinction between constitutional control and constitutional suffusion is not clear-cut in application. Statutory language may be semantically stretched to greater or lesser degrees. Depending on the constitutional norms involved, the prescription of legislative content may pre-empt legislative competence to a greater or lesser extent. State agencies obliged to adopt CCIs might be limited to administrative tribunals that follow court-analogous procedures – thereby providing opportunities for notice and argument prior to the adoption of a CCI – or might extend to all public officials. There are contingent correlations between the dimensions, as illustrated by Daly's distinction between Type A and Type B lawyers tracking across both the suffusion dimension and the semantic dimension. But it is theoretically possible and empirically observable that intensification can occur along one dimension but not another. The willingness of the Irish Supreme Court in *McDonald* to read in requirements of natural justice, thereby pre-empting legislative choices, reflects a technical control to respect constitutional supremacy rather than any broader commitment to suffuse the legal system with

[40] *R v Conway* 2010 SCC 22 (CanLII), [2010] 1 SCR 765, [82]. I am grateful to Paul Daly for explaining the Canadian doctrine to me and for drawing this case to my attention.

[41] See for instance Mark Tushnet, *Taking the Constitution Away from the Courts* (Princeton, Princeton University Press, 2008).

[42] See for instance Constitution of Ethiopia 1994 art 9(2).

constitutional values. For all these reasons, we can best assess the intensity of CCI by taking each dimension separately and then considering their cumulative effect.

Intensification of CCI on all dimensions involves greater amounts of norm-reshaping. Where that norm-reshaping is undertaken by judges – as under the first three dimensions – it would seem to connote an increase in judicial power. Courts hold ultimate authority over the interpretation of constitutional norms, so a judicial decision to give a wider reach to constitutional norms – suffusion rather than control – increases judicial power. The greater the semantic stretching that judges deem permissible, the greater their power. Constitutionally mandating certain words to be read into a statute restricts legislative power more than simply adopting a particular interpretation of words the legislature itself had chosen. If subordinate authorities under the fourth dimension follow judicial interpretations of the constitution, allowing those authorities to engage in CCI would also appear to increase judicial power. Against this analysis, however, we must bear in mind that the alternative to CCI remains a declaration of unconstitutionality – perhaps the most clearcut and far-reaching exercise of judicial power imaginable. All we can say with confidence is that intensification of CCI involves greater judicial activity in norm-reshaping. If intensification leads to judicial adoption of a CCI in circumstances where a declaration of unconstitutionality would not have been reached, then it involves an increase in judicial power. But if the adoption of a CCI has genuinely avoided a declaration of unconstitutionality, it remains impossible to calibrate whether the CCI – however intense – is a greater exercise of judicial power than would have been implicated by a declaration of unconstitutionality.

IV. Factors Motivating Adoption of Constitutionally Conforming Interpretation

A. Overview

Written judgments present a justification for a decision based on legal material interpreted in accordance with accepted norms. While these judgments may record what motivated judges to reach a particular conclusion, such transparency is not necessarily the case. It is also possible that judges are motivated by their own personal values, or by a desire to increase the power of the judiciary within the constitutional and political system. Writing about the US Supreme Court, Segal and Spaeth reject what they term the legal model in favour of an attitudinal model, attributing decisions of that court to the attitudes and values of the justices.[43] The attitudinal model, however, gives little purchase on the adoption of CCI and its

[43] Jeffrey A Segal and Harold J Spaeth, *The Supreme Court and the Attitudinal Model Revisited* (Cambridge, Cambridge University Press, 2002).

subsequent divergence, given that CCI itself is indifferent to substantive constitutional values (ie rights and freedoms, separation of powers, etc) and emerges across widely different systems in support of widely different values. In terms of reversing normative content with which a judge disagrees, a CCI is equally effectives as a declaration of unconstitutionality. A declaration of unconstitutionality might represent a more symbolic disavowal of the law. But a CCI might be less likely to prompt a legislative reintroduction of a similar law better protected against constitutional challenge. On balance, we have no reason to expect that attitudinal opposition to a law would favour a declaration of unconstitutionality over CCI.[44]

One possibly relevant attitude would be a belief on the part of judges that courts ought to have more power. The manifestation of this attitude, however, would be empirically indistinguishable from strategic decision-making on the part of judges, serving their own bureaucratic self-interest. In *Towards Juristocracy*, Hirschl argues that judicial empowerment through constitutionalisation is best understood as the by-product of a strategic interplay between political elites, economic elites, and 'judicial elites and national high courts that seek to enhance their political influence and international reputation'.[45] Hirschl focuses on the decision to introduce judicially interpreted and legally binding bills of rights, but CCI – almost universally a judicial innovation – might also be the result of strategic action on the part of judicial elites acting in their own bureaucratic self-interest to increase judicial power.

In any given case, it is difficult to disentangle legal, attitudinal, and strategic motivations. A strategic desire to enhance judicial power might well coincide with a sincerely held belief that judges ought to have more power, which in turn could be defended – and hence plausibly motivated – by sound legal argumentation. Norms of legal argumentation do not permit judges to justify their decisions on the grounds that they personally prefer a particular outcome or that they wish to increase the power of judges, so there will seldom be any direct evidence of attitudinal or strategic decision-making. Nevertheless, if we consider the corpus of decisions, both within and across systems, the broad trends are best explained as a product of largely converging but partially diverging legal motivations that overlap to different extents with the strategic / attitudinal objective of increasing judicial power. In this section, I draw on the national reports to identify the range of factors that may motivate the adoption of CCI. I repurpose the normative and conceptual justifications advanced in the reports as ideational factors, identifying two that might motivate adoption of CCI – idealistic commitments of constitutional order and reconciling the interests of parties to litigation – and one that might motivate rejection of CCI – illegitimate usurpation of legislative power. In relation to strategic factors, Hirschl shows how judges can be sophisticated strategic decision-makers, tailoring their judgments to reduce the risk of reversal by

[44] I am grateful to Yen-tu Su for pressing me on this point.

[45] Ran Hirschl, *Towards Juristocracy: The Origins and Consequences of the New Constitutionalism* (Cambridge, Harvard University Press, 2007) 43.

other branches while seeking 'to maintain or enhance [their] position vis-à-vis other major national decision-making bodies'.[46] Courts may take opportunities to 'strengthen their own position by extending the ambit of their jurisprudence and fortifying their status as crucial national policy-making bodies'.[47] Drawing on those insights, I explore two strategic factors in the context of CCI: enhancing judicial power relative to the legislature and enhancing the powers of constitutional and ordinary courts relative to each other.

B. Idealistic Commitments of Constitutional Order

The ideas of constitutional supremacy and legal unity present themselves as similar but slightly different normative foundations for CCI. Where constitutional supremacy pictures a hierarchically ordered legal system with the constitution limiting the permissible content of statutory norms, legal unity pictures a normatively integrated legal system where constitutional values infuse statutory norms. The difference between these pictures is ill-defined and a matter of degree, but the orientation of the former is that the constitution functions as a set of external limits on statutory norms while under the latter the constitution provides a font of norms that ought to infuse statutes. By selecting statutory interpretations that conform to the constitution, courts could be understood as underwriting either constitutional supremacy or legal unity. The canonical account of CCI in Taiwan captures both the supremacy and unity rationales: CCI is 'one kind of systematic interpretation and its purpose is to solve legal conflicts, harmonise the legal order, and ultimately implement the Constitution'.[48] But neither constitutional supremacy nor legal unity on its own suffices to justify CCI, since a declaration of unconstitutionality would be equally effective to that end. Responding to this deficiency, Klatt grounds the legitimacy of CCI in a combination of legal unity and *favor legis*, the principle of preserving legislation where possible.[49]

For Klatt, the principle of *favor legis* derives from the proposition that judges are bound *both* by statute *and* by the constitution. Faced with an unconstitutional statute – or an unconstitutional interpretation variant of a statute – these obligations pull in opposite directions. The competing obligations can best be reconciled by an approach that declares legislation unconstitutional only to the extent necessary. Where an interpretation variant exists that is constitutional, the court respects its role vis-à-vis the legislature by choosing that interpretation variant. While Klatt proposes the principle of *favor legis* as a complement to the principle of legal unity,

[46] ibid 47.

[47] ibid 48.

[48] Judicial Yuan Interpretation No. 437 (1997) (Justice Wang concurring), available at cons.judicial.gov.tw/en/docdata.aspx?fid=100&id=310618; Lin (n 7) s II(A).

[49] Matthias Klatt, 'The Legitimacy of Constitutionally Conforming Interpretation' in Klatt (n 2) s III(C).

it functions equally effectively as a complement to the principle of constitutional supremacy. Whether the prior objective is to ensure that statutes do not exceed constitutional limits or more broadly that constitutional values infuse the statute book thereby enhancing legal unity, *favor legis* recommends CCI over a declaration of unconstitutionality because CCI also respects the courts' obligation to give effect to the will of the legislature.

As we shall see below, the constitutional supremacy rationale coheres more with constitutional control while the legal unity rationale coheres more with constitutional suffusion. It is possible to characterise suffusion as a distortion of CCI or – from within the perspective of a particular system – illegitimate because it exceeds the foundational mandate to adopt CCI only in preference to a declaration of unconstitutionality that would otherwise be granted.[50] From this perspective, the proper justification for CCI is limited to preserving constitutional supremacy rather than advancing legal unity. Nevertheless, the legal unity rationale and constitutional suffusion model are so widely practised under the rubric of CCI that little is served, at least for an empirical study such as this, by deeming them illegitimate or distortions.

CCI in countries without a mastertext constitution[51] cannot, however, be motivated by the principle of *favor legis* because there is no possibility that a statute can be declared invalid. Similarly, neither constitutional supremacy nor legal unity in the senses explicated above can motivate CCI, since there is no mastertext constitution operating as a supreme legal norm or font of values to integrate into the rest of the legal system. Nevertheless, the constitutions of the UK and New Zealand both express values that are taken to be important, if not supreme, allowing us to understand the principle of legality as a response to the demand of legal unity. In the UK a statute ought not to be interpreted to authorise the doing of acts 'which adversely affect the legal rights of the citizen or the basic principles on which the law of the United Kingdom is based unless the statute conferring the power makes it clear that such was the intention of Parliament'.[52] In New Zealand, 'fundamental common law rights can be abrogated only by express words or necessary implication'.[53] In both these ways, courts interpret statutes to reflect important values, subject to the sovereignty of parliament.

This analysis of the principle of legality highlights the similarities between CCI and principles that operated in the classical legal tradition. Casey has shown how the Roman law principle that the prince could not be jurisdictionally or coercively bound to obey positive law was not a warrant for despotic government, partly because classical jurists interpreted the commands of the prince consistently with

[50] I am grateful to Chien-Liang Lee for pressing me on this point.

[51] John Gardner, *Law as a Leap of Faith: Essays on Law in General* (Oxford, Oxford University Press, 2012) 90.

[52] Friedman (n 11) s IV citing Lord Browne-Wilkinson in *R v Secretary of State for the Home Department, ex parte Pierson* [1998] AC 539, 575.

[53] Wilberg (n 11) s II(B)(iii).

unwritten legal principles.[54] For instance, Casey quotes the Italian jurist Baldus de Ubaldis as saying that 'nothing is presumed to please the emperor except what is just and true … and the emperor wishes all his actions to be ruled by divine and natural justice as well as human';[55] and interprets Aquinas as counselling jurists to understand all ordinances as guided and informed by right reason and the natural law. Casey also identifies a presumption that the prince would not act contrary to the existing law or custom (where the latter did not conflict with natural law). Helmholz identifies cases of statutory interpretation from the late 15th to 19th centuries which show the law of nature, conceptualised as above princes, being used as an interpretative guide that might lead to the acts of princes being interpreted in a manner at odds with the princes' interests and probable intentions.[56] Sometimes, a judge might go so far as 'to suppose a tacit condition in the lord's command that its effect was meant to stop short of iniquity'.[57] This mechanism is also common in western private law, in relation to the construction of wills and contracts.[58]

Casey draws the connection between these principles of classical law and CCI, in the form of the Irish double construction rule mentioned above in section III(D). But for present purposes, I wish to derive three somewhat different points. First, Waldron's argument for a contemporary *ius gentium* encompassed analysis that was 'typical of lawyerly thinking and lawyer's mentality the world over'.[59] In Waldron's view, a lawyer 'when he confronts a problem, tries to anatomize it, uncover its underlying structure and the order in which the issues entangled in the problem are best addressed'.[60] Classical legal principles evidence a thought process – interpreting the norms stipulated in one text in the light of other norms – that might qualify as an aspect of Waldron's typical lawyerly thinking. Given that this mental manoeuvre has been a feature of legal thinking in the western tradition for centuries, it is unsurprising that CCI would be adopted in western legal systems and, as western notions of constitutionalism migrated, in other jurisdictions also. Second, classical legal thought helps explicate how a different type of legal unity – conformity with non-posited, important if not legally supreme norms – underpins the principle of legality. In the UK and New Zealand, the values protected by the principle of legality are more limited than those of classical legal thought's natural law. But the interpretative move reflects a similar desire for legal unity, at least in terms of respect for basic principles of legality. Third, viewed in

[54] Conor Casey, 'What Pleases the Prince: The Relevance of Classical Legal Principles to Contemporary Public Law' (2023) Paper on file with author.

[55] ibid, citing Joseph Canning, *The Political Thought of Baldus de Ubaldis* (Cambridge, Cambridge University Press, 2002) 79.

[56] Richard H Helmholz, *Natural Law in Court: A History of Legal Theory in Practice* (Cambridge, Harvard University Press, 2015) 75–79.

[57] ibid 77.

[58] I am grateful to Ugljesa Grusic for this point.

[59] Waldron (n 1) 94.

[60] ibid 95.

this way, we can see CCI under both mastertext constitutions and the principle of legality as responding to the same desire for the legal unity of a system whose norms are interpreted in accordance with precepts of justice, the difference being the range and source of those precepts, as well as their legally superordinate status.

C. Reconciling the Interests of Parties to Litigation

A different type of justification for CCI lies in reconciling the interests of parties to litigation. Two scenarios illustrate the appeal of CCI from this perspective. CCI can narrow the scope of a statute so that the claimant avoids a detriment, while preserving the statute to meet many of the legislature's objectives. But CCI can also broaden the scope of a statute to allow the claimant a benefit that would not have been attainable through a declaration of unconstitutionality, while again preserving the statute to provide benefits to those whom the legislature intended to benefit. The following diagram illustrates these two scenarios.

Figure 1 Schematic Illustration of CCI

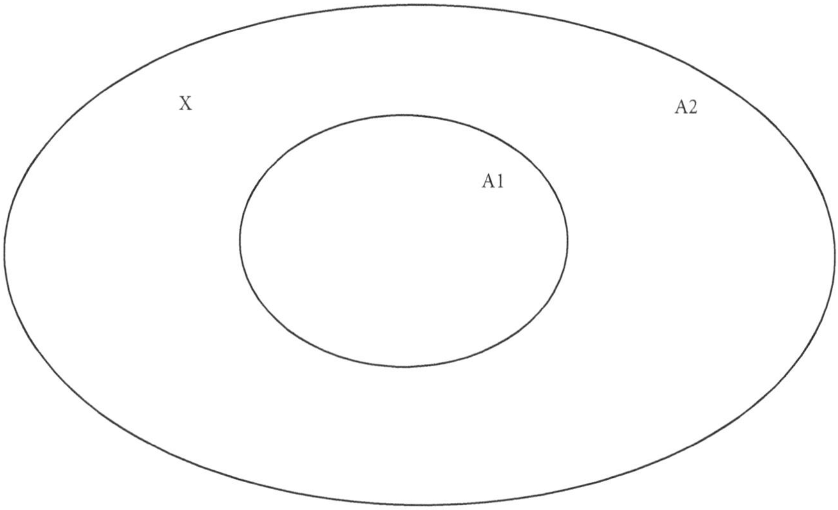

There is a statutory provision, A, which can be interpreted either narrowly (A1) or broadly (A2). X is the claimant. In scenario 1, X objects to being subject to A, arguing that it unconstitutionally imposes a detriment on them. Assume that A1 is a constitutional variant of A, while A2 is an unconstitutional variant. CCI allows the court to adopt A1 and preserve the validity of A, while providing a remedy to X on the grounds that they no longer fall within the scope of A. In litigation terms, there is a full victory for X but a mitigated loss for the legislature.

In scenario 2, X claims that they have been unconstitutionally deprived of the benefit of A. In this context, a declaration of unconstitutionality would not serve the interests of the claimant; such a declaration would merely remove the benefit of A from everyone, not provide those benefits to X. A suspended declaration of unconstitutionality would provide the legislature with a choice – remove the benefit entirely or provide it to the additional class of persons – which could ultimately benefit the litigant although this approach might lack retrospective effect and therefore fail to provide a remedy. But CCI can provide a claimant with a remedy immediately. If the court opts for the broader A2 interpretation, X then falls within the scope of A and receives the benefit alongside those whom the legislature intended to benefit.

The latter scenario is well illustrated by the result in the UK case of *Ghaidan v Godin Mendoza*.[61] As we saw above, *Ghaidan* involved a challenge to a provision of the Rent Act 1977, with the House of Lords dividing over whether the phrase 'living with the original tenant as his or her wife or husband' before that tenant's death could be semantically stretched to accommodate same-sex couples. For present purposes, the relevant point is that the decision extended a benefit which the legislature had not decided to confer. A declaration of incompatibility under the Human Rights Act 1998 is never a wholly satisfactory remedy for a litigant. But even a declaration of unconstitutionality with *erga omnes* effect would have done nothing to assist a litigant in the *Ghaidan* scenario: it would merely withdraw from opposite-sex couples the benefit of surviving to the tenancy. In these circumstances, CCI may be the only way of providing a meaningful benefit for a claimant who has suffered from an unconstitutionality.

This reason for CCI is mentioned in several of the National Reports, although perhaps fewer than might have been expected.[62] Writing about France, Carpentier comments that litigants may prefer CCI because it may 'be more profitable to the claimant to have the law remain in force, but with an altered meaning or scope, rather than have it repealed altogether. Sometimes a litigant prefers that a different law be applied to his case rather than there being no applicable law at all.'[63] In Indonesia, the Constitutional Court has identified a broader rationale that legal instruments sometimes require urgent change to protect constitutional rights but invalidation would leave a lacuna to be filled by a notoriously slow and unresponsive legislature.[64] The Czech Constitutional Court semantically stretched the definitions in a scheme of compensation for victims of Nazi persecution and their

[61] [2004] UKHL 30. I draw this account from Friedman (n 11) s III(B).

[62] Daniel Gosch suggests to me that this approach would be problematic in constitutional systems, such as the German, that accept a strict semantical barrier of interpretation (*Wortlautgrenze*), perhaps explaining why such cases do not feature prominently in the national reports.

[63] Mathieu Carpentier, 'France. The Dynamics of "Interpretative Reservations" in the Jurisprudence of the French Constitutional Council' in Klatt (n 2) s IV(A).

[64] Butt (n 17) ss I and IV.

relatives, with the result that a widow would qualify for compensation.[65] Ondřejek does not state that CCI provided a remedy to the widow that a declaration of unconstitutionality would have denied, but such seems to be the case.

The ideational force of these factors rests not on the idealistic commitments of constitutional order but rather on a pragmatic concern to give effective remedies and balance the interests of parties to litigation. To be sure, they rest on an underlying principle of respect for the constitutional order. But their orientation is not deep reflection on the nature of constitutional order but rather more simple propositions: (a) where a constitutional right has been infringed, a remedy should be provided; and (b) that remedy should be as minimally restrictive of the legislature's aims as possible. As such, where notions of legal unity and the principle of *favor legis* may motivate judges minded to reflect on deep questions of constitutional theory and structure, the factors considered in this sub-section may hold greater motivational force for pragmatic judges focused on the justice of the case before them. Of course, a judge could be simultaneously motivated by both types of factor.

D. Illegitimate Usurpation of Legislative Power

As well as the ideational factors motivating adoption of CCI, we must consider the ideational factors that might militate against adoption of CCI. This task requires repurposing the arguments from the National Reports for the illegitimacy of CCI as ideational factors counting against adoption of CCI. These arguments principally turn on the contention that CCI amounts to an illegitimate interference with legislative power, frequently formulated in terms of the court acting impermissibly as a positive legislator. We have seen in section III(A), however, that CCI never formally amounts to positive legislation and that every CCI substantively alters the obligations of those subject to the law. Fleshing out this argument somewhat, Schauer contends that the necessary indeterminacy in language means that CCI is always activist in character.[66] Most statutes will be partially indeterminate, but one plausible interpretation will be more plausible than another. If the more plausible interpretation would be inconsistent with the constitution, then CCI appears to prefer the worse interpretation to the better interpretation. The primary focus of Schauer's remarks is to establish that the US doctrine of constitutional avoidance does not truly avoid the constitutional decision.[67] But his critique goes beyond

[65] Judgment of the Constitutional Court of 7 May 1997, File No. Pl. ÚS 23/96 (conditions for compensation for victims of Nazi persecution) (author's translation); Ondřejek (n 8) s II.

[66] Frederick Schauer, 'United States. Constitutional Avoidance As Constitutional Conformation' in Klatt (n 2) s III.

[67] Weis correctly notes that the constitutional question cannot be avoided, but what CCI attempts to avoid is declarations of constitutional invalidity. Weis (n 11) s III(A)(i).

nomenclature to encompass the claim that CCI, at least if one believes that the text of the law is the law, involves a court in law-making.

The force of this illegitimacy argument is lessened considerably, however, where the alternative to CCI is a declaration of unconstitutionality. Subject to the level of intensification, a CCI will typically alter people's legal obligations less than would a declaration of unconstitutionality. For this reason, we would not expect legitimacy concerns to militate against adoption of CCI where it is accepted that a declaration of unconstitutionality is a judicially permissible means of altering people's legal obligations. This expectation is consistent with the fact that the US, where the practice of constitutional review has no clear textual foundation, sees greater resistance to CCI than any other jurisdiction in Volume 1.[68] If the alternative of a declaration of unconstitutionality were considered critical to the legitimacy of CCI, however, we would not see the principle of legality in the UK and New Zealand. These jurisdictions perhaps suggests that the illegitimacy arguments against CC per se are not perceived to carry great weight. The legitimacy concerns strengthen, however, as CCI itself intensifies along the dimensions explored in section III. Intensification involves greater judicial involvement in norm-reshaping at the expense of other constitutional actors. In the context of intensification, CCI becomes a subject of normative conflict, explaining why we see divergence between judges, between systems, and over time.

E. Strategic Incentives of Courts vis-à-vis Legislatures

As we saw in section III, CCI does not in principle expand the scope of judicial power over legislative power. As CCI intensifies, however, it gives courts a greater role in reshaping legislative directives. Accordingly, although the balance between judicial and legislative power does not provide judges with an incentive to adopt CCI in the first place, it does provide an incentive to intensify an existing doctrine of CCI.

Writing about Taiwan, Lin suggests a separate motivation for adoption of CCI. Treating CCI as non-expansive of judicial power, he suggests that the Taiwan Constitutional Court has sometimes deployed CCI to navigate intense political storms and avoid a head-on clash with the political branches.[69] He further describes CCI as sometimes an attempt – not always successful – to avoid political revenge.[70] This analysis identifies a different bureaucratic self-interest that could motivate the adoption of CCI, a desire to avoid provoking a more powerful branch of government and thereby preserve judicial power for exercise in a subsequent

[68] Schauer (n 63) s V. One possible explanation is that the practice of constitutional review itself rests on insecure foundations in the US compared to other jurisdictions. This insecurity may also problematise related constitutional approaches such as CCI.

[69] Lin (n 7) text before s I.

[70] Lin (n 7) s II(B).

case. The further relevance of this insight is that – where CCI is motivated by bureaucratic self-interest – that self-interest may warrant a narrow version of CCI as much as an expansive one. Everything will depend on the balance of power between different constitutional actors, with judges motivated by bureaucratic self-interest deciding whether it is an opportune moment for the consolidation or expansion of judicial power.

F. Strategic Incentives of Constitutional Courts and Ordinary Courts vis-à-vis One Another

Judicial incentives to adopt CCI come most clearly into view in the context of intra-judicial relationships between constitutional courts and ordinary courts. In a system of concentrated judicial review, CCI is only possible if either a constitutional court engages in statutory interpretation or an ordinary court engages in constitutional interpretation. There are ways of softening the intrusion by one type of court into the domain of the other type. For instance, a constitutional court's CCI might only bind the parties to the case; or an ordinary court could only adopt a CCI if the relevant constitutional meaning had already been determined by the constitutional court. But the expansion of judicial power – by either or both courts – is manifest. This dynamic has formed the basis for jurisdiction-specific criticism of CCI.[71] The purpose of this section is not to rehearse that legitimacy debate but rather to see how the bureaucratic self-interest of different types of court could motivate adoption of CCI.

While the expansion of power could always be an unarticulated motivation for adoption of CCI, it sometimes appears explicitly. In Italy in 1956, within the first four months of its existence, the Constitutional Court adopted CCI – upholding the constitutionality of a referred norm by giving it a different interpretation. In Valentini's analysis, this move extended the Constitutional Court's jurisdiction to the interpretation of ordinary statutes, while also advising 'regular courts to broaden their interpretation and enter the realm of constitutional values'.[72] She reports that subsequently, in 1965, a meeting of the Italian National Association of Magistrates invited ordinary judges, before raising questions of constitutional legitimacy, to utilise the Constitution as a normative resource, including CCI.[73] This meeting is an unusually clear example of a deliberate judicial strategy – as distinct from incidental to a decision in a particular case – to adopt CCI. The result was broader powers for both the Constitutional Court and the ordinary courts, leading to difficulties in harmonising constitutional and statutory interpretations that have been mediated differently at different times.

[71] Klatt (n 47) s IV(C); Bezemek and Gosch (n 2) s II.

[72] Chiara Valentini, 'Italy. Constitutionally Conforming Interpretation and Judicial Dialogue' in Klatt (n 2) s V(A).

[73] ibid s V(B).

Poland provides an even more striking example. Responding to the compromised Constitutional Court, a conference attended by judicial and academic figures in 2017 put forward a strategy that included implementation of dispersed constitutional review and extending the ordinary courts' use of CCI.[74] These moves were controversial; justifications were proffered partly on the basis of the constitutional text but more directly on the basis of the threat to constitutional governance posed by a flawed tribunal holding a monopoly on constitutional interpretation. Barczentewicz and Matczak see CCI as an important element of the strategy since 'it saturates sub-constitutional regulations with the constitutional axiology' particularly important in the context of expansive assertions of legislative power. Alongside the Italian example, the Polish case foregrounds and renders explicit the power-based explanations for adoption of CCI.

This section illustrates how bureaucratic self-interest can, whether on its own or in conjunction with one or more of the ideational factors considered in the previous section, motivate judges to adopt CCI. If we assume that courts act in their own bureaucratic self-interest, we can see that their incentives will sometimes be to take minimal steps and preserve the power they already have, but at other times to take assertive steps to expand their own power. The appropriate strategy will depend on the balance of power with other institutions – whether the legislature or other courts – at the relevant time.

V. Convergence and Divergence of Motivating Factors

In the previous section, I drew attention at various points to the ways in which judicial motivations – whether ideational or of bureaucratic self-interest – contribute to the commonality of CCI identified in section II or the divergence over intensification traced in section III. I shall now explore these connections more comprehensively and systematically. A wide range of ideational factors and bureaucratic incentives converge to motivate judges to adopt CCI: commitments to constitutional supremacy and/or legal unity, combined with a commitment to implementing the will of the legislature wherever possible; the desire to harmonise statutory requirements with higher law notions of justice; a pragmatic desire to give effective benefits to those who have suffered from unconstitutional legislation; and finally – in countries with centralised constitutional review – incentives for both constitutional and ordinary courts to expand their powers by undertaking at least some of the statutory or constitutional interpretation respectively assigned to the other courts. These factors appeal to different types of judges – constitutional idealists and constitutional pragmatists, as well as self-serving judges seeking to increase their own power. This congruence of factors explains how CCI has become a doctrine common to all judge-kind.

[74] Barczentewicz and Matczak (n 20) s V.

Ideational factors and bureaucratic incentives have different implications, however, for the extent to which CCI should intensify along different dimensions. At first blush, bureaucratic self-interest suggests that CCI should intensify along the first three dimensions: constitutional suffusion, semantic stretching, legislative pre-emption. It is less clear whether judges intent on expanding their own power should support diversifying the authority for constitutional interpretation. On the one hand, allowing stage agencies to engage in CCI might reduce judicial power; on the other hand, perhaps such state agencies could be expected to follow judicial interpretations, effectively expanding the reach of judicial power. The motivation provided by bureaucratic self-interest is not quite so unidirectional as this analysis suggests, however. Judges intent on increasing their own power must step carefully for fear of provoking a backlash: sometimes the imperative is to preserve rather than extend power. Nevertheless, in the long run, the incentives of bureaucratic self-interest would lead us to expect an expansion of CCI.

The ideational factors differ in their implications for intensification. A judge motivated by the idea that the entire legal system should consist of norms conforming to those in the mastertext constitution (legal unity) should be inclined to take a suffusing rather than controlling approach and should not be troubled by semantic stretching. Moreover, such a judge is unlikely to see difficulty with prescribing the scope of permissible legislation to the point of pre-empting legislative choices. A judge motivated by a narrower notion of constitutional supremacy or by a desire simply to balance the interests of parties to litigation while providing effective remedies should be inclined to favour a controlling rather than suffusing approach, should be more inclined to place limits on semantic stretching, should be slow to prescribe and pre-empt legislation and should balk at diversifying the *loci* of interpretative authority.

It would be difficult to disaggregate these motivations sufficiently to test the correlation between them and the extent to which CCI is intensified in a particular system. Different judges – potentially sitting on a collegiate court – are likely to be differently motivated. The decision of a collegiate court might well be the product of differing preferences over CCI. Even one judge could simultaneously act on different motivations. Judges who are primarily ideationally motivated are still likely to have some regard to bureaucratic self-interest, if only as a check on significant intensification. Conversely, the ideational and bureaucratic motivations may be covarying: judges who believe that the values of the mastertext constitution should suffuse the entire legal system are perhaps more likely to favour an expansion of judicial power; judges who favour a legalistic conception of the constitution as an external check on legislative action may likewise be more sceptical of expanding judicial power. And finally, as intensification increases so too do the legitimacy concerns over CCI that may prompt a backlash from other constitutional actors or a counteracting motivational force for judges themselves, leading sufficient judges to stymie intensification.

Nevertheless, linking judicial motivations to the intensification of CCI in this way generates several important insights about the development of judicial doctrine. First, because CCI is indifferent to substantive constitutional commitments – social rights or property rights; equal protection or laissez-faire liberalism – its development illuminates judicial attitudes to constitutionalism and judicial power for their own sake rather than as instruments in support of broader policy preferences or general moral commitments. Second, the general but contested trend towards intensification, with few if any jurisdictions intensifying on all four dimensions, suggests that the trend towards increased judicial power is real but not unqualified. Third, the level of variation between judges, between jurisdictions and between periods is inconsistent with the proposition that judges are motivated solely by bureaucratic self-interest. Judges are – at least partially and probably to a considerable extent – ideationally motivated actors who respond to deep understandings of what constitutions are and the role they should play in regulating public decision-making. Judicial idealists and judicial pragmatists may differ in their approach to CCI, but they each respond to fundamental ideas about law, its value and its function. Fourth, while we could attribute divergence over intensification of CCI to differing judicial assessments of how best to increase their power, it is at least equally plausible that such divergence is simply a continuation of the oldest debates in law and legal theory: between narrow and expansive approaches to law's scope and law's interpretation reflecting deep-seated commitments about the sort of thing law is.

VI. Conclusion

The purpose of this chapter has been to provide an explanation of why CCI emerges in such common form across diverse legal systems, only then to diverge – as much within systems as between systems – in relation to the appropriate degree of intensity with which CCI should be conducted. I have attributed the commonality to the convergence of several motivations supporting CCI in its original anodyne form, with different motivations suggesting different levels of intensification along four discrete but contingently related dimensions. This framework allows us to grapple with the reality of CCI more convincingly than the rather conclusory distinction between positive and negative legislation. It enables us meaningfully to compare the intensity of CCI between different judges, different systems, and different periods. By providing a more fine-grained account of CCI's intensity, it facilitates a more reasoned debate on whether particular instances of CCI represent an illegitimate intrusion on legislative power. That debate will turn, however, on prior commitments to a particular vision of law in general and constitutional law in particular. Those who conceive of law primarily as a human artifact are likely to favour less intense CCI. Those who conceive of law primarily as an aspiration towards a more just social ordering are likely to favour more intense CCI. Debates over the legitimacy of CCI are not amenable to technocratic or doctrinal resolution, a realisation that enhances our understanding of this surprisingly multi-textured doctrine, partly common to all judge-kind.

11

Placing Constitutionally Conforming Interpretation in its Larger Theoretical and Political Contexts

MICHEL ROSENFELD

I. Setting the Landscape Surrounding Discussions Relating to Constitutionally Conforming Interpretation

Constitutionally conforming interpretation (CCI) or its functional equivalents prevail in a very large number of jurisdictions as the national reports contained in the first volume of the present collective undertaking vividly attest to. On the surface at least, as ever more expansive legal pluralism prevails, the more urgent it becomes to search for harmony and reconciliation among superimposed, intersecting, or overlapping legal norms. And in this setting, CCI emerges as a presumptively useful and felicitous device. Subjection to clashing applicable legal norms not only impairs legal efficiency, but also potentially severely undermines adherence to the rule of law.

CCI's virtues are perhaps most manifest in the context of the established hierarchy and unity typical of nation-states adhering to constitutional democracy. If a parliamentary law can equally plausibly be interpreted as conforming to or violating the relevant jurisdiction's hierarchically superior constitution, it seems obvious that judicial adoption of the conforming interpretation is preferable from the combined standpoints of efficiency, legal legitimacy, and legal integrity. When one moves beyond the nation-state and confronts the interplay between international, transnational, and national legal regimes, matters become inevitably more complicated as issues of hierarchy and of unity loom as much more contested and open-ended.[1] Nevertheless, a strong case can still be made for CCI or variants

[1] See eg *Internationale Handelsgesellschaft Mbh v Einfuhr-Und Vorratsstelle Für Getreide Und Futtermittel [Solange I]* 37 BVerfGE 271 (1974) (German constitutional law prevails when in conflict with EU law); Case C-402/05 P *Yassin Abdullah Kadi and Al Barakaat International Foundation v Council and Commission* ECLI:EU:C:2008:461, [2008] ECR I–6351, 3 September 2008 (CJEU) (EU law

thereof. Indeed, from the standpoint of a European Union (EU) Member State, for example, it seems preferable wherever plausible to reconcile the nation-state constitution with adherence to EU law, the EU Charter of Rights, and conformity with the European Convention on Human Rights (ECHR). Undoubtedly, in the transnational setting the task is more challenging, but there have been conscious efforts towards harmony, including through dialogues among national constitutional judges and their EU and ECHR counterparts.[2] Upon further consideration, to the extent that it is desirable to allow for greater tolerance of diversity in the transnational sphere, ideally some form of CCI could be paired with a principled application of the 'margin of appreciation' standard amply developed in the jurisprudence of the European Court of Human Rights (ECtHR).[3] Accordingly, at the transnational level, core unity could be buttressed through some CCI variant whereas cross border differences that do not erode the core could be preserved through judicious deployment of the margin of appreciation standard.

If one agrees with the above overall logic, it becomes all the more intriguing and paradoxical that so much controversy surrounds CCI. And that remains the case even if one focuses exclusively on CCI's uses within the confines of the nation-state. Although the criticisms of CCI are manifold and diverse as attested by the various national reports in Volume 1, they ultimately seem to boil down to objections to what is perceived as illegitimate judicial intrusions into the legislative function meant to be exclusively entrusted to democratically accountable institutions.

Even under the most rudimentary positivistic conception of the rule of law, and in the absence of any hierarchy hovering over applicable duly legislatively created legal norms, the judicial function needs to be kept separate from its legislative counterpart.[4] Indeed, it is not for the legislator to decide upon the application of her law to individual cases. Application of a pertinent law to an individual case with its own set of facts is left to the judge, and unless the law in question dictates a single judicial outcome that logically discards all conceivably plausible alternatives, the judge's decision must comprise an interpretive choice. And that choice must thus advance one plausible construction of the law as against all others. Thus, for example, in the context of HLA Hart's well-known discussion of the putative law that provides that 'no vehicles are allowed in this park',[5] it is for a judge to decide an actual controversy over whether someone's use of roller skates in that

prevails over conflicting international law obligation); Antonia Baraggia, 'Conforming Interpretation in the EU Through the Lens of the CJEU's Case Law' in this volume.

[2] See Lech Garlicki, 'Cooperation of Courts: The Role of Supranational Jurisdictions in Europe' (2008) 6 *International Journal of Constitutional Law* 509.

[3] See *Handyside v United Kingdom* 1 EHRR 737 (1976) (UK allowed broader definition of indecency than one prevalent in Scandinavian countries).

[4] See Michel Rosenfeld, 'The Rule of Law and the Legitimacy of Constitutional Democracy' (2001) 74 *Southern California Law Review* 1307.

[5] See HLA Hart, 'Positivism and the Separation of Law and Morals' (1958) 71 *Harvard Law Review* 593, 607.

park violates the said law. Moreover, in common law jurisdictions where judicial decisions have precedential value, over time judicial interpretation, construction, and application of statutory law supplements the latter's legislative elaboration in a way that belies any neat cleavage between legislation and adjudication.

As long as there is no hierarchy among legal norms, although the legislator cannot avoid judicial input in the understanding and uses of parliamentary law, the legislator does retain the last word. Accordingly, in the last example, the law could be amended to specify that roller skates are not to be counted as vehicles under the now legislatively modified law. Under these circumstances, judicial intrusion could not be avoided – except in the relatively small number of cases where all judges and all legislators acting in good conscience would have to concur on the same single interpretation – but democratically accountable legislative correction or nullification would always be available.

Much more problematic is the inevitability of antimajoritarian judicial input in the context of a hierarchy of norms which formally or practically prevents the legislator from nullifying or correcting what he deems an unwarranted constitutional or legal interpretation or outcome. This problem is particularly acute in a country such as the US where the constitution is practically almost impossible to amend.[6] For instance, if a law is subject to two equally plausible interpretations, and a judge using constitutional avoidance[7] – which as Matthias Klatt persuasively argues is largely equivalent to CCI[8] – adopts the second rather than the first interpretation, then the legislator's ability to correct or nullify are likely to be severely limited. Suppose the legislator is intent on the first interpretation of the law in controversy, but that interpretation could not be reinstated through legislative means as under that interpretation the law has been judicially found to be unconstitutional. Suppose further that the legislator does not find the second interpretation consistent with her legislative aims. In that case the legislator is confined to two (from her standpoint) unsatisfactory options: either repeal the law or continue living with a version of it that significantly impairs her legislative objectives.

Consistent with these observations, one may conclude that where, like in the UK, parliamentary sovereignty prevails, CCI ought to be broadly accepted. In contrast, in places, like the US, where antimajoritarian judicial decisions are nearly impossible to overturn, CCI ought to be avoided as much as possible to constrain antimajoritarian intrusions to a minimum. Surprisingly, however, as the relevant national reports underscore, CCI is far from uncontroversial in the UK,[9] whereas constitutional avoidance is far less divisive in the US than certain

[6] See Norman Dorsen et al, *Comparative Constitutionalism: Cases and Materials* 4th edn (St Paul, West Academic, 2022) 86.

[7] See Frederick Schauer, 'United States: Constitutional Avoidance as Constitutional Conformation' in Matthias Klatt (ed), *Constitutionally Conforming Interpretation: Comparative Perspectives Volume 1: National Reports* (Oxford, Hart Publishing, 2023) 267.

[8] See Matthias Klatt, 'The Legitimacy of Constitutionally Conforming Interpretation' in Klatt (n 7) 3.

[9] See Nick Friedman, 'United Kingdom. In the Shadow of Parliamentary Sovereignty: The Human Rights Act and the Principle of Legality' in Klatt (n 7) 197.

downright constitutional judicial decisions.[10] This seemingly paradoxical contrast calls for closer inquiry which will be pursued below. But before proceeding further, it is necessary to briefly consider what stands at the opposite end of the spectrum of the conjunction between CCI and unexceptionable parliamentary sovereignty. That other end of the spectrum is carved out by the invocation of constitutional, supra-constitutional, national, transnational, or international legal norms deemed without exception applicable both vertically and horizontally to all legal matters whatever their place in any working legally pluralistic hierarchy or modus vivendi. In other words, how should CCI or its equivalents fare under the role of universally applicable legal rules or principles such as those considered to be part of *jus cogens* binding on all legal actors throughout the world?[11] One such rule is the absolute prohibition against torture.[12] Accordingly, all judicial interpretation whether in international law, constitutional law, or statutory law must be consistent with upholding the prohibition against torture. In this latter context, is not CCI indistinguishable from all other kinds of judicial interpretive interventions?

The short answer to this last question is in the affirmative. Whether dealing with a constitution, international, transnational, or statutory law, wherever more than one interpretation is plausible, the judge should only choose options consistent with the prohibition against torture. This conclusion is buttressed moreover by two principal considerations. First, particularly in the face of increased legal pluralism, harmonisation of the requirements imposed by various applicable legal regimes seems far preferable than serial nullifications leaving multiple gaps that may prove difficult to fill. Suppose a law explicitly allows the state to use all available methods of interrogation upon detaining an individual suspected of engaging in terrorist activity. A judge deciding a case challenging this law would either have to decide that it is unenforceable (which would create a legal vacuum) or to interpret it as allowing all 'available methods' falling short of torture.

The second principal consideration relates to the necessity to have recourse to antimajoritarian means in order to secure the presumably universally applicable

[10] See Schauer (n 7). Schauer argues that all constitutional avoidance requires constitutional interpretation. ibid 274. That is true in a formal sense, but not necessarily in a substantive one. For example, consider a jurisdiction in which it has long been established that hard core pornography is not constitutionally protected speech but that otherwise indecent depictions of sex or nudity are. If in that jurisdiction a law is enacted that prohibits all depictions of sex and nudity that are certain under generally accepted social norms to be considered offensive and indecent, a judge would either have to hold the law in question unconstitutional or to interpret the conjunction between indecent and offensive as being confined to instances that would also qualify as prohibited displays of hard-core pornography. In this example, although the judge is applying the constitution to interpret the law before her, she is in no way changing, adding, or subtracting anything to a long established (and presumably presently uncontested) understanding of the constitutional boundary between protected and unprotected depictions of sex and nudity.

[11] See Erika de Wet, 'The Constitutionalization of Public International Law' in Michel Rosenfeld and Andras Sajo (eds), *The Oxford Handbook of Comparative Constitutional Law* (Oxford, Oxford University Press, 2012) 1209; Stéphane Beaulac, 'Conforming Legal Interpretation based on International Law: The Use of Unwritten Principles, the Example of Equality of Arms' in this volume.

[12] ibid 1215.

legal norms embodied in *jus cogens* throughout the particular national, trans-national, or international setting at stake. Thus, even if large majorities clamour for the use of torture in the aftermath of a particularly violent terrorist attack, judges should refuse to enforce constitutional provisions, treaties, or ordinary parliamentary laws authorising torture. And in this context, CCI would amount to the functional equivalent of every other judicial effort to prevent or circumvent unwarranted legal toleration of torture. Going beyond the relatively easy case presented by torture, if there is a consensus on the universality of the legal mandate or prohibition involved, then adjusting and guiding judicial interpretation accordingly should be equally justifiable across the board. Conversely, if the presumptive universality of the legal norm at stake is highly contested, then the legal legitimacy of CCI should be no more or less questionable than that of all other antimajoritarian interpretive parsing out of constitutional, international, and national infra-constitutional law.

To get a better understanding of how CCI fares in its proper theoretical and political context, the remainder of this chapter proceeds as follows. Section II focuses on CCI and the potential and limitations of judicial interpretation. Section III explores the impact on CCI fostered by the concurrent internationalisation of constitutional law and constitutionalisation of international law.[13] Section IV zeroes in on CCI and questions of democracy. Finally, section V seeks to unravel the nexus between CCI and politics.

II. The Vicissitudes of Legal and Constitutional Interpretation

The legitimacy and integrity of CCI is largely dependent on one's theory of legal and constitutional interpretation coupled with one's willingness to embrace the presumption that the legislator seeks conformity with the constitution or other relevant hierarchically superior legal norm. If one adopts a view akin to that of the late Justice Antonin Scalia of the US Supreme Court, who insisted that the text of a statute should speak for itself and that declarations of legislative intent should be ignored by judges engaged in statutory adjudication,[14] then CCI would emerge as downright illegitimate. Moreover, by adding Scalia's 'plain meaning' statutory textualism to his 'original meaning' approach to constitutional interpretation,[15] judicial subjectivity and discretion could and ought to be altogether discarded. Accordingly, CCI would not only be unwarranted but also superfluous. The statute

[13] ibid; Wen-Chen Chang and Jiunn-Rong Yeh, 'Internationalization of Constitutional Law' in Rosenfeld and Sajo (n 11) 1165.

[14] See Jonathan R Siegel, 'The Legacy of Justice Scalia and His Textualist Ideal' (2017) 85 *The George Washington Law Review* 857, 862.

[15] See Antonin Scalia, 'Originalism: The Lesser Evil' (1989) 57 *University of Cincinnati Law Review* 849.

under judicial review would only have one correct meaning which would either be clearly consistent or clearly inconsistent with the one correct understanding of the constitution.

In contrast to Scalia, Ronald Dworkin has analogised judicial interpretation to the writing of a chain novel[16] which requires the (common law) judge to construct her forthcoming 'chapter' consistent with the already existing ones that precede it in order to achieve the 'best fit'.[17] Also, Dworkin calls upon judges to compose their chapter so as to preserve or further promote the 'integrity' of the chain novel analogous weaving together of judicial precedents.[18] Furthermore, focusing on the US Constitution Dworkin has asserted that it embraces a particular moral and political philosophy[19] and that it embodies certain general *concepts*, such as freedom of speech or equality, that can give rise to several plausible different *conceptions*.[20] Thus, for example, the concept of equality can be given a formal libertarian or a broadly redistributive liberal egalitarian conception. Dworkin insists that the US Constitution mandates a particular best suited conception of the general rights it enshrines and that every hard case has a single answer.[21] Whereas this last assertion is highly controversial,[22] tellingly Dworkin invokes the supra-human figure of a judge he names Hercules whom he postulates could assure the one correct result in every hard case.[23] For present purposes, an important implication of recourse to Hercules is that ordinary humanly fallible judges can in good faith disagree concerning the passage between concept and conception and regarding finding the best fit between the constitutional interpretation they are about to issue and all relevant preceding ones.

For Dworkin's Hercules CCI is an obvious choice given the importance of fit and integrity and the assurance of reaching the only right interpretive result. This is all the more so since Dworkin asserts that his principle of integrity charges legislators with the duty to make 'the total set of laws morally coherent' and judges to treat those laws as such 'so far as possible'.[24] Consistent with this perspective, ordinary fallible actual judges also should approximate Hercules as much as possible and do their best to achieve moral coherence and integrity. And accordingly, CCI looms as an equally justified tool in the hands of ordinary judges as it is in those of Hercules.

Standing sharply against the respective theories of interpretation promoted by Scalia and Dworkin, Critical Legal Studies (CLS) scholars have maintained that

[16] See Ronald Dworkin, *Law's Empire* (Cambridge, Harvard University Press, 1986) 229.
[17] ibid 230–31.
[18] ibid 176, 405.
[19] ibid 239.
[20] ibid 382.
[21] See Ronald Dworkin, *Taking Rights Seriously* (Cambridge, Harvard University Press, 1977) ch 4.
[22] See Michel Rosenfeld, 'Dworkin and the One Law Principle: A Pluralist Critique' (2005) 59 *Revue Internationale de Philosophie* 363.
[23] See Dworkin (n 16) 239, 264–65.
[24] ibid 176.

laws are inherently indeterminate and judicial interpretation is inescapably political.[25] Moreover, CLS considers all adjudication as political all the way up and down, and this in the sense of ordinary politics as contrasted with judicial politics or philosophy.[26] Under this approach, CCI becomes irrelevant and may be invoked or ignored whenever politically convenient. Since both the constitution and statutory law are believed to be sufficiently indeterminate to allow for politically contradictory interpretations – constitutional equality can be equally judicially manipulated to advantage the rich or the poor – CCI would have no substantive role to play. CCI could be therefore completely eliminated or preserved for purely rhetorical (political) purposes.

The three competing theories of interpretation outlined above have been elaborated with the US legal and constitutional system in mind. Notably, these theories are at least in part irrelevant or insufficient to account for constitutional or statutory interpretation in other jurisdictions. For example, Scalia's original meaning theory of constitutional interpretation seems completely irrelevant in Canada given the latter's adherence to the concept of 'the living tree' constitution.[27] Similarly, one can question whether Dworkin's chain novel metaphor can have much relevance in a civil law country that does not require adherence to judicial precedents. Finally, CLS's highly contested views may arguably sound more plausible in the context of the US's eighteenth century constitution than in those of more contemporary ones that emerge as wholistic and explicitly value laden such as Germany's Basic Law.[28]

With these differences in mind, it is still useful to conduct a brief critical assessment of the three contrasting theories outlined above for purposes of garnering certain general interpretive insights that may prove useful in evaluating CCI across diverse legal and constitutional regimes. Perhaps most obviously, Scalia's 'plain meaning' textualism and his 'original meaning' American constitutionalism are strikingly unpersuasive, and even he deviated from them in several of his judicial opinions.[29] As a general proposition, meaning never depends on text alone, but on text placed in its proper context. This becomes obvious when considering Hart's example about prohibiting vehicles in the park. If the purpose of such prohibition is to minimise noise in the park, then cars and motorcycles should be prohibited. If

[25] See eg Mark Kelman, 'Thrashing' (1984) 36 *Stanford Law Review* 293; Joseph William Singer, 'The Player and the Cards: Nihilism and Legal Theory' (1984) 94 *Yale Law Journal* 1.

[26] See Michel Rosenfeld, 'Judicial Politics Versus Ordinary Politics: Is the Constitutional Judge Caught in the Middle?' in Christine Landfried (ed), *Judicial Power* (Cambridge, Cambridge University Press, 2019) 36.

[27] See *Reference Re Same Sex Marriage*, 2004 SCC 79, para 22 (SCt of Canada).

[28] See Dieter Grimm, 'The Role of Fundamental Rights After Sixty-Five Years of Constitutional Jurisprudence in Germany' (2015) 13 *International Journal of Constitutional Law* 9.

[29] See eg *District of Columbia v Heller*, 554 US 570 (2008) and Stanley Fish, 'Antonin Scalia, Bernhard Schlink, and Lancelot Andrewes: Reading Heller' in Peter Goodrich and Michel Rosenfeld (eds), *Administering Interpretation: Derrida, Agamben, and the Political Theology of Law* (New York, Fordham University Press, 2019) 22 (Criticizing Scalia's opinion in *Heller* as failing under textualist and original meaning-based criteria).

instead the purpose is maximising safety, then bicycles and perhaps electric roller skates ought also to be added to the list. And if the purpose is peaceful enjoyment without fuelling agitation or controversy, then making a battle tested tank prevalent in a highly divisive war into a statue in the middle of the park ought arguably to be prohibited as it would provoke unease and antagonism among park users.

It might be objected that some texts do 'speak for themselves'. The most referred to example drawn from the US Constitution is the requirement that in order to be eligible to become president of the US a person must be at least 35 years old.[30] But even this text that does 'speak for itself' for an American audience could mean something different in the context of a different culture that pegs age to conception rather than to birth. Thus, for example, whereas presumably all Americans would agree that a person who is 34 years and six months old cannot then assume the presidency, those embedded in the alternative culture would concur that the person in question is constitutionally qualified. More generally, when a text appears to speak for itself what is really at stake is that there is consensus regarding the relevant context.

Scalia's appeal to conforming to 'original meaning' in constitutional interpretation raises numerous counterarguments both from within and beyond US constitutional adjudication. Most glaringly, Scalia's position has been rejected by some of his fellow US justices,[31] and as indicated above is irrelevant in most settings beyond US shores. More importantly, from a general interpretive standpoint, adherence to original meaning is unworkable when dealing with broadly phrased constitutional provisions regarding essentially contested concepts. Take, for instance, constitutional equality. For the last half century Americans, including US Supreme Court justices, have vehemently disagreed over whether preferential treatment based on race furthers, or is contrary to, the constitutionally mandated equal protection under law.[32] Suppose now that the US Equal Protection Clause had been adopted in 2000 rather than in 1868 (a time when racial segregation in education was broadly supported within American society),[33] how should a justice sympathetic to Scalia's approach determine the 'original meaning' of that Clause in 2200?

Turning to Dworkin's theory, some of his insights seem valid and valuable for the US and beyond whereas others seem unpersuasive in all or in many relevant contexts. Dworkin is right that for the most part in constitutional interpretation and to a large extent in statutory interpretation judicial decision making must incorporate some elements issued from the realms of moral and political

[30] US Const. art II, s 1, cl 5.

[31] See eg Stephen Breyer, *Reading the Constitution: Why I Chose Pragmatism, Not Textualism* (New York, Simon & Shuster, 2024).

[32] Significantly, the US Supreme Court has found affirmative action constitutional in some cases, see eg *Grutter v Bollinger* 539 U.S. 306 (2003), and unconstitutional in others, see eg *Students for Fair Admissions v Harvard* 600 U.S. 181 (2023).

[33] See *Plessy v Ferguson* 163 U.S. 537 (1896) (interpreting 1868 US Const. XIV Amend. 'Equal Protection' Clause as authorising state 'separate but equal' racial segregation laws).

philosophy. This is not to say that natural law must prevail as against legal positivism. Instead, this means, to put it in Wittgenstein's terminology,[34] that the language game of constitutional law must incorporate through translation or transpose certain propositions embedded within the language game of moral and political philosophy. Returning to the example of the question of the constitutional fate of preferential treatment for members of traditionally oppressed and disadvantaged groups under a generally phrased constitutional equality provision, any plausible cogent judicial answer must at least implicitly draw on the relevant corresponding philosophical debate.[35] Accordingly, a judge who understands or intuits justice as implying formal equality and formal equality of opportunity is much more likely to find preferential treatment constitutionally impermissible than a fellow judge who believes that justice requires equality of result or a Rawlsian understanding of fair equality of opportunity.[36] To be clear, the above example and most other ones do not require any merger of law and philosophy but only some convergence that does not contravene the distinctness and coherence of the two language games involved. Thus, the US judge enjoys greater latitude than the Canadian one in drawing on the philosophical debate relating to affirmative action and preferential treatment. And that is because constitutional equality in the US is framed in the most general terms whereas its Canadian counterpart explicitly bestows constitutional approval on affirmative action.[37]

Dworkin is also persuasive in his insistence that judges aim for 'fit' and for 'integrity'. Based on an understanding of the rule of law being built on the principles of predictability and fairness,[38] consistency and normative coherence ought to be aimed at whenever possible. To be sure, the means to achieve fit may well differ in common law and civil law jurisdictions. But the objective to realise the proper fit seems equally attainable through logic and analogical reasoning than through incorporation and further adapting and redirecting judicial precedents.

On the other hand, Dworkin is wrong both in his appraisal of the nexus between concept and conception in constitutional law and in his insistence that there is a single right answer to every hard case. Moreover, Dworkin is thus wrong both within the confines of US constitutional law and beyond. Any perfunctory perusal of the concepts of liberty, equality, or privacy within the confines of the

[34] See Ludwig Wittgenstein, *Philosophical Investigations* (GEM Anscombe tr, Oxford, Basil Blackwell Ltd, 1968) 2. 7.

[35] See Michel Rosenfeld, *Affirmative Action and Justice: A Philosophical and Constitutional Inquiry* (New Haven, Yale University Press, 1991).

[36] See John Rawls, *A Theory of Justice* (Cambridge, Harvard University Press, 1971) 73, 83–89. According to Rawls, formal equality of opportunity only requires that all those who compete for the same scarce good be uniformly subjected to the same generally applicable rules. Fair equality of opportunity, in contrast, requires that those who have experienced socially created competitive disadvantages be afforded corrective societal means in order to attain competitive parity.

[37] See Canadian Charter of Rights (1982) s 15(2). Arguably, to an important extent, the moral and political dimensions of affirmative action are much more settled within the constitution in Canada, thus leaving that country's judges with less interpretive latitude on the matter.

[38] See Rosenfeld (n 4) 1345–48.

US Constitution reveals wide ranging differences of conceptions among judges who have engaged with these concepts in the course of interpreting the constitution.[39] Also, Dworkin offers no proof that the relevant US constitutional framers chose one plausible conception of the enshrined concept over others. Finally, projecting the nexus between concept and conception beyond American shores, logic dictates that except in the rare cases in which a constitutionalised concept only yields one plausible conception, judges will have a contestable choice among several plausible fitting conceptions. To return to the affirmative action example, Canadian judges cannot embrace conceptions of equality that foreclose the legitimacy of affirmative action. But there are many different conceptions of affirmative action and Canadian judges are bound to choose among the latter in addressing the constitutional scope or limitations of the legitimate use of affirmative action under their constitutional equality provision.

To the extent that constitutionalisation of a general concept does not command adoption of one among several plausible conceptions of it, Dworkin's claim that every hard case can yield a single right answer proves patently false. This can be perhaps best illustrated through focus on Hercules. The errors of ordinary fallible judges relating to fit, integrity, and advancing the chain novel interpretive process over time can easily be imagined to be overcome by Hercules. Hercules possesses a comprehensive perspective and a full understanding of all nuances, potentials, and perils relating to interpretively linking the past, the present, and future. Hercules must also be assumed to have a failproof ability to navigate all the requisite transitions from the abstract to the concrete. But once one removes Dworkin's premise that constitutional concepts yield a single best conception, then Hercules is no better able than ordinary judges to pick among equally plausible conceptions. Dworkin himself prefers what amounts to a liberal egalitarian as against a libertarian understanding of the US Equal Protection Clause.[40] However, in view of the preceding discussion, this preference is based on a personal philosophical and constitutional vision and not on propositions that all concerned with fit and integrity would feel bound to accept. Hercules would excel in carrying out the best possible (or even the perfect) interpretation of constitutional equality under either a libertarian or a liberal egalitarian moral and political philosophy. But Hercules seems no better positioned than any real-life philosopher or judge to decisively settle the ideological dispute that divides libertarians from liberal egalitarians. In short, Hercules may well be the perfect libertarian or egalitarian constitutional adjudicator, yet he emerges without any infallible skills to decisively resolve normative and ideological divides within the realms of morals or politics.

The just presented critique of Dworkin does not alter the conclusion – sustained by his insights concerning, fit, integrity, and the dynamic between concept and

[39] Compare eg *Roe v Wade* 410 U.S. 113 (1973) (establishing a constitutional right to abortion) to *Dobbs v Jackson Women's Health Organization* 597 U.S. 215 (2022) (overruling 50 years of precedents and decreeing there is no constitutional right to abortion).

[40] See Dworkin (n 21) 232–38.

conception – that CCI should be sustained and promoted as an institutional tool bound to positively buttress the interpretive task. On further thought, on balance the preceding assessment of Dworkin's theory reinforces the conclusion regarding CCI. Indeed, the lack of certitude concerning the best conceptions and the best judicial resolution in hard cases, enhances the need for CCI as a vehicle for fruitful dialogue among judges and legislators. Since, as Dworkin emphasises, judges and legislators ought to aim for moral coherence, CCI furthers that aim amidst uncertainty and leaves the door open for legislators to maintain their input in the elaborations and corrections that may advance the quest for moral coherence.

Turning finally to CLS, one can concede that much judicial interpretation is indeterminate and that law cannot be purged of all politics. It does not follow from this, however, that judicial interpretation is reducible to mere politics. Two principal considerations underly this latter conclusion. First, as will be more fully explored in section V below, one must draw an important distinction between judicial politics or philosophy and ordinary politics.[41] Suffice it for now to point out that strict adherence to the dictates of judicial politics is bound to prompt judges to embrace certain interpretations that contradict their ordinary political leanings. Thus, a judge with a philosophy of restrictive interpretation of antimajoritarian constitutional rights cannot consistently and with integrity resort to expansive interpretations of such rights when that would better suit one of his strong ordinary politics convictions.

Second, as I have argued extensively elsewhere,[42] when combining the text and context of a constitutional or statutory provision that she must interpret a judge's options seems bound to be substantially limited. As already stressed, in most cases there is likely to be a multiplicity of plausible outcomes. But upon further consideration, such outcomes will prove for the most part to be limited in number. A judge may typically have a choice among a small number of streams of interpretation with each of which validating certain interpretations while excluding others. Take, for example, the question of equality between men and women in accordance with the US Constitution. Keeping in mind that the Equal Protection Clause was adopted in 1868, there are striking differences of interpretation between late nineteenth century judges and their late twentieth century counterparts. In the first of these periods the US Supreme Court held that women could be excluded from practicing law[43] and that it was reasonable to deny them the right to vote[44] (which was granted by constitutional amendment in 1920).[45] Although except for the grant of the right to vote none of the relevant constitutional provisions have changed, the social, political, and ideological context had radically changed by the 1970s. That

[41] See Rosenfeld (n 26).

[42] See Michel Rosenfeld, *Just Interpretations: Law Between Ethics and Politics* (Berkeley, University of California Press, 1998) ch 1.

[43] See *Bradwell v State of Illinois* 83 U.S. (16 Wall.) 130 (1873).

[44] See *Minor v Happersett* 88 U.S. (21 Wall.) 162 (1875).

[45] US Const. Amendment XIX (1920).

dramatic shift in context mandated a rejection of the earlier jurisprudence and an interpretive orientation squarely incompatible with the preceding one.[46] Though there is no guarantee that the newer context will remain stable or hold in the future against all regression, it is clear that a contemporary lawyer would be laughed out of court if he advocated a return to the late nineteenth judicial interpretive heritage in dealing with issues relating to equality between the sexes.

In the last analysis, consistent with these last observations and with the preceding discussion CCI can play a constructive role in the interpretation and application of statutory laws. This is all the more so if CCI is inserted in an institutional setting that facilitates dialogue between judges and legislators. That said, what remains unanswered thus far, and should become clearer in the course of the analysis below, is whether there are good other than interpretive reasons for the rejection of CCI.

III. The Concurrent Internationalisation of Constitutional Law and Constitutionalisation of International Law

As already briefly noted, international and transnational law play an important role *within* the legal precincts of the domestic nation-state constitutional order, but these supra-national legal regimes tend to weigh against full maintenance of the hierarchy and unity typically achievable within national settings. Viewed from a nation-state perspective, these supra-national legal regimes typically figure as being layered or segmented.[47] For example, EU law is supposed to achieve supremacy over inconsistent Member State law.[48] Unlike in a well-functioning federal republic where courts can assure preservation of hierarchy and unity among the federal unit and its federated counterparts, however, EU Member State constitutional courts have at times invoked resistance to EU law in cases in which they have deemed the latter in conflict with the commands of their own national constitution.[49] Because of this, EU law emerges as a *layered* regime that has been largely but not fully hierarchised and integrated within the otherwise unified constitutional confines of the EU Member States. On the other hand, the ECHR and other supra-national human rights conventions, such the (Inter)-American one, figure as *segmented* legal regimes. That is because these conventions enshrine human rights that are functionally equivalent to (and are superimposed on) the

[46] See eg *Craig v Boren* 429 U.S. 190 (1976); *United States v Virginia* 518 U.S. 515 (1996).

[47] See Michel Rosenfeld, 'Rethinking Constitutional Ordering in an Era of Legal and Ideological Pluralism' (2008) 6 *International Journal of Constitutional Law* 415, 425–27.

[48] See Case 6/64 *Flaminio Costa v ENEL* ECLI:EU:C:1964:66 (CJEU).

[49] See eg *Internationale Handelsgesellschaft Mbh v Einfuhr-Und Vorratsstelle Für Getreide Und Futtermittel [Solange I]* 37 BVerfGE 271 (1974) (German constitutional law prevails when in conflict with EU law).

fundamental rights component of domestic constitutions and render such human rights applicable within the boundaries of the Member States that have become signatories to the relevant convention.[50]

The presence of layered and segmented supra-national legal regimes calls for greater efforts at integration and smoothing out conflicts among the existing plurality of applicable legal regimes. This suggests embracing CCI or its functional equivalents and of enhancing their role given the much greater harmonisation challenges at stake.[51] This also raises the further crucial question of whether the transnational scene offers a common currency that can be put into use by both national and transnational judges working on harmonising the variety of legal regimes with which they have become confronted.

Although no consensus exists on the subject, one can garner practical and theoretical support for the proposition that a common currency has emerged throughout the legal regimes that adhere to the rule of law and that remain consistent with the dictates of constitutional democracy. This common currency is created and sustained by the combination of the internationalisation of constitutional law and the constitutionalisation of international law.[52] Both of these phenomena are associated with globalisation of the economy and the adoption of various international and regional covenants and conventions designed to promote and protect human rights in the aftermath of World War II.[53]

The internationalisation and constitutionalisation in question have sprung through differing means ranging from formal inclusion within a nation-state constitution to universal spread of *jus cogens* over and above any state consent to the relevant international law norms. Thus, for example, the post-apartheid South African Constitution explicitly incorporates international law prescriptions and encourages the country's constitutional judges to factor foreign constitutional jurisprudence when deciding domestic cases.[54] On the other hand, traditionally a nation-state cannot be bound by a public international law norm without its prior consent. However, what is categorised as *jus cogens*, including the prohibitions against torture, genocide, slavery, racial discrimination, apartheid, and violation of the basic laws pertaining to armed conflict, is unexceptionally binding on all nation-states regardless of consent.[55]

Because transnational norms are not backed by enforcement mechanisms readily available at the nation-state level, the CCI like availability in the hands of national judges seems particularly useful and desirable. Suppose, for instance, that

[50] See Gerald Neuman, 'Human Rights and Constitutional Rights: Harmony and Dissonance' (2003) 55 *Stanford Law Review* 1863, 1891–95.

[51] In some transnational institutional settings, CCI like intervention is explicitly foreclosed. Thus, in the EU context Member State judges must refer questions involving the interpretation of EU law to the EU Court of Justice (CJEU). See TEC art 267.

[52] See n 11 and n 13.

[53] See Chang and Yeh (n 13) 1170–71.

[54] 1996 Constitution of South Africa, art 39.

[55] See de Wet (n 11) 1215.

an international tribunal decides that a particular state that has not consented to refrain from torture has repeatedly violated the rights of its citizens to remain free from torture. In that case, there is no available supra-national mechanism whereby the dictates of *jus cogens* can be effectuated within the offending state. Suppose further, however, that the national law relied upon by the offending state could be plausibly interpreted as not authorising torture. Under such circumstances, a national judge whose *decisions* are routinely complied with could interpret the national law in question as foreclosing the legality of torture and could do so by implicit or explicit reference to the relevant *jus cogens* standards.

Let us now turn more specifically to the common currency that judges can avail themselves at both the national and supra-national level. In the most general terms, that common currency is framed by the four essential pillars of liberal constitutionalism. These include limitations on the powers of government, adherence to the rule of law, protection of a set of fundamental rights, and safeguarding the basic functioning of democracy.[56] There are of course many different ways to satisfy these four requirements, but an overlapping core emerges. For example, limitation or separation of powers can be fashioned for a parliamentary system as well as for a presidential one. Similarly, the fundamental rights protected by nation-state constitutions, UN covenants, and transnational regional human rights conventions may differ somewhat, but they all include certain key rights such as freedom of speech, freedom of religion, and equality rights. Accordingly, it seems obvious that in a country that has adhered to the ECHR a constitutional judge ought, if possible, interpret her own national freedom of speech provision consistent with the ECtHR's interpretation of the corresponding right under the ECHR. Moreover, the incentive for a CCI type reconciliation in the latter case is higher than in that of the national statutory alignment with the domestic constitution. Indeed, in the ECHR context, divergences in interpretations at the national and transnational levels may well lead to a proliferation of recourses to the ECtHR by citizens of the nation-state involved. And these recourses may well result in unwelcome ECtHR condemnations of the nation-state at stake for violations of their own citizens' ECHR rights.

The plausible common currency within the ambit of the four pillars of liberalism does not imply any commitment to any natural law jurisprudence. Instead, the common currency follows from acceptance of the premises underlying liberal constitutionalism and the nature of the structural features and of the bulk of fundamental rights that such constitutionalism typically deploys. It also bears emphasising that the common currency involved has been used aggressively, far beyond the usual scope of CCI, by judges engaged in constitutional and constitutional like interpretation. For example, reliance on this common currency has been put to use to justify binding constitutional review by judges in a country

[56] See Michel Rosenfeld, *A Pluralist Theory of Constitutional Justice: Assessing Liberal Democracy in Times of Rising Populism and Illiberalism* (Oxford, Oxford University Press, 2022) 1.

without a constitution,[57] to judicially invalidate constitutional amendments,[58] and even to judicially limit the scope of constitution making through formally legitimate exercises of constituent powers.[59] These bold and far-reaching judicial uses of this common currency have made it all the more controversial.[60] Before delving further into the controversies raised by invocations of the common currency in question below, suffice it for now to keep in mind the difference between the type of reconciliation sought through CCI and the constitutional fiats and ruptures just referred to.

The Israeli Supreme Court decision in its landmark *United Mizrahi Bank Ltd. v Migdal Village*[61] case perhaps best exemplifies the potential and pitfalls of judicial invocation of the common currency under discussion. Israel does not have a written constitution. The country's parliament, the Knesset, was empowered to enact a constitution since the country's declaration of independence in 1948,[62] but has thus far failed to do so. The Knesset, however, has enacted Basic Laws – two of which, respectively on 'Freedom of Occupation' and on 'Human Dignity and Freedom' were at issue in *Migdal* – which require an absolute majority vote for passage as opposed to the simple majority vote required, provided there is a quorum, for passage of ordinary laws. In *Migdal*, the Court decided that Basic Laws enjoy a 'constitutional super legislative status[63] and that therefore a subsequent ordinary law cannot supersede a prior Basic Law.[64] Furthermore, the Court also decided, albeit in the absence of any pronouncement or acknowledgment by the Knesset, that constitutional determination of the status of Basic Laws and resolution of conflicts between basic and ordinary laws were properly within the province of the courts.[65] In short, the Court in *Migdal* appropriates for itself two major tasks typically reserved to the constituent power: the constitutionalisation of rights and the apportionment of powers among distinct branches of government.

Chief Justice Barak's *Migdal* opinion suggests that Israel views itself as a constitutional democracy that has yet to settle on a full-fledged written constitution. In the meantime, the Knesset has acted in a piecemeal fashion to secure some of the most basic fundamental rights customarily protected by democratic constitutions, such as those in the two Basic Laws at stake in the case. Moreover, as it is the practice in the overwhelming majority of contemporary constitutional democracies, courts handle conflicts between parliamentary laws and constitutionally protected

[57] See *United Mizrahi Bank Ltd. v Migdal Village* CA 6821/93, 49 (4) P.D. 221 (1995) (Supreme Court of Israel).

[58] See Gabor Halmai, 'Unconstitutional Constitutional Amendments: Constitutional Courts as Guardians of the Constitution?' (2012) 19 *Constellations* 182–83.

[59] *Certification of the Constitution of the Republic of South Africa* 1996 (4) SALR 744 (CC).

[60] See Dorsen et al (n 6) 219–20 (recounting fierce Israeli reaction against 1995 Supreme Court self-anointment as constitutional reviewer).

[61] *United Mizrahi Bank Ltd. v Migdal Village* (n 57).

[62] ibid, para 35.

[63] ibid, para 36.

[64] ibid, para 35.

[65] ibid, para 77.

fundamental rights, thus making it logical for Israeli courts to assume this role in the context of challenges to Basic Laws.

The *Migdal* Court invoked two principal sources for purposes of legitimating the constitutionalisation of Basic Laws and entrusting constitutional review to itself. The first of these sources is a broad based consensus relating to constitutional essentials among post-World War II democracies, both with respect to the constitutional protection of certain basic fundamental rights and to reliance on constitutional adjudication to interpret such rights and to dispose of conflicts between parliamentary laws and constitutional rights.[66] The second source, in turn, which the Court invoked to justify declaring a law supported by the country's majority to be unconstitutional, was 'the values of society as they are understood by the culture and tradition of the people as they move forward through history'.[67] Chief Justice Barak specified, moreover, that the judge must not approach the values at stake subjectively, but instead objectively so as to reflect these as they inhere within the State of Israel 'as a Jewish and democratic state'.[68]

The first of the above mentioned two sources is plainly grounded on the internationalisation of constitutional law.[69] Chief Justice Barak's opinion highlights that there is a convergence among constitutional democracies over the protection of a bundle of core constitutional rights and over entrusting judges with specifying the meaning and proper bounds of these rights. Consistent with this and with the near worldwide adoption of the standard of proportionality,[70] judicial review of constitutional controversies has arguably gone global to a significant degree.[71] Because of this, filling domestic gaps with widespread widely shared foreign imports may well be left much more to judicial actors than to their political branches' counterparts.

In sharp contrast to the first source of legitimation of the constitutional status of Israel's Basic Laws, the second source referred to by the Court seems impervious to inclusion within a common currency framework. Chief Justice Barak alludes to the need for the constitutional judge to engage objectively with the societal values underlying the Basic Laws for purposes of achieving a proper judicial interpretation of the latter. If there were a national consensus on the values at stake, then the judge's task would be eminently manageable, and the values relied upon could presumably be seamlessly weaved into the requisite ongoing common currency based judicial process at stake – with the objectively articulated societal shared values providing the appropriate contextual setting. If, however, the polity were profoundly split over the values that the constitutional judge is supposed to rely

[66] ibid, para 58.
[67] ibid, para 81.
[68] ibid.
[69] See Chang and Yeh (n 13).
[70] See David M Beatty, *The Ultimate Rule of Law* (Oxford, Oxford University Press, 2004) ch 1.
[71] See generally, Anne-Marie Slaughter, *A New World Order* (Princeton, Princeton University Press, 2004).

on objectively in order to legitimate the constitutionalisation of basic rights and buttressing the Court as the constitutional adjudicator, then judicial review would fail to rise above ordinary politics.

As many have observed, Israel is sharply divided on fundamental values and those divisions may have had more than their fair share of the responsibility for Israel's failure to date to have adopted a full-fledged constitution – eg divisions among orthodox and secular Jews have led to an impasse on the proper constitutional handling of the relationship between the state and religion.[72] To the extent that a profound clash of values and a heretofore unbridgeable cultural gap has thus far prevented Israel from achieving a constitutional consensus, judicial invocation of common values and a shared culture may well be perceived as a judicial usurpation of ordinary politics that far strays from the strictures of the common currency.

Unsurprisingly, the *Migdal* decision has proved politically controversial and has given rise to a number of initiatives bent on depriving the Israeli Supreme Court of the power to engage in constitutional adjudication.[73] Most recently, prior to Israel's war with Hamas in Gaza, the Israeli government saw through legislation that would have largely deprived its Supreme Court of jurisdiction to engage in constitutional adjudication.[74] This initiative profoundly split the Israeli polity, and eventually led the Court to hold by a narrow majority that the disputed Knesset legislation was invalid because of separation of powers concerns with judicial independence[75] – a conclusion grounded in the common currency.

The Israeli example framed by the *Migdal* case and its aftermath well illustrate both the attractions and pitfalls of relying on a constitutional and constitutional like common currency. This example does not discredit the idea of a common currency in all settings, but it counsels recourse to it with caution. Thus, for example, reliance on the common currency and to CCI like adjudication seems much more defensible in a country signatory of the ECHR where the domestic judge seeks to harmonise a national fundamental right with its ECHR equivalent than in a politically, culturally, and religiously divided polity without any agreed upon constitution such as Israel.

In more recent years, a more profound challenge has been levelled against the idea of a common currency and of the viability or legitimacy of the internationalisation of constitutional law. This challenge is linked to the rise of populism

[72] See Gila Stopler, 'National Identity, Religion-State Relations: Israel in Comparative Perspective' in Gideon Sapir, Daphne Barak-Erez and Aharon Barak (eds), *Israeli Constitutional law in the Making* (Oxford, Hart Publishing, 2013) 503, 510 ('While some consider that the definition of Israel as a Jewish state constitutes an establishment of the Jewish religion in the state … others argue that the term "Jewish state"… merely designat[es] … Israel as the home of the Jewish people …').

[73] See Dorsen et al (n 6).

[74] See Yaniv Roznai and Amichai Cohen, 'Populist Constitutionalism and the Judicial Overhaul in Israel' (2023) 56 *Israel Law Review* 502.

[75] See *Movement for Quality Government v Knesset* (961 83 KB) HCJ 5658/23 (1 January 2024) (Supreme Court of Israel).

and of illiberalism.[76] To the extent that this rise leads straight into authoritarianism it signals a wholesale retreat from the four pillars of liberal constitutionalism and need not be further addressed here. However, in certain cases, the move to populism and to illiberalism has been accompanied by claims of maintained adherence to constitutional rule and to its four pillars. One such case is that of Hungary under prime minister Viktor Orban.[77] What is most salient about the latter cases for present purposes, is that whereas formally constitutional rule is maintained, substantively the content of each one of the four pillars is significantly altered to the point that it bears little resemblance with the mainstays of liberal constitutionalism. Thus, populism typically only designates part of the citizenry as belonging to 'The People' and this reframes the pillar of democracy.[78] Furthermore, illiberalism has given rise to redefining the rule of law as evinced by the dispute between Hungary and the EU authorities which was recently litigated before the CJEU.[79] Illiberalism has also led to the reframing of fundamental rights in ways that are inconsistent with the conception of such rights under liberal constitutionalism.[80]

It is beyond the scope of the present analysis to assess the full implications of the rise of populism and illiberalism within polities that have not (at least thus far) abandoned constitutional democracy. Suffice it for now to underscore that these developments raise weighty questions regarding the viability of the common currency approach and accordingly of the plausibility of meaningfully instituting CCI like judicial review at the supra-national level. In the most general terms, if the rise of populism and illiberalism is merely the precursor of a complete transition to authoritarianism, then it should have little conceptual import for polities that remain firmly within the bounds of liberal constitutionalism. If, on the contrary, the rise in question is bound to have some significant effect and to prompt increased focus inward in all constitutional democracies, then the idea of a common currency will have to be reevaluated. Be that as it may, in either case, the legitimacy of CCI and of judicial engagement in constitutional review is inevitably affected by questions of democracy and of politics to which I now turn.

[76] See eg Wojciech Sadurski, *Poland's Constitutional Breakdown* (Oxford, Oxford University Press, 2019), Ezra Klein, 'India is transforming. But into what?' *New York Times* (New York, 12 December 2023) (discussing rise in illiberalism), available at www.nytimes.com/2023/12/12/opinion/ezra-klein-podcast-pratap-bhanu-mehta.html; Mikolaj Barczentewicz and Marcin Matczak, 'Poland. Constitutionally Conforming Interpretation in Times of Constitutional Crisis' in Klatt (n 7); Raeesa Vakil, 'India. The Ultimate Interpreter: Democracy and Constitutionality in the Indian Supreme Court' in Klatt (n 7).

[77] See Renata Uitz, 'Can You Tell When an Illiberal Democracy is in the Making? An Appeal to Comparative Constitutional Scholarship from Hungary' (2015) 13 *International Journal of Constitutional Law* 279.

[78] See Daniele Albertazzi and Duncan Mcdonnell, *Populists in Power* (London, Routledge, 2015) 5 (defining populism as '[a] thin-centred ideology which pits a virtuous and homogeneous people against a set of elites and dangerous 'others' who are together depicted as depriving (or attempting to deprive) the sovereign people of their rights, values, prosperity, identity and voice').

[79] Case C-156/21 *Hungary v Parliament and Council* ECLI:EU:C:2022:97, [2023] 4 WLR 32 (CJEU).

[80] See Susanna Mancini and Michel Rosenfeld, 'Nationalism, Populism, Religion, and the Quest to Reframe Fundamental Rights' (2021) 42 *Cardozo Law Review* 463.

IV. Antimajoritarian Adjudication and Democracy

The strongest argument against CCI is grounded on the proposition that it is contrary to democracy. A democratically accountable parliament adopts a law and a democratically unaccountable judge rewrites it, modifying or frustrating the parliamentary majority's intent. Democracy, in turn, is inextricably linked to politics. In any complex society, democratic rule depends on political competition and will formation. Moreover, judicial review is also viewed as political – whether thoroughly so as CLS claims or partially or differently as further discussed below – but anti-democratic or at least antimajoritarian.

To properly assess the argument from democracy against CCI is rendered particularly difficult by the fact that all the key concepts involved, namely 'democracy', 'politics' and the 'politics (or lack thereof) of judicial interpretation', are all essentially contested concepts. Furthermore, even leaving aside the conflicts among various clashing conceptions of the concepts in question, comparative focus on CCI in different settings gives rise to certain unexpected paradoxes. For example, comparing the already mentioned differences between CCI (or its functional equivalent) in the UK and the US would logically suggest that from the standpoint of democracy it ought to be relatively unproblematic in the UK while quite troublesome in the US. Given parliamentary sovereignty in the UK, CCI would seem at worst as a minor irritant to, or postponement of, the workings of democracy. In sharp contrast, in the US – given that, as already noted, constitutional amendments are practically impossible in most circumstances – a judge's constitutionally based rewriting or limitation of a democratically adopted law becomes in most cases irreversible. Yet, in spite of this logic, as we have suggested, objections to CCI in the UK seem comparable to, if not more extensive than, those in the US.

Any thorough treatment of the larger conceptual issues raised by the above discussion is well beyond the scope of the present undertaking. Accordingly, I will briefly address certain essential aspects of democracy and politics that, while admittedly contestable, I believe are critical to properly anchor a productive theoretical and broader contextual assessment of CCI.

Any viable constitutionally grounded representative democracy must rely on a certain minimum of antimajoritarian norms and processes. Thus, for instance, even in the absence of a constitutional protection of free speech rights, free and fair parliamentary elections cannot be guaranteed without ensuring the free flow of relevant political information needed for voters to make informed choices.[81] Parliamentary majorities cannot be left alone to thwart the opposition's messaging relating to upcoming elections. Arguably therefore representative democracy should be understood as requiring an antimajoritarian component, and the latter ought to be considered as inherent to democracy itself. Furthermore, consistent

[81] See *Australian Capital Television v The Commonwealth of Australia*, High Court (Australia) (1992) 177 C.L.R. 106.

with the third pillar of liberal constitutionalism, certain fundamental rights cannot be adequately protected without antimajoritarian backing. For example, certain ethnic minorities may need antimajoritarian protection to obtain equal access to public employment as would certain religious minorities to benefit from freedom of religion.

To the extent that judges are less susceptible to majoritarian pressures than electorally accountable public officials, they seem best suited to be entrusted with constitutional democracy's requisite antimajoritarian functions. Whereas several scholars have criticised the powers of judges[82] and warned against the antidemocratic excesses of 'juristocracy',[83] reliance on judges still remains the best among what are to be sure imperfect alternatives. Indeed, separation of powers and 'checks and balances' loom as less well served if judges were prohibited to engage in any judicial review involving constitutional interpretation. Even in a setting where parliamentary supremacy knows no limits, a non-binding judicial declaration that a law violates the constitution could generate useful public debate and place political pressure on parliament to reform its law or to aim for closer adherence to the constitution in future legislation.

Leaving aside whether non-binding judicial declarations of unconstitutionality may suffice from a checks and balances standpoint, giving what is effectively the last word to judges does pose a vexing problem. Because of the near impossibility to supersede its decisions, the US Supreme Court has become for the most part what amounts to an 'unchecked checker', and its justices appointed for life appear anointed with unlimited antimajoritarian, if not undemocratic, power. More generally, whenever for all practical purposes judges have the last world, difficult questions arise both in terms of democracy and of politics. In short, from the standpoint of democracy, when does antimajoritarian adjudication become antidemocratic? And regarding politics, to be examined in section V, which as indicated above cannot be altogether expunged from judicial review, are there meaningful and workable distinctions between judicial politics and ordinary politics?

Regarding the first question, most obviously antimajoritarian norms are not only democratic but necessarily so when democracy depends on them, such as in the already mentioned case of guaranteeing a sufficient free flow of information to allow for meaningful votes in democratic elections. Furthermore, antimajoritarian norms are also not antidemocratic if all morally endowed persons ought to endorse them. Arguably, this includes the right against torture and what is required to accord a minimum of decency and dignity to fellow members of the same constitutional unit. Perhaps slightly more controversial, but still clearly not undemocratic, are rights accorded to democratic minorities that all ought to agree to if they acted as members of a constituent assembly operating under a modified Rawlsian veil of

[82] See Jeremy Waldron, 'The Core of the Case Against Judicial Review' (2006) 115 *Yale Law Journal* 1346, 1349–53.

[83] See Ran Hirschl, *Towards Juristocracy: The Origins and Consequences Of The New Constitutionalism* (Cambridge, Harvard University Press, 2004).

ignorance.[84] Thus, for example, as a member of the majority religion in my country, I may agree to vote for representatives that wish to suppress or discriminate against certain minority religions. But if as a hypothetical member of my country's constituent assembly without knowing my religion I had to vote on whether to adopt a freedom of religion provision that protects all religions within the polity, the fact that I may end up belonging to a minority religion should rationally suffice to prompt me to endorse the all-inclusive freedom of religion provision at stake.

Looking more closely at fundamental rights, there may be more controversy concerning which rights ought to be constitutionalised and concerning how rights that have been constitutionalised ought to be protected. More generally, the greater the politisation of the constitution and the constitutionalisation of politics, the more likely it seems that the antimajoritarian will turn into the antidemocratic. Thus, if constitutionalised fundamental rights are mainly confined to vertically applicable negative first-generation ones, these would seem much less likely to be credibly cast as antidemocratic than if they also encompassed second generation positive rights that are given broad horizontal effect. For example, a free speech right that prohibits state interference with political and artistic expression throughout the polity can easily be defended as not susceptible of crossing the line between antimajoritarian and antidemocratic. Conversely, an enforceable constitutional right to decent shelter[85] coupled with a horizontal requirement that prohibits private landlords from renting lodgings that do not meet the constitutional minimum the government must provide to its indigent population can be very plausibly characterised as antidemocratic. Indeed, in that latter case, satisfying constitutional rights and their implications for transactions among private actors involve policy and budgetary decisions traditionally left to democratically accountable legislators.

Wherever the line between merely antimajoritarian and antidemocratic may be drawn, so long as that line is not crossed allowing judges to have the last word ought to be accepted as presumably the best among imperfect available options. Consistent with this, CCI ought to be considered legitimate and in accordance with the four pillars of liberal constitutionalism. In short, where judicial intervention is antimajoritarian but not antidemocratic it ought to be considered to be theoretically justifiable. This ought to satisfy the objection against CCI from democracy but does not address the prudential question regarding CCI's desirability. On further thought, the question of desirability is ultimately to a large extent contextual in nature as it depends on constitutional particulars and societal attitudes and preferences. As already noted, an American would consider CCI in the UK as, at worse, a minor inconvenience or postponement relating to democratic resolution guaranteed by parliamentary sovereignty. Accordingly, the fact that many in the UK may happen to feel otherwise seems best explained by differences in the respective constitutional systems and in the respective societal expectations.

[84] See Rawls (n 36) 11.

[85] See *Government of the Republic of South Africa v Grootboom*, 2001 (1) SA 46; 2000 (11) BCLR 1169 (4 October 2000).

V. The Interplay between Judicial Politics and Ordinary Politics

The question of the politics surrounding constitutional adjudication has perennially been a vexing one, which is aggravated by the elusive and controverted boundaries between the antimajoritarian and the antidemocratic. Matters could be alleviated, however, if judges could be credibly considered apolitical or immersed in politics that are sufficiently distinguishable from ordinary politics. Assuming for the sake of argument that judges could remain apolitical, then the constitutionalisation of politics and the corresponding politicisation of the constitution would shrink the domain of ordinary politics, but judges would not risk usurping the legislators' function. Returning to the enforceable constitutional right to decent shelter, parliamentary policy and budgetary options would be restricted by judicial intervention but the latter would not be political in nature. Instead, such judicial intervention would be based on supra-political norms and practices with their own criteria of validity regardless of whether one regarded them as merely antimajoritarian or squarely antidemocratic.

As briefly alluded to already, one can draw a workable distinction between judicial politics or philosophy on the one hand and ordinary politics on the other. To begin with consider the following example. In the context of US federalism, some judges have a more expansive view of the limits of federal powers while others have a more restrictive view.[86] Accordingly, a judge with a restrictive judicial philosophy would have to uphold both a particular state's law that prohibits abortion and another state's law that legalises assisted suicide in case these two laws conflict with federal laws on the same subjects. Now, as a matter of ordinary politics, the judge in question may be conservative which would incline her to vote as a citizen in favour of banning both abortion and assisted suicide. Or else, that same judge may be politically progressive and thus inclined to vote against abortion restrictions and in favour of legalising assisted suicide.

The divide between judicial politics and ordinary politics stems initially from the insight that law and (ordinary) politics can be understood, to return to Wittgenstein's terminology already mentioned above, as distinct language games.[87] Relating to the already discussed HLA Hart example, there can be a political debate involving legislators and the general public regarding whether or not to prohibit certain or all vehicles in public parcs. The debate in question mirrors all political debates in which there is a division among the members of the polity and their legislative representatives over whether or not, and over how, to legislate on the subject matter at hand is conducted within the language game of ordinary

[86] Compare eg the majority and dissenting opinions in *United States v Lopez* 514 U.S. 549 (1995) (divided court holds that federal law banning guns in school zones is unconstitutional) and in *United States v Morrison* 529 U.S. 598 (2000) (violence against women federal law held unconstitutional).

[87] See Wittgenstein (n 34) 2, 7.

politics. But once a law is adopted, say banning vehicles from the park, the politics that preceded it are frozen and the law in question enters into the language game of law. Accordingly, one charged with having violated the law cannot invoke the political debate prior to its adoption, but is instead limited to raising defences and excuses that are entitled to consideration by law enforcers and judges, and that are thus within the boundaries of the language game of law. Furthermore, in this perspective, judicial interpretation carves out a distinct subset within the language game of law, and constitutional interpretation a subset within the domain of the language game of law delimited by judicial interpretation. For the sake of convenience, we can refer to the subset carved out by judicial interpretation generally as the language game of adjudication, and to that involving the constitutionality of infra-constitutional laws as the language game of constitutional adjudication.

The language game of adjudication whether constitutional or infra-constitutional comprises a politics of its own which is distinguishable from ordinary politics. Thus, as mentioned above, the late US justice Scalia advocated an 'original meaning' approach to constitutional interpretation and a 'plain meaning' approach to statutory interpretation. Other US judges reject Scalia's approach and embrace a judicial politics that advocates interpretation of constitutionally enshrined provisions in terms of their present-day connotations based on the conviction that broadly phrased constitutional norms are meant to be understood in terms of the evolving needs and aspirations of each succeeding generation.[88] Similarly, some judges refuse to be constrained by the plain meaning approach and look to legislative intent to guide them in their statutory interpretations.[89] Both these differing judicial politics (and the numerous others currently embraced throughout well-functioning constitutional democracies) must also adhere to workable criteria of fit and integrity. Thus, although a judge would remain within the language game of adjudication if he ceaselessly switched from an originalist to an adaptationist method of constitutional interpretation in order to attune his judicial politics to his ordinary politics predilections, this would contravene his obligation pursuant to the language game of adjudication to aim for the achievement of the best possible fit and to remain within reasonable bounds of integrity. In other words, a judge who remains within the constraints of the language game of adjudication, but who flouts fit and integrity may remain within the precincts of judicial politics *in form* but would fail to meet the basic requirements of judicial politics *in substance*.[90]

The insight that judicial politics is associated to adhesion to a language game of its own does not imply that it is entirely separable from ordinary politics. Actually, judicial politics is linked to ordinary politics in two principal different ways: one of these is internal, and the other external. The internal connection stems from the propriety of certain ordinary politics considerations within the realm of judicial politics. For example, if as a matter of judicial politics, a certain law could plausibly

[88] See Breyer (n 31).
[89] See Robert A Katzmann, *Judging Statutes* (Oxford, Oxford University Press, 2014) 1.
[90] See Rosenfeld (n 26) 59.

be interpreted as being constitutional or unconstitutional and one of the two alternatives would be particularly undesirable from an ordinary politics standpoint, then arguments from ordinary politics ought to be taken into account. An example of this is found in the US Supreme Court decision in a case that involved a constitutional challenge to a law that guaranteed medical insurance to dozens of millions of citizens who might otherwise be unable to afford necessary medical treatment.[91] Had the said law been held unconstitutional, given the divisions then prevailing in the US Congress, it would have been impossible to replace it with a suitable law that circumvented the constitutional infirmities of the would be struck down law. The US Supreme Court held the law in question constitutional in a 5-4 decision, with all judicial opinions emitted by the Court remaining within the four walls of judicial politics. As the oft repeated refrain that the 'constitution is not a suicide pact' instructs, consideration of dire ordinary politics potentially disastrous consequences ought to be weighed in when judicial politics offers a choice. In such a case, arguably there is no switch from one language game to another, but instead a translation from a proposition taken from the language game of ordinary politics into the grammar, syntax, and vocabulary of judicial politics.

This last point is perhaps best illustrated through an example of translation from the language game of philosophy to that of (constitutional) judicial politics. Justice and equality have been linked together at least since Aristotle.[92] On the other hand, as already briefly mentioned, the US Constitution guarantees to each person the generally and abstractly stated right to the 'equal protection' of the laws. With this in mind, for nearly a half a century justices on the US Supreme Court have disagreed over whether affirmative action requiring preferential treatment to members of traditionally oppressed groups comports with constitutional equality. Some justices have argued that such preferential treatment is in synchrony with realising the equality guaranteed by the constitution while others have insisted that any preference based on race is counter to equality and in violation of equal protection under law.[93] This divide mirrors the one between libertarian philosophers who claim that only formal equality resulting in equal treatment is justified and liberal egalitarian philosophers who maintain that discrepancies due to past unfair societal (or state sanctioned) discrimination or oppression ought to be rectified, thus justifying unequal treatment in the pursuit of what Rawls has termed fair equality of opportunity.[94] This entire philosophical debate is implicitly present in a translated form in the above referred to American judicial politics confrontation. Notably, however, the same translation could not legitimately take hold in Canada

[91] See *National Federation of Independent Business v Sebelius* 567 U.S. 519 (2012).

[92] See Aristotle, *The Nicomachean Ethics* (Martin Oswald tr, Oxford, Oxford University Press, 1980) Bk. V.

[93] See Rosenfeld (n 35) ch 7.

[94] See Rawls (n 36) 302.

as that country's constitution explicitly makes affirmative action legitimate in its equality provision.[95]

The second link between judicial and ordinary politics, which happens to be external, involves two separate kinds of phenomena. The first of these is that constitutional adjudication, even if fully accounted for within the realm of judicial politics, does have ordinary politics consequences. Moreover, these consequences can be important and even at times highly divisive and controversial. This was the case concerning the two US Supreme Court contradictory decisions on abortion – one recognising a constitutional right to it, and the other nearly 50 years later reversing its prior jurisprudence and decreeing that there is no such constitutional right.[96] From a judicial politics standpoint both of these decisions are fully accounted for in terms of competing judicial interpretive approaches regarding the US constitutional rights to due process and to equal protection.[97] In both cases, the justices were divided and invoked a multitude of judicial approaches, but in essence the contradiction between the two cases can be derived from long standing conflicting understandings of the two constitutional rights involved. Justices supporting an abortion right maintained that due process comprises a substantive liberty and privacy component as well as a procedural one, and that equal protection requires affording women the same right over their bodies as men have.[98] Justices rejecting an abortion right, in contrast, can rely on a purely procedural understanding of due process,[99] and maintain that the question of abortion does not raise issues of equality between men and women.[100] Instead, criminalisation of abortion produces unequal treatment between pregnant and non-pregnant persons, and most women are not pregnant most of the time.[101] Notwithstanding that the above sharp judicial disagreement can be understood as at all times fully encompassed within the bounds of judicial politics, both the recognition of a constitutional right to abortion and the subsequent retraction of such recognition have ignited intense divisive ordinary politics passions and initiatives.[102]

The second phenomenon associated to the external link between judicial and ordinary politics takes place in the relatively rare cases where there is a downright breakdown between the realm of judicial politics and that of ordinary politics. In other words, some judicial constitutional decisions so contravene deeply rooted

[95] 1982 Canadian Charter of Rights, s 15(2).

[96] See *Roe v Wade* 410 U.S. 113 (1973) (establishing constitutional right to abortion) and *Dobbs v Jackson Women's Health Organization* 597 U.S. 215 (2022) (overruling *Roe*).

[97] US Const. XIV Amendment (1868).

[98] See *Dobbs* (n 96) (Breyer, J., dissenting).

[99] See *Dobbs* (n 96) (Thomas, J., concurring).

[100] See *Dobbs* (n 96) (Alito, J., majority opinion).

[101] See *Dobbs* (n 96) (Alito J. citing to *Geduldig v Aiello*, 417 U.S. 484 (1974) which held that discrimination based on pregnancy did not amount to discrimination based on sex).

[102] See Laurence H Tribe, *Abortion: The Clash of Absolutes* (New York, W.W. Norton, 1992); Reva Siegel, 'Memory Games: Dabbs's Originalism as Anti-Democratic Living Constitutionalism – and Some Pathways for Resistance' (2023) 101 *Texas Law Review* 1127.

beliefs and commitments within the polity that there is open rebellion against what is widely perceived as an intolerable illegitimate judicial imposition going against the most deeply held convictions of vast majorities within the citizenry. A particularly telling example of this second phenomenon was Bavaria's refusal to implement the decision by the German Constitutional Court decreeing that displays of crucifixes in state school classrooms was unconstitutional under the Basic Law.[103] This rupture was all the more dramatic since the Basic Law explicitly empowers the German Constitutional Court as the ultimate authoritative interpreter of that country's constitution,[104] and since the court in question has traditionally been held in very high regard by the German citizenry.[105] To be clear, this second phenomenon is clearly distinct from the first one. As enormous as the controversies surrounding the US abortion decisions have been, they have not led to meaningful suggestions that the judicial decisions involved should be disregarded. Instead, the ordinary politics reactions have ranged from unrealistic appeals to adopt a constitutional amendment to protect or prohibit abortion to enactments of infra-constitutional laws in order to mitigate the consequences of the decried judicial decisions.[106] In contrast, simply disregarding binding judicial interpretations of the constitution, if more than merely aberrational as it was in the German case, seems bound to provoke a breakdown of the prevailing constitutional order.

The above detailed interplay between politics and constitutional adjudication is complex and varied, and its implications for CCI are neither obvious nor straightforward. Keeping this in mind, it seems helpful to keep questions of CCI's legitimacy in this context separate from those relating to its desirability. Both CCI's legitimacy and its desirability are affected by the levels of harmony within judicial and ordinary politics and among the two. In terms of legitimacy, the optimal scenario involves thorough vindication within judicial politics in substance coupled with diversity or consensus among judicial philosophies within the judiciary so long as differences do not verge into entrenched animosities among opposing judicial camps. Moreover, legitimacy is also likely to prevail if divisions over judicial philosophy remain intrinsic within the bounds of the appropriate language game, and if all concerned endeavour to achieve fit and integrity albeit through diverse plausible interpretive paths. At the other end of the spectrum, CCI's aspiration to legitimacy seems least likely to succeed where judicial politics that happen to be only in form barely dissimulate raw contentious ordinary politics struggles that linger just below the surface, and over which judges possess no special expertise.

[103] See *Classroom Crucifix II* 93 BVerfGE 1 (1995) and Michel Rosenfeld, 'Constitutional Adjudication in Europe and the United States: Paradoxes and Contrasts' (2004) 2 *International Journal of Constitutional Law* 633, 665, 668 (People in Bavaria refused to abide by ruling of German Constitutional Court prohibiting display of crucifix in state schools).

[104] German Basic Law (1949) art 93.

[105] See Rosenfeld (n 103) 633, 641.

[106] See Rosenfeld (n 103).

Turning to desirability, it is on the one hand enhanced by harmony within well working judicial politics in substance regimes in which disagreements do not impair overall consensus. On the other hand, CCI may be legitimate but not desirable in cases involving external links between judicial and ordinary politics as exemplified by the US abortion cases. The judicial roles in such cases are legitimate, but profoundly divisive ordinary politics ought to be avoided or mitigated whenever possible. Finally, in cases involving external links, such as that of the Bavarian crucifix display, CCI would be presumptively undesirable and conflict ought to be minimised wherever possible. Nevertheless, if the constitutional confrontation were unavoidable, even in this last situation CCI might prove occasionally desirable if it could yield a plausible judicial solution that would defuse a brewing explosive ordinary politics confrontation.

VI. Conclusion

Viewed from afar, CCI ought to be broadly embraced as offering unmatched means to promote legal and constitutional harmonisation and efficiency while better anchoring adherence to the rule of law. After the above closer examination of some of its most salient features in the various settings in which it may make a difference, however, what emerges is a more complex and nuanced picture of CCI's potential and likely pitfalls. Ultimately, CCI's legitimacy and desirability depend on a multiplicity of theoretical and contextual factors that differ from one setting to the next. For example, assume that two constitutional democracies are equivalent in all relevant respects, except that the first of them allows for easily amending the constitution while the second one makes such amendments practically nearly impossible. That difference alone ought to make it easier to justify CCI in the first polity than in the second. But imagine now that one more difference between these two polities is added. The first one experiences a high suspicion of the benefits of judicial review whereas the second one has great confidence in the latter. Whether or not that changes the prior conclusion regarding CCI's legitimacy or desirability, it certainly requires recalibration of the pertinent analysis.

Although the actual legitimacy and desirability of CCI is inextricably case specific, profitable criteria of evaluation and of guidance are suggested by the preceding examination of what I have claimed emerge as the most salient theoretical and contextual issues. As we have seen, under certain theories of judicial interpretation there is no place for CCI, whereas under certain others it is almost impossible to fashion a credible argument against CCI. Furthermore, paradoxically the spread of legal pluralism in the transnational and global arena makes judicial intervention that is the functional equivalent of CCI more urgent than in traditional legally unified nation-states. Yet, because of the layering and segmenting of transnational legal regimes, legitimation of judicial harmonisation faces more difficult obstacles when laws originate beyond the nation-state.

Transnational settings also magnify the objections to CCI from democracy. As emphasised above, the latter can be countered or mitigated by untangling the key difference between the antimajoritarian and the antidemocratic. Within the nation-state, as long as the constitution and the laws can be cogently defended as not being antidemocratic, a workable distinction can be maintained between what is antimajoritarian and thus likely consistent with CCI and what is antidemocratic and thus prone to count against CCI. On the transnational level, however, the more likely encounter with instances of 'democratic deficit'[107] may not only blur lines but also raise an additional weighty question. That question, though not directly addressed above as beyond the scope of the present analysis, ought nevertheless to be kept in mind. Are there any antimajoritarian *and* antidemocratic legal norms that ought to be entrusted to judges making them accordingly fit for CCI type handling? For example, are there transnationally imposed legal norms without the consent of the nation-state in which judges are entitled to interpret and apply them – whether forming part of *jus cogens* or some other body of law such as that of the EU that only requires the consent of a qualified majority of the Member States – that warrant judicial imposition and CCI type harmonisation?

Finally, as emphasised in the preceding analysis, politics plays a critical role in determining the legitimacy and desirability of CCI. Most important in that respect is the distinction between judicial and ordinary politics and the contrast between judicial politics in substance and judicial politics merely in form. Moreover, even when the legitimacy of CCI is at its highest given that judicial politics in substance unmistakably sorts out the antimajoritarian from the antidemocratic, external ordinary politics considerations may seriously undermine its desirability.

In the last analysis, CCI's legitimacy and desirability are prone to being enhanced in contexts of convergence of legal norms issued from all relevant applicable legal regimes. Conversely, the greater the divergence within and among constitutional and legal regimes, the more difficult it would likely become to sustain the legitimacy and desirability of CCI. Starting in the 1990's there was a worldwide spread of liberal constitutionalism and a thrust toward convergence (through constitutionalisation or otherwise) of transnational and international legal regimes.[108] More recently, however, with the surge in populism and illiberalism, there has been a turn to divergence and to inward looking balkanisation to fend off certain widely decried evils attributed to globalisation.[109] It is at present uncertain where these crosscurrents will lead, but it seems beyond serious dispute that they will significantly affect perceptions of both the legitimacy and the desirability of CCI.

[107] See David Marquand, *Parliament for Europe* (London, Jonathan Cape, 1979) 64 (referring to what has now become the EU).

[108] See Michel Rosenfeld, 'Illiberal Constitutionalism: Viable Alternative or Nemesis of The Modern Constitutional Ideal?' in Gary Jacobsohn and Miguel Schor (eds), *Comparative Constitutional Theory*, 2nd edn (London, Edward Elgar Publishing, 2024) (forthcoming).

[109] ibid.

12

Six Problems with Constitutionally Conforming Interpretation

MATTHIAS KLATT

I. Introduction

In the context of comparative constitutionalism, which has sharpened our focus on the diversity of context and institutional design, it is useful to reiterate a key outcome of this two-volume research project: Irrespective of whether a legal system is based on the common law or the civil law, whether it has a written or an unwritten constitution, whether the constitution is old or recently established, whether democracy and the rule of law are firmly established or endangered by modes of abusive constitutionalism, and whether constitutional review is exercised in a centralised or decentralised way, constitutionally conforming interpretation (CCI) is employed universally.

In a multitude of contexts, the 19 jurisdictions examined in Volume 1 demonstrate that CCI is applied in a strikingly similar manner.[1] This diagnosis is supported by the finding that even the formulation of CCI across jurisdictions is markedly similar.[2] This is a significant finding, given that empirical studies, informed by phenomenalism and an observer's perspective, frequently undervalue a category of normative and analytical constitutional theory that is shaped by universalism and a participant's perspective.[3]

The contributions to the present volume serve to reinforce the diagnosis of similarity and provide further detail. It can be stated that the legal system of Israel

[1] Oran Doyle, 'Partly Laws Common to all Judge-Kind: The Commonality and Divergence of Constitutionally Conforming Interpretation' in this volume s I; Doyle adds that the commonality of CCI still goes hand in hand with significant divergence as to the limits of CCI.

[2] cf the two examples cited by ibid s II.

[3] On the two perspectives and their role in legal scholarship more generally see Matthias Klatt, 'Integrative Jurisprudence: Legal Scholarship and the Triadic Nature of Law' (2020) 33(4) *Ratio Juris* 380; Matthias Klatt, 'Robert Alexy's Philosophy of Law as System' in Matthias Klatt (ed), *Institutionalized Reason: The Jurisprudence of Robert Alexy* (Oxford, Oxford University Press, 2012) 13.

is also included in the list of those in which CCI is applied.[4] The majority of legal systems recognise an obligation for all state officials and agencies to apply CCI.[5] In some cases, the obligations of ordinary courts are subject to the fulfilment of certain conditions.[6] CCI can be used not only ex post, but also ex ante.[7] Furthermore, CCI is applied also *within* the constitution, across different hierarchical levels of constitutional law.[8] It is applied not only regarding material constitutional law, but also formal, organisational constitutional law.[9] CCI is employed as a remedy in instances of abusive amendments.[10]

Beyond the nation state, CCI is used in international law.[11] In the multilevel system of EU law, a variety of types of CCI are employed with the objective of ensuring compliance with the supremacy of EU law.[12] Rosenfeld has aptly identified the tensions that CCI faces in transnational legal systems.[13] On the one hand, the decline of hierarchy and integration is occurring concurrently with the emergence of pluralism. Conversely, the necessity for CCI is especially pronounced in the context of pluralism. Rosenfeld endeavours to reconcile this inconsistency through the institution of a common currency, as exemplified to some extent in the ECHR system. This argument is compelling. In contrast, his claim that populism and illiberalism in countries such as India, Poland, and Hungary are undermining the viability of the common currency is less convincing. This may be the case in purely factual terms; however, no argument against CCI can be derived from this from a normative perspective. On the contrary, it is precisely at this juncture that the protection of liberal constitutional values through the instrument of CCI becomes especially crucial.

[4] Hillel Sommer and Yaniv Roznai, 'What is the "Doomsday Weapon" – Annulment or Interpretation?: A Critical Perspective on Constitutionally Conforming Interpretation in Israel' in this volume.

[5] Hanna Wilberg, 'Aotearoa New Zealand. Legislators' Understanding as a Constraint on Interpretive Presumptions' in Matthias Klatt (ed), *Constitutionally Conforming Interpretation – Comparative Perspectives Volume 1: National Reports* (Oxford, Hart Publishing, 2023) 408; Chien-Chih Lin, 'Taiwan. Constitutionally Conforming Interpretation and Judicial Sleight of Hand' in Klatt (ibid) 330; Mikolaj Barczentewicz and Marcin Matczak, 'Poland. Constitutionally Conforming Interpretation in Times of Constitutional Crisis' in Klatt (ibid) 141; Pavel Ondřejek, 'Czech Republic: Insights from the Constitutional Court's Post-Transition Practice of Constitutionally Conforming Interpretation' in Klatt (ibid) 58; cf Doyle (n 1) s III(E); Doyle criticises this broad obligation.

[6] Wilberg (n 5) 408; Virgílio Afonso da Silva, 'There is No Such Thing as the Duty to Save a Statute' in this volume s III(B).

[7] Eoin Carolan, 'Constitutionally Conforming Interpretation and the Invisible Constitution' in this volume s II(B).

[8] Sommer and Roznai (n 4) s I.

[9] ibid s IV.

[10] Silvia Suteu, 'Constitutionally Conforming Interpretation and Constitutional Amendments' in this volume s IV(A).

[11] Stéphane Beaulac, 'Conforming Legal Interpretation based on International Law: The Use of Unwritten Principles, the Example of Equality of Arms' in this volume.

[12] Antonia Baraggia, 'Conforming Interpretation in the EU Through the Lens of the CJEU's Case Law' in this volume s I.

[13] Michel Rosenfeld, 'Placing Constitutionally Conforming Interpretation in its Larger Theoretical and Political Contexts' in this volume s III.

It would be inaccurate to suggest that the influence of CCI is limited to a select few areas of the law; rather, it is a pervasive phenomenon that can be observed across a diverse range of legal contexts.[14] The intensity of the criticism is at odds with the perception of the pervasive use of this legal approach.[15]

Nevertheless, the criticism is not unexpected when one considers that questions of legal methodology are inherently related to those of constitutional law. The approach of CCI also exemplifies foundational decisions regarding the structure of constitutional design, functioning as a magnifying glass that intensifies the impact of these decisions. What is the role of constitutional norms within the legal system? To whom is the responsibility for ensuring the fulfilment of this function and the supervision of its performance primarily attributed? What is the relationship between the stability and dynamics of the legal system? What is the role of the judicial system in establishing the interpretation of legal norms?

This final chapter addresses six issues related to CCI that remain challenging: the reconstruction of the law as a system (section II), the presumption of constitutionality (section III), the principle *favor legis* (section IV), the reversed type of CCI (section V), the balancing of competences as a means to resolve authority-related conflicts among the various state organs (section VI), and the separate method of constitutionally conforming further development of the law (section VII).

II. The Law as a System

A. Basic Principles

The legitimacy of CCI depends on a reconstruction of law as a hierarchically structured system of norms.[16] This reconstruction aims to guarantee that the law exhibits two distinct characteristics: consistency and coherence. While consistency necessitates the absence of logical contradictions between the norms of a system, coherence binds the norms and their meaning substantively to the fundamental values enshrined in the constitution. As evidenced in the national reports, consistency[17] and coherence[18] are widely accepted as a foundation for CCI.[19]

[14] cf Beaulac (n 11) s II: 'It is a feature of legal interpretation around the world', citing the Supreme Court of Canada.

[15] Rosenfeld (n 13) s I: 'It becomes all the more intriguing and paradoxical that so much controversy surrounds CCI'.

[16] Matthias Klatt, 'The Legitimacy of Constitutionally Conforming Interpretation' in Klatt (n 5) s II(B).

[17] ibid s III(B) fns 97–99.

[18] ibid s III(B) fns 122–127.

[19] In addition to the works cross-referenced above in fns 17 and 18, see Sommer and Roznai (n 4) s IV. The authors refer to Aharon Barak, *Constitutional Interpretation* (Jerusalem, Nevo Publishing, 1994) 116–17.

In her analysis of hierarchically structured legal systems, Weis identifies consistency as an essential element: 'It is foundational that legislation and the common law are *subordinate* to, and must be *consistent* with, the Constitution.'[20] This is harmonious with my previous analysis of hierarchy and consistency as two key elements of legal systems.[21] In order to supplement my earlier analysis, I will now mention a typology of legal hierarchies.[22] In a previous discussion, I highlighted Kelsen's distinction between the hierarchy of conditions and the hierarchy of derogation.[23] Guastini has proposed an alternative typology. Guastini differentiates between the concepts of 'material hierarchy' and 'axiological hierarchy.'[24] Pino has effectively demonstrated that these concepts of hierarchy serve as the foundation for CCI.[25]

B. The System's Significance for Constitutionally Conforming Interpretation

Some criticism has been proposed, and given the foundational function of consistency and coherence for the legitimacy of CCI, it is imperative to address this criticism. In response to my analysis, Afonso da Silva has proposed that the unity of the legal system 'does not really play a relevant role in the justification of CCI.'[26] He asserts that the primary objective of CCI is to avoid contradictions and to ensure the compatibility of ordinary legislation with the constitution. CCI 'says nothing about what to do when contradiction arises.'[27]

This is, in fact, the case. Nevertheless, this does not signify that the systemic unity of the law is irrelevant in justifying CCI. The fact that unity is not a sufficient condition for CCI does not negate its role as a necessary condition. In the absence of the concept of systemic unity of the law, it would be impossible to establish the postulates for consistency and coherence. In the absence of these postulates, it is not possible to justify the concept of CCI. In light of these considerations, it becomes evident that the unity of the system of law plays a significant role.

[20] Lael K Weis, 'Australia: Techniques of Developing Legislation and the Common Law to Align with Constitutional Legal Norms' in Klatt (ed), *Constitutionally Conforming Interpretation* (n 5) 382, emphases added.

[21] Klatt, 'The Legitimacy of Constitutionally Conforming Interpretation' (n 16) 11–16; Giorgio Pino, *L'interpretazione nel diritto: Come un trattato* (Torino, G. Giappichelli editore, 2021) 294 (hierarchy of norms as the fundament of interpretazione adeguatrice); on the significance of subordination, see also Riccardo Guastini, 'Invalidity' (1994) 7(2) *Ratio Juris* 212, 220.

[22] I am grateful to my colleague Professor Giorgio Pino, who introduced me to this literature in a valued conversation during my time as a visiting fellow at Roma Tre in the spring of 2024.

[23] Klatt, 'The Legitimacy of Constitutionally Conforming Interpretation' (n 16) 12–13.

[24] cf Guastini, 'Invalidity' (n 21) 217–19; Riccardo Guastini, 'On Legal Order: Some Criticism of the Received View' (2000) 3 *Ethical Theory and Moral Practice* 265, 270–71.

[25] Giorgio Pino, *Teoria analitica del diritto I: La norma giuridica* (Jura. Studi. Testi classici, Pisa, ETS, 2016) 177; Pino, *L'interpretazione nel diritto* (n 21) 294–99.

[26] Afonso da Silva (n 6) s II(B).

[27] ibid.

C. Coherence and Legal Systems as Value-Orders

i. *Values as Source of Uncertainty*

In order to achieve coherence with the constitutional values, CCI must adopt a holistic and integrity-driven approach to legal interpretation.[28] This holistic approach is pervasive in the legal systems that have been the subject of our reporting.[29] As Baraggia illustrates, value-conforming interpretation represents the latest trend in CJEU adjudication.[30]

Nevertheless, the concept of coherence and its associated notion of interpreting legal systems as value orders are the subject of criticism. In reference to Canadian case law, Daly asserts that:

> Lurking in many of these cases is the idea that recourse to 'values' – be they international, constitutional or something else entirely – is dangerous because it inherently increases judicial discretion and augments uncertainty.[31]

In light of this diagnosis, I submit that this concern may indeed be justified in specific legal systems, depending on the quality of the argumentation presented by the courts when invoking values. Conversely, it is frequently feasible to ascertain the import of values and to discern their impact through a rational perspective. Value argumentation does not inherently preclude a substantial degree of rationality and legal certainty. Moreover, in legal systems that are confronted with evolving circumstances and developments, 'it is imperative that statutory interpretation remain alive to the Constitution's deep-rooted transformative objectives and values'.[32]

ii. *Law as a Hodgepodge*

Some scholars, adopting an observer perspective, assert that the absence of a coherent system presents a significant challenge to the implementation of CCI. Suteu makes reference to Raz's descriptive point about the law as a hodgepodge: '[…] contrary to the hierarchical, ordered, predictable constitutional hinterland presupposed by proponents of CCI, many real-world constitutions actually contain a hodgepodge of norms.'[33] In particular, she asserts that a 'neat hierarchy'

[28] cf Weis (n 20) 386–87; Rosenfeld (n 13) s II.

[29] Klatt, 'The Legitimacy of Constitutionally Conforming Interpretation' (n 16) 14 and references in fn 127; Doyle (n 1) s III(B); Stacey (n 29) 356 ('validity-first approach'); Barczentewicz and Matczak (n 5) 138–39 ('axiological consistency'); Ondřejek (n 5) 62 ('value system').

[30] Baraggia (n 12) s IV.

[31] Paul Daly, 'Canada. Legal Coherence versus Legal Certainty' in Klatt (ed), *Constitutionally Conforming Interpretation* (n 5) 264.

[32] Richard Stacey, 'South Africa. The Siren Call of Constitutionally Compliant Interpretation: Statutory Validity at the Expense of Constitutional Values' in Klatt (ed), *Constitutionally Conforming Interpretation* (n 5) 376.

[33] Suteu (n 10) s II(B).

is absent in certain scenarios of constitutional amendment review.[34] A legislative constitutional amendment proposal that is subject to abstract, a priori amendment review by the constitutional court could be halted in its progress, yet it would still retain its sub-constitutional normative value.[35]

It is unclear how these considerations could be considered convincing objections. The general argument may be empirically accurate to a certain extent with regard to the factual state of affairs, contingent on the specific characteristics of particular legal systems. Nevertheless, from a normative perspective, it is imperative that legal interpreters reconstruct the law as a system. The reconstruction of the law as a consistent and coherent system is an active process undertaken by the individual engaged in the interpretation and application of the legal norm.[36] This normative perspective is not subject to challenge on the basis of empirical descriptions.

With regard to Suteu's scenario, it is only once a legislative amendment proposal has been fully adopted in accordance with the constitutional procedures that it can be considered to form part of the legal system. During the interim period between the proposal and adoption stages, the established hierarchy of norms remains intact, as the proposal does not alter the constitution prior to its adoption. In the event that an a priori amendment review is conducted, the competence of the constitutional court to control the amendment proposal may be contested, even vigorously, as evidenced by the examples from Romania and India cited by Suteu.

However, the question of competence is a separate issue, and regardless of how it is resolved, the implications for the hierarchical system of norms will be evident. In the event that the proposal is halted by the court, the legislative attempt to alter the constitution will be unsuccessful. Even in the unlikely event that it were feasible to reinterpret the amendment proposal as the successful adoption of some sub-constitutional normative value, the established hierarchy between constitutional and sub-constitutional law would remain unambiguous, presenting no challenges for CCI.

iii. Fragmented International Law

Vidmar emphasises that the fragmentation of public international law has resulted in an unsystematic and discordant 'cacophony', so that 'unity of international law is neither achieved nor sought'.[37] It is evident that legal interpreters who adhere to the normative ideal of consistency and coherence encounter heightened challenges in this domain.

Nevertheless, as Pino has helpfully reminded us, the concept of normative hierarchy should not be dismissed too hastily, even in the context of complex and

[34] ibid s II(A).

[35] ibid.

[36] Klatt, 'The Legitimacy of Constitutionally Conforming Interpretation' (n 16) 15.

[37] Jure Vidmar, 'Constitution Conforming Interpretation and the Constitutionalisation of International Law: Certain Public Law Elements Short of Constitutionalism' in this volume s V(A).

intricate situations.[38] It is incumbent upon legal interpreters to pursue a more systematic reconstruction of the various regimes and their impact upon one another and upon national legal systems. This may be more straightforward in certain regional human rights systems, such as the Inter-American system or the European Convention system, which both exhibit a notable degree of constitutionalisation, and more challenging in other areas. However, it is noteworthy that Vidmar himself, throughout his chapter, cites numerous elements of public international law that appear to contradict his anti-systematic stance.[39]

III. The Presumption of Constitutionality

A. Basic Principles

As evidenced by the contributions to Volume 1, a significant number of legal systems operate on the assumption that all legislation is constitutional.[40] The CCI method serves to safeguard this presumption. Additional support for the presumption of constitutionality can be found in both Pino's and Barak's seminal works on legal interpretation.[41] Beaulac illustrates that a comparable presumption can be applied with regard to conformity with international law, and Doyle recalls that a presumption was accepted in ancient Roman law.[42] Arguably, the most compelling support can be found in Dworkin's principle of integrity. As Rosenfeld emphasises, for Dworkin's Hercules CCI is an obvious choice.[43]

B. Irrelevance of the Actual Intentions

Nevertheless, the criticism of the presumption of constitutionality persists. Wilberg highlights the fact that a mere 'rhetorical reliance on presumed intent adds to the confusion and uncertainty' whenever presumption 'are couched in terms of presumed legislative intent' despite the fact that they are used to act in a counter-majoritarian way.[44]

[38] Pino, *Teoria analitica del diritto I* (n 25) 168.

[39] Vidmar (n 37) s IV(A) (*jus cogens* as 'hierarchically superior' which 'can have interpretative effects on the system'); s IV(B) (general principles ensure 'at least a minimum' of coherence); s III (*erga omnes* obligations as creating a 'vertical relationship').

[40] Klatt, 'The Legitimacy of Constitutionally Conforming Interpretation' (n 16) 8, with further references in fns 69–79.

[41] Pino, *L'interpretazione nel diritto* (n 21) 297; for the reference to Barak, see Sommer and Roznai (n 4) s III with fn 35.

[42] Beaulac (n 11) s II; Doyle (n 1) s IV(B) with fns 54–55.

[43] Rosenfeld (n 13) s II with fns 16–24.

[44] Wilberg (n 5) 417.

Notwithstanding the discrepancy between the presumed and actual intent of the legislator, the presumption does not, in and of itself, become mere rhetoric. The presumption is not concerned with the legislator's actual intent, but rather with what ought to be intended in light of the context of the legal system.[45] The presumption is not an empirical argument; rather, it is a normative argument.[46] Carolan most effectively illustrates this point when he asserts that the presumption of constitutionality operates 'as a maxim rather than as a claim or assessment about the behaviour of legislators'.[47] He underlines that even though the intent to act constitutionally 'may not factually be the case', this does 'not really matter for interpretive purposes'.[48]

C. Conditions for the Presumption

Further criticism is offered by Afonso da Silva. He posits that the presumption of constitutionality was not, in fact, a presumption at all, given that it did not set forth any conditions that must be met for the presumption to be valid.[49] Nevertheless, this objection is open to question. It is typical for constitutions to establish significant formal and procedural conditions that must be fulfilled in order to enact them. These conditions can be considered the 'given clause' which Afonso da Silva has missed.

D. Proof and Rebuttal

A second aspect of Afonso da Silva's criticism pertains to the potential for rebut ting the presumption. He asserts that the possibility of rebutting a presumption of constitutionality is untenable in light of the fact that the latter is not susceptible to proof. He draws a comparison between this presumption and a civil code presumption that a child be deemed 'legitimate' if born at least 180 days after the date of the marriage. In contrast to the aforementioned presumption, the presumption of constitutionality cannot be refuted through the use of a DNA test, for example.[50] Thus far, there is no DNA test for constitutionality, which lends credence to this argument.

However, the argument is flawed in that it limits the scope of proof or rebuttal to scientific tests, thereby excluding other potential means of substantiation. The means of substantiating or refuting the presumption of constitutionality is through

[45] Klatt, 'The Legitimacy of Constitutionally Conforming Interpretation' (n 16) 9–10; Frederick Schauer, 'Ashwander Revisited' (1995) *The Supreme Court Review* 71, 93.

[46] Otherwise, it would be possible for the legislator to 'recite itself into validity', see Weis (n 20) 391.

[47] Carolan (n 7) s II(A).

[48] ibid.

[49] Afonso da Silva (n 6) s II(A)(i).

[50] ibid s II(A)(ii).

the process of legal argumentation. Indeed, Afonso da Silva himself acknowledges this possibility in a footnote. He posits that, from an argumentative perspective, it would be preferable to conceptualise the presumption as a default rather than as a presumption.[51] However, if he merely employs a distinct designation for the analogous theoretical construct, this does not appear to be a cause for concern.

E. Presumptions and Amendments

Finally, Suteu raises the question of the role of the presumption of constitutionality in the context of constitutional amendments that have been formally adopted through the appropriate legal process but may be unconstitutional in substance.[52] In particular, Suteu highlights a scenario of abusive amendments, in which a malevolent legislator attempts to transition towards an illiberal democracy in subtle and incremental steps. The crux of the critique is that the presumption of constitutionality is ill-equipped to address the actions of a malevolent legislator who seeks to contravene the constitution. Paradoxically, the presumption would actually serve to facilitate the passage of such amendments.[53]

Nevertheless, it is unclear how this scenario would pose 'difficult questions for advocates of CCI', as Suteu asserts.[54] In any case, the presumption is subject to rebuttal. If compelling reasons are to be considered in determining the material (or, indeed, formal) unconstitutionality of an amendment, the presumption would not be applicable. As a presumption, it functions in favour of constitutionality only through a prima facie mechanism.[55] Lifante-Vidal has most clearly articulated this point: '[The] presumption does not have the same force in all circumstances. In the case of legislation passed in historical periods of authoritarian government rule, the presumption of constitutionality ceases to be well-founded.'[56]

A second proposition put forth by Suteu is untenable for the same reason. In a case from the Indian Supreme Court, Suteu posits that the Court's reliance on CCI has been 'inconsistent and unpredictable.'[57] In a particularly egregious instance, the Court implicitly relied on the presumption of constitutionality while strategically opting not to adjudicate the constitutional question. The objection is that the presumption encourages a kind of Pilatus-move on the part of courts that wish to avoid clarifying a constitutional matter. This was considered a disadvantage of CCI.

[51] ibid s II(A)(ii), fn 8.
[52] Suteu (n 10) s II(B).
[53] cf ibid s III(A).
[54] ibid s II(B).
[55] Klatt, 'The Legitimacy of Constitutionally Conforming Interpretation' (n 16) 10 and fn 89.
[56] Isabel Lifante-Vidal, 'Spain. Constitutionally Conforming Interpretation and Interpretative Judgements in the Spanish Constitutional Court' in Klatt (ed), *Constitutionally Conforming Interpretation* (n 5) 193.
[57] Suteu (n 10) s III(C); see the whole section for more examples stating inconsistent practice of CCI.

It bears reiterating that the presumption is rebuttable. Furthermore, it is important to note that problematic practice does not disprove a theory; rather, it demonstrates the necessity for it.[58] In contrast with Vakil's assertion on this matter, which Suteu references explicitly, it is poor practice and not the presumption of constitutionality that 'sometimes leads to reduced enforcement of rights.'[59]

F. Two Ways of Rebuttal

One might inquire at this juncture whether my argument was self-contradictory. This question arises for the following reason: It is my contention that the presumption is not an empirical argument, but rather a normative one. Consequently, an intent to act unconstitutionally does not negate the presumption.[60] Conversely, I also argue that the presumption is rebuttable and therefore that courts cannot evade their constitutional obligations by invoking the presumption. The impression of self-contradiction arises from the apparent discrepancy between the assertion that the presumption is fixed and unchanging, as per the initial claim, and the assertion that it is flexible and amenable to rebuttal, as per the second claim.

The impression of self-contradiction is negated, however, when it is recognised that there is a distinction between two methods of rebuttal. A presumption can be rebutted in one of two ways: either by demonstrating that the intent of the legislators in question was subjective and abusive, thereby ignoring the unconstitutionality of their actions, or by presenting objective and normative reasons for why their actions were unconstitutional. It is not contradictory to argue that, due to the necessity of claiming constitutionality, subjective intent cannot rebut the presumption, and that objective unconstitutionality can.

IV. The Principle *Favor Legis*

A. Basic Principles

The principle *favor legis* provides insight into why CCI is a superior alternative to annulment as a means of resolving inconsistencies or incoherencies within a legal system.[61] This principle requires the legal interpreter to endeavour to preserve the

[58] For another example, see Simon Butt, 'Indonesia. "Conditional" Decisions in the Constitutional Court' in Klatt (ed), *Constitutionally Conforming Interpretation* (n 5) 308, 325: lack of transparency and failure to make explicit the interpretation variants and provide a justified choice among them.

[59] Raeesa Vakil, 'India. The Ultimate Interpreter: Democracy and Constitutionality in the Indian Supreme Court' in Klatt (ed), *Constitutionally Conforming Interpretation* (n 5) 305; Suteu (n 10) s III(C) with text to fn 75.

[60] See above, and my argument of a necessary claim to constitutionality in Klatt, 'The Legitimacy of Constitutionally Conforming Interpretation' (n 16) 10.

[61] ibid 16; cf Doyle (n 1) s IV(B).

norm to the greatest extent possible. It is particularly important to note that the CCI operates not only at the level of multiple legal norms, but also at the level of the individual legal norm.[62] It offers a superior safeguard of the separation of powers and legal certainty and stability of positive law in comparison to the alternative of annulment. These advantages may explain why this principle is similarly pervasive in the legal systems under consideration.[63] Further evidence in support of this principle can be found in the case of Israel.[64] The principle of *favor legis* can also be used to explain why the obligation to repeal national legislation that is incompatible with EU law is superseded by the requirement to apply the CCI.[65]

B. Unfaithfulness in Disguise

Criticism has been presented against this CCI foundation as well.[66] In his argument, Afonso da Silva posits that 'that deference to the will of the legislature and respect for the separation of powers' inherent in *favor legis* were 'only catchphrases' and 'unconvincing disguise'.[67] According to him, the principle *favor legis* allowed courts to 'correct, restrict or extend the work of the legislature'[68] while paying lip service to a purported faithfulness to the legislator.

It is respectfully objected that Afonso da Silva may have misapprehended the principle *favor legis*. He makes the following assertion:

> CCI gives rise to a 'duty to save ordinary statutes' that will almost never be compatible with the idea of deference towards the legislature, because either what the statute 'says' (or the legislature 'wants') is compatible with the constitution (and in this case there is no room for CCI), or it is not compatible with the constitution (and in this case performing CCI will most likely make the statute 'say' what it is neither written nor wanted).[69]

This argument presents several problematic elements. First, it is important to note that CCI does not consider the part of the norm that is upheld, but rather the

[62] Compare the difference between 'reading down' and 'severance' in Australian doctrine, Weis (n 20) 389.

[63] Klatt, 'The Legitimacy of Constitutionally Conforming Interpretation' (n 16) 16–17 with fns 45–147.

[64] See the rule *ut res magis valeat quam pereat*, Sommer and Roznai (n 4) s IV.

[65] Baraggia (n 12) s II.

[66] For a further critical argument see Doyle (n 1) s IV(B). Doyle claims that *favor legis* had a limited applicability. Given that CCI's function was to avoid annulment, CCI had a legitimate basis only in preference to a declaration of constitutionality that would otherwise be granted. From this Doyle infers that *favor legis* could not operate in legal systems without a mastertext constitution since there was lacking both the constitution as a yardstick and the possibility to declare a statute invalid. I shall not consider this argument further here, since Doyle himself tones down his objection by pointing to the counter-examples of the UK and New Zealand.

[67] Afonso da Silva (n 6) s II(C).

[68] ibid.

[69] ibid s V.

part that is excluded on the grounds that it is not constitutional. Afonso da Silva's argument appears to assume that *favor legis* permitted not only the exclusion of unconstitutional meaning variants from consideration, but also the rewriting of the remaining constitutional meaning variants.

However, this is not the case. The doctrine of *favor legis* requires the court to adhere to the remainder of the norm, regardless of its individual meaning, rather than nullifying the norm in its entirety, even if only some interpretations would render it unconstitutional. It is unclear why a court would refrain from upholding those parts of a norm's meaning that are compatible with the Constitution. It would appear that a particular rationale for such actions is necessary, and it is unclear what such a rationale might be. Ultimately, judges are bound not only to the Constitution but also to the statute. If the two obligations pull in opposite directions, the most effective solution is to declare the statute unconstitutional only to the extent that is necessary.[70] In this manner, CCI demonstrates its respect for the concerns expressed by Afonso da Silva, namely the obligation to give effect to the legislative will.

Afonso da Silva's remark is potentially influenced by a broader concern regarding the reconciliation of arguments from law's real dimension (wording, subjective telos) with arguments from law's ideal dimension (objective telos, justice). This general problem, however, is *always* inherent to *any* application of the law.[71] As Carolan has argued, 'the use of non-textual sources of meaning is in many respects a familiar and established part of any act of judicial interpretation of a statute'.[72]

Moreover, the meaning of a statute (in the sense of what the statute 'says', as Afonso da Silva has it) is always dependent on interpretation. The meaning, in an elaborated sense that considers all relevant factors, does not exist independently of or prior to interpretation. The question of whether the meaning is or is not compatible with the constitution must be answered through legal interpretation and argumentation.

In contrast, Afonso da Silva's argument presupposes the exclusion of interpretation altogether, or at the very least, an interpretation that would deviate from the written or intended meaning. The decision of the individual tasked with applying the law to refrain from deviating from the intended meaning of the original historical legislator, for instance, is also an interpretive decision that requires justification. This is regardless of whether the approach taken is a strict, positivistic, and 'real-dimension only' one. Moreover, it appears challenging to maintain that, within the discursive process of justification, the constitution, as the supreme law of the land, will have no bearing on the available means and methods.

[70] Klatt, 'The Legitimacy of Constitutionally Conforming Interpretation' (n 16) 16–17; cf Doyle (n 1) s IV(B).

[71] Matthias Klatt, 'The Rule of Dual-Natured Law' in Eveline T Feteris et al (eds), *Legal Argumentation and the Rule of Law* (The Hague, Eleven International Publishing, 2016) 37–41; see also Carolan (n 7) s III: 'That a question of legal judgment may involve degrees of ambiguity, or admit of more than one possible meaning or outcome, is thus true of both the textual and non-textual elements of a constitutional order.'

[72] Carolan (n 7) s III.

C. A Mere Quarrel about Terminology?

However, it is necessary to determine whether my previous analysis of Afonso da Silva's criticism accurately represents his objection. While maintaining the aforementioned criticism of *favor legis*, he simultaneously appears to endorse the CCI as a valid legal approach. He makes the following assertions:

> A court that resorts to CCI actually gives its own interpretation to an enacted law to make it compatible with the constitution as interpreted by the same court. There is nothing necessarily wrong with this; after all, it is exactly the task of a court in the context of constitutional adjudication to interpret legal provisions and to assess whether they are compatible with the constitution […].[73]
>
> There is nothing wrong with having the constitution as an interpretive parameter. Indeed, this is a duty anywhere where the constitution is considered the supreme law of the land, with which all other laws must comply.[74]
>
> Whenever a court concludes that a given legal provision can be interpreted in (at least) two different ways, that these interpretations are equivalent (questions of constitutional interpretation aside), and that adducing constitutional reasons makes one interpretation incompatible with the constitution, there seems to be no controversy at all: the interpretation in conformity with the constitution should prevail.[75]

From these remarks, it can be inferred that Afonso da Silva is in agreement with the use of CCI as an interpretive argument. It can be inferred that his vehement criticism is not directed at the substance of interpretive work, but rather at the label of *favor legis*, which purported to demonstrate fidelity to the legislator but ultimately failed to do so. It should be noted, however, that even an integrative, holistic, dual-nature approach to legal interpretation necessarily engages with the material enacted by the legislature.

It is a fallacy to assume that once an ideal dimension of legal argumentation is accepted, the weight of real-dimension arguments in legal interpretation, such as will and wording, are entirely disregarded.[76] On the contrary, as illustrated by the Radbruch formula of legal argumentation, real-dimension arguments are accorded default priority in the balancing of canones.[77] The number of possible interpretations that judges may choose from in this complex and holistic model is, in fact, more limited than many critics have claimed.[78]

It is therefore erroneous to assert that my proposed account of interpretation would amount to unfaithfulness. What is meant by *favor legis*, or faithfulness to the law? At least two versions of the concept are possible, either as a positivist

[73] Afonso da Silva (n 6) s II(C), emphases omitted.
[74] ibid s V.
[75] ibid.
[76] I discuss this myth in details in Matthias Klatt, '5 1/2 Myths of Legal Non-Positivism' (2024) *Analisi e Diritto* 53, 60–65.
[77] For details, see Klatt, 'The Rule of Dual-Natured Law' (n 71) 37–39.
[78] Rosenfeld (n 13) s II with fn 42.

or a non-positivist concept. In the non-positivist version, *favor legis* cannot be interpreted as fidelity to a narrow, original intent and the literal, uninterpreted text of the law. Rather, it must be understood as fidelity to the dual nature of law, which encompasses and builds upon the enacted norm as well as considerations of justice.

D. Constitutionally Conforming Interpretation and the Other Canons

Ultimately, Afonso da Silva's criticism seems to be based on a single scenario, as evidenced by the concluding paragraph of his chapter. In that particular scenario, CCI stands in stark contrast to all the other canons. It appears that such a scenario is uncommon and an overly simplified representation of reality. In the majority of cases, the evidence is not so clearly aligned that all interpretive canons point in one direction, while only CCI points in another.

It would be inaccurate to describe CCI as an external disruption to a legal argument that is otherwise neat and tidy. CCI is an internal factor in the process of legal interpretation, operating through systematic and objective-teleological interpretation, which are two of the recognised canons. Moreover, in cases of considerable complexity, the standard set of canons (in the absence of CCI) will not provide a clear direction, but rather numerous possibilities. The interpreter is thus tasked with making a well-founded selection among the canons, weighing the arguments according to their respective significance in the individual case. The character of the task remains unchanged by the introduction of CCI.

In the event that the exceptional circumstances outlined by Afonso da Silva materialise, it is our position that we would not apply CCI. Instead, we would pursue a constitutionally conforming further development of the law, given that the fourth condition for CCI would not be met.[79] In conclusion, Afonso da Silva's argument against *favor legis* can be seen as an argument against constitutionally conforming further development. This is a distinct issue in itself.[80]

V. Reversed Conforming Interpretation

A. Basic Principles

A reversed conforming interpretation is defined as the process of interpreting the constitution in a manner that aligns with the doctrines set forth in a statute. The

[79] On the fourth condition, see Klatt, 'The Legitimacy of Constitutionally Conforming Interpretation' (n 16) 6.

[80] See s VII below.

question of how this is possible, given the established hierarchy of norms, remains unanswered. The act of interpreting a higher-ranked norm in conformity with a lower-ranked norm appears to invert the established hierarchy, which is a clear contravention of the superior status of the constitution.[81] It is therefore evident that there is a need to re-examine the aforementioned proposition.

Nevertheless, some contributors have indicated that this possibility exists. In Taiwan, a reserved conforming interpretation is a viable option for specific constitutional terms that have particular requirements outlined in a statute.[82] Additionally, the possibility for statutory laws to influence the interpretation of constitutional terms has been observed in South Africa[83] and in the Czech Republic.[84] In the context of international courts, a reversed conforming interpretation is employed in order to manage interactions between international laws and national legal systems. The doctrine of the margin of appreciation as interpreted by the ECHR can be understood in this way, as it permits the national legal system to exert influence over the interpretation of international law.[85]

B. Analysis

Upon closer examination, however, the inversion appears to be acceptable in a very limited set of cases. As illustrated by the case of Taiwan, the inversion primarily pertains to references made to the statutory definitions of constitutional terms.[86] This can be reconstructed such that the constitution itself delegates the specification of a constitutional meaning to the ordinary legislator. In this manner, the legislative specification of constitutional requirements is ultimately justified by the higher-ranked constitution. This reconstruction eliminates the impression of acting contrary to the established hierarchy of norms.

It is imperative to insist that the reversed conforming interpretation necessitates the existence of a constitutional licence empowering the legislator to determine the constitutional meaning. The inversion must be based on a command stated in the constitution, whether explicitly or implicitly. A particularly noteworthy example is that of the Czech Republic, where socio-economic constitutional rights may be asserted only within the confines of statutory laws that implement these rights.[87]

[81] Klatt, 'The Legitimacy of Constitutionally Conforming Interpretation' (n 16) 13; see also Lin (n 5) 350: The inversion seems to 'substitute legislative intent for constitutional intent'; Stacey (n 29) 357: 'inconsistent with the principles of constitutional supremacy and the rule of law'.

[82] Lin (n 5) 349.

[83] Stacey (n 29) 357.

[84] Ondřejek (n 5) 64–65.

[85] Cormac Mac Amhlaigh, 'EU Constitutional Conflicts and Constitutionally Conforming Interpretation' in this volume s II.

[86] Lin (n 5) 349; see also Pino, *L'interpretazione nel diritto* (n 21) 298–99 with fn 67.

[87] Ondřejek (n 5) 64.

Furthermore, it is of the utmost importance that the practice of reversed constitutional interpretation be utilised exclusively in extraordinary circumstances. Otherwise, a shift in the interpretation of the Constitution towards the statute may result in a 'weakening of the protections afforded by constitutional rights.'[88] If it remains the exception, it can be argued that the coherence of the legal system can be strengthened overall by the inversion, as Ondřejek has asserted.[89]

VI. The Balancing of Competences

A. Basic Principles

The competence conflicts between the legislature and the various courts involved in the use of CCI pose a significant risk to the rule of law and the principle of democracy.[90] It is noteworthy that one of the outcomes of Volume 1 is that CCIs do not, in principle, expand the scope of judicial power over legislative power.[91] Nevertheless, the competence conflicts represent a pivotal point of contention in the broader debate surrounding the legitimacy of the CCI.[92] The question of competence conflicts assumes particular significance.

A significant feature of balancing as a legal methodology is the presence of a conflict between competing principles that can be conceptualised in terms of their relative weight. In instances where the issue of weight is raised in the context of constitutional concerns, it can be reasonably assumed that a balancing act is at play. The following sections will demonstrate how considerations of weight play a significant role in the ongoing debate surrounding the legitimacy of CCI.

B. Annulment or Constitutionally Conforming Interpretation?

The question of whether CCI or its alternative, annulment, constituted a more serious infringement with the legislature's competence to decide is a matter of debate.[93] Some scholars[94] assert that CCI represents a more serious infringement, while

[88] See the apt warning by Stacey (n 29) 357; see also Pino, *L'interpretazione nel diritto* (n 21) 298: 'weakens the material hierarchy'.

[89] Ondřejek (n 5) 64.

[90] Rosenfeld (n 13) s IV: 'The strongest argument against CCI is grounded on the proposition that it is contrary to democracy'.

[91] Doyle (n 1) s IV(E).

[92] Eszter Bodnár, 'Hungary. Conflicts over Competence' in Klatt (ed), *Constitutionally Conforming Interpretation* (n 5) 90, 100–108.

[93] Klatt, 'The Legitimacy of Constitutionally Conforming Interpretation' (n 16) 28 with fns 216–222.

[94] Sommer and Roznai (n 4) s I; Mathieu Carpentier, 'France. The Dynamics of "Interpretative Reservations" in the Jurisprudence of the French Constitutional Council' in Klatt (ed), *Constitutionally Conforming Interpretation* (n 5) 82.

others posit that it should not be regarded as a constitutional remedy, but rather as an integral component of the established norms governing statutory interpretation. From this latter perspective, the notion of infringement with respect to the legislature is significantly mitigated, such that the lesser infringement is avoiding annulment with the help of CCI.[95] CCI then seems to be 'far preferable than serial nullifications leaving multiple gaps that may prove difficult to fill'.[96]

One argument in favour of the view that annulment was the lesser infringement with respect to the legislature's competence is the claim that a strong use of CCI could impede the legislature's ability to enact legislation in accordance with its public policy objectives, particularly in those areas that are sensitive to fundamental rights.[97] Doyle's theory of CCI intensity is based on the observation that CCI can, at times, make. '[...] detailed prescriptions about what is constitutionally permissible, thereby pre-empting legislative action.'[98] This is consistent with my theory of balancing competences. These considerations can be formulated as rules of thumb for the external justification of weights allocated to the competing competences. To illustrate, consider the following example: A greater degree of detail in a CCI is indicative of a more significant infringement of legislative competence.

C. The Potential for Legislative Response

Those who espouse the view that annulment represents a less serious infringement contend that the legislature then has the opportunity to fill the resulting gap, thereby ensuring that the meaning of the statute is more consistent with its policy goals than a judicially imposed meaning.[99] In light of these considerations, it is pertinent to inquire whether this potential for legislative response is similarly applicable in cases of CCI.

It would be reasonable to assume that this potential for legislative response is also applicable in cases of CCI. One critique of this assumption, however, is that CCI may constrain the legislature's future autonomy.[100] Nevertheless, comparable constraints may also result from the annulment: Any future statute that fills the gap will be limited by the 'need to stay within the parameters of constitutionality identified in the decision to strike down the offending provision'.[101] With regard to

[95] This perspective is Aahron Barak's and reported by Sommer and Roznai (n 4) s IV; see also Bodnár (n 92) 102.

[96] Rosenfeld (n 13) s I.

[97] cf Wilberg (n 5) 416; see also the worry raised by Sommer and Roznai (n 4) s VI, who claim following Landfried that with CCI, the '"ball has left the hands" of the political authority'; Carolan (n 7) s II(B): 'imposes constraints on the legislature's future freedom of action'.

[98] Doyle (n 1) s III(D).

[99] Christine Landfried, 'Constitutional Review and Legislation in the Federal Republic of Germany' in Christine Landfried (ed), *Constitutional review and legislation: An international comparison* (Baden-Baden, Nomos, 1988) 154.

[100] Carolan (n 7) s II(B).

[101] ibid.

the extent of the legislature's capacity to respond to either annulment or CCI, there is no inherent distinction between the two.[102]

Rosenfeld posits that the potential for legislative response was constrained to legal systems devoid of a hierarchical structure. Hierarchical systems, in contrast, 'prevent [...] the legislator from nullifying or correcting what he deems an unwarranted constitutional or legal interpretation or outcome'.[103] It is important to note that the latter consequence will only occur if the constitution prescribes a single, definitive solution, thereby eliminating any discretion on the part of the legislature.

This is, however, an exceedingly uncommon occurrence. In the majority of cases, even in systems with a clear hierarchical structure, the constitution will still afford the legislature a certain degree of discretion. The most significant form of discretion is structural, manifesting in instances of stalemate in the balancing of constitutional principles.[104] Given the frequency of stalemates, the preventive effect upon the legislature is not a particularly pressing concern.

In any case, suggesting that the legislature might respond could potentially lead to further complications in specific instances. In certain instances, the financial implications of introducing new legislation or a reduction in legislative capacity may effectively preclude this possibility.[105] This exclusion, in turn, reinforces the court's authority to engage in CCI.

This is also the case when it can be reasonably anticipated that the legislature will be unable to fill the gap in a reasonable time frame for any reason. In such a scenario, the nullification of the legislation would almost certainly precipitate a 'prolonged legal vacuum'.[106] It is imperative that CCI be engaged to prevent the creation of a vacuum that could result in the ineffective protection of fundamental rights. The protection of fundamental rights is also a relevant factor in general when determining whether to choose between the options of CCI and annulment. In many cases, the parties involved in a specific legal dispute will only benefit from CCI, rather than from a gap in the law or a later legislative action.[107]

D. Achieving Institutional Practical Concordance

In light of the aforementioned considerations, it can be reasonably inferred that the dimension of weight is pertinent and, consequently, balancing is at play.

[102] ibid: 'its capacity to (respond) is similarly constrained'.
[103] Rosenfeld (n 13) s I.
[104] Matthias Klatt and Moritz Meister, *The Constitutional Structure of Proportionality* (Oxford, Oxford University Press, 2012) 79–80, 161.
[105] For these factors, see Lin (n 5) 335.
[106] Butt (n 58) 308.
[107] Doyle (n 1) s IV(C).

As previously demonstrated in my contribution to Volume 1, it is possible to resolve these competence conflicts with the help of a formal balancing exercise, in accordance with the ideal of institutional practical concordance.[108] My theory of institutional practical concordance is consistent with the principle of sincere cooperation as it is understood in EU law.[109] This approach allows for a dynamic and flexible model that helps to overcome the impasse between positions that always give either the court or the legislator the last word. Furthermore, it assists in making a rational decision between the options of annulment and CCI.[110]

It is noteworthy that the model of balancing competences is capable of addressing the criticism raised by Afonso da Silva. He takes issue with the CCI on the grounds that it was necessary to account for the plurality of constitutional designs.[111] This is undoubtedly a significant requirement. Nevertheless, the intrinsic mechanisms of balancing competences are the optimal means of accommodating pluralism. The theory is sufficiently flexible to accommodate the nuances of different local legal systems. To illustrate, two of these mechanisms are worthy of mention: The abstract weights of competences can be differentiated in accordance with the specific characteristics of a given legal system.

Moreover, the outcome of the formal balancing is a conditional preference relation, and the conditions can effectively capture differences in the local context. They make the balancing sensitive to the circumstances of the case or category of cases in which CCI is being used.[112] In conclusion, the aforementioned considerations demonstrate that the formal balancing approach is an effective method for achieving institutional practical concordance.

E. The Necessity of Theory

The necessity of such a theory is substantiated by an analysis of the country reports. For Canada, the theory provides a solution to the puzzle of how to integrate 'Type A lawyers, with their laser-like focus on legal certainty, and Type B lawyers, with their heartfelt desire for legal coherence'.[113] In Indonesia, for instance, the Constitutional Court, when formulating legal norms with the assistance of the CCI,

> […] often does not comprehensively explain precisely why those norms are required by the Constitution. It also does not discuss competing interpretations and the extent to

[108] For details, see Klatt, 'The Legitimacy of Constitutionally Conforming Interpretation' (n 16) 25–31.
[109] Baraggia (n 12) s II.
[110] This problem is enlisted as one of the main problems of CCI by Pino, *L'interpretazione nel diritto* (n 21) 297.
[111] Afonso da Silva (n 6) s IV.
[112] cf Klatt, 'The Legitimacy of Constitutionally Conforming Interpretation' (n 16) 27.
[113] Daly (n 28) 264.

> which they might be constitutionally supported. [...] Problematically, the Court has not matched its self-allocation of greater powers with convincing reasoning in conditional cases. In particular, it has not squarely considered whether conditional decisions affect the separation of powers and, if so, what the consequences of this might be.[114]

The necessity for theoretical orientation is made evident by the presence of such poor practice examples. It is only through the lens of such a theory that we can challenge the notion that CCI was merely a power play orchestrated by judges, who freely choose meanings in accordance with their individual political biases.[115]

In light of the necessity for a balanced account that can provide normative guidance for the participants in adjudicative practice, it is unsurprising that the country reports frequently mention legal factors that enable us to determine the weight of the competing competences.[116] For example, Rosenfeld makes a distinction between what he terms 'judicial politics' and 'ordinary politics'.[117] This distinction could inform a differentiation of competence weights according to the specifics of the case in question.[118] Another factor to consider is the situation of convergence or divergence among the norms of different legal regimes.[119] The complexity of the statute in question, as well as its age, also influence the weight that a court should afford to a CCI.[120]

It can be argued that one of the more intuitively appealing situations in which a court's competence to engage in CCI is strengthened is mentioned in a number of country reports. In India, the 'declining functionality of the Indian Parliament' is referenced in this context.[121] In Indonesia, the competence of a slow, dysfunctional, and noncompliant legislature will be 'outweighed by the imperative of effectively upholding constitutional rights,' thus allowing the court's competence to engage in CCI to take precedence.[122]

A notable illustration of this phenomenon can be observed in the constitutional crisis that unfolded in Poland. In this case, the malfunctioning and politicised constitutional court only served to reinforce the authority of the ordinary court in its capacity to interpret legislation in a manner that aligns with the Constitution.[123] In this context, it is evident that the constitutional crisis in Poland has led to a situation where the ordinary courts have been granted greater competence to interpret legislation in a manner that is consistent with the Constitution.

[114] Butt (n 58) 325; see also Carpentier (n 94) 82: 'the Council's very loose reasoning'.
[115] cf Rosenfeld (n 13) s II; see also Doyle (n 1) s IV(A).
[116] Klatt, 'The Legitimacy of Constitutionally Conforming Interpretation' (n 16) 27–29.
[117] Rosenfeld (n 13) s V.
[118] See also the fourth factor enlisted by Lin (n 5) 339.
[119] Rosenfeld (n 13) s VI.
[120] Lin (n 5) 338.
[121] Vakil (n 59) 303.
[122] Butt (n 58) 326.
[123] Barczentewicz and Matczak (n 5) 145–46.

VII. Further Development of the Law

A. Basic Principles

In accordance with the prevailing understanding of CCI, this legal method is not a viable means of wholly rewriting the legal norm.[124] The wording of the norm and its fundamental objectives represent the outer limits of the scope of application of CCI.[125] This does not imply that any application beyond these limits was illegitimate. In lieu of the aforementioned limits, a distinct legal methodology commences, namely, constitution-conforming further development of the law (CCFD).

The quasi-legislative (as opposed to interpretive) character of a further development of the law is evident, for example, in the case of South Africa. In order for a court to read words into or delete words from the meaning of a statute, it must first declare the statute invalid. Only then, in the second instance, may the court remedy the defect by reading words into or out of the statute.[126] It is evident that by conferring upon courts the authority to engage in CCFD, a legal system will effectively disavow the Kelsenian notion of constitutional courts as 'negative legislators'.[127]

Not all legal systems provide a sufficiently clear delineation between the processes of interpretation and further development. In Australia, CCI is a legal concept that encompasses 'at least some practices that involve the development of judge-made law rather than discerning the meaning of non-judge-made sources'.[128] In Taiwan, a 'second type' of CCI is accepted that is, analytically speaking, not interpretation but further development.[129] Additionally, in Israel, further developments fall under the category of CCI.[130] A similar argument can be made with regard to the semantic stretching employed in the famous UK case *Ghaidan*[131] and the Spanish[132] practice of the judicial filling of axiological gaps.

[124] This is the fourth condition for legitimate CCI, see Klatt, 'The Legitimacy of Constitutionally Conforming Interpretation' (n 16) 6; for the legislative purpose as constraining CCI, see Wilberg (n 5) 425; see also Weis (n 20) 404: 'no licence for a court to adjust the meaning [...] which the court might think to be unwise or ill-considered'.

[125] For my theory of the limits of the wording, defining the borderline between interpretation and further development generally, see Matthias Klatt, *Making the Law Explicit: The Normativity of Legal Argumentation* (European Academy of Legal Theory Series vol 7, Oxford, Hart Publishing, 2008).

[126] Stacey (n 29) 362.

[127] Doyle (n 1) s III(A).

[128] Weis (n 20) 382.

[129] Lin (n 5) 332.

[130] Sommer and Roznai (n 4) s IV.

[131] cf Doyle (n 1) s III(C).

[132] Alfonso García Figueroa, 'Constitutionally Conforming Argumentation and Legalism' in this volume s II(C).

B. Misdirected Criticism

The distinction between interpretation and further development demonstrates that a significant portion, if not the majority, of the criticism directed against CCI is, in essence, a critique of CCFD. This is exemplified by Afonso da Silva's objection to CCI, which asserted that the court's interpretation of an unwritten exception into a written rule was not a matter of pure interpretation.[133] Indeed, if the text is not ambiguous and if the limit of the wording is transgressed – as illustrated by Afonso da Silva's example – then this is not an instance of CCI, but rather, an instance of CCFD. The same is true of criticism directed against the 'manipulative' decisions of the STF in Brazil.[134] Such interpretations go beyond the possible meaning of the norms and contravene the 'degree of judicial law-making or law-remaking' necessitated by the US-American[135] avoidance canon.

An additional illustration of misguided criticism can be observed in the contention that the Romanian Constitutional Court was exceeding the boundaries of interpretation by effectively enacting an informal constitutional amendment while purporting to merely interpret a vague constitutional text.[136] As Afonso da Silva correctly asserts, in all of these instances, 'speaking of CCI is insincere (or simply wrong)'.[137] It is wrong or insincere because the legal method applied is a CCFD.

C. Constitutionally Conforming Argumentation

Redirecting the criticism towards CCFD instead of CCI does not yet address the substance of the criticism. The substance has been succinctly articulated by Afonso da Silva, who asserts that the objective of CCFD is to rectify the actions of the legislature, typically by limiting or expanding the scope of legal provisions.[138]

This analysis may be regarded as a critique if one is inclined to concur with the view that CCFD was not a competence of the courts, in accordance with the rule of law and the principle of the separation of powers. This leads us back to the issue of balancing competences.[139] It is evident that CCFD infringes more seriously on the legislature's competence than CCI. Nevertheless, it is not evident

[133] See his discussion of a hypothetical case in Afonso da Silva (n 6) s III(A).

[134] cf Diego W Arguelhes and Rafael B de Lima, 'Brazil. From Restraint to Preemption?' in Klatt (ed), *Constitutionally Conforming Interpretation* (n 5) 236.

[135] Frederick Schauer, 'United States. Constitutional Avoidance as Constitutional Conformation' in Klatt (ed), *Constitutionally Conforming Interpretation* (n 5) 276.

[136] cf Suteu (n 10) s IV(B).

[137] Afonso da Silva (n 6) s V.

[138] ibid. It is worth noting that Afonso da Silva does not object to the result as such. On the contrary, he agrees that a court may have very good reasons to apply CCFD in some contexts.

[139] See s VII above.

that CCFD is more invasive than annulment, as Sommer and Roznai assert.[140] As with CCI, the legitimacy of CCFD will be determined by a balancing of competences.

In the case of CCFD, it can be argued that the infringement of legislative competence is more significant than in the case of CCI. Consequently, the significance of the courts' authority to engage in CCFD must be substantiated by more substantial justifications. In his analysis, Carolan has identified an important aspect of this mechanism in the following rule: '[…] the further from the master-text that a constitutionally-conforming meaning is derived, the greater is the interpretive burden on the court.'[141]

The principal conclusion to be drawn from the critical objections is as follows: It is imperative that courts enhance the quality of their justifications for both CCI and CCFD, particularly in light of the necessity to provide a more detailed and comprehensive account of the legal considerations pertaining to the relative weight of the various competences in question. It is imperative that the legal considerations pertaining to the relative merits of the competing competences be explicitly articulated, and that any counter-considerations be addressed and refuted in a transparent, consistent, and conclusive manner.

In this regard, there is, in fact, little difference between the approaches adopted by CCI and CCFD. In essence, they both exemplify what Figueroa has aptly termed 'constitutionally conforming argumentation'.[142]

[140] Sommer and Roznai (n 4) ss I, VI.
[141] Carolan (n 7) s III.
[142] García Figueroa (n 132) s II(C).

INDEX

NB – 'constitutionally conforming interpretation' is abbreviated as CCI in this index

www.ingramcontent.com/pod-product-compliance
Lightning Source LLC
LaVergne TN
LVHW012212130925
821035LV00003B/165